Computer Hardware and Organization: An Introduction

M. E. SLOAN

Michigan Technological University

SCIENCE RESEARCH ASSOCIATES, INC.
Chicago, Palo Alto, Toronto
Henley-on-Thames, Sydney, Paris, Stuttgart

A Subsidiary of IBM

We wish to acknowledge the following for permission to reprint material:

Figures 11.5 and 11.6: From *Hewlett-Packard Journal,* June 1972. © 1972, Hewlett-Packard Company. Used with permission.
Figures 11.7, 11.8, and 11.9. From *Intel MCS-40 Users Manual for Logic Designers,* © 1975, Intel Corporation. Used with permission.
Figures 11.11, 11.12, 11.13, and 11.14: From *PDP8/e, PDP8/m, and PDP8/f Small Computer Handbook,* © 1973, Digital Equipment Corporation. Used with permission.

Library of Congress Cataloging in Publication Data

Sloan, Martha E.
    Computer hardware and organization.

    Bibliography: p.
    Includes index.
    1. Computers.   I. Title.
TK7885.S56   621.3819′5   75-34109
ISBN 0-574-21065-2

CONTENTS

3 Combinational Logic Circuits and Logic Technologies

4 Sequential Logic

PART II THE PROGRAMMING LEVEL

PART III   THE SYSTEMS LEVEL

9   Memory

10   Input/Output

11   Computer Systems

PREFACE

This text is intended for an introductory course in computer hardware and computer organization. Students are assumed to have taken the usual mathematics courses taught in American schools through at least the first two years of high school. The text is suited for college freshmen or sophomores but, with the optional sections, can be used for juniors and seniors.

At Michigan Technological University, this text is used in a one-term introductory course in computer engineering usually taken by three types of students. Electrical engineering students who intend to specialize in computer engineering take the course to survey areas of computer engineering that do not require a background in electronic circuits or in advanced mathematical techniques. Other electrical engineering and a few other engineering students who are not primarily interested in computer engineering take the course for an understanding of computer hardware. Computer science students also take the course as a computer hardware course. The text is supplemented by a laboratory program. Students design and construct several simple logic circuits and write a few machine language and assembly language programs.

The theme of the text is computer structure. The structure of a computer is examined at several progressive levels. Structures at one level become the components of a higher level. The text begins at the logic level, skipping over the electronic circuit level, a discussion of which would require the student to have a background in physics, circuit analysis, and electronics that is not needed for the rest of the book. Unlike most other introductory computer hardware texts, the text does not begin with number representation. This topic is covered in an appendix where it may serve as a review for students who are familiar with it; many students have learned binary arithmetic in high school or elsewhere. An instructor may choose to begin with this appendix. More advanced aspects of number representation for computers are treated in context as they are needed.

The main chapters are prefaced with an overview that allows the student to prepare a mental framework for the material of the chapter in accordance with the principles of cognitive learning theory. Each chapter ends with a summary, references, and problems. The section of the text needed for each problem is shown in parentheses to facilitate assigning problems. Answers for selected odd-numbered problems are given in appendix B. Since this is an introductory text, most references are to other texts rather than to the original research papers.

Chapter 1 presents an overview of the structural levels of the computer. The logic level discussions (chapters 2 through 5) cover combinational logic circuit analysis and design; logic technologies and integrated circuit implementations of standard logic functions; flipflops and sequential circuits, concentrating on common computer circuits such as registers and counters; and construction of logic systems from register-transfer modules. Chapter 6 consolidates the material on the logic level by discussing the arithmetic circuits needed for a computer. The programming level is treated in chapters 7 through 8, which discuss the machine language and assembly language programming sublevels. Memories and microprogramming, input/output devices and interrupt handling, and the organization of minicomputers and microprocessors are developed in chapters 9, 10, and 11, respectively—the systems level. The back matter includes tables of instructions and codes for the PDP-8, a review of binary arithmetic, and a glossary.

The discussion in chapters 7 and 8 centers on minicomputers since we think students should have hands-on experience with a computer, and minicomputers are both relatively inexpensive and widely available for student use in most universities. The discussion of programming is made as general as possible, using the PDP-8 (the most widely used minicomputer) as a continuing example. Instruction sets of other popular minicomputers and microcomputers are also discussed. The instructor can readily supplement this material with information about any computer available for class use.

Many people helped in the development of this text. At Michigan Tech Arnold Lee reviewed an early version of the manuscript, and Ted Grzelak taught two classes from a later version and contributed many helpful suggestions. Harold Stone of the University of Massachusetts encouraged me throughout the developmental process. Dale Anderson (Iowa State University), Jay Bayne (California Polytechnic State University), John Keown (Southern Technical Institute, Marietta), Donald P. Leach (Foothill College), Robert J. Smith, II (Lawrence Livermore Laboratory), Michael G. Thomason (University of Tennessee, Knoxville), John Wakerly (Stanford University), and Gerald E. Williams (formerly of Riverside City College) also reviewed the manuscript and contributed many improvements. Also essential to the book's development was the careful typing of Ruth Tepsa and Phyllis Brumm.

1 Overview

What are you able to build with your blocks?
Castles and palaces, temples and docks.

　　　　　　　　　　　　　　　　　Robert Louis Stevenson

The theme of this book is the diversity of levels in the structures of digital computers and other digital systems. This chapter defines the levels that we will study and provides an overview of the book.

1.1 INTRODUCTION

Modern digital computers are complex systems. To understand them, we will view them as a hierarchy of system levels, as first described by Bell and Newell (1971). We will consider four basic levels: electronic circuits, logic, programming, and computer systems. (The logic level is further divided into three sublevels: combinational logic, sequential logic, and register-transfer logic.) Since a thorough understanding of electronic circuits requires some advanced knowledge of physics and mathematics, we will concentrate on the other three levels, which are unique to computers and to digital technology.

The levels nest together in a hierarchy. At each level the system may be described in terms of appropriate components, structures, and system behavior. The components at a particular level obey certain physical or mathematical laws and combine to make structures. Together, the components and structures determine the behavior of the system at that level. Each level also has a distinct language or languages to describe components and their connections.

TABLE 1.1

HIERARCHY OF SYSTEM LEVELS WITH EXAMPLES
OF STRUCTURES AND COMPONENTS

LEVEL	STRUCTURES	COMPONENTS
Computer systems	Computers, networks	Controls, processors, memories
Programming	Programs	Instructions, subroutines, memories, operators
Logic Register-transfer	Circuits—arithmetic unit	Registers, data operators
Sequential	Circuits—counters, registers	Flipflops—*RS, JK, T, D*
Combinational	Circuits—encoders, decoders	Gates—AND, OR, NOT, NOR, NAND
Electronic Circuit	Circuits—gates, multivibrators (flipflops), amplifiers	Active—transistors, voltage sources Passive—resistors, capacitors, inductors, diodes

Table 1.1 shows the system levels with examples of their components and structures. Note that structures at one level can become components at another level. For example, gates and flipflops are both structures at the electronic circuit level, but gates are components at the combinational logic sublevel and flipflops are components at the sequential logic sublevel.

The purpose of this book is to study each computer level (except the electronic circuit level) briefly, yet in enough detail to show its characteristics and importance to computer systems. Because digital technology is rapidly changing, not all the levels we will study are well established or well understood. While the lowest levels have been organized or codified for several decades, the newer levels—particularly the register-transfer level and the computer systems level—change constantly. New levels may yet emerge. In addition, the levels described here cannot completely describe computer system behavior, since they exclude mechanical devices, such as card readers, teletype terminals, and line printers. We will study such devices briefly in chapter 10 to see how they interact with other structures and to improve our knowledge of computer hardware.

The study of computer systems is similar to the study of human systems. Humans, too, can be studied at many levels, for example the anatomical, the neurological, the biochemical, the psychological, the sociological, and the anthropological, to name just a few. An attempt to classify such a study would yield a hierarchy in which some structures at one level, say the biochemical, become components at another level, say the physiological. In other cases, the hierarchy is not clear. Just as there are careers in human systems that involve primarily one level, so there are careers in computer systems that concentrate on one level, such as programming or logic design. Yet a knowledge of the impact of one level on the entire system is important in order to analyze, design, and use systems successfully.

The rest of this chapter contains brief overviews of system levels. All the ideas introduced here will be discussed in more detail in later chapters. Some of the words and concepts may be unfamiliar to you now but will become familiar as you progress through the book. This chapter is intended to provide a framework for understanding the hierarchy of system levels; it is not intended to introduce any level rigorously.

1.2   ELECTRONIC CIRCUIT LEVEL

The lowest level shown in table 1.1 is the electronic circuit level. (A lower level might combine electromagnetic theory and quantum mechanics to explain the operation of the components at this level.) Its components can be passive (such as resistors, capacitors, inductors, and diodes) or active (such as voltage or current sources and transistors). Circuit behavior is characterized by continuous waveforms of voltage and current, which can be described by differential equations.

We will not consider the electronic circuit level in any detail since it requires a knowledge of circuit analysis and physics beyond that assumed for this book. However, we will consider how the technologies chosen to implement electronic circuit design, for example metal-oxide-semiconductor (MOS) technology, affect other levels of computer operation.

1.3   LOGIC LEVEL

The concept of logic level is unique to digital technology. The preceding electronic circuit level, in contrast, is useful for many technologies. The difference between the two levels is most obvious in circuit behavior. At the logic level, circuit behavior is described by discrete binary variables that are called 0 and 1, or low and high, regardless of the exact voltages to which they correspond. At the electronic circuit level, circuit behavior is described by continuous waveforms that require analysis by differential equations, a far more complex form of mathematics.

If operation of a logic circuit depends only on the current values of the inputs, it is called *combinational logic*. The mathematics necessary to describe combinational logic is switching algebra. The components perform logical operations such as logical addition (OR) and logical multiplication (AND), which are analogous to conventional addition and multiplication. (We will define these operations precisely in chapter 2.) The components that implement the operations are connected at their terminals in much the same way that electronic components are connected. The signals are considered to be discrete 0s or 1s.

After learning to analyze and design combinational logic circuits with switching algebra, we will look at some simple map and table methods for combinational logic. We will also look at integrated circuits that have several combinational logic circuits on single chips of silicon. We will consider how integrated circuits have modified older methods of combinational logic design.

The *sequential logic* sublevel characterizes logic circuits whose behavior depends in part on the past history of the circuit. In addition to the logic components used at the combinational logic sublevel, the sequential logic sublevel requires memory or delay components, such as flipflops. A flipflop is a small storage unit whose output can be either 0 or 1. Difference equations, the discrete analog of the differential equations used at the electronic circuit level, describe circuit behavior.

We will study two basic types of sequential logic circuits—*registers* and *counters*. Ordinarily, computers and other digital systems operate with a basic unit of information called a *word*. For a given system a word has a standard number of bits, usually ranging from 4 to 64, where each bit can be either 0 or 1. Registers store information and usually hold one word, but they can be shorter or longer as needed. Counters, as their name implies, count computer operations or time intervals and are basic to the timing and control of a computer.

While both the combinational logic sublevel and the sequential logic sublevel have been standardized for nearly as long a time as electronic computers have existed, the last logic sublevel, the register-transfer level, is new and uncertain. Its components are registers and transfer paths between registers. The behavior of a register-transfer system is represented by the sequence of bit values. Contents of the registers can be combined by logical operations, arithmetic operations, or simple transfers. A set of expressions specify the rules for register transfers. Register-transfer level descriptions of computers are becoming more common, and a number of register-transfer languages have been developed. Unfortunately, notation is not standard. Later we will look at one register-transfer language and at register-transfer hardware.

1.4 PROGRAMMING LEVEL

The programming level may be the most familiar to you since you probably have some experience in programming in a high-level language such as FORTRAN. This level is unique not only to digital technology, but even more narrowly, to digital devices with central processors that interpret a programming language. Some digital devices, such as simple digital voltmeters, do not have central processors; they have a logic level but not a programming level. As we will see in chapter 11, a major current trend is to replace digital systems based solely on logic with digital systems based on microprocessors, or small central processors.

We may regard instructions and subroutines as the basic components of the programming level since they are the components of programs. An alternate view is to consider programming level components to be memories and operations. *Memories* store *data structures* such as student records. *Operations* transform the data structures and produce new data structures. The behavior of the programming level is the sequence of data values. A *program* (that is, a sequence of instructions) prescribes the operations to be performed on given data structures. A control structure specifies the order of execution of instructions, allowing for program branching.

The programming level has a hierarchy of sublevels, as shown in table 1.2. The lowest sublevel, *microprogramming,* involves *micro-instructions,* which are components of the basic instructions of a computer. *Machine language* programs are written with the basic instruction set of the computer and can be expressed as the actual bit patterns of 1s and 0s used by the computer hardware. Since bit patterns or numbers are difficult to remember, we often represent machine language instructions with symbols called *mnemonics.* For each instruction both an address and the numerical form of the instruction must be specified. *Assembly language* is shorthand notation for machine language that allows mnemonic instead of numeric

TABLE 1.2

HIERARCHY OF LANGUAGE SUBLEVELS OF PROGRAMMING LEVEL

LANGUAGE SUBLEVEL	EXAMPLE
Compiler languages	FORTRAN, PL/I, COBOL
Interpreter languages	BASIC, APL
Assembly language	
Machine language	Unique to each computer
Microprogramming languages	

instructions, and symbolic instead of numeric addresses. Assembly language programs are run with the help of a program, called an *assembler,* that performs many needed housekeeping functions for the programmer.

The three lowest programming sublevels—microprogramming, machine, and assembly language—are unique for each computer. In contrast the higher sublevels—*interpreter* and *compiler* languages—can be used on many computers. These two languages differ in the way they are implemented. Compilers usually translate a source program written in the compiler language, such as FORTRAN, directly into an equivalent machine language program which is executed. Interpreters usually translate and execute source language statements, written in an interpreter language such as BASIC, one at a time.

The programming level differs markedly from the logic level since it is linguistic rather than physical. It allows us to name things, to abbreviate, and to interpret instructions, none of which we could do at lower levels. Because the programming level differs so from other levels, people can become expert programmers with little or no understanding of logic or electronic circuit behavior.

Most of today's computer science focuses on the programming level. This level comprises a hierarchy of language levels and a diversity of languages that rivals the natural languages of the world. No universal programming language yet exists, although some notations for programming languages are becoming standard. This book will be concerned with programming primarily at the machine language and assembly language levels. We will illustrate machine and assembly language programming with programs for the PDP-8, a simple minicomputer.

1.5 COMPUTER SYSTEMS LEVEL

The highest level, and the one least understood, is the computer systems level. It is somewhat surprising that we do not understand this level better since it is the most visible level when we look at a computer or digital system. Its components are input/output devices, processors, memories, controls, and other hardware. Its behavior is the processing of information expressed in *bits, characters, words,* and the like, and is measured in flow rates and capacities. The computer systems level more closely resembles the logic level than the programming level in its operation. The major difficulty in describing behavior at this level is the very large number of states needed to represent the components. There is no standard notation for describing the computer systems level.

Figure 1.1 shows the organization of a simple computer at the computer systems level. The computer has four main units—control, arithmetic, memory, and input/output—connected by links called *buses.* The *control unit* controls the other units by sending signals on control buses in response to status information it receives from other units. The *arithmetic unit* performs arithmetic and logical operations on data it receives from memory or *input/output* devices. The control unit and the arithmetic unit together compose the *central processing unit.* Input/output devices are located outside the computer and transfer information between the computer and the outside world.

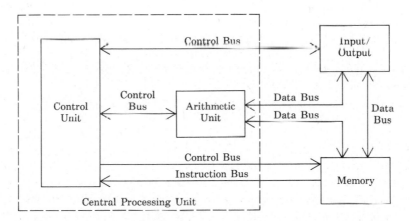

Fig. 1.1 Computer systems level — organization of a simple computer

1.6 SUMMARY

This chapter has given an overview of the book and has introduced a variety of terms and concepts. We have scanned only major ones here but will encounter others in later chapters. The basic notion of this chapter is that computers can be viewed as a hierarchy of levels. The lowest level, for our purposes, is the electronic circuit level in which electronic components are assembled to form logic devices. The next level, the logic level, has three sublevels—combinational, sequential, and register-transfer logic. The combinational logic sublevel concerns logic systems whose current operation is independent of the previous history of the system. The sequential logic sublevel deals with logic components whose operation depends on its past operation. The register-transfer sublevel concerns the transfer of information between large logic units, called registers. The programming level, which is least like the other levels, describes the transformation of stored information in the form of data structures. The highest level, the computer systems level, describes the interconnection and operation of large units, such as memories and processors.

Concepts

combinational logic	programming
computer systems	register-transfer logic
electronic circuits	sequential logic

1.7 REFERENCES

The original classification of the levels of computer structure described here was made by Bell and Newell (1971). Their book remains the best description of computer structures, especially at the top two levels, and contains excellent case studies of a wide variety of computers. Bell, Grason, and Newell (1972) is the best reference on the register-transfer level. McCluskey (1965), Bartee (1972), and Hill and Peterson (1973 and 1974) discuss the electronic circuit level and relate it to the logic level. Additional references for each level will be given after we have looked at the level in more detail.

part I

The Logic Level

2 Combinational Logic

2.1 OVERVIEW

We will first examine the combinational logic sublevel of the logic level, in particular, the logic or switching functions of one or more input variables. The number of functions grows exponentially with the number of input variables; with only five binary inputs, for example, there are more than 4 billion possible switching functions. Since this large number of functions would be difficult to handle, we look for ways of expressing any logic function with just a few basic operations. Fortunately, we can express any logic function with just one basic operation. Consequently, with just one type of logic device we can build circuits to implement any logic function. In this chapter we will look at a few standard implementations of logic functions.

Having learned that we can build logic circuits to implement any switching function with one or more standard logic devices, we next consider the most economical ways of building logic circuits, including simplifying or minimizing logic functions and the circuits that implement them. These minimization techniques were most appropriate several years ago when they corresponded directly to the types of logic devices then being used. We examine three minimization techniques—algebraic simplification (which resembles methods used in ordinary or high school algebra), a map method, and a tabular method. The map and tabular methods are straightforward and can be applied directly to any function. Minimization for modern logic devices is less straightforward, as we will learn in the next chapter.

2.2 INTRODUCTION

Consider a system with r inputs and one output as shown in figure 2.1. The inputs and outputs are binary variables; that is, at any given time each input and each output is either 0 or 1. The system implements *combinational logic* if the output is a function of only the current values of the system inputs. The output of a combinational logic system does not depend on previous values of system inputs. The system implements *sequential logic* if the output depends on the values of the inputs at some previous time. A combination lock with several dials (fig. 2.2a), which is often used for bicycles, is an example of combinational logic. A combination lock with just one dial that must be turned to several numbers in sequence (fig. 2.2b) is an example of sequential logic.

2.3 BASIC SWITCHING FUNCTIONS

The mathematics of logic was developed by George Boole, an English mathematician (1815–1864), to describe thinking. Boole was concerned with statements that could be either true or false. In his 1854 publication, *An Investigation of the Laws of Thought,* he described

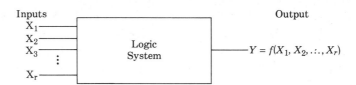

Fig. 2.1 Logic system with r inputs and one output

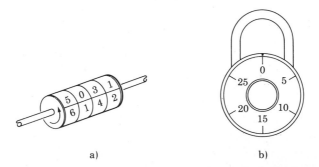

a)   b)

Fig. 2.2 Examples of locks with combinational logic (a) and sequential logic (b)

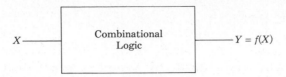

Fig. 2.3   A combinational logic system with one input variable

a symbolic notation useful in logic problems and mathematics for dealing with the symbolic statements. In 1938, Claude Shannon, a mathematician at Bell Laboratories, adapted Boolean algebra to analyze switching networks. Terms such as truth table are historical reminders of the development of the mathematics, now usually called *switching algebra,* used in digital technology.

A *truth table* shows the output of a logic system for every possible combination of inputs. The output of a logic system with r binary inputs can be any one of 2^{2^r} functions. The simplest case is a logic system with just one input, as shown in figure 2.3. Such a logic system could implement any one of $2^{2^1} = 4$ functions, as shown in table 2.1. Each of the four functions is a *unary* function, a function of one variable. Table 2.1 shows unary functions of binary variables; that is, each function has just one variable and the variable is binary or two-valued.

The four functions are simple. Two are constant: $Y = 0$, called the *null* function, and $Y = 1$, called the *unity* function. The function $Y = X$ is called the *identity* function. The remaining function is defined as the *complement* of X and is written $\overline{X}$. We will also refer to the complement of X as *NOT X*. $\overline{X}$ is 0 when X is 1; $\overline{X}$ is 1 when X is 0. Thus $\overline{X}$ is not X; its value is what X is not.

The next simplest case is a logic system with two binary inputs, shown in figure 2.4. Its output can be any one of $2^{2^2} = 16$ binary functions, as shown in table 2.2. Binary functions are functions of

TABLE 2.1

Truth Table for the Four Functions
of One Binary Variable

Input	Outputs			
X	$Y = 0$	$Y = X$	$Y = \overline{X}$	$Y = 1$
0	0	0	1	1
1	0	1	0	1

TABLE 2.2

Truth Tables for the 16 Functions of Two Binary Variables

Inputs		ZERO	AND		X		Y	XOR	OR	NOR	COIN.	NOT Y		NOT X		NAND	ONE
X Y		f_0	f_1	f_2	f_3	f_4	f_5	f_6	f_7	f_8	f_9	f_{10}	f_{11}	f_{12}	f_{13}	f_{14}	f_{15}
0 0		0	0	0	0	0	0	0	0	1	1	1	1	1	1	1	1
0 1		0	0	0	0	1	1	1	1	0	0	0	0	1	1	1	1
1 0		0	0	1	1	0	0	1	1	0	0	1	1	0	0	1	1
1 1		0	1	0	1	0	1	0	1	0	1	0	1	0	1	0	1
Symbol			·	/		/		⊕	+	→	⊙	−		−		↑	

Outputs

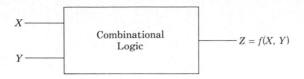

Fig. 2.4   A combinational logic system with two input variables

two variables. We can obtain the 16 truth tables of table 2.2 by counting in binary from 0 to 15, starting with the first column. Each output function is numbered correspondingly from 0 to 15. All 16 functions have names, many of which you may know. We will quickly mention the functions that are least useful for digital circuits and then carefully consider the more important ones. f_0, the null function, and f_{15}, the unity function, are the same as their counterparts in the one-variable system. $f_3 - X$ and $f_5 - Y$ are also simple functions. f_2 and f_4 are *inhibition* functions for X but not Y, and Y but not X, respectively. f_{11} and f_{13} are *implication* functions for Y implies X, and X implies Y, respectively. Inhibition and implication are more important for philosophy than for digital circuits.

The other functions are the most useful to us for components of logic circuits. We could try to implement the 2^{2^r} switching functions of r variables by producing separate logic circuits for each switching function, but this would require maintaining a large stockpile of circuits. For four inputs we would need $2^{2^4} = 65,536$ different circuits, and for five inputs we would need more than 4 billion circuits. If we took advantage of symmetry and stocked only different types of circuits, we could cut these numbers somewhat, but we would still need more than 30 million different circuit types for five inputs. A more promising approach is to construct the circuits we need from several building blocks.

The remaining eight functions include two unary and six binary operations that can be realized as useful components. The other eight operations can be expressed in terms of these functions, which are discussed below. In section 2.6 it will be shown that only a subset of these functions, called a *complete* set, is needed to express any combinational logic function.

1. NOT

$$f(X) = \overline{X}$$

X	$\overline{X}$
0	1
1	0

The *NOT* or complement operation is unary; that is, it is a function of only one variable. $f(Y) = \bar{Y}$ is the second unary function.

2. AND

$$f(X,Y) = XY = X \cdot Y$$

X	Y	XY
0	0	0
0	1	0
1	0	0
1	1	1

The *AND* operation, or the logical product, has an output of 1 only when both inputs equal 1. AND is represented as XY or $X \cdot Y$.

3. OR

$$f(X,Y) = X + Y$$

X	Y	X + Y
0	0	0
0	1	1
1	0	1
1	1	1

The *OR* operation, or the logical sum, has an output of 1 when either input or both inputs equal 1. OR is represented as $X + Y$; note the difference between OR and arithmetic addition.

These first three functions—NOT, AND, and OR—are the basic functions of switching algebra. The next four functions are also useful and, as we will see in the next chapter, can be easily implemented as integrated circuits.

4. NAND

$$f(X,Y) = X \uparrow Y = \overline{XY}$$

X	Y	X ↑ Y
0	0	1
0	1	1
1	0	1
1	1	0

NAND equals 1 except when both inputs equal 1. It is the complement of AND, NOT AND, and can be represented as $X \uparrow Y$ or $\overline{XY}$. (The NAND symbol is a Sheffer stroke.)

5. NOR

$$f(X,Y) = X \downarrow Y = \overline{X + Y}$$

X	Y	$X \downarrow Y$
0	0	1
0	1	0
1	0	0
1	1	0

NOR equals 1 only when both inputs are zero. It is the complement of OR, NOT OR, and can be represented as $X \downarrow Y$ or as $\overline{X + Y}$. (The NOR symbol is a Pierce arrow.)

6. EXCLUSIVE OR (XOR)

$$f(X,Y) = X \oplus Y$$

X	Y	$X \oplus Y$
0	0	0
0	1	1
1	0	1
1	1	0

XOR equals 1 only when exactly one input is 1. It is represented by $X \oplus Y$. (The XOR symbol is a ring sum.)

7. COINCIDENCE

$$f(X,Y) = X \odot Y = \overline{X \oplus Y}$$

X	Y	$X \odot Y$
0	0	1
0	1	0
1	0	0
1	1	1

COINCIDENCE equals 1 only when both inputs have the same value; that is, the inputs coincide. COINCIDENCE is the complement of EXCLUSIVE OR. It is represented by $X \odot Y$ or $\overline{X \oplus Y}$.

The standard symbols (American National Standard ANSI Y32.14-1973 and IEEE 91-1973) for the logic gates that implement these basic operations are shown in figure 2.5. (A *gate* is a logic device with one or more inputs and one output.) Only the standard distinctive-shape symbols are shown. There are also standard rectangular-shape symbols that consist of rectangles with letters or other symbols naming the functions inside. A small circle on an input or output line denotes the complementing of the signal on that line;

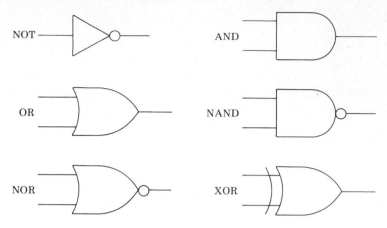

Fig. 2.5   ANSI symbols for logic gates

that is, a small circle denotes NOT. The NOT operation alone is represented by a triangle followed by a circle. The triangle symbolizes the amplification that may be present in the gate, and the circle symbolizes complementation. When NOT follows another logic operation, such as AND, the other symbol is followed by a circle to produce a composite symbol (here NAND). Alternatively, small circles may be placed on gate inputs to show that input signals should be complemented before the gate operation is formed. Figure 2.6 shows an AND gate whose Y input is complemented before the AND operation is done. No special symbol represents COINCIDENCE; an XOR gate followed by a small circle can be used, as shown in figure 2.7.

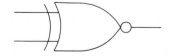

Fig. 2.6   AND gate with Y input complemented

Fig. 2.7   COINCIDENCE symbol

2.4   COMPOSITE FUNCTIONS

So far we have discussed binary or unary operations involving at most two variables. More complex functions can be produced by applying binary or unary operators successively to functions. To do this, we note that the functions are binary variables so they can become the arguments in any operation.

Example 2.1

$$f(A,B) = A \oplus B$$
$$g(C,D) = C + D$$
$$h(E,F) = EF$$

We can form the composition of f and g by h:

$$h(f(A,B), g(C,D)) = h(A,B,C,D) = (A \oplus B)(C + D)$$

To evaluate h, we can substitute all possible input values for its arguments and carry out the indicated operations. For this we need precedence rules, similar to those in ordinary (high school) algebra which stipulate that multiplication must be done before addition, and so on. For example, the arithmetic expression

$$2 + 3 \times 4$$

is evaluated as 14 because the multiplication of 3×4 takes precedence over addition. Similarly, the expression

$$2 \times 5 + 3$$

is evaluated as 13. The order of multiplication and addition can be altered by parentheses. For example,

$$(2 + 3) \times 4 = 20 \quad \text{and} \quad 2 \times (5 + 3) = 16$$

Operations within parentheses take precedence over and are performed before unparenthesized operations.

Similarly, in logic, parenthesized operations take precedence over unparenthesized operations. Logical multiplication (AND) takes precedence over logical addition (OR). Complementation (NOT) of a variable is always evaluated before combining the variable with either AND or OR, just as in ordinary algebra a negative number would be evaluated before multiplication or addition.

The following precedence rules apply:

1. Consider the NOT operator applied to an expression as putting parentheses around the expression. (Do not put parentheses around a single complemented variable.)

2. Evaluate expressions within parentheses working from inner to outer parentheses in the following order:

   a. First evaluate NOTs of values from left to right.
   b. Then evaluate ANDs of pairs of values from left to right.
   c. Then evaluate ORs of pairs of values from left to right.

3. Substitute the values resulting from evaluations of parenthesized expressions into the remaining expressions and evaluate in the same order, that is:

   a. First evaluate NOTs from left to right.
   b. Then evaluate ANDs from left to right.
   c. Then evaluate ORs from left to right.

Example 2.2

Evaluate

$$f(W,X,Y,Z) = (WX + \overline{\overline{X}Y})\,Z + \overline{W\overline{X} + \overline{YZ}}$$

for $W = 1$, $X = 1$, $Y = 0$, $Z = 1$.

1. Place parentheses around the complemented expressions.

$$f(W,X,Y,Z) = (WX + (\overline{\overline{X}Y}))\,Z + (\overline{W\overline{X} + (\overline{YZ})})$$

2. Evaluate the inner parenthesized expressions, $(\overline{\overline{X}Y})$ and $(\overline{YZ})$.

$$\overline{X} = \overline{1} = 0$$
$$\overline{X}Y = 0 \cdot 0 = 0$$
$$\overline{\overline{X}Y} = \overline{0} = 1$$
$$YZ = 0 \cdot 1 = 0$$
$$\overline{YZ} = \overline{0} = 1$$

3. Evaluate the outer parenthesized expressions.

$$WX = 1 \cdot 1 = 1$$
$$WX + \overline{\overline{X}Y} = 1 + 1 = 1$$
$$W\overline{X} = 1 \cdot 0 = 0$$
$$W\overline{X} + \overline{YZ} = 0 + 1 = 1$$
$$(\overline{W\overline{X} + \overline{YZ}}) = \overline{1} = 0$$

4. Substitute the values of the parenthesized expressions into the remaining expressions and evaluate the entire function.

$$f(W,X,Y,Z) = 1 \cdot Z + 0 = 1 \cdot 1 + 0$$
$$= 1 + 0 = 1$$

Example 2.3

Evaluate

$$f(A,B,C,D) = AC + \overline{B(C\overline{D})} + \overline{(A\overline{B} + BC)D}$$

for $A = B = 1$, $C = D = 0$.

1. Place parentheses around the complemented expressions.

$$f(A,B,C,D) = AC + (\overline{B(C\overline{D})}) + ((\overline{A\overline{B} + BC)D})$$

2. Evaluate the parenthesized expressions, proceeding from inner to outer expressions.

$$C\overline{D} = 0 \cdot \overline{0} = 0 \cdot 1 = 0$$
$$B(C\overline{D}) = 1 \cdot 0 = 0$$
$$(\overline{B(C\overline{D})}) = \overline{0} - 1$$
$$A\overline{B} + BC = 1 \cdot \overline{1} + 1 \cdot 0 = 1 \cdot 0 + 1 \cdot 0 = 0 + 0 = 0$$
$$(A\overline{B} + BC)D = 0 \cdot 0 = 0$$
$$(\overline{(A\overline{B} + BC)D}) = \overline{0} = 1$$

3. Substitute the values of the parenthesized expressions into the remaining expressions and evaluate the function.

$$f(A,B,C,D) \quad AC + 1 + 1$$
$$= 1 \cdot 0 + 1 + 1$$
$$= 0 + 1 + 1$$
$$= 1$$

In this example we did not need to carry out the entire evaluation. As soon as we found that one of the terms in the sum, $B(C\overline{D})$, was 1, we knew the function was 1. In general, whenever one term of a logical sum is 1, the sum is 1. Similarly, whenever one factor of a logical product is 0, the product is 0. These observations can greatly simplify the evaluation.

Evaluating expressions involving NAND, NOR, or XOR functions is more complicated. Always put parentheses around expressions involving NAND, NOR, or XOR to show the intended operands. Then the expressions can be evaluated by the preceding rules.

Example 2.4

Evaluate

$$f(A,B,C,D) = (A \uparrow (B\overline{C})) \oplus ((A\overline{B}) \downarrow (C\overline{D}))$$

for $A = 1$, $B = 0$, $C = 1$, $D = 1$.

1. There are no complemented expressions.

2. Evaluate the parenthesized expressions proceeding from inner to outer parentheses.

$$B\overline{C} = 0 \cdot \overline{1} = 0 \cdot 0 = 0$$
$$A \uparrow (B\overline{C}) = A \uparrow 0 = 1 \uparrow 0 = 1$$
$$A\overline{B} = 1 \cdot \overline{0} = 1 \cdot 1 = 1$$
$$C\overline{D} = 1 \cdot \overline{1} = 1 \cdot 0 = 0$$
$$(A\overline{B}) \downarrow (C\overline{D}) = 1 \downarrow 0 = 0$$

3. Evaluate the function:

$$f(A,B,C,D) = 1 \oplus 0 = 1$$

2.4.1 Generalization of Basic Operations

Analysis of composite functions has suggested that we can generalize the basic binary operations to operations on n variables. We summarize the generalizations below. The truth tables are left as an exercise.

1. The value of the AND function is 1 only when all n variables are 1. AND is an all-or-nothing operation.

2. The value of the OR function is 1 when any of its n variables is 1. OR is an any-or-all operation.

3. The value of the NAND function is 0 when all n variables are 1 and is 1 otherwise. NAND is the complement of AND.

4. The value of the NOR function is 1 only when all n variables are 0. NOR is the complement of OR.

5. The value of the XOR function is 1 when an odd number of its variables are 1 and is 0 when an even number of variables are 1. This characteristic makes the XOR function useful to

check whether the number of 1s in a word is odd or even, a property called the *parity* of the word. XOR is an odd operation.

6. The COINCIDENCE function is the complement of the XOR function. We cannot form a simple generalization about its value as a function of the evenness or oddness of its 1 inputs. You can convince yourself of this by evaluating and considering $X \odot (Y \odot Z)$.

All of these logical operations—AND, OR, NAND, NOR, XOR, and COINCIDENCE—are *associative*. The principle of associativity assures that the order in which we combine variables in a single operation makes no difference. For example, $W(X(YZ)) = ((WX)Y)Z = (WX)(YZ) = WXYZ$.

2.4.2 Logical Equivalence

Two functions defined for the same arguments are logically equivalent if and only if they are equal for all possible combinations of the arguments. We can easily show logical equivalence by comparing truth tables for the two functions.

Example 2.5

$$f(X,Y,Z) = (X \downarrow Y) \downarrow (Y \uparrow Z)$$
$$g(X,Y,Z) = \overline{X}YZ + XYZ$$

X	Y	Z	$X \downarrow Y$	$Y \uparrow Z$	$f(X,Y,Z)$	$\overline{X}YZ$	XYZ	$g(X,Y,Z)$
0	0	0	1	1	0	0	0	0
0	0	1	1	1	0	0	0	0
0	1	0	0	1	0	0	0	0
0	1	1	0	0	1	1	0	1
1	0	0	0	1	0	0	0	0
1	0	1	0	1	0	0	0	0
1	1	0	0	1	0	0	0	0
1	1	1	0	0	1	0	1	1

The truth tables for $f(X,Y,Z)$ and $g(X,Y,Z)$ show that f and g are logically equivalent.

2.4.3 Analysis of Complex Logic Circuits

We can easily write an expression for the output of a complex combinational logic circuit. We will adopt the convention that the circuit

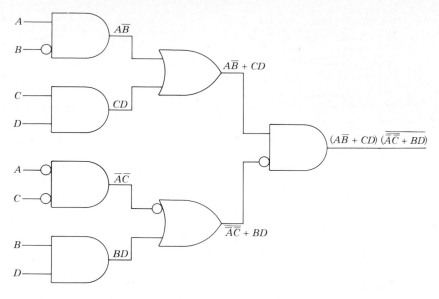

Fig. 2.8   Derivation of an output expression from a combinational logic circuit

is organized from left to right; that is, the inputs to the first gates are on the left, and the output of the final gate is on the right. The procedure for writing the output expression is:

1. Write the output of each gate, starting at the left.
2. Use parentheses where needed for clarification.

Example 2.6

Write the output for the logic circuit of figure 2.8.

The figure shows the steps of the solution. We start by writing the outputs of the four AND gates on the left. Circles on the inputs complement the input lines so the output of the top gate is $A\overline{B}$. Then we write the outputs of the two OR gates in the center. Finally we write the output of the right AND gate. Note that parentheses are needed to clarify the inputs to the AND gate. The output expression is:

$$f(A,B,C,D) = (A\overline{B} + CD)\,(\overline{\overline{A}\overline{C} + BD})$$

Similarly, we can design a combinational logic circuit to implement a given output expression. We proceed from the output back to the input. For each operation we must have a gate. The procedure is:

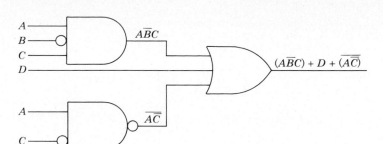

Fig. 2.9 Implementation of a logic expression

1. Use a gate to implement each operation, starting with the last operation. Begin with unparenthesized operations and proceed from outer to inner parentheses.
2. Use the principle of associativity to combine inputs to the same operation.

Example 2.7

Construct a logic circuit to implement

$$f(A,B,C,D) = (A\overline{B}C) + D + (\overline{\overline{A}\,\overline{C}})$$

The solution is shown in figure 2.9. The final operation is the OR operation. We first construct a single OR gate with three inputs to implement the two + signs. One of the inputs is the single variable D. The other two inputs come from an AND gate to implement $A\overline{B}C$ and from a NAND gate to implement $\overline{A}\,\overline{C}$.

2.5 SWITCHING ALGEBRA

Switching algebra is the mathematics that describes the operation of logic circuits. It consists of a set of symbols and a set of rules for manipulating the symbols. The symbols are a set of binary variables and the AND, OR, and NOT operations. The binary variables, such as X, Y, or Z, can occur with or without NOTs. We use the term *literal* to refer to a variable with or without an associated NOT; thus X and $\overline{X}$ are different literals. The postulates and theorems that follow are valid for any literals.

2.5.1 Postulates

1. All literals must have a value of either 0 or 1. Hence,

$$X = 0 \text{ if } X \neq 1; \qquad\qquad X = 1 \text{ if } X \neq 0$$

2. The NOT operation is defined as:

$$\overline{0} = 1 \qquad\qquad \overline{1} = 0$$

3. The logical operations + and · are defined as:

OR (+)	AND (·)
$0 + 0 = 0$	$0 \cdot 0 = 0$
$0 + 1 = 1$	$0 \cdot 1 = 0$
$1 + 0 = 1$	$1 \cdot 0 = 0$
$1 + 1 = 1$	$1 \cdot 1 = 1$

There are two versions of each theorem—an OR version and an AND version. We leave detailed examination of switching algebra theorems to more advanced texts. The theorems are listed in table 2.3.

Many of these rules are the same as those of ordinary algebra. Associativity and commutativity, for example, are valid for both ordinary algebra and switching algebra. However, note that switching algebra differs in the following cases:

1. In ordinary algebra, multiplication distributes over addition, $X(Y + Z) = XY + XZ$; but addition does not distribute over

TABLE 2.3

SWITCHING ALGEBRA THEOREMS

OR Version	AND Version	Theorem
$X + 0 = X$	$X \cdot 1 = X$	Identities
$X + 1 = 1$	$X \cdot 0 = 0$	Null elements
$X + X = X$	$X \cdot X = X$	Idempotence
$X + \overline{X} = 1$	$X \cdot \overline{X} = 0$	Complements
$\overline{\overline{X}} = X$	$\overline{\overline{X}} = X$	Involution
$X + Y = Y + X$	$XY = YX$	Commutative
$X + (Y + Z) = (X + Y) + Z$	$X(YZ) = (XY)Z$	Associative
$X + YZ = (X + Y)(X + Z)$	$X(Y + Z) = XY + XZ$	Distributive
$X + XY = X$	$X(X + Y) = X$	Absorption 1
$X + \overline{X}Y = X + Y$	$X(\overline{X} + Y) = XY$	Absorption 2
$XY + \overline{X}Z + YZ = XY + \overline{X}Z$	$(X + Y)(\overline{X} + Z)(Y + Z) = (X + Y)(\overline{X} + Z)$	Consensus
$\overline{X + Y} = \overline{X}\overline{Y}$	$\overline{XY} = \overline{X} + \overline{Y}$	DeMorgan's

multiplication, $X + YZ \neq (X + Y)(X + Z)$. In switching algebra, AND distributes over OR and OR distributes over AND.
2. Idempotence, absorption, and consensus do not hold in ordinary algebra.
3. Cancellation does not hold in switching algebra. That is, $XY = XZ$ does not imply $Y = Z$.

2.5.2 DeMorgan's Theorems

DeMorgan's theorems are especially useful for digital circuits. The OR version states that

$$\overline{X + Y} = \overline{X}\overline{Y}$$

The complement of the sum of two variables equals the product of the complements of the variables.
The AND version states that

$$\overline{XY} = \overline{X} + \overline{Y}$$

The complement of the product of two variables equals the sum of the complements of the variables.

DeMorgan's theorems are used to find alternate forms of an expression, especially to remove complements. They are also useful in converting expressions from ANDs and ORs to NANDs and NORs.

Example 2.8

Express $A\overline{B}$ with NOR.

The OR version of DeMorgan's theorem states that the complement of the sum of two variables (that is, the NOR of two variables) equals the product of the complements of the variables. Thus,

$$\overline{A + B} = A\overline{B} \qquad \text{or} \qquad A \downarrow B = A\overline{B}$$

2.5.3 Duality

Two forms were given for each postulate and theorem. Alternatively, we can say that each rule has a *dual* obtained by:

1. interchanging AND and OR,
2. interchanging 0 and 1, and
3. leaving the literals unchanged.

   More generally, any switching algebra function has a dual formed in the same way. If we denote a function by f and its dual by f_d, we may say that $f(X,Y,0,1, +, \cdot)$ has a dual $f_d\ (X,Y,1,0,\cdot,+\ )$.

Example 2.9

$$f = (X + 1)(Y + \bar{Z})$$
$$f_d = X \cdot 0 + Y \cdot \bar{Z}$$

Note that f and f_d in the example are not logically equivalent as shown by the truth tables of table 2.4. In general, a function and its dual are not logically equivalent.

2.5.4   Proof of Theorems

Switching algebra theorems can be proved either by perfect induction or by deduction. *Perfect induction* is a brute force display of the logical equivalence of both sides of the equation, usually as truth tables. It is cumbersome for equations with more than two or three variables. *Deduction* involves successive application of postulates and previously proved theorems to show the validity of an equation.

Example 2.10

Proof of OR version of absorption 2

1. by perfect induction:

$$X + \bar{X}Y = X + Y$$

X	Y	$\bar{X}Y$	$X + \bar{X}Y$	$X + Y$
0	0	0	0	0
0	1	1	1	1
1	0	0	1	1
1	1	0	1	1

2. by deduction, assuming distributive law, complement, and identity:

$$X + \bar{X}Y = \begin{cases} (X + \bar{X})(X + Y) & \text{Distributive} \\ 1 \cdot (X + Y) & \text{Complement} \\ X + Y & \text{Identity} \end{cases}$$

The deductive method can also be used to prove the equivalence of general expressions.

TABLE 2.4

LOGICAL EQUIVALENCE OF EXAMPLE 2.9

X	Y	Z	$X + 1$	$Y + \bar{Z}$	f	f_d
0	0	0	1	1	1	0
0	0	1	1	0	0	0
0	1	0	1	1	1	1
0	1	1	1	1	1	0
1	0	0	1	1	1	0
1	0	1	1	0	0	0
1	1	0	1	1	1	1
1	1	1	1	1	1	0

Example 2.11

Show that

$$WX + \overline{W}XY\bar{Z} + W\bar{X}\bar{Y}Z + \bar{Y}\bar{Z} = (X + \bar{Y})(W + \bar{Z})$$

$WX + \overline{W}XY\bar{Z} + W\bar{X}\bar{Y}Z + \bar{Y}\bar{Z}$

$= (WX + WX\bar{Y}\bar{Z} + WX\bar{Y}Z + WXY\bar{Z}) + \overline{W}XY\bar{Z}$
$\quad + W\bar{X}\bar{Y}Z + (\bar{Y}\bar{Z} + \bar{Y}\bar{Z}\overline{W}X + \bar{Y}\bar{Z}W\bar{X} + \bar{Y}\bar{Z}WX)$

$\qquad\qquad\qquad\qquad\qquad\qquad\qquad$ Absorption 1

$= WX + \bar{Y}\bar{Z} + W\bar{Y}(X\bar{Z} + \bar{X}\bar{Z} + XZ + \bar{X}Z)$
$\quad + X\bar{Z}(\overline{W}Y + \overline{W}\,\overline{Y} + W\overline{Y} + WY)$
$\qquad\qquad\qquad\qquad\qquad\qquad\qquad$ Commutative
$\qquad\qquad\qquad\qquad\qquad\qquad\qquad$ and Distributive

$= WX + \bar{Y}\bar{Z} + W\bar{Y}[X(Z + \bar{Z}) + \bar{X}(Z + \bar{Z})]$
$\quad + X\bar{Z}[W(Y + \bar{Y}) + \overline{W}(Y + \bar{Y})]$
$\qquad\qquad\qquad\qquad\qquad\qquad\qquad$ Commutative
$\qquad\qquad\qquad\qquad\qquad\qquad\qquad$ and Distributive

$= WX + \bar{Y}\bar{Z} + W\bar{Y} + X\bar{Z}$
$\qquad\qquad\qquad\qquad\qquad\qquad\qquad$ Complement

$= W(X + \bar{Y}) + \bar{Z}(X + \bar{Y})$
$\qquad\qquad\qquad\qquad\qquad\qquad\qquad$ Distributive

$$WX + \overline{W}XY\bar{Z} + W\bar{X}\bar{Y}Z + \bar{Y}\bar{Z} = (X + \bar{Y})(W + \bar{Z})$$
$\qquad\qquad\qquad\qquad\qquad\qquad\qquad$ Distributive

The equation is valid.

2.5.5   Generalized DeMorgan's Theorem

DeMorgan's theorem can be extended to apply to three or more variables.

$$\overline{X_1 + X_2 + X_3 + \cdots + X_n} = \overline{X}_1\overline{X}_2\overline{X}_3 \ldots \overline{X}_n$$
$$\overline{X_1X_2 \ldots X_n} = \overline{X}_1 + \overline{X}_2 + \overline{X}_3 + \cdots + \overline{X}_n$$

The complement of a general function can be obtained by complementing all literals, interchanging AND and OR, and interchanging 0 and 1. Note that this procedure differs from the one used for finding the dual. For the dual, literals are unchanged; for the complement, literals are complemented.

$$\overline{f(X,Y,0,1,+,\cdot)} = f(\overline{X},\overline{Y},1,0,\cdot,+)$$

Example 2.12

$$f = XY + \overline{Z}(X + \overline{Y})$$
$$\bar{f} = \overline{XY + \overline{Z}(X + \overline{Y})} = (\overline{X} + \overline{Y})(Z + \overline{X}Y)$$
$$f_d = (X + Y)(\overline{Z} + X\overline{Y})$$
$$\overline{f_d} = \overline{(X + Y)(\overline{Z} + X\overline{Y})} = \overline{X}\overline{Y} + Z(\overline{X} + Y)$$

2.6   CANONICAL FORMS AND GATE IMPLEMENTATIONS

We saw in section 2.3 that functions can be shown by truth tables. In this section, we examine two standard or *canonical* forms used to express any combinational logic function. To do this, we first note that with any row in a truth table we can associate two terms. The first, called a *minterm,* is a logical product of all literals in the row. We get a minterm by complementing (barring) any variables that are 0 for the row and leaving unbarred any variables that are 1 for the row. Then we form the logical product of all literals defined by this process; that is, we AND them together.

Maxterms are complements of minterms. Thus a maxterm is the logical sum of the complements of all literals in the row. We get a maxterm by barring all variables that are 1 for the row and leaving unbarred all variables that are 0 for the row. We then form the logical sum of all literals defined by this process; that is, we OR them together. Table 2.5 shows minterms and maxterms for three variables.

We can now write the output function for any table that has a 1 output for only one row by simply writing the minterm for that

TABLE 2.5

TRUTH TABLE FOR THREE VARIABLES
SHOWING MINTERMS AND MAXTERMS

Row Number	X	Y	Z	Minterms	Maxterms
0	0	0	0	$\overline{X}\overline{Y}\overline{Z}$	$X + Y + Z$
1	0	0	1	$\overline{X}\overline{Y}Z$	$X + Y + \overline{Z}$
2	0	1	0	$\overline{X}Y\overline{Z}$	$X + \overline{Y} + Z$
3	0	1	1	$\overline{X}YZ$	$X + \overline{Y} + \overline{Z}$
4	1	0	0	$X\overline{Y}\overline{Z}$	$\overline{X} + Y + Z$
5	1	0	1	$X\overline{Y}Z$	$\overline{X} + Y + \overline{Z}$
6	1	1	0	$XY\overline{Z}$	$\overline{X} + \overline{Y} + Z$
7	1	1	1	XYZ	$\overline{X} + \overline{Y} + \overline{Z}$

row. Similarly, we can write the output function for any table that has a 0 output for only one row by writing the maxterm for that row.

Example 2.13

Row number	X Y Z	Function f_1	Row number	X Y Z	Function f_2
0	0 0 0	0	0	0 0 0	1
1	0 0 1	0	1	0 0 1	1
2	0 1 0	1	2	0 1 0	1
3	0 1 1	0	3	0 1 1	1
4	1 0 0	0	4	1 0 0	1
5	1 0 1	0	5	1 0 1	1
6	1 1 0	0	6	1 1 0	0
7	1 1 1	0	7	1 1 1	1

$$f_1 = \overline{X}Y\overline{Z} \qquad\qquad f_2 = \overline{X} + \overline{Y} + Z$$

We can write the output function for more complex tables by combining minterms or maxterms. An output function that is 1 for several rows of the truth table is written as a logical sum of minterms for all rows for which the function is 1. This form is the canonical *sum-of-products* (AND-OR) form. We use a *decimal expression* to show which minterms are included in the sum. The Greek letter sigma, Σ, is used for the sum. The decimal expression $\Sigma(1,2,4)$ means that the minterms of rows 1, 2, and 4 are ORed together.

Example 2.14

Row number	X	Y	Z	Function f_3	Minterms with output 1
0	0	0	0	0	
1	0	0	1	1	$\overline{X}\overline{Y}Z$
2	0	1	0	1	$\overline{X}Y\overline{Z}$
3	0	1	1	0	
4	1	0	0	0	
5	1	0	1	1	$X\overline{Y}Z$
6	1	1	0	1	$XY\overline{Z}$
7	1	1	1	1	XYZ

$$f_3 = \overline{X}\overline{Y}Z + \overline{X}Y\overline{Z} + X\overline{Y}Z + XY\overline{Z} + XYZ = \Sigma(1,2,5,6,7)$$

Similarly, an output function that is 0 for several rows of the truth table is written as a logical product of all maxterms for which the output is 0. This is the canonical *product-of-sums* (OR-AND) form. The Greek letter pi, π, is used for the product. The decimal expression $\pi(0,6,7)$ means that the maxterms of rows 0, 6, and 7 are ANDed together.

Example 2.15

Row number	X	Y	Z	Function f_3	Maxterms with output 0
0	0	0	0	0	$X + Y + Z$
1	0	0	1	1	
2	0	1	0	1	
3	0	1	1	0	$X + \overline{Y} + \overline{Z}$
4	1	0	0	0	$\overline{X} + Y + Z$
5	1	0	1	1	
6	1	1	0	1	
7	1	1	1	1	

$$f_3 = (X + Y + Z)(X + \overline{Y} + \overline{Z})(\overline{X} + Y + Z) = \pi(0,3,4)$$

The two forms of examples 2.14 and 2.15 represent the same function f_3. It is important to note that the sum-of-products form uses minterms of rows for which the function is 1; the product-of-sums form uses maxterms of rows for which the function is 0. We can express any logic function in *both* sum-of-products and product-of-sums forms using ANDs, ORs, and NOTs. Thus AND, OR, and NOT are a *complete set,* that is, a set of logic operators that can express any logic function.

We can implement sum-of-product and product-of-sum functions easily in *two-level* circuits, that is, circuits that have two stages of gates. Sum-of-product implementations have several AND gates forming the minterms followed by an OR gate to form the sum. Product-of-sum implementations have several OR gates to form the maxterms followed by an AND gate for the product. Figure 2.10 shows the AND-OR and OR-AND implementations of the function f_3. Two conventions are used in figure 2.10. First, all inputs labeled X (or Y or Z) are common; that is, if $X = 1$ is the X input to any gate, $X = 1$ is the X input to all gates. Second, we assume that we have X, Y, Z, $\overline{X}$, $\overline{Y}$, and $\overline{Z}$ available for inputs; this is called *double-rail* inputs. If we have only X, Y, and Z available for inputs, we have *single-rail* inputs and must use *inverters* (NOT gates) to complement inputs.

Often we prefer to design circuits with NAND or NOR gates (which are easily implemented with integrated circuits) instead of AND, OR, and NOT gates. We can simply substitute NANDs for both ANDs and ORs in the AND-OR implementation. Similarly, NORs can replace all ORs and ANDs in the OR-AND implementation. Examples are shown in figure 2.11. Note that only the substitutions described are valid. We cannot generalize about the replacements of AND and OR by NAND and NOR.

NANDs alone can implement OR-AND functions and NORs alone can implement AND-OR functions, but more than two levels of logic may be required. We can realize the NOT, AND, and OR functions by either NAND or NOR as shown in figure 2.12. Hence either NAND or NOR is a complete set that can express any switching function. Other aspects of logic design with NANDs and NORs may be found in advanced texts.

2.7 ALGEBRAIC SIMPLIFICATION

In the last section, we saw that any combinational logic function can be expressed in two canonical forms. The canonical expressions can then be implemented by two-level circuits. These circuits, however, are usually not the most economical implementations of the logic functions. In the next three sections we discuss ways of simplifying or minimizing logic functions to achieve economical implementations. *Simplifying* means finding an expression with fewer terms or fewer literals. *Minimizing* means finding an expression that is best

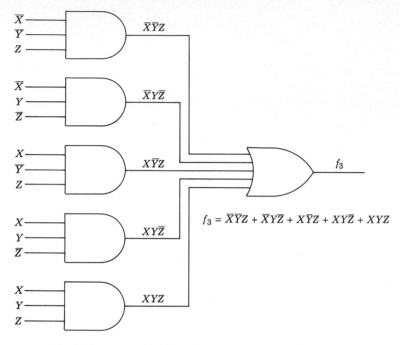

Fig. 2.10a   Sum-of products (AND-OR) implementation of f_3

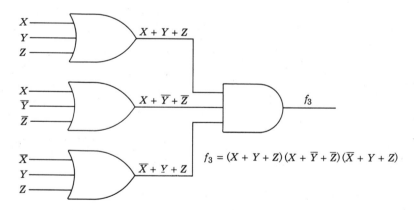

Fig. 2.10b   Product-of-sums (OR-AND) implementation of f_3

by some minimization criterion. Usually we will try to minimize first the number of terms in the expression and then the number of literals. This procedure corresponds to minimizing first the number of logic gates and then the number of inputs in the implementation. This

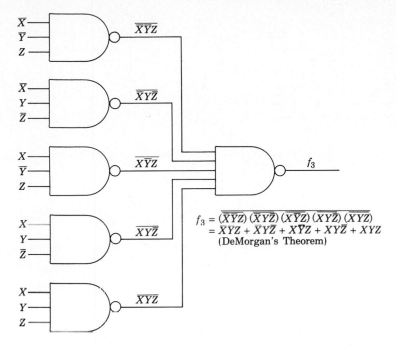

Fig. 2.11a   NAND-NAND realization of an AND-OR function

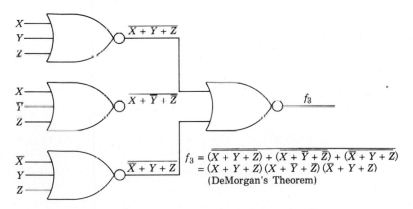

Fig. 2.11b   NOR-NOR realization of an OR-AND function

minimization criterion is the classic one developed in the early years of switching theory. It was well suited to the discrete components available at that time. In the next chapter we will consider minimization criteria that are better suited to modern components. Here we will discuss three methods:

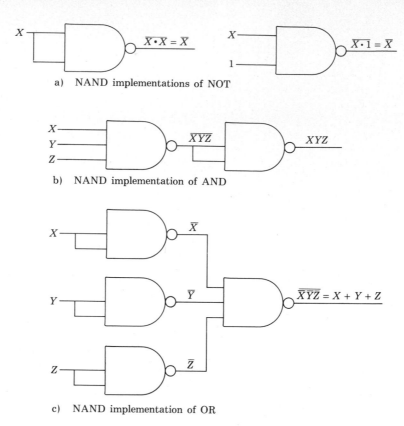

a) NAND implementations of NOT

b) NAND implementation of AND

c) NAND implementation of OR

Fig. 2.12   Implementation of NOT, AND, and OR with NANDs and NORs

1. algebraic simplification
2. Karnaugh maps
3. Quine-McCluskey tables

We introduced algebraic simplification in section 2.5. The basic method for simplifying algebraic expressions is to apply theorems and postulates. The most useful reductions come from repeated applications of $XY + X\overline{Y} = X$ to reduce sums, or its dual $(X + Y)$ $(X + \overline{Y}) = X$ to reduce products. The consensus theorems $XY + \overline{X}Z + YZ = XY + \overline{X}Z$ and $(X + Y)$ $(\overline{X} + Z)$ $(Y + Z) = (X + Y)$ $(\overline{X} + Z)$ can also be used to eliminate terms.

Example 2.16

$$f_1 = ABD + AB\overline{D} + \overline{A}C + \overline{A}BC + ABC$$

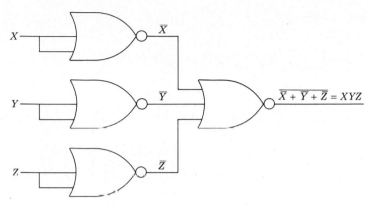

d) NOR implementations of NOT

e) NOR implementation of AND

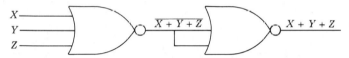

f) NOR implementation of OR

(Fig. 2.12 continued)

Substitute: AB for $AB\bar{D} + AB\bar{D}$ and BC for $ABC + \bar{A}BC$

$$f_1 = AB + \bar{A}C + BC$$

Apply consensus.

$$f_1 = AB + \bar{A}C$$

The original expression required five AND gates and one OR gate for implementation. The minimized expression requires two AND gates and one OR gate (fig. 2.13). The number of literals has been reduced from 14 to 4, and the variable D has been eliminated.

Example 2.17

$$f_2 = (A + B + \bar{C})(A + B + C)$$
$$(A + \bar{B} + C)(\bar{A} + \bar{B} + C)$$

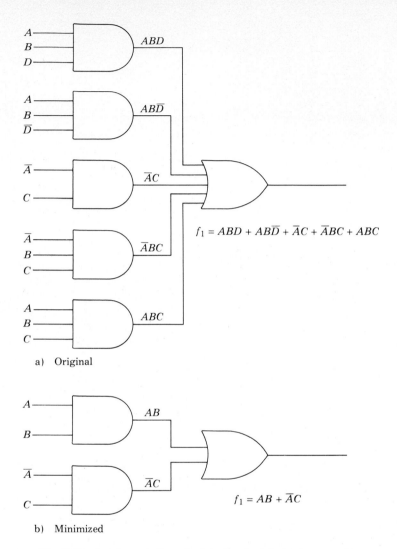

$$f_1 = ABD + AB\overline{D} + \overline{A}C + \overline{A}BC + ABC$$

a)   Original

$$f_1 = AB + \overline{A}C$$

b)   Minimized

Fig. 2.13   Implementation of original and minimized expression

Since $X = X \cdot X$, we can expand f_2 as follows:

$$f_2 = (A + B + C)(A + B + \overline{C})(A + B + C)$$
$$(A + \overline{B} + C)(A + \overline{B} + C)(\overline{A} + \overline{B} + C)$$

Substitute: $A + B$ for $(A + B + C)(A + B + \overline{C})$

$A + C$ for $(A + B + C)(A + \overline{B} + C)$

and $\overline{B} + C$ for $(A + \overline{B} + C)(\overline{A} + \overline{B} + C)$

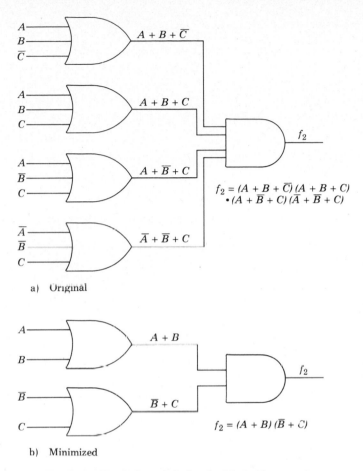

$f_2 = (A + B + \overline{C}) (A + B + C)$
  $\cdot (A + \overline{B} + C) (\overline{A} + \overline{B} + C)$

a)   Original

$f_2 = (A + B) (\overline{B} + C)$

b)   Minimized

Fig. 2.14   Circuit for original and minimized expression

$$f_2 = (A + B) (A + C) (\overline{B} + C)$$

Apply consensus.

$$f_2 = (A + B) (\overline{B} + C)$$

Instead of $X \cdot X = X$, we could have used each sum in as many reductions as we liked. Figure 2.14 shows circuits for the original and minimized expressions. Implementation of the minimized expression requires two OR gates and one AND gate instead of four OR gates and one AND gate. Literals have been reduced from 12 to 4.

Algebraic minimization can be tedious. Consider the following example.

Example 2.18

$$f_3 = ABC\overline{D} + AB\overline{C}D + A\overline{B}C\overline{D} + A\overline{B}\,\overline{C}D$$
$$+ \,\overline{A}BCD + \overline{A}B\overline{C}D + \overline{A}\,\overline{B}CD + \overline{A}\,\overline{B}C\overline{D}$$

We can apply $XY + X\overline{Y} = X$ to 10 pairs of terms by using some terms two or three times.

$$\begin{array}{ll}
ABC\overline{D} + AB\overline{C}\,\overline{D} = AB\overline{D} & A\overline{B}C\overline{D} + A\overline{B}\,\overline{C}\,\overline{D} = A\overline{B}\,\overline{D} \\
ABC\overline{D} + A\overline{B}C\overline{D} = AC\overline{D} & \overline{A}BCD + \overline{A}\,\overline{B}CD = \overline{A}CD \\
AB\overline{C}\,\overline{D} + A\overline{B}\,\overline{C}\,\overline{D} = A\overline{C}\,\overline{D} & \overline{A}B\overline{C}D + \overline{A}\,\overline{B}\,\overline{C}D = \overline{A}\,\overline{C}D \\
A\overline{B}C\overline{D} + \overline{A}\,\overline{B}C\overline{D} = \overline{B}C\overline{D} & \overline{A}BC\overline{D} + \overline{A}B\overline{C}\,\overline{D} = \overline{A}B\overline{C} \\
A\overline{B}\,\overline{C}\,\overline{D} + \overline{A}\,\overline{B}\,\overline{C}\,\overline{D} = \overline{B}\,\overline{C}\,\overline{D} & \overline{A}BCD + \overline{A}B\overline{C}\,\overline{D} = \overline{A}BC
\end{array}$$

Since all four-literal terms have been combined with others, we can now sum the three-literal terms. Otherwise we would have to include any uncombined four-literal terms in the sum.

$$f_3 = AB\overline{D} + AC\overline{D} + A\overline{C}\,\overline{D} + \overline{B}C\overline{D} + \overline{B}\,\overline{C}\,\overline{D}$$
$$+ \,A\overline{B}\,\overline{D} + \overline{A}CD + \overline{A}\,\overline{C}D + \overline{A}B\overline{C} + \overline{A}BC$$

We again apply $XY + X\overline{Y} = X$.

$$\begin{array}{ll}
AB\overline{D} + A\overline{B}\,\overline{D} = A\overline{D} & \overline{B}C\overline{D} + \overline{B}\,\overline{C}\,\overline{D} = \overline{C}\,\overline{D} \\
AC\overline{D} + A\overline{C}\,\overline{D} = A\overline{D} & \overline{A}CD + \overline{A}\,\overline{C}D = \overline{A}C \\
AC\overline{D} + \overline{A}C\overline{D} = C\overline{D} & \overline{A}BC + \overline{A}B\overline{C} = \overline{A}C
\end{array}$$

All three-literal terms have been combined. Hence we sum the resulting two-literal terms, ignoring repetition.

$$f_3 = A\overline{D} + C\overline{D} + \overline{A}C$$

Apply consensus, $XY + \overline{X}Z + YZ = XY + \overline{X}Z$,

with $X = A; \; Y = \overline{D}, \, Z = C.$

$$f_3 = A\overline{D} + \overline{A}C$$

Algebraic simplification, besides being tedious, does not clearly show which terms should be combined. We prefer methods that help us quickly identify possible combinations. One such method is the Karnaugh map.

2.8   KARNAUGH MAP

The *Karnaugh map* was developed by Maurice Karnaugh, an electrical engineer at Bell Laboratories. It resembles a rigid version of a Venn diagram, which you may recall from set theory. It is a graphic display of a truth table arranged so that adjacent terms differ in only one literal. The map is divided by rows and columns into single cells.

Forms of the Karnaugh map for one, two, three, and four variables and their corresponding truth tables are shown in figures 2.15 through 2.18, respectively. (Karnaugh maps for more than four variables will be discussed later.) One version of each map shows the cell number corresponding to the row number of the truth table. The second version of each map shows the minterm corresponding to each cell. A minterm on a Karnaugh map is a cell whose output is 1, called a *1 cell*. We could also show the maxterm corresponding to each cell. A maxterm on a Karnaugh map is a cell whose output is 0, called a *0 cell*. Ordinarily, Karnaugh maps show output function, as in the example of figure 2.19.

We can construct the minterm for each 1 cell (cell with output 1) from the row and column headings by writing the logical product of the unbarred literal for each 1 and the barred literal for each 0.

Example 2.18

Write the minterm for the 1 cell of the second column and fourth row of the four-variable map of figure 2.19. The cell corresponds to

Row Number	X	Minterm
0	0	$\overline{X}$
1	1	X

a)   Truth table

X

0	1
0	1

b)   Karnaugh map showing cell numbers

X

0	1
$\overline{X}$	X

c)   Karnaugh map showing minterms

Fig. 2.15   One-variable truth table and Karnaugh maps

Row Number	X	Y	Minterms
0	0	0	$\overline{X}\overline{Y}$
1	0	1	$\overline{X}Y$
2	1	0	$X\overline{Y}$
3	1	1	XY

a)   Truth table

b)   Karnaugh map showing cell numbers

c)   Karnaugh map showing minterms

Fig. 2.16   Two-variable truth table and Karnaugh maps

$W = 0$, $X = 1$, $Y = 1$, $Z = 0$. Thus W and Z are barred; X and Y are unbarred. We form the logical product. The minterm is $\overline{W}XY\overline{Z}$.

We can construct the maxterm for each 0 cell (cell with output 0) by writing the logical sum of the unbarred literal for each 0 and the barred literal for each 1.

Example 2.19

Write the maxterm for the 0 cell of the fourth column and third row of the four-variable map of figure 2.19.

The cell corresponds to $W = 1$, $X = 0$, $Y = 1$, $Z = 1$. Thus W, Y, and Z are barred; X is unbarred. We form the logical sum. The maxterm is $\overline{W} + X + \overline{Y} + \overline{Z}$.

The cells of the Karnaugh maps for three and four variables are arranged so that only one variable changes in a single vertical or horizontal move. The variables change from 00 to 01 to 11 to 10. In a single move, either a 0 changes to 1 or a 1 changes to 0. If the variables were ordered instead in the usual binary fashion (00,

Row Number	X	Y	Z	Minterm
0	0	0	0	$\bar{X}\bar{Y}\bar{Z}$
1	0	0	1	$\bar{X}\bar{Y}Z$
2	0	1	0	$\bar{X}Y\bar{Z}$
3	0	1	1	$\bar{X}YZ$
4	1	0	0	$X\bar{Y}\bar{Z}$
5	1	0	1	$X\bar{Y}Z$
6	1	1	0	$XY\bar{Z}$
7	1	1	1	XYZ

a)   Truth table

	XY			
Z	00	01	11	10
0	0	2	6	4
1	1	3	7	5

b)   Karnaugh map showing cell numbers

	XY			
Z	00	01	11	10
0	$\bar{X}\bar{Y}\bar{Z}$	$\bar{X}Y\bar{Z}$	$XY\bar{Z}$	$X\bar{Y}\bar{Z}$
1	$\bar{X}\bar{Y}Z$	$\bar{X}YZ$	XYZ	$X\bar{Y}Z$

c)   Karnaugh map showing minterms

Fig. 2.17   Three-variable truth table and Karnaugh maps

01, 10, 11), two variables would change in the single move from 01 to 10.

To allow the combining of terms that differ in only one variable, the columns and rows are ordered as shown. The right and left ends of the Karnaugh map are considered adjacent as there is only one variable change between 00 and 10. Similarly, the top and bottom of the map are considered adjacent. Although we must represent the map as flat, it is best to think of the map as on a sphere. Then the adjacencies are clear.

A Karnaugh map shows cells that can be combined. The general rule is that 1s (or 0s) may be combined if they form rectangles of 2^k cells for integer k. That is, cells may be combined in rectangles of 2, 4, 8, or 16 cells on Karnaugh maps with four or fewer variables. We always look for the largest rectangle covering any 1 cell (or 0 cell).

Row Number	W	X	Y	Z	Minterms
0	0	0	0	0	$\overline{W}\overline{X}\overline{Y}\overline{Z}$
1	0	0	0	1	$\overline{W}\overline{X}\overline{Y}Z$
2	0	0	1	0	$\overline{W}\overline{X}Y\overline{Z}$
3	0	0	1	1	$\overline{W}\overline{X}YZ$
4	0	1	0	0	$\overline{W}X\overline{Y}\overline{Z}$
5	0	1	0	1	$\overline{W}X\overline{Y}Z$
6	0	1	1	0	$\overline{W}XY\overline{Z}$
7	0	1	1	1	$\overline{W}XYZ$
8	1	0	0	0	$W\overline{X}\overline{Y}\overline{Z}$
9	1	0	0	1	$W\overline{X}\overline{Y}Z$
10	1	0	1	0	$W\overline{X}Y\overline{Z}$
11	1	0	1	1	$W\overline{X}YZ$
12	1	1	0	0	$WX\overline{Y}\overline{Z}$
13	1	1	0	1	$WX\overline{Y}Z$
14	1	1	1	0	$WXY\overline{Z}$
15	1	1	1	1	$WXYZ$

a)   Truth table

YZ＼WX	00	01	11	10
00	0	4	12	8
01	1	5	13	9
11	3	7	15	11
10	2	6	14	10

b)   Karnaugh map showing cell numbers

YZ＼WX	00	01	11	10
00	$\overline{W}\overline{X}\overline{Y}\overline{Z}$	$\overline{W}X\overline{Y}\overline{Z}$	$WX\overline{Y}\overline{Z}$	$W\overline{X}\overline{Y}\overline{Z}$
01	$\overline{W}\overline{X}\overline{Y}Z$	$\overline{W}X\overline{Y}Z$	$WX\overline{Y}Z$	$W\overline{X}\overline{Y}Z$
11	$\overline{W}\overline{X}YZ$	$\overline{W}XYZ$	$WXYZ$	$W\overline{X}YZ$
10	$\overline{W}\overline{X}Y\overline{Z}$	$\overline{W}XY\overline{Z}$	$WXY\overline{Z}$	$W\overline{X}Y\overline{Z}$

c)   Karnaugh map showing minterms

Fig. 2.18   Four-variable truth table and Karnaugh maps

Pairs of cells may be combined vertically or horizontally but not diagonally. (See figure 2.20.) Combining pairs on a Karnaugh map is a graphical simplification corresponding to $XY + X\overline{Y} = X$, or elimination of one variable. On a four-variable map we can combine pairs such as $WXYZ + WXY\overline{Z} = WXY$. We show the combination by drawing a loop around the combined cells. Cells can be combined

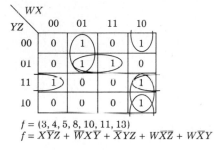

WX YZ	00	01	11	10
00	1	1	1	1
01	1	1	0	0
11	1	0	0	0
10	1	1	0	0

$$f = \Sigma(0, 1, 2, 3, 4, 5, 6, 8, 12)$$
$$f = \pi(7, 9, 10, 11, 13, 14, 15)$$

Fig. 2.19   Example of a four-variable Karnaugh map

WX YZ	00	01	11	10
00	0	1	0	1
01	0	1	1	0
11	1	0	0	1
10	0	0	0	1

$$f = (3, 4, 5, 8, 10, 11, 13)$$
$$f = X\overline{Y}Z + \overline{W}X\overline{Y} + \overline{X}YZ + WX\overline{Z} + W\overline{X}Y$$

Fig. 2.20   Four-variable map showing blocks of two cells

into more than one pair. The top and bottom cells of a column may be combined. The leftmost and rightmost cells of a row may be combined.

We label a pair on a Karnaugh map by writing all the literals that are the same for the pair. For example, the pair in the lower right corner of figure 2.20 combines $W\overline{X}YZ$ and $W\overline{X}Y\overline{Z}$. Since only the Z variable changes, we eliminate Z and label the pair $W\overline{X}Y$. Similarly, the pair on the ends of the third row combines $WXYZ$ and $\overline{W}XYZ$. This pair is labeled XYZ for the three variables that are the same in the pair.

Combinations of four cells are shown in figure 2.21. The simplifications correspond to $XYZ + X Y\overline{Z} + X\overline{Y}Z + X\overline{Y}\overline{Z} = X$, or elimination of two variables. On a four-variable map these simplifications correspond to $WXYZ + WXY\overline{Z} + WX\overline{Y}Z + WX\overline{Y}\overline{Z} = WX$. They occur either in 4×1 rectangles or in 2×2 squares. The combinations involving corner cells (fig. 2.21c) and top-bottom or left-right cells are the hardest to spot. We label blocks of four on a Karnaugh map by writing the variables that are constant for the block. For example,

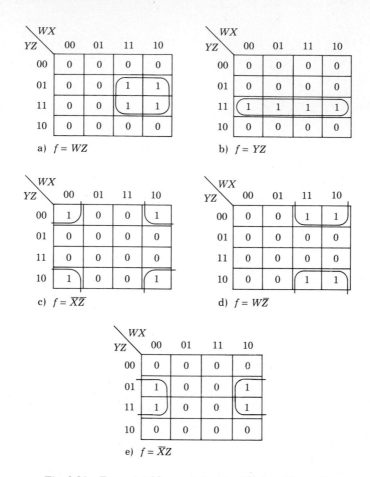

Fig. 2.21 Four-variable maps showing blocks of four cells

the block in figure 2.21a combines $WX\overline{Y}Z$, $W\overline{X}\overline{Y}Z$, $WXYZ$, and $W\overline{X}YZ$. It is labeled WZ for the two constant literals.

Combinations of eight cells representing elimination of three variables are shown in figure 2.22. The only possible pattern on a four-variable Karnaugh map is a 2 × 4 rectangle. Again the patterns combining cells on the edges of the map are most difficult to see. The block of eight is labeled for its constant variables. On a four-variable Karnaugh map, only one variable in a block of eight will be constant. It will be the label of the block. Figure 2.22 shows four examples.

A four-variable Karnaugh map has only one possible combination of 16 cells, as shown in figure 2.23. The label for the block of 16

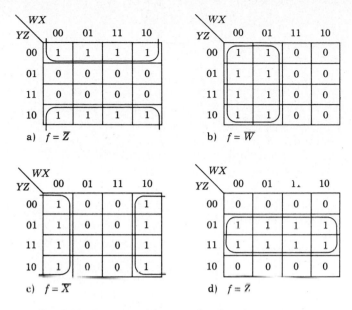

Fig. 2.22 Four-variable maps showing blocks of eight cells

cells is 1. Karnaugh maps with five or more variables can have several blocks of 16. They would be labeled with their constant variable.

We note that the larger blocks correspond to products with fewer literals. For the four-variable map, blocks of eight correspond to one literal; blocks of four correspond to products of two literals; blocks of two correspond to products of three literals; and single 1 cells correspond to products of four literals. In gate implementations, the larger blocks are implemented as gates with fewer inputs. Thus we will prefer to cover 1 cells with blocks that are as large as possible.

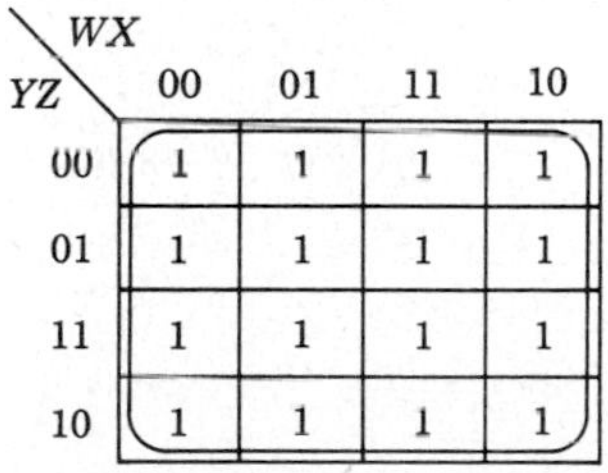

Fig. 2.23 Four-variable map showing block of 16 cells

2.8.1 Minimization by Karnaugh Maps

Karnaugh maps can help minimize most functions through a simple, almost intuitive procedure.

1. Map the function.
2. Starting with n equal to the number of variables on the map and decreasing, outline all rectangular blocks of size 2^n that are not subsets of rectangular blocks of size larger than 2^n.
3. Choose a subset of the blocks outlined that:
   a. covers all the 1 cells of the function,
   b. contains the fewest blocks, and
   c. contains the fewest literals of all subsets with the fewest blocks.

Example 2.18

Minimize

$$f_3 = \overline{A}\overline{B}CD + ABC\overline{D} + \overline{A}BCD + \overline{A}BC\overline{D} + AB\overline{C}D$$
$$+ \overline{A}\overline{B}C\overline{D} + A\overline{B}\overline{C}D + A\overline{B}CD$$

Algebraic simplification of this function is tedious. On a Karnaugh map minimization is easy. We first map the function as shown by the 1 cells in figure 2.24. In this example all terms of the function are 1 cells. If the function contained a term like $\overline{A}BC$, we would put 1s in the cells for both $\overline{A}BCD$ and $\overline{A}BC\overline{D}$. Then we would circle the three blocks of four. Note that we do not circle any pairs within a single block of four. The four blocks shown in figure 2.24 are $\overline{A}C$, $C\overline{D}$, and $A\overline{D}$. Hence

$$f = \overline{A}C + C\overline{D} + A\overline{D}$$

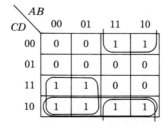

Fig. 2.24 Karnaugh map for example 2.18

However, we note that $\overline{A}C$ and $A\overline{D}$ cover all the 1 cells. $C\overline{D}$ is thus redundant and

$$f = \overline{A}C + A\overline{D}$$

Example 2.18 makes it easy to see from the Karnaugh map which cells to combine and which products to include in the simplified output function. Because most functions are more complex, we need a systematic procedure for finding the best output expression. Example 2.19 shows a more complex function, which we will try to minimize with the help of some definitions and a more detailed procedure.

Example 2.19

$$f_4(A,B,C,D) = \Sigma(2,4,6,8,9,10,12,13)$$

Figure 2.25 is a Karnaugh map of f_4.

An *implicant* is a product that, if 1, implies the function is 1. Thus, $\overline{A}BC\overline{D}$ is an implicant of f_4.

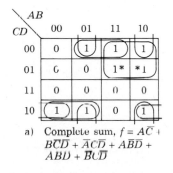

a) Complete sum, $f = A\overline{C}$ +
$B\overline{C}D + \overline{A}C\overline{D} + A\overline{B}\overline{D}$ +
$ABD + B\overline{C}\overline{D}$

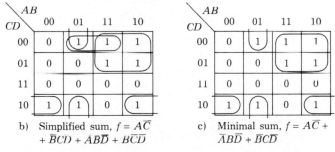

b) Simplified sum, $f = A\overline{C}$
$+ B\overline{C}D + A\overline{B}\overline{D} + B\overline{C}\overline{D}$

c) Minimal sum, $f = A\overline{C}$ +
$\overline{A}B\overline{D} + B\overline{C}D$

Fig. 2.25   Minimization of $f(A,B,C,D) = \Sigma(2,4,6,8,9,10,12,13)$

A *prime implicant* is implied by no other implicant. Graphically, it is the largest block that covers a given 1 cell. Algebraically, it is the implicant with the smallest number of literals that implies a given 1 cell. $\overline{A}BC\overline{D}$ is not a prime implicant of f_4 but $\overline{A}C\overline{D}$ is because $\overline{A}C\overline{D}$ implies $\overline{A}\overline{B}C\overline{D} + \overline{A}BC\overline{D}$. All prime implicants of f_4 are circled in figure 2.25a.

A *complete sum* is the sum of all prime implicants. The complete sum for f_4 is shown below the map in figure 2.25a.

A *simplified sum* is equal to the complete sum but contains fewer literals. Figure 2.25b shows a simplified sum that is not minimal.

A *minimal sum* is equal to the complete sum but contains the smallest number of product terms. Figure 2.25c shows a minimal sum for f_4. Although unique in this example, the minimal sum is not necessarily unique in general. Hence it is called a *minimal* sum instead of a minimum sum. Figure 2.26 shows two minimal sums for one function.

A *distinguished 1 cell* is a 1 cell covered by only one prime implicant. These cells are starred in figure 2.25a. There are no distinguished 1 cells in figure 2.26.

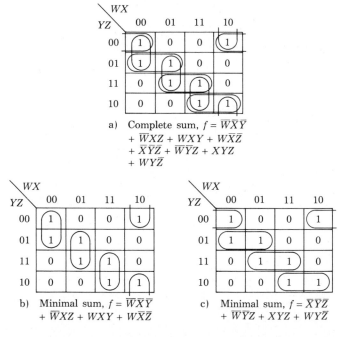

a) Complete sum, $f = \overline{W}\overline{X}\overline{Y}$
   $+ \overline{W}XZ + WXY + W\overline{X}\overline{Z}$
   $+ \overline{X}\overline{Y}\overline{Z} + \overline{W}\overline{Y}Z + XYZ$
   $+ WY\overline{Z}$

b) Minimal sum, $f = \overline{W}\overline{X}\overline{Y}$
   $+ \overline{W}XZ + WXY + W\overline{X}\overline{Z}$

c) Minimal sum, $f = \overline{X}\overline{Y}\overline{Z}$
   $+ \overline{W}\overline{Y}Z + XYZ + WY\overline{Z}$

Fig. 2.26 A function with two minimal sums

An *essential prime implicant* is a prime implicant that includes a distinguished 1 cell.

Two prime implicants are *equal* if they cover the same set of remaining 1 cells. In figure 2.27d, prime implicants $\overline{Y}Z$ and $X\overline{Y}$ are equal.

Prime implicant PI_1 *dominates* prime implicant PI_2 if PI_1 covers the same remaining 1 cell(s) as PI_2 and at least one other remaining 1 cell. Figure 2.28 gives examples of dominance.

A *don't care cell* (denoted by d or -) may be either 0 or 1 as desired in the minimization. A don't care cell represents an input condition that we do not consider important. It may be an input condition that cannot occur.

2.8.2 Minimization Procedure

The following steps illustrate the minimization procedure for the Karnaugh map:

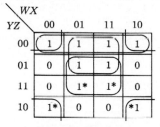

a) Prime implicants are circled, and distinguished 1 cells are asterisked. Complete sum, $f = \overline{X}\overline{Z} + \overline{Y}Z + X\overline{Y} + XZ$

b) Essential prime implicants (EPI) $\overline{X}\overline{Z}$ and XZ

c) Cells covered by EPI are changed to dashes

d) Remaining prime implicants, $\overline{Y}Z$ and $X\overline{Y}$, are equal; choose either. Minimal sum, $f = \overline{X}\overline{Z} + XZ + \overline{Y}Z$

Fig. 2.27 Equal prime implicants

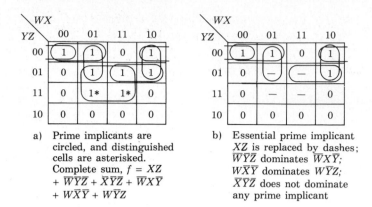

a) Prime implicants are circled, and distinguished cells are asterisked. Complete sum, $f = XZ + \overline{W}\overline{Y}\overline{Z} + \overline{X}\overline{Y}\overline{Z} + \overline{W}X\overline{Y} + W\overline{X}\overline{Y} + W\overline{Y}Z$

b) Essential prime implicant XZ is replaced by dashes; $\overline{W}\overline{Y}\overline{Z}$ dominates $\overline{W}X\overline{Y}$; $W\overline{X}\overline{Y}$ dominates $W\overline{Y}Z$; $\overline{X}\overline{Y}\overline{Z}$ does not dominate any prime implicant

Fig. 2.28 Dominant prime implicants

1. Assume all don't cares are 1s.
2. Generate all prime implicants.
3. Star all distinguished 1 cells; ignore distinguished d cells.
4. Sum all essential prime implicants.
5. Change all 1 cells covered by essential prime implicants to don't cares.
6. Discard the smaller of two equal prime implicants; discard either of two equal prime implicants of the same size.
7. Discard dominated prime implicants if smaller than dominant prime implicants.
8. Repeat steps 3 through 7 until no more prime implicants can be included in the sum. If all 1 cells are covered by essential prime implicants, you are finished.
9. If all 1 cells are not yet covered, arbitrarily pick one of the remaining prime implicants as essential and repeat steps 5 through 8.
10. Pick the set of sums formed in step 9 that has the fewest terms.
11. Pick one of the set of sums formed in step 10 with the fewest literals as a minimal sum.

Figure 2.29 gives a flowchart of this minimization procedure. While the procedure seems long, its application is straightforward. Usually only the first eight steps are needed, as in the following example.

Example 2.20

$$f(W,X,Y,Z) = \Sigma(0,2,3,4,5,8,10,11,12,13,14,15)$$

Figure 2.30a shows a Karnaugh map of f; its prime implicants are circled in figure 2.30b. $\overline{W}X\overline{Y}Z$ and $\overline{W}XYZ$ are distinguished 1 cells. Therefore, $\overline{X}Y$ and $X\overline{Y}$ are essential prime implicants and must be included in the minimal sum. After the 1 cells covered by $\overline{X}Y$ and $X\overline{Y}$ are changed to don't cares in figure 2.30c, the remaining prime implicants are circled in figure 2.30d. We note that $\overline{Y}\overline{Z}$ equals $\overline{X}\overline{Z}$ since both cover $\overline{W}\overline{X}\overline{Y}\overline{Z}$ and $W\overline{X}\overline{Y}\overline{Z}$ but no other remaining 1 cells. Similarly, WX equals WY since both cover $WXY\overline{Z}$ and $WXYZ$ but no other remaining 1 cells. There are no dominance relationships. We arbitrarily choose $\overline{X}\overline{Z}$ and WX and hence discard $\overline{Y}\overline{Z}$ and WY. $\overline{W}\overline{X}\overline{Y}\overline{Z}$ and $WXYZ$ are now distinguished 1 cells (fig. 2.30e). Thus $\overline{X}\overline{Z}$ and WX are essential prime implicants and must be included in the minimal sum, mapped in figure 2.30g.

2.8.3 Don't Care Conditions

The Karnaugh map minimization procedure treats don't cares as 1s. However, we do not want to include a product that covers only ds, nor do we want to consider a prime implicant as essential simply because it covers one or more distinguished d cells. In other words, we want to include d cells to allow us to form bigger blocks of 1s since bigger blocks have fewer literals and thus require fewer inputs in their realization. We do not want to include ds if doing so will lead to more terms or terms with more literals.

Example 2.21

$$f(V,W,X,Y,Z) = \Sigma(4,5,9,12,13,16,20,21,24,25,26,28)$$
$$+ \, d(8,14,15,17,22,23,29,30,31)$$

Figure 2.31 shows the Karnaugh map of f. Since f is a function of five variables, two four-variable Karnaugh maps are drawn. Though shown side by side, the maps should be considered as one on top of the other. Then a 1 cell can be combined with another directly below. We thus have three directions for combining 1 cells—vertically, horizontally, and above-below (out of the plane of the page).

Distinguished 1 cells $\overline{V}\overline{W}X\overline{Y}Z$, $V\overline{W}\overline{X}\overline{Y}Z$, $\overline{V}\overline{W}X\overline{Y}\overline{Z}$, and $V\overline{W}\overline{X}YZ$ require the inclusion of essential prime implicants, $X\overline{Y}$, $W\overline{Y}$, $V\overline{Y}$, and $VW\overline{Z}$, respectively. Distinguished d cells are $\overline{V}WXYZ$ and $\overline{V}WXY\overline{Z}$ in WX, $V\overline{W}XYZ$ and $V\overline{W}X\overline{Y}Z$ in VX, and $V\overline{W}\overline{X}\overline{Y}Z$ in $V\overline{Y}$. We do not include WX or VX to cover the first four distinguished d cells; $V\overline{Y}$ has already been included to cover a distinguished 1 cell. Since

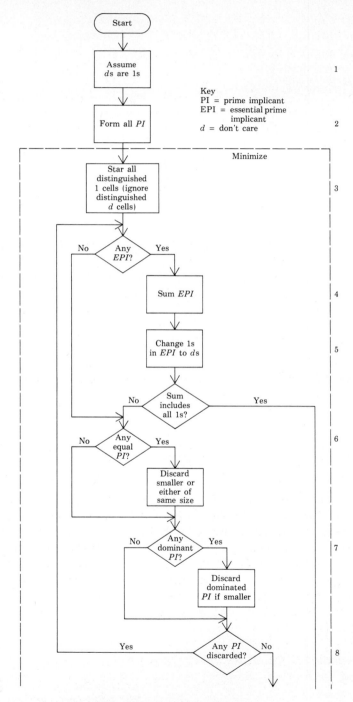

Key
PI = prime implicant
EPI = essential prime
        implicant
d = don't care

Fig. 2.29 Flowchart of minimization

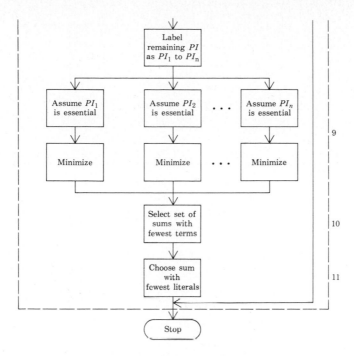

(Fig. 2.29 continued)

the essential prime implicants cover all 1 cells, the sum of the essential prime implicants is the minimal sum.

$$f = X\bar{Y} + W\bar{Y} + V\bar{Y} + VW\bar{Z}$$

2.8.4   Product-of-Sums Minimization

The Karnaugh minimization of a product-of-sums function is the dual of the procedure for minimization of sum-of-product functions that we have just discussed. Thus we will look for blocks of 0s and treat ds as 0s. The blocks are sums instead of products. When writing each sum, we write the complement of the expression we would have written for blocks of 1s. That is, columns or rows headed by 0s are written as unbarred variables, and columns or rows headed by 1s are written as barred variables. We write a product of sums instead of a sum of products. The sums are called *implicates* instead of implicants.

Example 2.21   (product-of-sums version)

$$f(V,W,X,Y,Z) = \pi(0,1,2,3,6,7,10,11,18,19,27)$$
$$+ \ d(8,14,15,17,22,23,29,30,31)$$

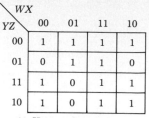

	00	01	11	10
00	1	1	1	1
01	0	1	1	0
11	1	0	1	1
10	1	0	1	1

a) Karnaugh map

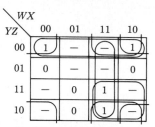

b) Prime implicants are circled, and distinguished 1 cells are asterisked. Complete sum, $f = \overline{Y}\overline{Z} + WX + \overline{X}\overline{Z} + X\overline{Y} + WY + W\overline{Z} + \overline{X}Y$

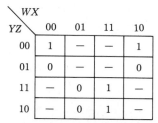

c) Cells covered by essential prime implicants, $\overline{X}Y$ and $X\overline{Y}$, are changed to don't cares

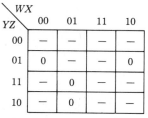

d) Of remaining prime implicants, $\overline{Y}\overline{Z} = \overline{X}\overline{Z}$, $WX = WY$. Choose $\overline{X}\overline{Z}$ and WX; discard $\overline{Y}\overline{Z}$ and WY.

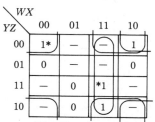

e) $\overline{W}\overline{X}\overline{Y}\overline{Z}$ and $WXYZ$ are now distinguished 1 cells; hence $\overline{X}\overline{Z}$ and WX are secondary essential prime implicants.

	00	01	11	10
00	—	—	—	—
01	0	—	—	0
11	—	0	—	—
10	—	0	—	—

f) Cells covered by $\overline{X}\overline{Z}$ and WX are changed to don't cares; no 1 cells remain.

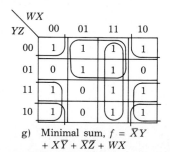

g) Minimal sum, $f = \overline{X}Y + X\overline{Y} + \overline{X}\overline{Z} + WX$

Fig. 2.30 Karnaugh maps for example 2.20

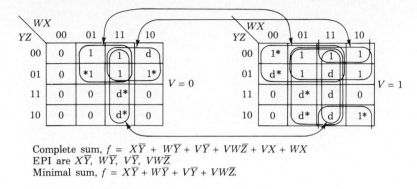

Complete sum, $f = X\overline{Y} + W\overline{Y} + V\overline{Y} + VW\overline{Z} + VX + WX$
EPI are $X\overline{Y}$, $W\overline{Y}$, $V\overline{Y}$, $VW\overline{Z}$.
Minimal sum, $f = X\overline{Y} + W\overline{Y} + V\overline{Y} + VW\overline{Z}$.

Fig. 2.31 Karnaugh map for example 2.21

Figure 2.32a shows the prime implicates of the function. $(\overline{Y} + \overline{Z})$ and $(W + \overline{Y})$ are essential prime implicates; $(Y + Z)$ covers distinguished 0 cell $\overline{V} + \overline{W} + X + \overline{Y} + \overline{Z}$. $(W + \overline{Y})$ covers distinguished 0 cell $\overline{V} + W + X + \overline{Y} + Z$. Figure 2.32b shows the map after $(\overline{Y} + Z)$ and $(W + \overline{Y})$ have been changed to don't cares. $V + W + X$ dominates $W + X + \overline{Z}$; hence we remove $W + X + \overline{Z}$. $V + X + Z$ dominates $V + \overline{Y}$ but $(V + \overline{Y})$ is larger in area so we do not remove it. Figure 2.32c shows the map of the remaining prime implicates. The secondary essential prime implicate is $(V + W + X)$ because of distinguished 0 cell $V + W + X + Y + Z$. Figure 2.32d shows the map after $(V + W + X)$ has been changed to ds. Both $(V + \overline{Y})$ and $(V + X + Z)$ cover the remaining 0 cell and hence are equal. We choose $(V + \overline{Y})$ since it is larger in area and has fewer literals.

Minimal product, $f = (\overline{Y} + \overline{Z})(V + W + X)(V + \overline{Y})(W + \overline{Y})$

Note that expansion of the minimal product yields:

$$f = VW\overline{Y} + V\overline{Y} + W\overline{Y} + VX\overline{Y} + WXY$$
$$+ X\overline{Y} + VWXY + VW\overline{Z} + V\overline{Y}\overline{Z} + W\overline{Y}\overline{Z}$$
$$+ VWX\overline{Z} + X\overline{Y}\overline{Z} + VW\overline{Y}\overline{Z} + VW\overline{Y}\overline{Z} + WX\overline{Y}\overline{Z}$$

which simplifies to

$$f = V\overline{Y} + W\overline{Y} + X\overline{Y} + VW\overline{Z}$$

the minimal sum.

In general, however, the expansion of the minimal product does not equal the minimal sum since d cells may be considered as 0s in one minimization and 1s in the other. Any expression may have

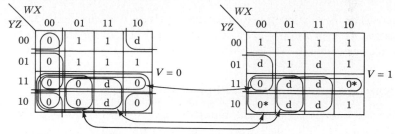

a) Essential prime implicates are $(\overline{Y} + \overline{Z})$ and $(W + \overline{Y})$.

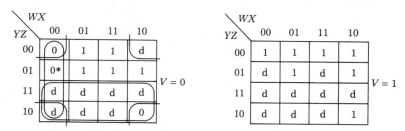

b) $(\overline{Y} + \overline{Z})$ and $(W + \overline{Y})$ are changed to ds, and implicates with only d cells are removed. $(V + W + X)$ dominates $(W + X + \overline{Z})$.
$(V + X + Z)$ dominates $(V + \overline{Y})$ but $(V + \overline{Y})$ is larger in area.

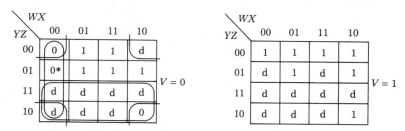

c) $(W + X + \overline{Z})$ is removed, and secondary distinguished 0 cell is $(V + W + X + Y + \overline{Z})$. Secondary EPI is $(V + W + X)$.

d) Secondary EPI is changed to ds.
$(V + \overline{Y})$ and $(V + X + Z)$ cover remaining 0 cell.
Choose $(V + \overline{Y})$ since it is the larger of the two equal implicates.
Minimal product $= (\overline{Y} + \overline{Z})\,(W + \overline{Y})\,(V + W + X)\,(V + \overline{Y})$.

Fig. 2.32 Example of product-of-sums minimization

more than one minimal sum or more than one minimal product because of a different treatment of d cells or different choices of equal prime implicants or implicates.

2.8.5 Karnaugh Maps for Additional Variables

Karnaugh maps are not well suited for six or more variables. Figure 2.33 shows a Karnaugh map for a function of six variables. The

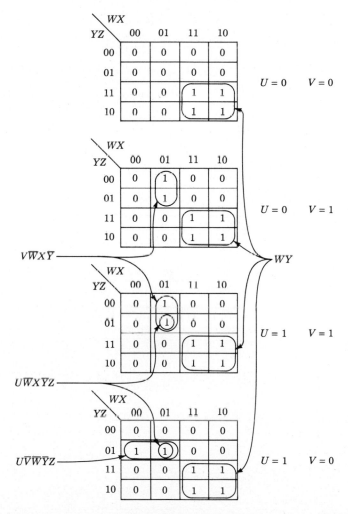

Fig. 2.33 Six-variable Karnaugh map for
$$f(U,V,W,X,Y,Z) = WY + V\overline{W}X\overline{Y} + U\overline{V}\,\overline{W}\,\overline{Y}Z + U\overline{W}X\overline{Y}Z$$

four-variable maps should be considered as stacked on top of each other in the order shown. Then, much as in three-dimensional tic-tac-toe, we can look for combinations that appear in two or four of the maps.

Beyond six variables the basic Karnaugh map is hard to use. In space there are only three axes to use. Since there are two directions for each axis, six variables can be plotted, but no more. If we wish to plot more than six variable functions on a Karnaugh map, we must go to an extended Karnaugh map, as shown in figure 2.34. The criterion for this map is symmetries rather than adjacencies. Any two 1 cells (or 0 cells) may be combined provided they are symmetric with respect to any line that divides the Karnaugh map into halves,

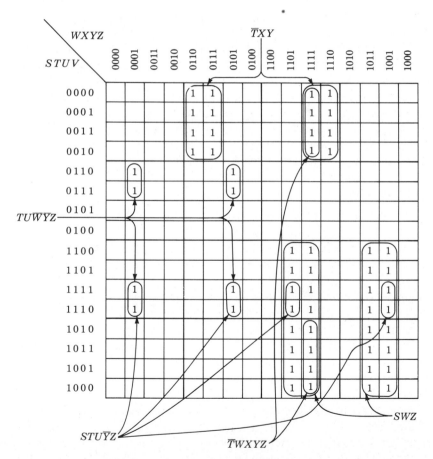

Fig. 2.34 Eight-variable extended Karnaugh map for
$f(S,T,U,V,W,X,Y,Z) + SWZ + \overline{STX}Y + TU\overline{WYZ} + STU\overline{YZ} + \overline{T}WXYZ$

quarters, eighths, or any other division of 2^{-n}. Examples are shown in the figure. Such symmetries are hard to see, and hence the extended Karnaugh map is hard to use accurately.

2.9   QUINE-McCLUSKEY TABLES

The Karnaugh map takes advantage of our ability to see patterns. Unfortunately, it is difficult to use for more than about four to six variables. In addition, we are likely to make errors by missing patterns connecting two 1s on opposite sides of the map. Hence it is desirable to have a method that is completely algorithmical and thus does not rely on human intuition. The Quine-McCluskey tabular method of minimization meets this requirement. It is especially useful for functions with several variables and can be readily programmed for a computer.

The Quine-McCluskey method follows steps similar to the Karnaugh map method. First, prime implicants (or implicates) are found. Then the essential prime implicants (or implicates) are identified and are necessarily included in the minimal sum (or product). Third, the remaining prime implicants (or implicates) are examined for 1s (or 0s) that can be deleted because of dominance or equality. After successive reductions, a minimal sum (or product) is finally obtained. This process is best illustrated by an example.

Example 2.22

$$f = \Sigma(0,2,4,6,7,8,9,10,11,12,13,14,16,18,19,29,30,31)$$

To find the prime implicants, we represent each fundamental product by the binary number of its row in the truth table. For example, $\overline{V}WX\overline{Y}\overline{Z}$ is represented by 01100. Then we group the resulting numbers by the number of 1s and separate the groups by lines. (See table 2.6.) We now have six groups, corresponding to numbers with zero to five 1s. Figure 2.35 shows a Karnaugh map of this function.

Once the numbers are grouped, we can form pairs by combining any two numbers that differ in only one bit position. To do this, we compare each number with every number in the group below it and check for differences in just one bit position. The number 0 combines with all numbers in the following group, yielding pairs (0,2), (0,4), (0,8), and (0,16) as shown in table 2.7. As we combine numbers into pairs, we check each number combined. The pairs have a dash for a don't care condition in the bit position in which the original numbers differed.

TABLE 2.6

GROUPING OF 1 CELLS

$f = \Sigma(0,2,4,6,7,8,9,10,11,12,13,14,16,18,19,29,30,31)$

1 Cells	V	W	X	Y	Z
0	0	0	0	0	0 ✓
2	0	0	0	1	0 ✓
4	0	0	1	0	0 ✓
8	0	1	0	0	0 ✓
16	1	0	0	0	0 ✓
6	0	0	1	1	0 ✓
9	0	1	0	0	1 ✓
10	0	1	0	1	0 ✓
12	0	1	1	0	0 ✓
18	1	0	0	1	0 ✓
7	0	0	1	1	1 ✓
11	0	1	0	1	1 ✓
13	0	1	1	0	1 ✓
14	0	1	1	1	0 ✓
19	1	0	0	1	1 ✓
29	1	1	1	0	1 ✓
30	1	1	1	1	0 ✓
31	1	1	1	1	1 ✓

We next combine pairs into groups of four. We look for two pairs that have a dash in the same position and differ in only one other position. They will combine to give numbers with two dashes. As before, we compare each number in one group with numbers in the group below. All pairs can be formed in more than one way. By convention, we list them only once with numbers ordered in increasing

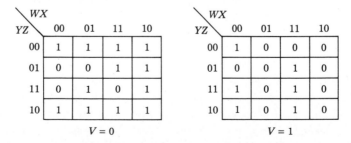

Fig. 2.35   Karnaugh map of example 2.22

TABLE 2.7

Grouping of Pairs

$$f = \Sigma(0,2,4,6,7,8,9,10,11,12,13,14,16,18,19,29,30,31)$$

Pairs	V	W	X	Y	Z
0,2	0	0	0	–	0 ✓
0,4	0	0	–	0	0 ✓
0,8	0	–	0	0	0 ✓
0,16	–	0	0	0	0 ✓
2,6	0	0	–	1	0 ✓
2,10	0	–	0	1	0 ✓
2,18	–	0	0	1	0 ✓
4,6	0	0	1	–	0 ✓
4,12	0	–	1	0	0 ✓
8,9	0	1	0	0	– ✓
8,10	0	1	0	–	0 ✓
8,12	0	1	–	0	0 ✓
16,18	1	0	0	–	0 ✓
6,7	0	0	1	1	– J
6,14	0	–	1	1	0 ✓
9,11	0	1	0	–	1 ✓
9,13	0	1	–	0	1 ✓
10,11	0	1	0	1	– ✓
10,14	0	1	–	1	0 ✓
12,13	0	1	1	0	– ✓
12,14	0	1	1	–	0 ✓
18,19	1	0	0	1	– I
13,29	–	1	1	0	1 H
14,30	–	1	1	1	0 G
29,31	1	1	1	–	1 F
30,31	1	1	1	1	– E

sequence. We must take care to check all four pairs that contribute to each group of four. This is usually easy to do. When we have found pair (0,2) combining with (4,6) to yield (0,2,4,6) or 00--0, we look for another pair with two of these numbers; we find (0,4) and know to look for (2,6). (See table 2.8.)

We then look for blocks of eight. Blocks of eight are formed from groups of four that have dashes in the same two positions and differ in just one other position. They combine to have dashes in three positions. Only one occurs in our example; it is shown in table 2.9. We must check all blocks of four that can combine to give a block of eight; note that six blocks are checked. In a general problem, we would next look for blocks of 16, and so on, but clearly there are none in this example.

TABLE 2.8

BLOCKS OF FOUR

Blocks of Four	V	W	X	Y	Z	
0,2,4,6	0	0	–	–	0	✓
0,2,8,10	0	–	0	–	0	✓
0,2,16,18	–	0	0	–	0	D
0,4,8,12	0	–	–	0	0	✓
2,6,10,14	0	–	–	1	0	✓
4,6,12,14	0	–	1	–	0	✓
8,9,10,11	0	1	0	–	–	C
8,9,12,13	0	1	–	0	–	B
8,10,12,14	0	1	–	–	0	✓

The result of this process has been to find the prime implicants; these are the unchecked blocks of eight, four, and two. In a more general problem, there might also be unchecked single numbers, or blocks of 16, 32, and more. We give each unchecked block a letter for convenient reference in the tables that follow. However, at this point, we can also write the prime implicants from the tables by barring each literal that is 0, writing each literal that is 1, and omitting each literal that is –. Thus $A = \bar{V}\bar{Z}$ and $B = \bar{V}W\bar{Y}$.

The process has been much slower and more tedious than the corresponding procedure for the Karnaugh map. In the Karnaugh map we looked for big blocks, but in the Quine-McCluskey method we must build them from combining first 1 cells, then pairs, then blocks of four, and so forth.

We now want to find the essential prime implicants. We list all prime implicants in table 2.10. The rows of the table are prime implicants, and the columns are the 1 cells of the function. We say that a row covers a column if the row is 1 for the column; for example, row D covers columns 0, 2, 16, and 18. We place crosses at the intersections of each column and the rows that cover it. We then circle each column with only one cross. These columns are *distinguished columns,* corresponding to distinguished 1 cells in the Karnaugh map procedure. We star each row that covers a distinguished

TABLE 2.9

BLOCKS OF EIGHT

Blocks of Eight	V	W	X	Y	Z	
0,2,4,6,8,10,12,14	0	–	–	–	0	A

TABLE 2.10

PRIME IMPLICANTS

Prime Implicants		0	2	④	6	⑦	8	9	10	⑪	12	13	14	⑯	18	⑲	29	30	31
0,2,4, 6,8,10, 12,14*	A	X	X	X	X		X		X		X		X						
8,9,12,13	B						X	X			X	X							
8,9, 10,11*	C						X	X	X	X									
0,2, 16,18*	D	X	X											X	X				
30,31	E																	X	X
29,31	F																X		X
14,30	G												X					X	
13,29	H											X					X		
18,19*	I														X	X			
6,7*	J				X	X													

column. These rows are essential rows, representing essential prime implicants that must be in our minimal sum. Essential prime implicants in this example are $A = \overline{VZ}$, $C = \overline{V}W\overline{X}$, $D = \overline{W}\overline{X}\overline{Z}$, $I = V\overline{W}\overline{X}Y$, and $J = \overline{VW}XY$.

We next delete all distinguished columns and essential rows since the 1 cells covered by them are included in the minimal sum. We also delete all columns covered by the essential rows for the same reason. The result is a reduced table (table 2.11). It corresponds to a reduced Karnaugh map after all essential prime implicants have been removed.

We next look for instances of equality (similar to equality in the Karnaugh map) where two remaining rows cover the same columns. There are none. We look for instances of dominance (corresponding to dominance in the Karnaugh map) where one row covers all remaining columns covered by another row and at least one more. E dominates G; we discard G. H dominates B; however, B, being a block of four, covers more 1 cells and has fewer literals than does H. Hence we do not discard B.

TABLE 2.11

First Reduced Table

Prime Implicants		13	29	30	31
8,9,12,13	B	X			
30,31	E			X	X
29,31	F		X		X
14,30	G			X	
13,29	H	X	X		

We form another reduced table (table 2.12). Now E is an essential row to cover the distinguished column 30. We add E to our minimal sum and remove row E and columns 30 and 31 from the table, thus forming another reduced table (table 2.13). H covers both remaining columns so we add H to our minimal sum. All columns have been covered so we are finished.

The Quine-McCluskey procedure can be used for forming minimal products and for functions with don't care conditions, just as the Karnaugh map can. McCluskey (1965) has an extensive discussion of the Quine-McCluskey method.

$$\begin{aligned} \text{Minimal sum} &= A + C + D + I + J + E + H \\ &= \overline{V}Z + \overline{V}W\overline{X} + \overline{W}\overline{X}\overline{Z} + V\overline{W}\overline{X}Y \\ &\quad + \overline{V}\overline{W}XY + VWXY + WX\overline{Y}Z \end{aligned}$$

2.10   SUMMARY

In this chapter we examined combinational logic systems with n binary inputs and one output that could be any of 2^{2^n} switching functions. We examined 16 switching functions of two variables in

TABLE 2.12

Second Reduced Table

Prime Implicants		13	29	30	31
8,9,12,13	B	X			
30,31	E*			X	X
29,31	F		X		X
13,29	H	X	X		

TABLE 2.13

FINAL REDUCED TABLE

Prime Implicants		13	29
8,9,12,13	B	X	
29,31	F		X
13,29	H	X	X

detail and found that each could be implemented with a subset of the switching functions known as a complete set. AND, OR, and NOT are a complete set; NAND is a complete set; and NOR is a complete set. Complex functions can be constructed by successively applying operators to functions; precedence rules are needed to specify unambiguously the order in which operators should be applied. Two composite functions can be examined for logical equivalence. They are logically equivalent if they are defined for the same arguments and are equal for all possible combinations of the arguments. This condition is most easily shown by comparing truth tables for the two functions.

Switching algebra is the mathematics that describes the operation of logic circuits. It comprises a set of symbols and a set of rules for manipulating the symbols. The rules are both postulates and theorems—for example, absorption, consensus, idempotence, DeMorgan's. Switching algebra differs from ordinary algebra by the lack of cancellation, among other things. Theorems can be proved by perfect induction (listing all possibilities) or deduction.

Any combinational logic function can be expressed in two canonical forms—a sum-of-products (AND-OR) form and a product-of-sums (OR-AND) form. These forms can be implemented as logic circuits with two gate levels.

Combinational logic functions can be minimized by algebraic techniques, Karnaugh maps, or Quine-McCluskey tables. The criterion for minimization is to minimize first the number of terms and next the total number of literals. Algebraic simplification involves the successive application of theorems and postulates to reduce the expression; it is tedious and error prone. Karnaugh maps take advantage of the ability of the human eye to spot patterns, but the maps are hard to use for functions of more than four to six variables. The Quine-McCluskey approach is algorithmic and can easily be implemented on a computer; it is tedious to do by hand.

We did not consider the problem of logic circuits with more than one output. Minimization of multiple output circuits requires examination of each output to detect common terms that can be combined to yield the minimum number of gates for the total outputs. Karnaugh map and Quine-McCluskey techniques for this procedure are given in some of the references.

Concepts

AND	logical equivalence
canonical forms	maxterm
cell	minimal sum
COINCIDENCE	minimization
combinational logic	minterm
complement	NAND
complete set	NOR
complete sum	NOT
decimal expression	OR
DeMorgan's theorems	perfect induction
distinguished 1 cell	precedence rules
dominance	prime implicant
don't care	product-of-sums
double-rail	Quine-McCluskey
dual	sequential logic
equality	single-rail
essential prime implicant	sum-of-products
gate	switching algebra
implicant	truth table
implicate	two-level
inverter	unary
Karnaugh map	XOR
literal	

2.11 REFERENCES

McCluskey (1965) is a classic text that, naturally, is especially thorough on explanation of the Quine-McCluskey method. Booth (1971) and Bartee (1972) discuss combinational logic at about the level of this text; Booth also treats multiple output minimization. Williams (1970) covers Boolean algebra and its application to computers. Kohonen (1972), Peatman (1972), Hill and Peterson (1974), and Nagle, Carroll, and Irwin (1975) are more advanced texts. Harrison (1965) gives a thorough theoretical coverage.

2.12 PROBLEMS

2.1 Evaluate $\overline{\overline{\overline{A}B\overline{C}D}} + \overline{\overline{A}BCD(\overline{B\overline{C}D} + \overline{\overline{A}CD})}$ for $A = 0, B = 1,$
$C = 1, D = 0.$ (2.4)

2.2 Evaluate $\overline{A\overline{BC}(D\overline{E}F(\overline{BC\overline{F}} + \overline{B}D))}$ for $A = 0, B = 0, C = 1,$
$D = 1, E = 0, F = 0.$ (2.4)

2.3 Evaluate $(A \oplus \overline{B}C)\uparrow(BD\downarrow\overline{A}C)$ for $A = B = 1, C = D = 0.$ (2.4)

2.4 Evaluate $((AB)\downarrow\overline{C}) \oplus (C\downarrow(D \oplus \overline{A}))$ for $A = 1, B = 0,$
$C = 1, D = 1.$ (2.4)

2.5 Show the three-variable truth tables for the generalized functions $f(X,Y,Z) =$

a. XYZ
b. $X + Y + Z$
c. $X\uparrow Y\uparrow Z$
d. $X\downarrow Y\downarrow Z$
e. $X \oplus (Y \oplus Z)$
f. $X\odot(Y\odot Z)$ (2.4)

2.6 Show the four-variable truth tables for the generalized functions $f(W,X,Y,Z) =$

a. $WXYZ$
b. $W + X + Y + Z$
c. $W + (X + (Y + Z))$
d. $W\cdot(X\cdot(Y\cdot Z))$ (2.4)

2.7 Design a circuit for problem 2.3.   (2.4)

2.8 Design a circuit for problem 2.4.   (2.4)

2.9 Algebraically check the validity of the equation:
$(X + \overline{Y})(\overline{X} + Z)(Y + \overline{Z}) = (\overline{X} + Y)(X + \overline{Z})(\overline{Y} + Z)$ (2.5)

2.10 Algebraically check the validity of the equation:
$$XY + \overline{X}\overline{Y}Z = (X + Z)(Y + Z)$$ (2.5)

2.11 Algebraically check the validity of the equation:

$$(X + Y)(Y + Z)(X + Z) = (\bar{X} + \bar{Y})(\bar{X} + \bar{Z})(\bar{Y} + \bar{Z}) \quad (2.5)$$

2.12 Algebraically check the validity of the equation:

$$(XY)(YZ)(XZ) = (\overline{\bar{X} + \bar{Y}})(\overline{\bar{X} + \bar{Z}})(\overline{\bar{Y} + \bar{Z}}) \quad (2.5)$$

2.13 For the function $f(W,X,Y,Z) = \bar{W}XY + W(X + Y)\bar{Z}$ find

a. the dual function, f_d;
b. the complement of the function, $\bar{f}$;
c. the complement of the dual function, $\bar{f_d}$.
d. Are any of these functions logically equivalent?   (2.5)

2.14 For the function $f(X,Y,Z) = XYZ + \bar{X}Y\bar{Z} + \bar{X}\bar{Y}Z + X\bar{Y}\bar{Z}$ find

a. the dual function, f_d;
b. the complement of the function, $\bar{f}$;
c. the complement of the dual function, $\bar{f_d}$.
d. Are any of these functions logically equivalent?   (2.5)

2.15 For the logic function $f(W,Y,Z) = \Sigma(0,1,7)$,

a. show the truth table;
b. write the sum-of-products form;
c. write the product-of-sums form;
d. show circuits for items (a) and (c).   (2.6)

2.16 Design circuits for the two canonical forms of

$$f(A,B,C) = \pi(1,3,4) \quad (2.6)$$

2.17 A combinational logic circuit with four inputs—W, X, Y, and Z—produces a 1 output if and only if an odd number of the inputs are 1.

a. Show the truth table.
b. Find a canonical sum-of-products expression for the output.
c. Find a canonical product-of-sums expression for the output.
d. Find a minimal function.   (2.7)

2.18 A combinational logic circuit has two inputs—Y_i and Z_i. It has four outputs—W_o, X_o, Y_o, and Z_o. The output $W_o X_o Y_o Z_o$ is the square of the input $Y_i Z_i$. That is, input 10 produces output 0100. Design a minimal circuit.   (2.8)

2.19 In hockey, icing may not be called on a team that, because of penalties, has one or two fewer players on the ice than the other team has. Devise a logic circuit that will produce a 1 output whenever icing may not be called on team A. Each team always has four, five, or six players on the ice and zero, one, or two players in the penalty box. (Hint: Inputs should be the number of players serving penalties on team A and the number of players serving penalties on team B.)   (2.8)

2.20 People have any one of four basic blood types—A, B, AB, and O. Type O can donate blood to any type but receive only O. Type AB can receive blood from any type but can donate only to AB. A can donate to A or AB and receive from A or O. B can donate to B or AB and receive from B or O. Design a logic circuit that will accept as inputs the blood types of a desired donor-receiver pair and will output a 1 if the transfusion is permissible by these rules. Only four inputs are needed.
        (2.8)

2.21 A triply redundant circuit is to be built to increase the reliability of a combinational logic circuit. Three identical circuits will feed their outputs, Y_1, Y_2, and Y_3, into a majority voter circuit, M. The output, Z, of the majority voter circuit will, as the name implies, always agree with at least two inputs. Hence, if no more than one of the original circuits is incorrect, the final output Z should be correct. The figure below represents this problem.

   a. Form the truth table for the majority voter circuit.
   b. Write a simplified sum-of-products expression for Z.
   c. Implement the majority voter circuit.   (2.8)

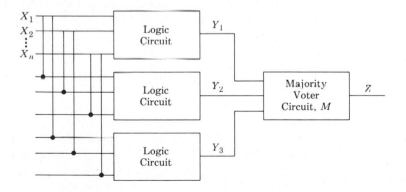

2.22 a. Find a function $f(X,Y,Z)$ that meets the conditions below:

  i. f has the maximum number of prime implicants;
  ii. f contains the minterm XYZ.

 b. Find a minimal sum for f and state how many prime implicants it has. (2.8)

2.23 a. Find a function $g(X,Y,Z)$ that meets the conditions below:

  i. g has the maximum number of essential prime implicants;
  ii. g contains the minterm XYZ.

 b. Find a minimal sum for g and state how many prime implicants it has. (2.8)

2.24 a. Construct the four-variable Karnaugh map for

$$f(W,X,Y,Z) = \Sigma(0,2,5,7,8,9,11) + d(3,4,13,14)$$

 b. Find the complete sum.
 c. Find a minimal sum.
 d. Find a minimal product. (2.8)

2.25 a. Construct the four-variable Karnaugh map for

$$f(W,X,Y,Z) = \Sigma(1,2,3,4,5,6,13,14,15) + d(8,10)$$

 b. Find the complete sum.
 c. Find the minimal sum.
 d. Find a minimal product.
 e. Would the circuits implementing your minimal sum and minimal product have the same output for all inputs? Why or why not? (2.8)

2.26 The binary code shown below is used for an input/output device called a flexowriter. Other code words (not shown) are used for punctuation.

A	011000	I	001100	Q	011101
B	010011	J	011010	R	001010
C	001110	K	011110	S	010100
D	010010	L	001001	T	000001
E	010000	M	000111	U	011100
F	010110	N	000110	V	001111
G	001011	O	000011	W	011001
H	000101	P	001101	X	010111

Y	010101	2	111100	6	110110
Z	010001	3	111000	7	111010
0	011111	4	110100	8	110000
1	101010	5	110010	9	011011

a. Design a minimal sum-of-products circuit that will accept a word of this code as an input and produce a 1 output if and only if that code word is a vowel (*A, E, I, O,* or *U*).

b. Repeat (a) assuming that only letters can be inputs. In other words, assume that all code words for numbers and punctuation are don't cares.

c. Design a minimal sum-of-products circuit that will output a 1 if and only if a number (0 through 9) is received.

d. Design a minimal product-of-sums circuit that will give a 1 output for vowels and a 0 output for other letters with all other inputs assumed to be don't cares. (2.8)

2.27 Seven-segment displays, as shown below, are found on many laboratory instruments. Design a logic circuitry that will accept numbers 0 through 9 in binary form and yield outputs to light segments of the display. You have considerable flexibility in your design since the inputs corresponding to decimal numbers 10 through 15 are don't care conditions. A brute force solution of this problem is easy; a minimal solution takes some thought. Try to design a circuit that has the minimum number of gates for all seven outputs rather than for each output considered singly. (The position of 1 is not standard. For your design, consider it to be on the right, that is, segments *B* and *C*.) (2.8)

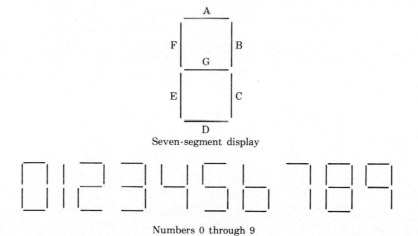

Seven-segment display

Numbers 0 through 9

2.28   Using a Karnaugh map, minimize

$$f(W,X,Y,Z) = WXYZ + \overline{WX}\overline{YZ} + W\overline{Y} + \overline{YZ} + WY\overline{Z} + \overline{WX} \tag{2.8}$$

2.29   Using a Karnaugh map of

$$f(W,X,Y,Z) = \Sigma(0,2,4,8,10,12,14) + d(1,3,7,15)$$

find

a. a minimal sum;
b. a minimal product. (2.8)

2.30   Using a Karnaugh map of

$$f(W,X,Y,Z) = \pi(0,1,2,5,6,8,12) + d(3,9,11)$$

find

a. a minimal sum;
b. a minimal product. (2.8)

2.31   Using a Karnaugh map of

$$f(V,W,X,Y,Z) = \pi(0,1,3,6,7,8,9,11,15,16,18,19,20,21)$$
$$+ d(4,25,26,28,30)$$

find

a. a minimal sum;
b. a minimal product. (2.8)

2.32   Using a Karnaugh map of

$$f(V,W,X,Y,Z) = \Sigma(1,2,4,7,9,11,17,18,19,21,26,28,30)$$
$$+ d(0,8,16,24,25)$$

find

a. a minimal sum;
b. a minimal product. (2.8)

2.33   Consider the function $f(V,W,X,Y,Z) =$

$$\Sigma(1,3,4,5,6,7,9,11,12,13,14,17,20,21,22,23,25,26,27,28,31).$$

a. Show f on a Karnaugh map.
b. On the map, star the distinguished 1 cells and circle the essential prime implicants.

c. Find a minimal sum for f by the minimization procedure for Karnaugh maps. Write the sum and show it on a map.
d. Find a minimal sum for f by the Quine-McCluskey method. Write it and show it on a Karnaugh map.
e. For a two-level AND-OR realization, how many gates and gate inputs are required if f is realized using

   i. the canonical sum?
   ii. your sum from (c)?
   iii. your sum from (d)?   (2.9)

2.34 Minimize $f(A,B,C,D,E) =$

$$\Sigma(0,1,5,8,9,13,16,17,20,21,22,23,29,30,31)$$

by

a. Karnaugh map;
b. Quine-McCluskey table.   (2.9)

2.35 Minimize $f(V,W,X,Y,Z) =$

$$\pi(2,3,4,6,7,10,11,12,19,20,21,22,23,27,28,29)$$

by

a. Karnaugh map;
b. Quine-McCluskey table.   (2.9)

3 Combinational
Logic Circuits and
Logic Technologies

3.1 OVERVIEW

Our discussion of logic and logic circuits thus far has been theoretical. This chapter considers more practical aspects of logic circuits that will interest those concerned with hardware design more than those concerned primarily with computer theory and software. It is not essential to later chapters and may be skipped.

In this chapter we will inspect some problems that affect realization of logic circuits. We will consider the ways that we can assign the logic values 0 and 1 to the voltages of some logic technology. We will consider the problems presented by nonideal logic components—delay and timing problems, power limitations, and noise. We will study and compare the major logic technologies. The discussion of logic problems and technologies will also apply to the sequential logic circuits of chapter 4.

Design with actual logic components depends on the devices that are available. Minimization is done more intuitively since there is no straightforward procedure for minimizing logic designs with current components. Although design can be done with the basic gates of chapter 2, other available logic components can lead to better designs. We will look at some available logic components and consider how they are used to implement logic functions.

3.2 PRACTICAL CONSIDERATIONS

Our treatment of logic gates and circuits in chapter 2 was idealized. We did not consider the physical voltages corresponding to the binary signals 0 and 1. We assumed there were no limitations on the number of gate inputs or outputs and we ignored timing problems. In this section, we will examine some practical considerations that affect the use or design of combinational logic circuits.

3.2.1 Voltage Assignments

The binary signals 0 and 1 do not ordinarily correspond to voltages of 0 and 1 volt. Rather we assign the values 0 and 1 to two stable voltage ranges of the gate. We denote the higher (more positive) of the two voltage ranges by H and the lower by L. In between is a transition range in which the logic value of the voltage is not defined. Figure 3.1 shows an example of the voltage ranges. In practice, H and L may both be positive or negative, or just one may be positive as shown. The ranges are necessary since signals always have fluctuations in voltage, called *noise*.

We can assign the values 0 and 1 to the voltage ranges H and L in two ways. The assignment of 1 to H and 0 to L is called *positive logic*. The converse assignment of 0 to H and 1 to L is called *negative logic*. For example, consider a logic technology for which the high-voltage range is from 2.4 to 4.5 volts (v), and the low-voltage range is from 0.4 to 0.8 v. The two possible assignments are:

Positive logic	$1 = 2.4 - 4.5$ v	$0 = 0.4 - 0.8$ v
Negative logic	$1 = 0.4 - 0.8$ v	$0 = 2.4 - 4.5$ v

We can implement two logic functions with one logic device, choosing either positive or negative logic. For example, consider a gate that produces outputs as shown by the truth table of table 3.1. This

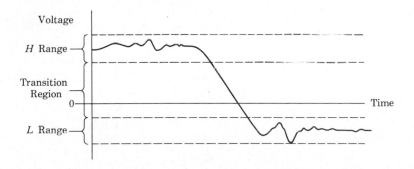

Fig. 3.1 Voltage ranges H and L

TABLE 3.1

TRUTH TABLE OF GATE

Inputs		Output
X	Y	Z
L	L	L
L	H	H
H	L	H
H	H	H

gate is an OR gate for positive logic but an AND gate for negative logic, as can be seen from the truth tables of table 3.2.

We can construct truth tables for the six main binary functions for both positive and negative logic. (See table 3.3.) From the tables we conclude that:

1. positive AND is negative OR;
2. positive OR is negative AND;
3. positive NAND is negative NOR;
4. positive NOR is negative NAND;
5. positive XOR is negative COINCIDENCE;
6. positive COINCIDENCE is negative XOR.

Because one function with inputs H and L can correspond to different logic functions for positive and negative logic, we can implement two logic functions with the same physical device. For example, a gate that gives an H output only when both inputs are H can be used as an AND gate for positive logic and as an OR gate for negative logic. A gate responds to voltage levels; we can designate these levels as we like. Manufacturers often label gates as AND/OR or NAND/NOR to show that they can be used to implement two functions, depending on the choice of logic. Alternatively, manufac-

TABLE 3.2

GATE TRUTH TABLES FOR POSITIVE AND NEGATIVE LOGIC

Positive logic $H = 1, L = 0$			Negative logic $H = 0, L = 1$		
X	Y	Z = X + Y	X	Y	Z = XY
0	0	0	1	1	1
0	1	1	1	0	0
1	0	1	0	1	0
1	1	1	0	0	0

TABLE 3.3

TRUTH TABLES FOR POSITIVE AND NEGATIVE LOGIC

Inputs	Outputs					
X Y	AND	OR	NAND	NOR	XOR	COINCIDENCE
a) Positive logic, $L = 0$, $H = 1$						
L L	L	L	H	H	L	H
L H	L	H	H	L	H	L
H L	L	H	H	L	H	L
H H	H	H	L	L	L	H
b) Negative logic, $H = 0$, $L = 1$						
L L	L	L	H	H	H	L
L H	H	L	L	H	L	H
H L	H	L	L	H	L	H
H H	H	H	L	L	H	L

turers sometimes specify positive logic in describing gates. We then understand that the gate functions described are for positive logic but that the gates can also be used for other functions in negative logic.

We use positive logic in this book unless stated otherwise.

3.2.2 Timing

No assumptions were made in chapter 2 about the time response of logic circuits because we did not consider response to a time series of inputs. In practice, of course, logic circuits must respond to a series of inputs. The speed of response of individual gates strongly affects the overall speed of the computer or digital system. We will be concerned with two types of time delays. The first delay, T_R, *rise time,* is the time required for the voltage to rise from 10% to 90% of its nominal final value. Figure 3.2b shows the rise time for the X input of the OR gate of figure 3.2a. (Similarly we could define T_F, *fall time,* as the time required for the voltage to fall from 90% of its initial value to 10%; this is not shown.) T_F may differ significantly from T_R. The second delay, T_D, *propagation delay,* measures the time required for the output to respond to the input. Propagation delay is defined as the time between the 50% points on the input

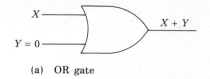

(a)   OR gate

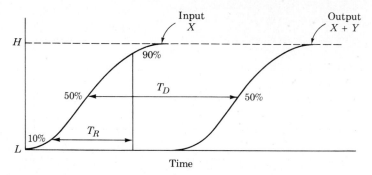

(b)   Input and output waveforms of OR gate

Fig.3.2   OR gate with input and output waveforms illustrating rise time, T_R, and propagation delay, T_D

and output signals. Figure 3.2b shows the propagation delay of the OR gate as the time interval required for the output to rise to 50% of its final value after the input has reached 50% of its final value. Propagation delays may differ for 0 to 1 transitions and 1 to 0 transitions. Manufacturers usually specify both delays.

We can model any logic gate as a delayless ideal gate followed by a time delay. Figure 3.3a shows a logic circuit consisting of three ideal gates followed by their inherent propagation delays. We would like to know the propagation delay of the complete logic circuit. Figure 3.3b shows how this is determined for the case $T_2 > T_1 > T_3$. The maximum propagation delay of a logic circuit is the largest sum of the propagation delays for the gates through which any input signal passes. In the case shown, the maximum propagation delay is $T_2 + T_3$ for inputs $\overline{X}$ and $\overline{Y}$. The maximum delay would be even greater if complemented inputs were not available, for then the delay of inverters would be added. The additive nature of propagation delay tends to make two-level circuits more attractive than three- or four-level circuits.

The speed at which a computer or digital system can operate is inversely proportional to the propagation delays of the logic circuitry.

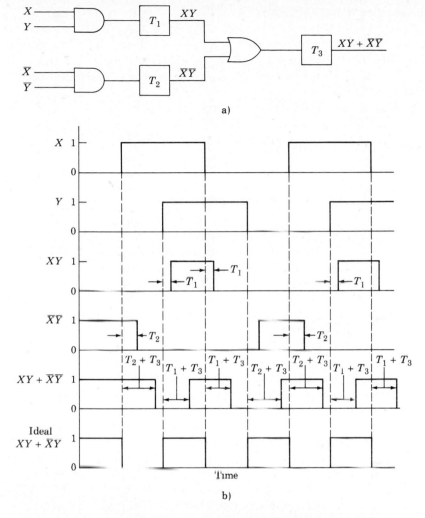

Fig. 3.3   Combinational logic network comprising ideal gates followed by their inherent propagation delays (a) and timing diagram (b)

The basic relationship is that frequency is the reciprocal of time; frequency = 1/time. A rule of thumb is that a computer can operate at about one-third the rate determined by its maximum propagation delay. Thus, a computer whose worst delay is 300 nanoseconds (ns) can operate at about $(1/3) \times (1/300) \times 10^{+9}$ hertz (Hz) or about 1.1 megahertz (MHz).

3.2.3   Power Requirements

The power required to operate a logic gate is a major factor in choosing between different types of gates, as will be discussed in the next section on logic technologies. The usual measure is power dissipation per gate in milliwatts (mw).

When several gates are connected together, we must consider not only the power dissipated by each gate but also the transfer of power through the circuit. Logic devices can accept a limited number of input signals and can drive a limited number of output signals. These limitations are usually described in terms of an arbitrarily defined *unit load,* the power required for one specific gate. We can describe the number of inputs of a particular gate as its *fan-in.* Each logic technology, such as those discussed in the next section, has a practical limit on the number of inputs possible. We define the maximum number of unit load inputs that a given logic technology can handle as its *maximum fan-in.*

Similarly, the *fan-out* of a particular gate in a logic circuit is the number of gates which its output drives. The maximum number of unit loads that the output of gates of a given logic technology can drive is called its *maximum fan-out.* Most TTL gates, which will be discussed in the next section, have a fan-out of 10. Thus they can be connected to 10 unit loads. The input of a typical simple gate, such as a NAND with four inputs, presents one unit load. Inputs of some more complex logic devices, such as those discussed later in the chapter, may be two, three, or four unit loads. Thus the output of a TTL gate could drive either the inputs of 10 simple gates or two to five inputs of more complex devices.

3.2.4   Noise Immunity

Logic gates are subject to two types of noise. Internal noise is generated by the logic circuit itself. Circuits that generate little noise are said to have good *internal noise immunity.* Logic gates also receive noise from their environments. Resistance to external noise, called *external noise immunity,* is important for devices that must operate in high-noise environments, such as aircraft.

Manufacturers often specify a *noise margin* between guaranteed output voltage levels and permitted input voltage levels. They will guarantee minimum 1 outputs and maximum 0 outputs provided that loading and input voltage conditions are met. Input voltage conditions are the maximum 0 input voltage and the minimum 1 output voltage allowed. The difference between the guaranteed out-

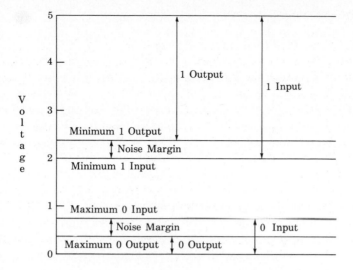

Fig. 3.4 Noise margins for TTL gates

put voltage and the permitted input voltage for a 0 or a 1 is the noise margin. It provides a margin for unavoidable noise.

For example, consider the voltage characteristics of a standard line of transistor-transistor-logic (TTL) circuits. The permitted input and guaranteed output voltages are as follows:

Logic state	Input voltages	Output voltages
0	less than 0.8 v	less than 0.4 v
1	more than 2.0 v	more than 2.4 v

These voltages are shown in figure 3.4. There is a noise margin of 0.4 v between the permitted input voltage and the guaranteed output voltage for both 0 and 1. This means that even if there is 0.4 v of noise on the wire connecting the output of one gate to the input of the next, the input voltage will still be within the permitted range. For example, if a 0 output encounters 0.3 v of noise on the wire connecting it to another gate, it will not exceed 0.7 v, a permitted 0 output.

3.3 LOGIC TECHNOLOGIES

Most logic circuits today are realized with *integrated circuits* instead of discrete components. These circuits combine many components on one semiconductor chip. They are roughly divided into three classes by the number of components on one integrated circuit or *chip*.

1. *Small-scale integrated* circuits (SSI) have 1 to 11 gates per chip.
2. *Medium-scale integrated* circuits (MSI) have 12 to 99 gates per chip.
3. *Large-scale integrated* circuits (LSI) have 100 or more gates per chip.

Several technologies are used to construct integrated circuits. In this section we will discuss and compare current major technologies. Because the evolution of semiconductor technologies has been and continues to be very rapid, we cannot compare technologies that will remain valid for a long time. The technologies we study here are used for the combinational logic devices we studied in chapter 2, the sequential logic devices that we will study in chapter 4, and the semiconductor memories that we will discuss in chapter 9.

3.3.1 Bipolar Technologies

We can divide logic technologies into bipolar technologies that are based on conventional transistors, and MOS technologies that are based on a newer type of transistor constructed from metal-oxide-semiconductors.

Transistor-Transistor-Logic The most widely used logic technology has been transistor-transistor-logic (TTL). It is a modification of an older technology, diode-transistor-logic (DTL), and is compatible with DTL. A main advantage of TTL is its high speed; it allows operation at speeds from 5 MHz to more than 50 MHz, depending on the series of TTL selected. It has good drive capability with a typical fan-out of 10 so that it can be used flexibly in complex circuits. Its noise immunity, both internal and external, is good. Because of these basic advantages, TTL is very popular, but MOS has become a strong competitor recently. Prices of TTL circuits have been reduced, and the types of available TTL circuits have increased significantly.

The most widely used family of digital logic integrated circuits is the 54/74 series of TTL. It has several variations—a low power series, 54L/74L; a high-speed series, 54H/74H; a higher speed series called Schottky-clamped, 54S/74S; and a standard series, 54/74.

The 54/74 series also has some three-state circuits. *Three-state logic* (TSL) has three stable states—0, 1, and a disabled state that prevents

TABLE 3.4

COMPARISON OF TTL 54/74 SERIES

Typical characteristics	54/74	54L/74L	54H/74H	54S/74S
Propagation delay (ns)	10	33	6	3
Power dissipation per gate (mw)	10	1	23	19
Speed-power product (ns × mw)	100	33	138	57
Noise margin (dc v)	1	1	1	1
Fan-out	10	10	10	10

data transfer. TSL is used to interface several devices to a bus. When a device is in the disabled state, it is effectively disconnected from the bus.

Table 3.4 compares these TTL series. One important characteristic is the *speed-power product,* a single figure of merit that measures both speed (actually delay) and power. On this basis the Schottky-clamped series is best. All 54/74 series have similar noise margin and fan-out. However, fan-out is expressed in terms of gates of each series. A standard 54/74 gate can drive 10 standard 54/74 gates or 40 low power 54L/74L gates. Some gates may be obtained in versions called *buffers* that have greater fan-out. In general, the fan-out of one series in loads of another series depends on the relative power dissipations of the two series.

Emitter-Coupled-Logic Emitter-coupled-logic (ECL), another bipolar logic, is popular for its high speed and flexibility. It is currently the only logic technology available for speeds above 75 MHz. A fan-out of 25 allows it to drive many gates and thus be used flexibly. Both the output and its complement are usually available so inverters can be avoided. ECL circuits generate very little noise in switching and thus have excellent internal noise immunity.

ECL has several disadvantages, however. Its power dissipation is high. Its external noise immunity is poor compared with that of other logic technologies because it has only a small voltage difference between logic states. It uses a negative voltage supply; consequently, its voltage levels H and L are both negative and must be interfaced to make them compatible with the positive voltages of TTL and CMOS.

3.3.2 MOS Technologies

MOS technologies offer some advantages over bipolar technologies. MOS consumes less power; MOS gates can be made much smaller so that many more gates can be put on a single chip. Unfortunately, MOS devices are fundamentally slower than bipolar devices.

MOS technologies can be classified into *PMOS, NMOS,* and *CMOS.* PMOS and NMOS are named for their respective *p*-channels and *n*-channels; they are duals. CMOS, or complementary MOS, has both *p*-channel and *n*-channel devices so arranged that they compensate and draw minimum power.

PMOS technology was the earliest MOS technology. PMOS devices are simple and allow a high density of gates per chip. They are limited in operating speed to a few megahertz. They usually require two power supplies and are not compatible with TTL.

NMOS offers several advantages over PMOS. It consumes less power, offers higher speed, is about half the size, and is compatible with TTL. Despite these advantages, NMOS has been slower to develop because it is more difficult and expensive to manufacture.

CMOS combines both PMOS and NMOS devices in such a way that they compensate and require almost no power except when they switch from one state to another. CMOS is compatible with TTL and requires only one power supply. It requires slightly more area per gate than PMOS or NMOS, but it is still much smaller than TTL. It can operate at somewhat higher speeds, up to 20 MHz. It has high noise immunity and excellent fan-outs—50 or more. CMOS is the best technology for low speed, low power applications.

Table 3.5 compares TTL, ECL, PMOS, and CMOS technologies. It is necessarily a simplification, and its data will be rapidly outdated as the technologies evolve. Other factors to consider in choosing a logic technology include temperature range and packaging. All four logic families can be obtained in versions capable of operating from −55°C to 125°C. Integrated circuits are now usually produced on chips of silicon ranging from 40 × 40 mils for very simple circuits to 160 × 160 mils for complex circuits. The silicon chip is then encased in a ceramic or plastic *dual-in-line* package which typically has from 14 to 40 leads. (See figure 3.5.) The variety of available circuits can best be determined from manufacturers' catalogs.

3.4 STANDARD LOGIC CIRCUITS

Logic design with integrated circuits differs from the classical approach for discrete logic components discussed in chapter 2. In clas-

TABLE 3.5

Typical Characteristics of Logic Technologies

Parameter	TTL	ECL	PMOS	CMOS
Cost	Low to medium	Low to medium	Medium to high	Medium to high
Propagation delay per gate (ns)	5-10	1-2	300	70
Operating speed (MHz)	5-75	Up to 200	Less than 2	Up to 20
Power dissipation per gate (mw)	1-25	30-200	0.2-10	0.002-3 proportional to frequency
Fan out	10	25	20	50
Supply voltage (v)	+5	-5.2	-27, -13	+5 to +15
External noise immunity	Good	Fair	Excellent	Excellent
Internal noise immunity	Good	Excellent	Good	Good

sical design, there is a straightforward minimization criterion of minimum gates with minimum inputs. The algebraic expression for a function can be minimized algorithmically and implemented with a few types of discrete components. Integrated circuits, however, are necessarily restricted to chips that implement a large number of standard functions. The criterion for minimization is not as clear and usually cannot be used algorithmically. Because minimization of integrated circuit systems cannot be done algorithmically, intuition and experience are helpful in design with integrated circuits. Possible criteria for minimizing integrated circuit systems are:

1. Use the fewest chips. This criterion is simple and is similar to that for discrete components.
2. Use the least expensive combination of chips. This criterion makes sense but can be difficult to determine.
3. Use the fewest interconnections. This criterion is good for designing reliable systems since most integrated circuit system failures occur at the connections between chips. Chips themselves are highly reliable.

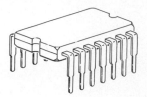

Fig. 3.5 Dual-in-line package

Advantages of integrated circuits are:

1. They can usually be designed more rapidly than discrete components.
2. Systems of integrated circuits can be analyzed more rapidly since their building blocks are larger and fewer than those of discrete circuits.
3. Systems of integrated circuits can easily be modularized and extended to larger circuits.
4. The reliability of integrated circuits is better than that of discrete circuits since most failures occur at external connections between devices.
5. The cost of integrated circuits is much lower than that of discrete circuits.

These advantages make it important for us to know something about available integrated circuits. In this section we will discuss a few standard chips and their applications. All chips used for examples are available in the TTL 54/74 series. Most are available in other logic technologies.

3.4.1 NAND, NOR, AND, OR, and NOT Gates

Most logic lines offer a wide variety of NAND, NOR, AND, OR, and NOT gates. Because NAND gates are the easiest to construct with TTL, NAND is the basic gate offered. Recall that NAND in positive logic is the same as NOR in negative logic. Small-scale integrated circuits usually have two or more gates per chip because it costs less to produce two gates on one chip than on separate chips. Gates are packaged in pairs (dual), threes (triple), fours (quad), or sixes (hex). Figure 3.6 shows a dual four-input NAND gate. Common NAND circuits are:

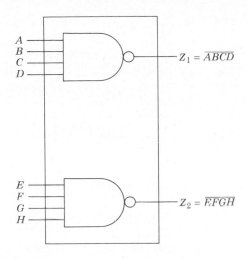

Fig. 3.6   A dual four-input NAND gate

1. quad two-input NAND
2. triple three-input NAND
3. dual four-input NAND
4. eight-input NAND

NOR, OR, and AND gates are packaged in similar arrangements although not as many alternatives may be offered. NOT gates are often packaged in sixes.

TTL NAND and AND gates are sometimes constructed with an open collector output. The outputs of open collector TTL gates can be simply wired together. The result is the same as though the outputs had been combined in an AND gate. This connection is called a *wired AND*. A wired-AND connection offers the advantages of an AND gate without its cost or propagation delay, but TTL gates with open collector outputs are somewhat slower than other TTL gates. Some ECL gates offer a similar function—a wired OR.

The manufacturer specifies what should be done with unused inputs. Often an unused input, such as the fourth input on a four-input NAND gate implementing a three-variable function, is connected or tied to another input. Then the gate receives two identical inputs, and the output is unchanged (except for XOR or COINCI-DENCE). Otherwise an unused input may be tied to a 0 or 1 so long as the function is not changed. For example, an unused NAND input could be tied to a 1 but not to a 0.

3.4.2 AND-OR-INVERT Gates

TTL integrated circuits have a gate called *AND-OR-INVERT (AOI)*. AOI gates combine the functions of AND, OR, and INVERT in a single gate with just one propagation delay. Figure 3.7 shows the function implemented by one AOI gate. The figure shows the AND operation followed by the NOR operation; however, these operations are performed by one gate with one delay. The gate shown is called a *two-wide, three-input* AOI gate because it has the equivalent of two three-input AND gates. (Wide refers to the number of equivalent AND gates; input refers to the number of inputs to each equivalent AND.) Other AOI gates are available with expander inputs that allow constructing AOI gates with the equivalent of more AND gates. Typical AOI gates can provide outputs:

$$Y = \overline{AB + CD + X}$$
$$Y = \overline{AB + CE + EF + GH + X}$$
$$Y = \overline{ABCD + EFGH + X}$$
$$Y = \overline{ABC + DEF}$$

X indicates an input from an expander. Attaching an expander increases the propagation delay, but the delay usually remains less than the combined delays of the equivalent AND and NOR gates.

The output function of an AND-OR-INVERT gate is the complement of a sum-of-products (AND-OR) function. We can design with AOI gates by combining all 0s on a Karnaugh map in exactly the same way as we would combine 1s for an AND-OR implementation. We do not label them as we would 0s combined for an OR-AND implementation.

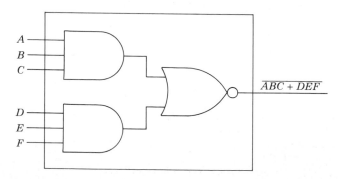

Fig. 3.7   A two-wide, three-input AND-OR-INVERT gate equivalent

Example 3.1

Implement $f(A,B,C,D) = \Sigma(0,1,3,7,8,9,11,15)$ with an AOI gate.

The Karnaugh map of this function is shown in figure 3.8. To implement it with an AOI gate, we combine 0s. There are three blocks of 0s but we can cover the 0s with only two of them. We choose $B\bar{C}$ and $C\bar{D}$. We implement the function with a two-wide, two-input AOI gate as

$$f(A,B,C,D) = \overline{B\bar{C} + C\bar{D}}$$

The implementation is shown in figure 3.8.

Alternatively, we can get the AND-OR implementation of $\bar{f}$, the complement of f, and then complement the result to get f.

3.5 DECODERS

Decoders are versatile circuits that convert information from n inputs to a maximum of 2^n output lines. Decoders are used to route data

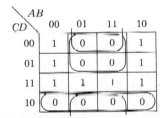

(a) Karnaugh map for f = $\Sigma(0,1,3,7,8,9,11,15)$

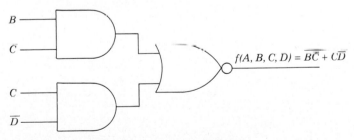

(b) Implementation of f with an AOI gate

Fig. 3.8 Implementation of a function with an AOI gate

to desired output lines, to address memories, and to convert information from one code to another. A wide variety of integrated circuit decoders are available for the most common decoding tasks. Figure 3.9 shows a 1-of-2^n decoder, so named because one n-bit address can activate one of 2^n outputs. Figure 3.10 shows a 1-of-4 decoder; here the inputs X and Y can select any of four outputs. The *enable* input in figure 3.10 enables or turns on the circuit. Regardless of the values of inputs X and Y, no output is activated unless the enable signal is 1.

Figure 3.11 shows a 1-of-16 decoder. This decoder has two enable inputs, $1G$ and $2G$, both of which must be low in order for the decoder to function. An enable signal that enables when it is low is called an *active low enable*. The input line for an active low signal has a circle to show inversion.

A decoder with a data input is called a *demultiplexer* and can route input data to any one of 2^n outputs as selected by the n-bit input address. Figure 3.12 shows a demultiplexer application of a decoder. The first n inputs specify the n-bit destination address for the data; the last input is for the data. Data are routed to the output line designated by the n-bit address.

Another application of a decoder is to change information that is coded in one form to another. An example is a BCD-to-seven-segment decoder which changes inputs in BCD (*binary-coded decimal,* or the usual binary numbers from zero to nine) into outputs that will light the appropriate segments of a seven-segment display for each number. Problem 2.27 considered the classic discrete design for a BCD-to-seven-segment decoder. We can obtain such a decoder as an integrated circuit as shown in figure 3.13. The chip offers ripple blanking inputs and blanking inputs, features that are useful for BCD displays on calculators. Ripple blanking inputs suppress leading zeros to insure that any number shown starts with a nonzero numeral. Blanking inputs can control display brightness.

Decoders are used to convert numbers from one code to another.

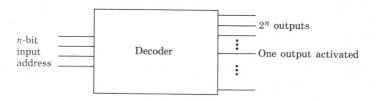

Fig. 3.9   A 1-of-2^n decoder

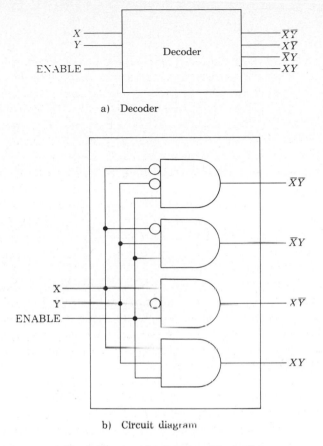

a) Decoder

b) Circuit diagram

Fig. 3.10   A 1-of-4 decoder with enable input

One example is conversion from standard binary to Gray code. Table 3.6 shows 4-bit versions of the two codes. *Gray code* is designed to have just one bit change between the representations of any two adjacent numbers. In binary, for example, four bits change between the representation of seven (0111) and the representation of eight (1000). In Gray code just one bit changes between the representation of seven (0100) and the representation of eight (1100). In the 4-bit Gray code only one bit changes between the representations of fifteen (1000) and zero (0000). Gray codes are often used for computer input/output devices because the property of just one bit changing provides good error characteristics and convenient representation of angular data. We will discuss Gray code devices in chapter 10.

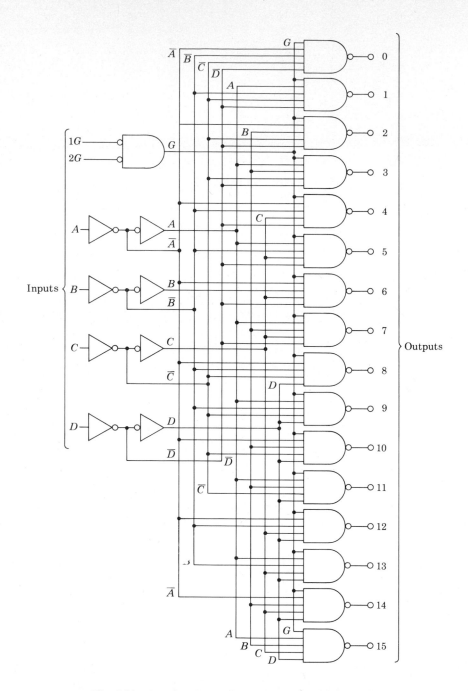

Fig. 3.11   A 1-of-16 decoder with enable inputs 1G and 2G

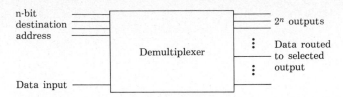

Fig. 3.12 Demultiplexer

We can easily design decoders to convert between Gray and binary by means of a Karnaugh map. However, the simplest design involves EXCLUSIVE OR gates because Gray-coded numbers are simply expressed as XOR combinations of their binary equivalents. For the 4-bit case the Gray equivalent of a given binary number is:

$$G_0 = B_0 \oplus B_1$$
$$G_1 = B_1 \oplus B_2$$
$$G_2 = B_2 \oplus B_3$$
$$G_3 = B_3$$

Subscript 0 is for the least significant bit, subscript 1 for the next least significant bit, and so forth.

TABLE 3.6

4-BIT BINARY AND GRAY CODES

Decimal	Binary $B_3B_2B_1B_0$	Gray $G_3G_2G_1G_0$
0	0 0 0 0	0 0 0 0
1	0 0 0 1	0 0 0 1
2	0 0 1 0	0 0 1 1
3	0 0 1 1	0 0 1 0
4	0 1 0 0	0 1 1 0
5	0 1 0 1	0 1 1 1
6	0 1 1 0	0 1 0 1
7	0 1 1 1	0 1 0 0
8	1 0 0 0	1 1 0 0
9	1 0 0 1	1 1 0 1
10	1 0 1 0	1 1 1 1
11	1 0 1 1	1 1 1 0
12	1 1 0 0	1 0 1 0
13	1 1 0 1	1 0 1 1
14	1 1 1 0	1 0 0 1
15	1 1 1 1	1 0 0 0

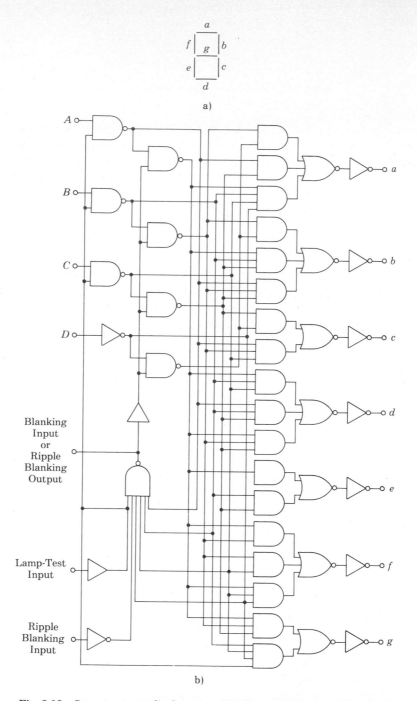

Fig. 3.13   Seven-segment display (a) and BCD-to-seven-segment decoder (b)

The 4-bit binary equivalent of a Gray-coded number is:

$$B_0 = G_0 \oplus G_1 \oplus G_2 \oplus G_3$$
$$B_1 = G_1 \oplus G_2 \oplus G_3$$
$$B_2 = G_2 \oplus G_3$$
$$B_3 = G_3$$

Circuits for binary-Gray conversion and Gray-binary conversion corresponding to these equations are shown in figures 3.14 and 3.15, respectively. Alternatively, we can construct decoders that accept a 4-bit input in one code and give a 1 output on the corresponding one of 16 lines in another code. The decoder design is simple because Gray code is simply a permutation of binary code. It is left as an exercise.

Other codes are better suited to coding decimal numbers. Table 3.7 shows three common codes for decimal numbers. We discussed the binary-coded-decimal code earlier; it is just the 4-bit binary equivalent of the decimal digit. *Excess-three code* is the binary equivalent of the decimal digit plus three. For example, five is represented by 1000; the binary equivalent of five plus three equals eight. Excess-three code represents the digits 0 to 9 by the middle 10 of the 16

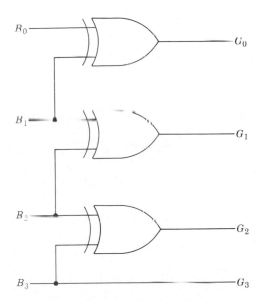

Fig. 3.14 Binary-Gray conversion

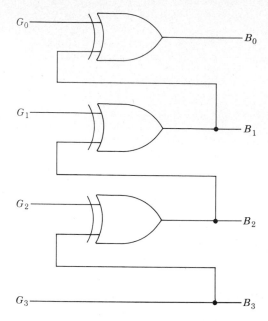

Fig. 3.15   Gray-binary conversion

4-bit binary numbers. The code has a property called *nines comple-ment;* that is, the excess-three representation of any number is the complement of the representation of the difference between nine and that number. For example, the representation of four is 0111; the complement of the representation of nine minus four equals five or 1000. The third code is *excess-three Gray,* the Gray code of the binary equivalent of the sum of the decimal number plus three. The excess-three Gray code for two is obtained by adding two plus three equals five, and taking the Gray code of five (1000). Excess-three Gray code has the property that the representation for nine (1010) differs by only one bit from the representation for zero (0010). Excess-three Gray code thus has the same advantages for decimal coding that Gray code has for coding numbers from 0 to 15, or more generally, numbers from 0 to 2^n-1 for any n.

Figure 3.16 shows decoders for these three codes, with four input lines and 10 output lines, called four-line-to-ten-line decoders, for converting numbers from each of these three codes to decimal.

TABLE 3.7

Decimal	Binary-coded decimal	Excess-three	Excess-three Gray
0	0 0 0 0	0 0 1 1	0 0 1 0
1	0 0 0 1	0 1 0 0	0 1 1 0
2	0 0 1 0	0 1 0 1	0 1 1 1
3	0 0 1 1	0 1 1 0	0 1 0 1
4	0 1 0 0	0 1 1 1	0 1 0 0
5	0 1 0 1	1 0 0 0	1 1 0 0
6	0 1 1 0	1 0 0 1	1 1 0 1
7	0 1 1 1	1 0 1 0	1 1 1 1
8	1 0 0 0	1 0 1 1	1 1 1 0
9	1 0 0 1	1 1 0 0	1 0 1 0

3.6 MULTIPLEXERS

Another standard circuit is a *multiplexer,* which is nearly the opposite of a decoder. A multiplexer is conceptually a switch that can connect one of 2^n inputs to the output. Figure 3.17 shows a multiplexer with 2^n inputs plus an enable input and one output. A common application of a multiplexer is as a *data selector,* as shown in figure 3.18. In the figure the four data select inputs select which of the 16 data inputs will be sent to the output. This data selector can be used, for example, to select which of 16 teletypes would go to a computer input. Figure 3.19 shows a 16-input data selector.

Another use of multiplexers is for function generation. We would like to implement general logic functions, often called *random logic,* with integrated circuits. In chapter 2, we learned how to implement any of the 2^{2^n} logic functions of n input variables with two canonical expressions, the sum-of-products (AND-OR) and the product-of-sums (OR-AND). We can realize these expressions with standard MSI OR and AND (or NOR or NAND) chips, but many unreliable external connections are needed. For this reason we will look at two different realizations with MSI chips—one with a decoder and an OR gate and the other with a multiplexer.

Figure 3.20 shows an example of function generation with a decoder and an OR gate. The decoder is used to generate the 2^n minterms, which are then connected externally to a 2^n-input OR gate. The

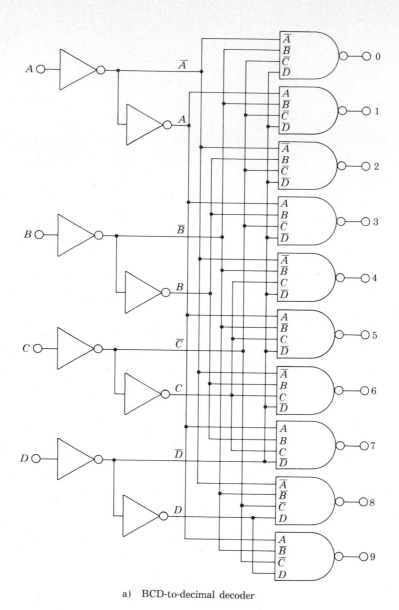

a)   BCD-to-decimal decoder

Fig. 3.16   Three four-line-to-ten-line decoders

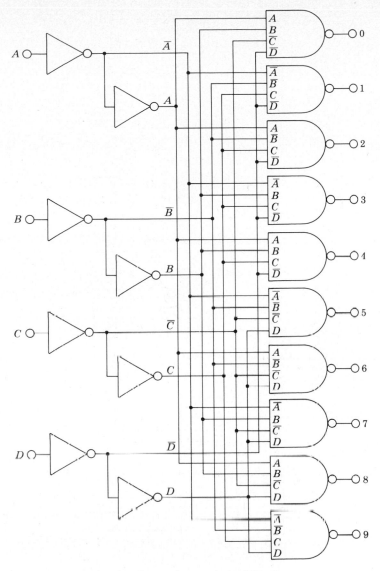

b) Excess-three-to-decimal decoder

(Fig. 3.16 continued)

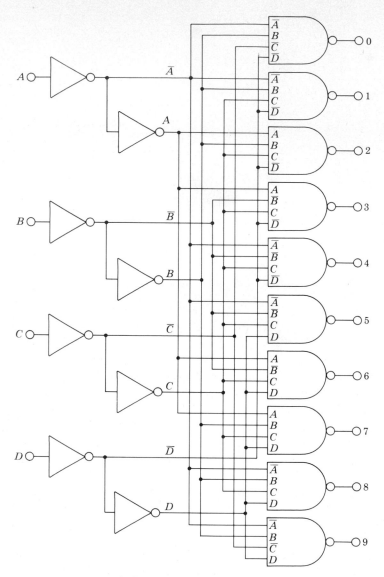

c)   Excess-three Gray-to-decimal decoder

(Fig. 3.16 continued)

Fig. 3.17 Multiplexer with 2^n inputs, and an enable input

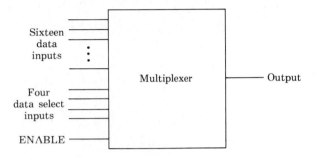

Fig. 3.18 Data selector application of multiplexer

example shown is a 1-of-4 decoder generating the function $Z = X \oplus Y$. The main disadvantages of this realization are the external connections to the OR gate. The connections are inherently unreliable, and the OR gate requires a large fan-in of 2^n possible inputs. (By using inverters, we could use an OR gate with only 2^{n-1} maximum inputs.) However, if the function to be implemented has only a small number of minterms, an OR gate with fewer inputs may be used.

Figure 3.21 shows a realization of the same function $Z = X \oplus Y$ with a two-input multiplexer. The name "two-input multiplexer" refers to the top two inputs, I_0 and I_1, rather than to the X input. The signals to I_0 and I_1 may be Y, $\overline{Y}$, 0, or 1. Appropriate choice of the input signals allows realization of any of the 16 possible logic functions of two input variables. The figure shows that inputs $I_0 = Y$ and $I_1 = \overline{Y}$ generate $X \oplus Y$. Since the logic gates are all connected inside the multiplexer, the circuit is reliable.

To implement a two-variable function $f(X,Y)$ with a multiplexer, proceed as follows:

1. Construct a standard two-variable Karnaugh map of the function.

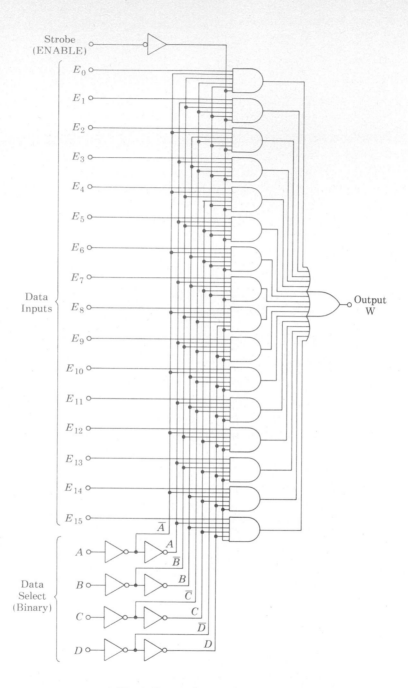

Fig. 3.19   16-input data selector

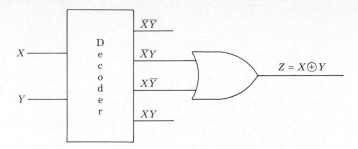

Fig. 3.20 Function generation with decoder and OR gate

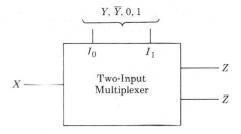

a) Two-input multiplexer

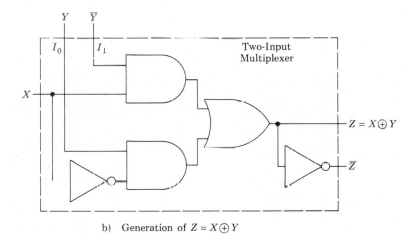

b) Generation of $Z = X \oplus Y$

Fig. 3.21 Function generation with a multiplexer

2. Put inputs I_0 and I_1 above the 0 and 1 values of the first variable, X.
3. Examine each column of the map.
   a. If the column has two 0s, the input should be 0.
   b. If the column has two 1s, the input should be 1.
   c. If the column matches the values of the second variable, Y, the input should be Y.
   d. If the column is the complement of the second variable, Y, the input should be $\bar{Y}$.

Example 3.2

Implement the function $f(X,Y) = \bar{X}\bar{Y}$ with a multiplexer.

Figure 3.22a shows the Karnaugh map for this function. Input I_0 should be $\bar{Y}$, and input I_1 should be 0. Parts b, c, and d of figure 3.22 show the implementation of other two-variable functions. Generation of functions of more than two variables requires larger multiplexers. The multiplexer size selection rule is as follows:

A logic function of n variables requires a 2^{n-1} input multiplexer.

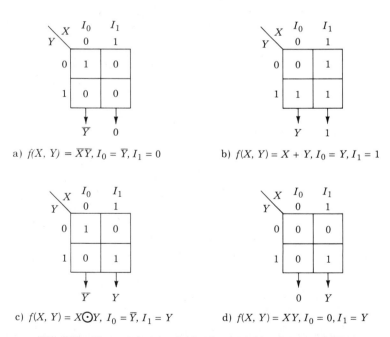

a) $f(X, Y) = \bar{X}\bar{Y}, I_0 = \bar{Y}, I_1 = 0$

b) $f(X, Y) = X + Y, I_0 = Y, I_1 = 1$

c) $f(X, Y) = X \odot Y, I_0 = \bar{Y}, I_1 = Y$

d) $f(X, Y) = XY, I_0 = 0, I_1 = Y$

Fig. 3.22   Karnaugh maps for implementation of two variables

For example, if $n = 4$, then a $2^{4-1} = 2^3 =$ eight-input multiplexer can implement any logic function of four variables. This rule assumes that both the variable and the complement of at least one input variable are available; otherwise a larger multiplexer may be required.

Implementation of three-variable and four-variable functions with multiplexers follows a procedure much like that for two-variable functions. Examples of multiplexers for three- and four-variable functions are shown in figures 3.23a and 3.24a. In each case one variable, its complement, 0, and 1 are available to be applied to inputs shown on the top of the multiplexer. The remaining variables are applied to inputs shown on the side of the multiplexer. The multiplexer may have an enable input as shown in figure 3.23a. Implementation of functions of more than four variables is usually a more complex

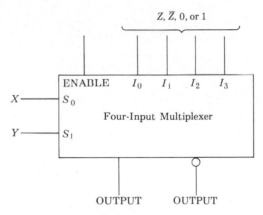

a) Four-input multiplexer

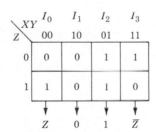

b) Determination of inputs for
implementation of a function

Fig. 3.23 Implementation of a function with a four-input multiplexer

procedure and involves two or more levels of multiplexers. To implement a three- or four-variable function with a multiplexer, proceed as follows:

1. Construct a map of the function with columns for the first two variables of a three-variable function or the first three variables of a four-variable function. The map has two rows for the last variable. Figures 3.23b and 3.24b show the maps.

2. Put the I inputs above the values of the corresponding first two or three variables. Figures 3.23b and 3.24b show one convention for inputs that differs from standard binary order.

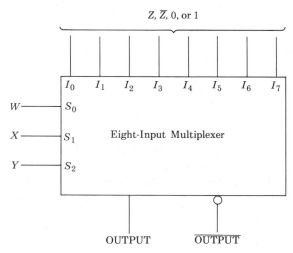

a) Eight-input multiplexer

WXY	I_0	I_1	I_2	I_3	I_4	I_5	I_6	I_7
Z	000	100	010	110	001	101	011	111
0	0	1	1	0	0	0	1	1
1	0	0	1	1	1	0	1	0
	↓	↓	↓	↓	↓	↓	↓	↓
	0	$\overline{Z}$	1	Z	Z	0	1	$\overline{Z}$

b) Determination of multiplexer inputs from a map

Fig. 3.24 Implementation of a function with an eight-input multiplexer

3. Examine each column of the map.
   a. If the column has two 0s, the input should be 0.
   b. If the column has two 1s, the input should be 1.
   c. If the column matches the value of the last variable, Z, the input should be Z.
   d. If the column is the complement of the last variable, Z, the input should be $\bar{Z}$.

Example 3.3

Implement $f(X,Y,Z) = \bar{X}\bar{Y}Z + \bar{X}Y + XY\bar{Z}$ with a four-input multiplexer.

This function is mapped in figure 3.23. The inputs should be $I_0 = Z$, $I_1 = 0$, $I_2 = 1$, $I_3 = \bar{Z}$.

Example 3.4

Implement $f(W,X,Y,Z) = \bar{W}X + XY\bar{Z} + \bar{W}YZ + X\bar{Y}Z + W\bar{X}\bar{Y}Z$ with an eight-input multiplexer.

The function is mapped in figure 3.24. For the input convention shown, the inputs should be $I_0 = I_5 = 0$, $I_1 = I_7 = \bar{Z}$, $I_2 = I_6 = 1$, $I_3 = I_4 = Z$. Note that the I inputs correspond to all possible combinations of the variables W, X, and Y. Since different manufacturers may use different input conventions, a multiplexer user must study the multiplexer circuit diagram carefully to learn the correspondence.

Table 3.8 summarizes the requirements for a random logic function generation with decoders and OR gates or with multiplexers. The decoder generation requires a 1-of-2^n decoder plus a 2^n-input OR gate to sum the minterms. The multiplexer requires a (2^{n-1})-input multiplexer. The multiplexer design is simpler, avoids troublesome interconnections, and gives both an output and its complement.

TABLE 3.8

RANDOM LOGIC FUNCTION GENERATION

Realization	Number of logic variables				
	1	2	3	4	5
Decoder					
Decoder size	1-of-2	1-of-4	1-of-8	1-of-16	1-of-32
OR gate inputs	2	4	8	16	32
Multiplexer					
Multiplexer inputs	—	2	4	8	16

3.7   SUMMARY

Several practical considerations affect logic circuit operation. The binary values 0 and 1 can be assigned to the voltage ranges H and L to give either positive logic ($H = 1$, $L = 0$) or negative logic ($H = 0$, $L = 1$). The maximum propagation delay of a computer or logic system is the largest sum of individual gate delays, T_D, through which one signal passes. It is inversely proportional to the maximum operating rate of the digital system. Logic devices can receive power from a maximum number of input devices (the maximum fan-in) and can drive a maximum number of output devices (the maximum fan-out). Internal noise immunity and external noise immunity measure the device's resistance to fluctuations in the signal.

We examined five current logic technologies, two bipolar and three MOS. TTL (transistor-transistor-logic) is the most widely used because of its speed and flexibility. ECL (emitter-coupled-logic) offers the highest speed and has high fan-out but has poor noise immunity and is not directly compatible with other logic lines. MOS technologies—PMOS (p-channel), NMOS (n-channel), and CMOS (complementary)—operate at very low power with good noise immunity but are limited in speed.

Integrated circuits that package many circuit components on single chips are commercially available for a wide variety of standard functions. We looked at small-scale integrated circuits for the basic logic functions of chapter 2. The formal minimization procedures of chapter 2 do not apply directly to integrated circuits; more intuitive notions of minimization and design are necessary. Circuits can be designed with special integrated circuit chips that combine several functions. AND-OR-INVERT circuits allow designing the complement of sum-of-products expressions with a single propagation delay. Decoders provide rapid selection of as many as 2^n output lines with an n-bit address. They can convert information coded as binary-coded-decimal (the binary numbers zero to nine), Gray (a code in which adjacent numbers differ by just one bit), or excess-three (the binary equivalent of the number plus three) into other forms. Decoders can be used as demultiplexers to send data to a desired output. Multiplexers act as switches that can connect one of 2^n inputs to the output. Data selectors are multiplexers that can select which of the 2^n inputs will be connected to the output. Generation of a random logic function of n variables requires a 1-of-2^n decoder and an OR gate or a 2^{n-1} multiplexer.

Concepts

active low	internal noise immunity
AOI	LSI
BCD	MOS
bipolar	MSI
CMOS	multiplexer
data selector	negative logic
decoder	NMOS
demultiplexer	noise margin
ECL	PMOS
enable	positive logic
excess-three code	propagation delay
external noise immunity	rise time
fall time	SSI
fan-in	three-state logic
fan-out	TTL
Gray code	wired-AND
integrated circuit	

3.8 REFERENCES

Discussions of practical considerations affecting logic circuits at the level of this book can be found in Booth (1971), Bartee (1972), and Abrams and Stein (1973). Information on logic families is given in Peatman (1972), Garrett (1970), Su (1973), Hnatek (1973), Blakeslee (1975), and Gschwind and McCluskey (1975). The integrated circuit manufacturers' manuals, such as Texas Instruments (no date), are the best sources of current data on integrated circuits. Designing with TTL is discussed in Peatman (1972), Greene et al (1972), Wickes (1968), Morris and Miller (1971), and Blakeslee (1975). Carr and Mize (1972) describe MOS design. Barna and Porat (1973) present detailed discussions of design with common integrated circuits.

3.9 PROBLEMS

3.1 A logic technology has voltage ranges −5 to −4 and +12 to +15 v. Show the assignments for positive and negative logic.

$$(3.2)$$

3.2 Construct the truth table for a device that will be a NAND gate for positive logic and a NOR gate for negative logic. (3.2)

3.3 If AND gates cost $0.75 and OR gates with four inputs cost $1.00, how much will it cost for the gates needed to realize $f(W,X,Y,Z) = XY + WY + YZ + XZ + WZ$? (3.2)

3.4 Assume that AND and OR gates with fan-ins and fan-outs of 4 cost $1.25 each and that AND and OR gates with fan-ins and fan-outs of 2 cost $1.00. What is the minimum cost for a two-level or three-level logic network that will realize $f(W,X,Y,Z) = WX + WY + XY + YZ$? (3.2)

3.5 Draw a timing diagram for the circuit below. Assume $T_1 > T_2 > T_3$. (3.2)

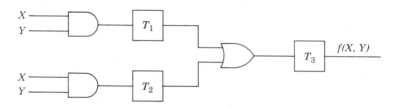

3.6 The figure below shows a series of logic subunits connected in series. Each logic subunit has an input X_i, an external output Y_i, and an output S_i that becomes the input to the next logic subunit. Each subunit has a propagation delay T and negligible rise time.

a. What is the propagation delay between X_1 and Y_5?
b. What is the maximum operating speed of the overall logic unit? (3.2)

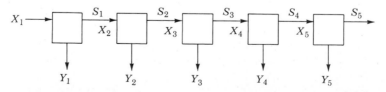

3.7 The circuit below illustrates a condition called a *static hazard*. If the inputs change simultaneously from $X = Y = 0$, $Z = 1$ to $X = Y = 1$, $Z = 0$, the output should remain 1. However, if $T_1 > T_2$, the output will be zero for a period of length $|T_2 - T_1|$. This improper output occurs because the output of delay T_2 goes to 0 before the output of delay T_1 goes to 1. Show with timing diagrams that a static hazard for some sequence of inputs always exists when $T_1 \neq T_2$. (3.2)

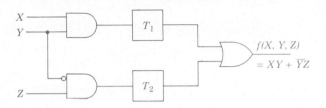

3.8 Obtain a manufacturer's figures for any logic line showing the characteristics in table 3.5 for his product line. (3.3)

3.9 Using only four-input NAND gates and inverters, design a six-input NAND gate. (3.4)

3.10 Using only NAND gates, implement $f(A,B,C) = AB + AC + BC$. (3.4)

3.11 We wish to implement

$$f(A,B,C,D) = \overline{A}\overline{B} + \overline{B}\overline{C} + \overline{A}\overline{C} + AB + A\overline{C} + B\overline{C}$$

at minimum cost. Integrated circuits cost as follows:

Quad two-input AND	$0.50
Triple three-input AND	$0.60
Dual four-input AND	$0.50
Quad two-input OR	$0.50
Triple three-input OR	$0.60
Dual four-input OR	$0.50

a. Sketch a minimum cost circuit. Draw a dotted line around all gates on one integrated circuit.
b. List the integrated circuits required. (3.4)

3.12 We wish to implement

$$f(A,B,C,D) = \Sigma(1,2,4,5,6,7,8,9,10,11,14,15)$$

at minimum cost. Integrated circuits cost as follows:

Quad two-input AND	$0.50
Triple three-input AND	$0.60
Dual four-input AND	$0.50
Quad two-input OR	$0.50
Triple three-input OR	$0.60
Dual four-input OR	$0.50

a. Sketch a minimum cost circuit. Draw a dotted line around all gates on one integrated circuit.
b. List the integrated circuits required. (3.4)

3.13 Implement $f(A,B,C,D) = \Sigma(1,3,5,7,9,11,12,13,14,15)$ with a two-wide, two-input AOI gate. (3.5)

3.14 Implement $f(A,B,C,D) = \Sigma(0,1,2,4,8,9,10,11,12,14,15)$ with a four-wide, three-input AOI gate. (3.5)

3.15 Design a decoder to convert 4-bit Gray code inputs to one of 16 binary outputs. (3.5)

3.16 Design a decoder to convert excess-three coded inputs to the seven-segment outputs corresponding to the decimal equivalent of each excess-three input. (3.5)

3.17 Tabulate the inputs I_0 and I_1 in figure 3.21 to realize all 16 possible logic functions of two input variables. (3.6)

3.18 Show the internal circuitry of a four-input multiplexer that will realize all logic functions of three variables. (3.6)

3.19 Determine the inputs $I_0, \ldots, I_7$ of the eight-input multiplexer shown below to implement $f(W,X,Y,Z) = \Sigma(0,1,2,5,8,10,13,14)$. The inputs can be 0, 1, Z, or $\overline{Z}$. Assume that I_0 to I_7 correspond to $\overline{W}\overline{X}\overline{Y}$, $W\overline{X}\overline{Y}$, $\overline{W}X\overline{Y}$, $WX\overline{Y}$, $\overline{W}\overline{X}Y$, $W\overline{X}Y$, $\overline{W}XY$, and WXY, respectively. (3.6)

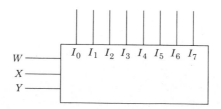

3.20 Determine the inputs $I_0, \ldots, I_7$ of an eight-input multiplexer to implement $f(W,X,Y,Z) = Y\bar{Z} + \bar{W}X\bar{Y} + W\bar{X}Z$.   (3.6)

3.21 A four-input multiplexer is to implement $f(X,Y,Z) = \bar{X}Y\bar{Z} + X\bar{Y}\bar{Z} + XZ$. Inputs I_0, I_1, I_2, and I_3 correspond to $\bar{X}\bar{Y}$, $\bar{X}Y$, $X\bar{Y}$, and XY, respectively. Select the inputs for I_0 through I_3 from 0, 1, $\bar{Z}$, and Z.   (3.6)

3.22 An eight-input multiplexer is to implement $f(W,X,Y,Z) = \Sigma(2,3,5,6,8,10,11,13,14)$. Inputs I_0 through I_7 have the same correspondence as in problem 3.19. Select inputs for I_0 through I_7 from 0, 1, Z, and $\bar{Z}$.   (3.6)

4 Sequential Logic

4.1 OVERVIEW

In chapter 2 we discussed the distinction between combinational and sequential logic. Combinational logic circuits depend only on the current values of the inputs. Sequential logic circuits depend on the current inputs and on the past history of the circuit. We compared sequential logic to a combinational lock requiring several turns and stops to open. Opening the lock thus involves going through a sequence of steps, and at any time the state of the lock may depend on several previous states.

We will begin our discussion of sequential logic circuits with simple two-state devices called *flipflops*. We will study four common flipflops and the clock signals that control them. General sequential logic circuits can be divided into combinational logic circuits and a storage network as shown in figure 4.1. The storage network may be either flipflops or just time delays.

Our approach will be to look at the use of flipflops and combinational logic in two basic computer circuits—registers that store information and counters that count time intervals. We will study a few variations of registers and counters from a simple, almost intuitive viewpoint. Then in optional sections we will introduce concepts from mathematical systems theory that will enable us to analyze and design simple sequential circuits.

4.2 RS Flipflops

Flipflops are the main storage devices in sequential circuits. There are many types of flipflops, all of which share two common properties.

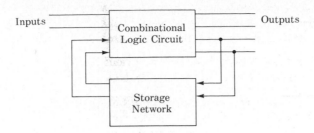

Fig. 4.1   A general sequential logic circuit

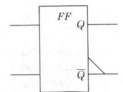

Fig. 4.2   A general flipflop

1. Flipflops are bistable devices. The input(s) to a flipflop can cause
   it to assume either the 1 (set) state or the 0 (reset) state. The
   flipflop will remain in that state until new inputs change the
   state.
2. Flipflops have two outputs that are complements of each other.
   By convention we give the same name to the flipflop state and
   to one output.

Figure 4.2 shows the general form of a flipflop. We call this flipflop
Q for the Q output. The $\bar{Q}$ output is shown with a diagonal line
at the output to indicate complementation, as required by ANSI*
standards. The diagonal line is omitted when it is otherwise clear
that the output is complemented.

We begin our discussion of specific flipflops with the RS flipflop.
We can model an RS flipflop with two NOR gates and two associated
time delays as shown in figure 4.3. We can consider the delays, ΔT
seconds, as the inherent time delays required for the NOR gates to
switch or we can assume that we have built delays into the circuit.
We have labeled the outputs Q and $\bar{Q}$ to provide the two complementary outputs of a flipflop circuit. This circuit looks like the general

---

*ANSI Y32.14-1973/IEEE STD 91-1973, *Graphic Symbols for Logic Diagrams*.

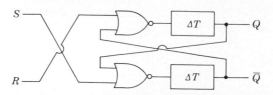

Fig. 4.3 A NOR circuit model of an RS flipflop

sequential circuit of figure 4.1, as the outputs of the combinational logic circuit (the two NOR gates) are fed back to the inputs through delay elements. We have taken our outputs at the end of the delays rather than at the outputs of the combinational logic circuit, but this is a minor matter that does not affect circuit operation.

Because of the delays and because the Q and $\bar{Q}$ outputs are fed back to the inputs, the circuit behavior at any time depends both on the inputs and on the state Q of the circuit. More precisely, at any time the outputs of the NOR gates depend on the current values of the inputs S and R and the output (or state) Q. The current outputs of the NOR gates move through the delay ΔT to become the next value of the output (state) Q. We denote the *next state* of Q as Q^n. If we change the circuit inputs at time t, the next state will be the state existing after the circuit has stabilized, usually $2\Delta T$ seconds later. We assume that all inputs remain constant for at least $2\Delta T$ seconds after any input change so that the circuit may stabilize.

We thus expect that the next state of the circuit, Q^n, depends on the *current inputs* S and R and the *current state* Q, that is, $Q^n = f(S,R,Q)$. We want to know what the function is. As each of the three variables is binary, there are eight possible cases to inspect.

Case 1: S = 0, R = 0, Q = 0 The current output of the top NOR is 0; ΔT seconds later, after the NOR output has passed through the delay, Q will stay 0. The current output of the bottom NOR is 1; in ΔT seconds, $\bar{Q}$ will stay 1. Thus the next state Q^n is 0, the same as the current state Q.

Case 2: S = 0, R = 0, Q = 1 The current output of the top NOR is 1; in ΔT seconds, after the NOR output has passed through the delay, Q will stay 1. The current output of the bottom NOR is 0; in ΔT seconds, $\bar{Q}$ will stay 0. Thus the next state Q^n is 1, the same as the current state Q.

Case 3: S = 0, R = 1, Q = 0 The current output of the top NOR is 0; in ΔT seconds, Q will stay 0. The output of the bottom

NOR is 1; in ΔT seconds, $\bar{Q}$ will stay 1. Thus the next state Q^n is 0.

Case 4: S = 0, R = 1, Q = 1 The output of the top NOR is 0; after ΔT seconds, Q will change from 1 to 0. Then the output of the bottom NOR will be 1, and $2\Delta T$ seconds after the inputs have been applied, $\bar{Q}$ will go to 1. Thus the next state Q^n is 0.

Case 5: S = 1, R = 0, Q = 0 The output of the bottom NOR is 0; after ΔT seconds, $\bar{Q}$ will change from 1 to 0. Then the output of the top NOR will change from 0 to 1, and $2\Delta T$ seconds after the inputs were applied, Q will change from 0 to 1. Thus Q^n is 1.

Case 6: S = 1, R = 0, Q = 1 The output of the bottom NOR is 0; ΔT seconds later $\bar{Q}$ stays 0. The output of the top NOR is 1; ΔT seconds later Q stays 1. Q^n is 1.

Case 7: S = 1, R = 1, Q = 0 The outputs of both NORs are 0. After ΔT seconds, both Q and $\bar{Q}$ become 0. Since Q and $\bar{Q}$ should be complements, we do not want this condition to occur. Q^n is not defined.

Case 8: S = 1, R = 1, Q = 1 As in the previous case, both NOR outputs are 0 and after ΔT seconds, both Q and $\bar{Q}$ become 0. This is not an allowable condition. Q^n is not defined.

We can summarize the response of the NOR representation of an *RS* flipflop:

1. When both S and R are 0, the next state Q^n is the same as the current state Q. This property allows the flipflop to hold either a 0 or a 1 that has been previously entered after both inputs have been removed.
2. When $R = 1$ and $S = 0$, Q^n is 0. (We call this *resetting* the flipflop.)
3. When $S = 1$ and $R = 0$, the next state Q^n is 1. (We call this *setting* the flipflop.)
4. The input condition with both S and R equal to 1 is not allowed.

Additional insight into the behavior of this NOR circuit model of an *RS* flipflop is gained by looking at a timing diagram, shown in figure 4.4. The waveforms are idealized; all changes in waveforms are assumed to occur instantaneously. Note that Q does not change until ΔT or $2\Delta T$ seconds after the input changes. In other words,

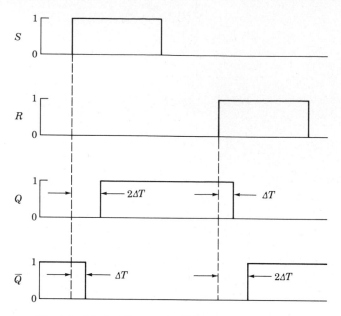

Fig. 4.4   Timing diagram for NOR model of RS flipflop

it takes one or two delays of ΔT seconds for the current state Q to change to the next state Q^n.

The distinction between the current state Q and the next state Q^n is sometimes tricky for the novice. The next state Q^n is not a circuit variable like S, R, and Q. We cannot measure the next state Q^n of a circuit from outside the circuit. If we could take readings inside our circuit model, we could measure the output of the top NOR gate. We know the top NOR gate output now is the next state Q^n, which will be Q in ΔT seconds. We have a sliding time frame. Starting at $t = 0$, we have current inputs S and R and a current state Q. We can calculate the next state Q^n. After $2\Delta T$ seconds, the current state Q will change to the value of the original Q^n. We then use our new current inputs and current state to calculate another next state Q^n. After $2\Delta T$ seconds, the current state will change to equal that next state, and so we proceed. The current state cannot change instantly to the next state. Thus, for example, setting S to 1 will not instantly change the current state to 1. Setting S to 1 and R to 0 leads to a next state Q^n of 1. Table 4.1 shows RS flipflop response to a series of inputs that occur at intervals greater than $2\Delta T$.

TABLE 4.1

RS FLIPFLOP RESPONSE TO SERIES OF INPUTS

t	0	1	2	3	4	5	6	7
S	0	1	0	0	0	1	1	1
R	0	0	0	1	0	0	0	0
Q	0	0	1	1	0	0	1	1
Q^n	0	1	1	0	0	1	1	1

Table 4.1 assumes that the inputs have just changed at each time t shown; thus the flipflop has not changed in response to inputs at time t. At $t = 0$, the flipflop is in the 0 state, and both inputs are 0. Hence the flipflop remains in the 0 state for $t = 1$. The $S = 1$ input at $t = 1$ sets the flipflop state to 1 for $t = 2$. The $S = R = 0$ inputs at $t = 2$ hold the flipflop in the 1 state for $t = 3$. The $R = 1$ input at $t = 3$ resets the flipflop to the 0 state for $t = 4$. The reader should be able to explain the rest of the table.

A formal way of displaying the behavior of a sequential circuit is by a *transition table*, which shows the next state or states of a sequential circuit as a function of current states and current inputs. Table 4.2a shows a transition table for an *RS* flipflop. The abbreviated transition table (table 4.2b) omits the current state column Q and shows the dependence of the next state Q^n on the current state Q in the Q^n column.

As an aid in finding a function that relates Q^n to S, R, and Q, we can plot a Karnaugh map (fig. 4.5, left) from the transition table 4.2a with disallowed conditions entered as don't care conditions. (We don't care what happens because we guarantee they won't occur.) We then minimize the map (fig. 4.5, right) and obtain a function called the *characteristic function* of the *RS* flipflop:

$$Q^n = S + \bar{R}Q$$

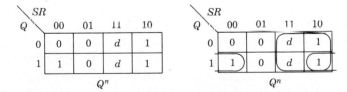

Fig. 4.5 Karnaugh map for *RS* flipflop (left) and minimization of Karnaugh map, $Q^n = S + \bar{R}Q$ (right)

TABLE 4.2a

TRANSITION TABLE FOR RS FLIPFLOP

	Current inputs S R	Current state Q	Next state Q^n
	0 0	0	0
	0 0	1	1
	0 1	0	0
	0 1	1	0
	1 0	0	1
	1 0	1	1
Disallowed {1 1	0	Indeterminate
input conditions {1 1	1	Indeterminate

TABLE 4.2b

ABBREVIATED TRANSITION TABLE FOR RS FLIPFLOP

	Current inputs S R	Next state Q^n
	0 0	Q
	0 1	0
	1 0	1
Disallowed	1 1	Indeterminate

The characteristic function of a flipflop expresses the next state Q^n as a function of the current state and current inputs.

We have now looked at a variety of descriptions of an RS flipflop—a model, a description in words, a timing diagram, a response to a sequence of inputs, two transition tables, a Karnaugh map, and a characteristic function. All these descriptions give insight into the behavior of the flipflop. Figure 4.6 summarizes these descriptions.

4.3 CLOCKED FLIPFLOPS

Inputs to flipflops can be either pulse or level signals. A *pulse* is a signal that is on for a specific length of time that may be short compared with the interval between pulses. Pulses may occur at fixed intervals of time as determined by a clock (*synchronous* operation) or may appear at arbitrary times (*asynchronous* operation). Level signals are either 0 or 1 for arbitrary periods of time; they may change at arbitrary times. The distinction between pulse and level signals is a matter of degree rather than a clear difference.

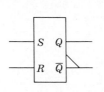

1. If both inputs are 0, the flipflop stays in its current state.
2. If S is 1 and R is 0, the next state is 1.
3. If S is 0 and R is 1, the next state is 0.
4. Both inputs cannot be 1 at the same time.

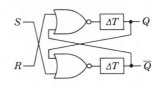

a) Device symbol   b) Word description   c) Model

Current Inputs	Current State	Next State
SR	Q	Q^n
00	0	0
00	1	1
01	0	0
01	1	0
10	0	1
10	1	1
11	0	d
11	1	d

Current Inputs	Next State
SR	Q^n
00	Q
01	0
10	1
11	d

$\overset{\displaystyle SR}{Q}$	00	01	11	10
0	0	0	d	1
1	1	0	d	1

Q^n

f) Karnaugh map

d) Transition table   e) Shortened transition table   g) Characteristic function

$$Q^n = S + \bar{R}Q$$

Fig. 4.6 Summary of RS flipflop

Flipflops that are controlled by pulse signals other than clock signals operate in *pulse* mode. Circuits that are controlled by level signals operate in *level* mode. Pulse and level mode circuits are more complex than synchronous circuits. We will study primarily synchronous circuits.

4.3.1 RS Flipflops

The RS flipflop we have been considering responds to any S or R input of sufficient duration. No CLOCK or ENABLE signal has been necessary, hence the flipflop has operated asynchronously. RS and other flipflops more commonly operate synchronously. Figure 4.7a shows a model of an RS flipflop with both synchronous and

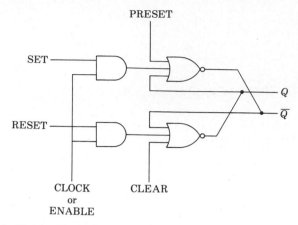

a)   Model with synchronous and asynchronous inputs

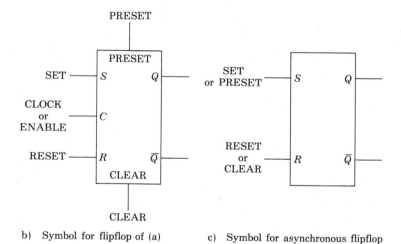

b)   Symbol for flipflop of (a)   c)   Symbol for asynchronous flipflop

Fig. 4.7   Synchronous and asynchronous RS flipflops

asynchronous inputs. S (SET) and R (RESET) now become synchronous inputs. They are ANDed with a CLOCK or ENABLE input,
and thus the flipflop cannot change state unless the CLOCK or
ENABLE input is 1. Two asynchronous inputs—PRESET and
CLEAR—have been added. The PRESET input can set the flipflop
to 1 regardless of the state of the CLOCK or ENABLE signal. Similarly, the CLEAR input can reset the flipflop to 0 independent of

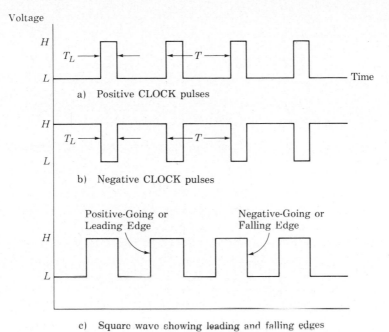

a)   Positive CLOCK pulses

b)   Negative CLOCK pulses

c)   Square wave showing leading and falling edges

Fig. 4.8   Types of CLOCK pulses

the CLOCK signal. Figure 4.7b shows a flipflop symbol with both synchronous and asynchronous inputs. A C input is for the CLOCK or ENABLE signal. The asynchronous inputs are commonly shown at the top and bottom of the symbol to distinguish them from synchronous inputs. However, if there is no CLOCK or ENABLE input, the asynchronous inputs are shown at the left side, as shown in figure 4.7c, and may be called SET and RESET.

CLOCK signals for digital computers were originally short pulses as shown in figure 4.8a and b. The pulse length T_L is short but must be long enough to change the flipflop state. Flipflop inputs must be constant during the time T_L while the pulse is on. The pulse period T determines the operating speed of the computer. T may be almost any duration but must be long enough to allow all flipflop changes to stabilize before the next pulse occurs. Since most flipflops can change state in nanoseconds (1 nanosecond = 10^{-9} second), T_L may be several nanoseconds. T can be any desired period longer than several nanoseconds.

Many integrated circuits use the CLOCK signals shown in figure 4.8. These signals are called *square waves;* the term "square" refers

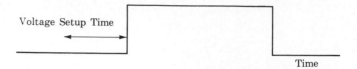

Fig. 4.9 Setup time for positive-going edge-triggered flipflops

to the equal periods of on and off. The two important parts of the square wave are its edges. The change from the lower voltage L to the higher voltage H is called the *leading edge,* or the *rising edge,* or the *positive-going edge.* The change from H to L is called the *trailing edge, falling edge,* or *negative-going edge. Edge-triggered* flipflops respond to either the rising edge (positive edge triggered) or the falling edge (negative edge triggered) but not both. The inputs to an edge-triggered flipflop must stay constant for a short period immediately before the triggering edge. This period, called the *setup time,* is shown in figure 4.9 for a flipflop that responds to the positive-going edge.

4.3.2 Master-Slave Flipflops

Flipflop circuits frequently have flipflop outputs fed back to the flipflop inputs or to combinational logic circuitry leading to the flipflop inputs, as was shown in figure 4.1. Changes in flipflop outputs are fed back to the flipflop inputs, thus resulting in further changes in flipflop outputs and, consequently, additional changes in inputs, and so on. If these changes produce unpredictable (and hence undesirable) output sequences, the condition is called a *race.* A race can lead to oscillations of the circuit. One way to avoid races is to use *master-slave* flipflops.

A NOR gate model of a master-slave RS flipflop is shown in figure 4.10. The model has two parts, the master and the slave. When the CLOCK signal is 1, the inputs to the master are enabled since the CLOCK signal is ANDed with the inputs S_1 and R_1. The master flipflop can change in response to the inputs and can produce intermediate outputs I and $\bar{I}$. While the CLOCK signal is on, the slave flipflop is cut off from the master since the inputs to the slave are ANDed with the inverted CLOCK signal.

When the CLOCK signal goes to 0, the master is cut off from the slave. The inputs to the slave are now enabled by the inverted CLOCK signal. The slave inputs are simply the intermediate outputs of the master. Since the master has been cut off, the intermediate outputs will not change while the slave changes. The slave changes

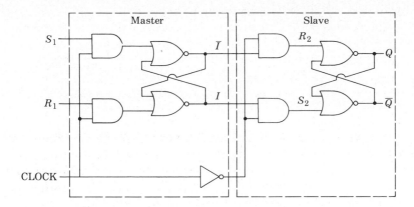

Fig. 4.10   NOR model of master-slave RS flipflop

in response to its inputs I and $\overline{I}$ and produces changes in the outputs Q and $\overline{Q}$. Even if the outputs Q and $\overline{Q}$ are fed back to the inputs S_1 and R_1 of the master, no changes can propagate through the circuit because the master and slave never change simultaneously. The name "master-slave" means that the master determines the behavior of the slave. The master responds to circuit inputs; the slave responds to the master.

A block diagram of a master-slave flipflop is shown in figure 4.11. It shows two positive edge-triggered flipflops combined to construct

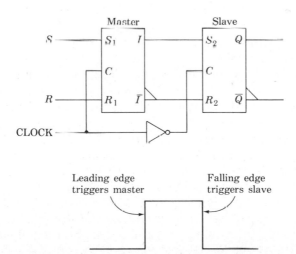

Fig. 4.11   Master-slave RS flipflop and clock pulse applied to master-slave flipflop

a master-slave flipflop. The leading edge of the CLOCK pulse triggers the master; the trailing edge triggers the slave. Note that the combination of two basic flipflops is one master-slave flipflop.

4.4   D, T, AND JK FLIPFLOPS

The main problem with the RS flipflop, whether clocked or not, is that both inputs may not be 1 at the same time. In this section we will look at three common flipflops that avoid this problem. The models shown are intended to illustrate flipflop behavior and are not intended to represent actual flipflop construction. All three flipflops are usually clocked.

4.4.1   D Flipflop

One way to avoid presenting 1 signals to both flipflop inputs is to allow just one flipflop input. The D flipflop, as modeled in figure 4.12c, has just one data input; it functions as an RS flipflop with complementary inputs. The D flipflop is always a clocked flipflop as its symbol shows in figure 4.12a. The input to the D flipflop at the time of the CLOCK pulse determines the output until the next CLOCK pulse. If D is 1, Q^n is 1; if D is 0, Q^n is 0. The characteristic equation is

$$Q^n = DC + \bar{C}Q$$

Delay flipflops are often used to transfer data. Figure 4.12 summarizes the D flipflop.

4.4.2   T Flipflops

The T flipflop also has just one data input, a toggle input. The behavior of the T flipflop is also simple. If $T = 1$, the flipflop changes state. If $T = 0$, the flipflop stays in its current state. Thus

$$Q^n = T \oplus Q$$

Because the state changes when the input is 1, the T flipflop is called a *toggle* flipflop. Figure 4.13 summarizes an asynchronous T flipflop. The T flipflop can also be clocked. T flipflops are not available as integrated circuits but are easily constructed from JK flipflops.

4.4.3   JK Flipflops

The JK flipflop is a two-input clocked flipflop that is much like a clocked RS flipflop. It solves the problem of simultaneous 1 inputs

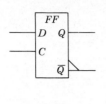

a) Device symbol

1. If D is 1 and C is 1, the next state is 1.
2. If D is 0, and C is 1, the next state is 0.
3. If C is 0, the flip-flop stays in its current state.

b) Word description

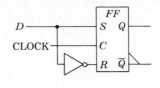

c) Model

Current Inputs		Current State	Next State
D	C	Q	Q^n
0	0	0	0
0	0	1	1
0	1	0	0
0	1	1	0
1	0	0	0
1	0	1	1
1	1	0	1
1	1	1	1

d) Transition table

Current Inputs		Next State
D	C	Q^n
0	0	Q
0	1	0
1	0	Q
1	1	1

e) Shortened transition table

DC				
Q	00	01	11	10
0	0	0	1	0
1	1	0	1	1

Q^n

f) Karnaugh map

$$Q^n = DC + \overline{C}Q$$

g) Characteristic equation

Fig. 4.12 Summary of D flipflop

by assigning next-state values for both 1 inputs. When both inputs are 1, the JK flipflop acts like a T flipflop. Thus with both inputs 1, the flipflop changes state at each CLOCK pulse. For all other inputs, the next state is the same as for the clocked RS flipflop. The flipflop can be modeled by a clocked RS flipflop with the inputs ANDed with the outputs as shown in figure 4.14c. The characteristic equation is

$$Q^n = J\overline{Q} + \overline{K}Q$$

with the understanding that all changes must be enabled by a CLOCK pulse. Because of its flexibility, the JK flipflop is popular and many integrated circuit versions are available. Figure 4.14 summarizes JK flipflops.

In the sections that follow, we will discuss some common uses of flipflop circuits in digital computers and other digital systems. First we examine the operation of such circuits as registers and counters from a simple, intuitive viewpoint. Later, we introduce formal analysis and design of sequential circuits.

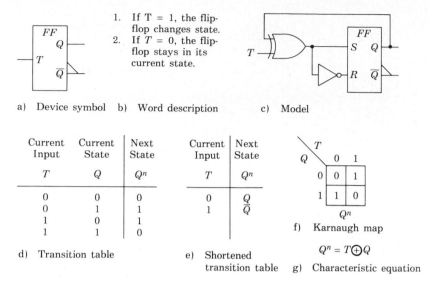

a) Device symbol   b) Word description   c) Model

Current Input	Current State	Next State
T	Q	Q^n
0	0	0
0	1	1
1	0	1
1	1	0

d) Transition table

Current Input	Next State
T	Q^n
0	Q
1	$\overline{Q}$

e) Shortened transition table

	T	
Q	0	1
0	0	1
1	1	0

Q^n

f) Karnaugh map

$$Q^n = T \oplus Q$$

g) Characteristic equation

Fig. 4.13   Summary of T flipflop

Most of the circuits inspected can be made from several types of flipflops. The choice of flipflop for a given application is complex and depends on considerations that we will not examine. Although we may show a circuit with just one type of flipflop, it can usually be built from other flipflop types. Similarly, the examples will illustrate many possible features, but for simplicity, each circuit will contain only a few.

4.5   REGISTERS

A major use of flipflops in digital computers is to construct registers that store information. A register is a row of associated flipflops. Information can be transferred into and out of registers with n flipflops either in series (1 bit per clock period) or in parallel (all n bits in one clock period). There are four possible ways to transfer information into and out of a register, as shown in figure 4.15.

The serial-input, serial-output arrangement of figure 4.15a is the slowest, since n clock periods (one for each of n bits) are required to input or output the information. We are willing to accept such slow information transfer only when we are transferring information

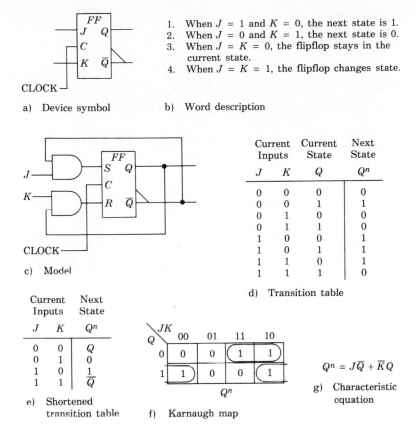

a) Device symbol

b) Word description

1. When $J = 1$ and $K = 0$, the next state is 1.
2. When $J = 0$ and $K = 1$, the next state is 0.
3. When $J = K = 0$, the flipflop stays in the current state.
4. When $J = K = 1$, the flipflop changes state.

c) Model

Current Inputs		Current State	Next State
J	K	Q	Q^n
0	0	0	0
0	0	1	1
0	1	0	0
0	1	1	0
1	0	0	1
1	0	1	1
1	1	0	1
1	1	1	0

d) Transition table

Current Inputs		Next State
J	K	Q^n
0	0	Q
0	1	0
1	0	1
1	1	$\overline{Q}$

e) Shortened transition table

f) Karnaugh map

$$Q^n = J\overline{Q} + \overline{K}Q$$

g) Characteristic equation

Fig. 4.14 Summary of JK flipflop

from and to slow input/output devices, such as teletypes. The main advantage of this connection is that the logic circuitry for the inputs and outputs is simple in that only one set of input logic circuits and one set of output logic circuits are needed.

The parallel-input, serial-output arrangement of figure 4.15b can receive n bits of information in one clock period but takes n clock periods to output them. It is most useful when transferring data from a high-speed device to a low-speed device. Conversely, the serial-input, parallel-output arrangement of figure 4.15c can transfer data from a low-speed device to a high-speed device.

The fully parallel information transfer possible with the arrangement of figure 4.15d is the fastest method of transfer. Just one clock

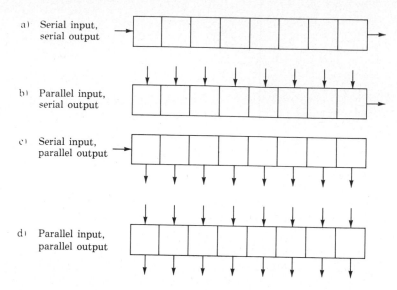

a) Serial input, serial output

b) Parallel input, serial output

c) Serial input, parallel output

d) Parallel input, parallel output

Fig. 4.15 Register information transfer

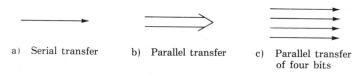

a) Serial transfer   b) Parallel transfer   c) Parallel transfer of four bits

Fig. 4.16 Transfer notation

period is required for either information input or information output. However, the logic circuitry required for this arrangement is complicated. For both input and output, n copies of any needed logic circuits are required.

We will use a special transfer notation for showing serial and parallel transfers in system diagrams later in the text. Figure 4.16 shows the notation. A single arrow (fig. 4.16a) means serial transfer, 1 bit at a time. A double arrow (fig. 4.16b) means parallel transfer, n bits at a time. The size of n will usually be indicated in discussion of the system or in a statement of system specifications. Sometimes we show n lines for parallel transfer of n bits. Figure 4.16c shows parallel transfer of 4 bits.

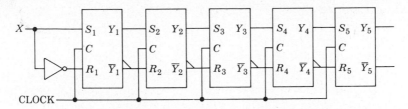

Fig. 4.17   A 5-bit shift register constructed from RS flipflops

4.5.1   Shift Registers

Shift registers transfer information serially. Figure 4.17 shows the
5-bit shift register Y constructed from RS flipflops. The input X is
entered into the first stage of the shift register, one bit at each CLOCK
signal. If $X = 1$, $S_1 = 1$ and Y_1 becomes 1 at the CLOCK pulse.
If $X = 0$, $R_1 = 1$ and Y_1 becomes 0 at the CLOCK pulse. At each
CLOCK pulse, the information stored in the first stage transfers to
the second stage. Y_1 is the S input to the second stage, and Y_1 is
the R input to the second stage. If $Y_1 = 1$, then $S_2 = 1$ and
$R_2 = 0$, so Y_2 becomes 1 at the CLOCK signal. If $Y_1 = 0$, then
$S_2 = 0$ and $R_2 = 1$, so Y_2 becomes 0 at the CLOCK signal. Similarly
at each CLOCK pulse, Y_2 is transferred to Y_3, Y_3 is transferred to
Y_4, and so on.

Table 4.3 shows the contents of the five-stage shift register for
an input series. The contents of the shift register are shown when
they are stable after a CLOCK pulse. Shifts occur at the CLOCK
pulses. This shift register is called a *shift-right register* since information shifts from left to right. Similarly, shift registers that move

TABLE 4.3

INPUT AND CONTENTS OF 5-BIT SHIFT REGISTER
BETWEEN SUCCESSIVE CLOCK PULSES

Input X	Shift Register				
	Y_1	Y_2	Y_3	Y_4	Y_5
1	0	0	0	0	0
0	1	0	0	0	0
1	0	1	0	0	0
1	1	0	1	0	0
1	1	1	0	1	0
0	1	1	1	0	1
1	0	1	1	1	0

information from right to left are called *shift-left registers.* Integrated circuit shift registers are often designed so that the same register can shift either right or left by changing the inputs.

Shift registers must be carefully designed so that information shifts only once at each CLOCK pulse. If the shift register stages change state too fast, bits can ripple or race across the shift register. The master-slave configuration is one solution to this problem.

Figure 4.18 shows an 8-bit shift register for serial transfer of data constructed from RS master-slave flipflops. It accepts data as the logical product of two input lines, A and B; AB is the first S input and $\overline{A}\overline{B}$ is the first R input. Data are shifted when the clock is positive.

4.5.2 Parallel Transfers

Information can be transferred in parallel either from or to external sources or between registers. Figure 4.19 shows a circuit for transferring external data into a 4-bit register. Since the register bits are Y_1, Y_2, Y_3, and Y_4, we can refer to the register as Y. Similarly, we can call the 4-bit input X. The clock is called a *transfer clock* to emphasize its role in transferring data. Since we do not usually want to transfer data at every period of the basic computer clock, we may use a transfer clock to send signals only when instructed by special control circuits. At each pulse of the transfer clock, the data X are transferred into the register Y. The mechanism is the same as for the shift register just discussed. Since each X bit is the S input to its stage and $\overline{X}$ is the R input, each Y bit becomes its X input at the transfer signal.

Parallel transfer of information between registers is shown in figure 4.20. At the transfer clock signal, information is transferred from the 4-bit X register to the 4-bit Y register. The reader should be able to explain the transfer.

4.6 COUNTERS

Binary counters are important components of digital circuits. They occur in many variations. We will look at two types of counters in this section—modulo 2^n counters and BCD counters.

4.6.1 Modulo 2^n Counters

A four-stage counter constructed of T flipflops is shown in figure 4.21. This counter is called a *modulo 16* counter because it counts

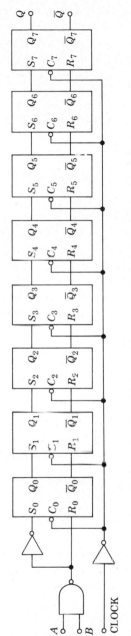

Fig. 4.18 An 8-bit shift register constructed from RS master-slave flipflops

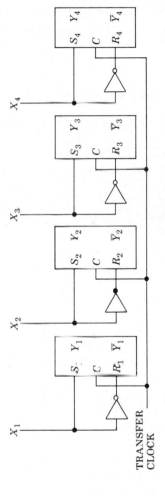

Fig. 4.19 Parallel transfer of information from external inputs X_1, X_2, X_3, and X_4, to 4-bit register Y

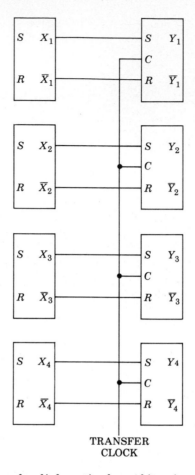

Fig. 4.20   Parallel transfer of information from 4-bit register **X** to 4-bit register **Y**

in binary from 0 to the decimal number 15. More generally, counters of n stages are modulo 2^n counters. Toggle flipflops give this counter a simple design since they possess the desired property of changing the output for every 1 input. The counter has a CLEAR line to start it at 0.

We will assume that the flipflops are negative edge-triggered, hence each flipflop changes state when its input changes from 1 to 0. The input to T_0 is a series of CLOCK pulses. Let us consider the counter operation beginning with 0s in each stage. The negative edge of the first CLOCK pulse will cause Q_0 to become 1. The negative edge

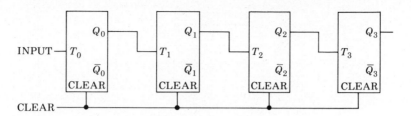

Fig. 4.21   A four-stage modulo 16 counter constructed of T flipflops

of the second CLOCK pulse will reset Q_0 to 0; the negative edge from the transition of Q_0 from 1 to 0 will set Q_1 to 1. The negative edge of the third CLOCK pulse will set Q_0 to 1. The negative edge of the fourth CLOCK pulse will reset Q_0 to 0; the negative edge of the Q_0 output will reset Q_1 to 0; the negative edge of the Q_1 output will set Q_2 to 1. This operation is shown in figure 4.22 and table 4.4. Note that the counter counts from left to right. The least

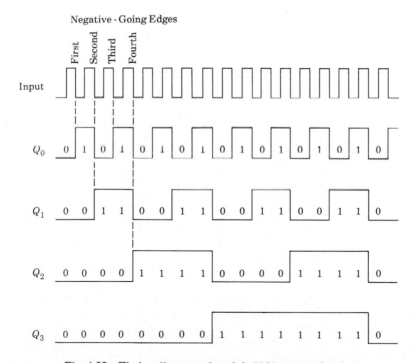

Fig. 4.22   Timing diagram of modulo 16 binary ripple counter

TABLE 4.4

OUTPUT OF MODULO 16 BINARY COUNTER FOR
SUCCESSIVE CLOCK PULSES

Q_3	Q_2	Q_1	Q_0
0	0	0	0
0	0	0	1
0	0	1	0
0	0	1	1
0	1	0	0
0	1	0	1
0	1	1	0
0	1	1	1
1	0	0	0
1	0	0	1
1	0	1	0
1	0	1	1
1	1	0	0
1	1	0	1
1	1	1	0
1	1	1	1

significant bit is on the left and the most significant bit is on the right. Each stage of the counter is called a *divide-by-2 stage;* you will see that the output waveform changes just half as rapidly as the previous stage. The counter is called a *ripple counter* since changes ripple across the counter.

A modulo 16 ripple counter using *JK* flipflops is shown in figure 4.23. The ENABLE signal must be 1 for the flipflop to count the input pulses. Counters called *up-down counters* (not shown) use two ENABLE lines and some logic circuits to count up or down. When the UP ENABLE signal is 1, the counter counts 0, 1, 2, 3, ...

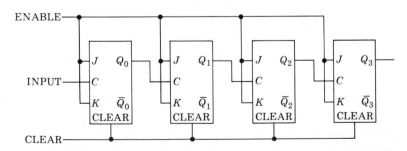

Fig. 4.23   A modulo 16 ripple counter constructed from *JK* flipflops

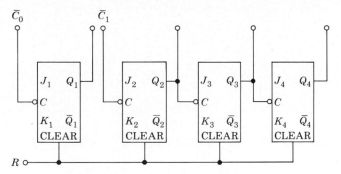

NOTE: All J and K inputs are connected to 1.

Fig. 4.24   A 4-bit binary counter composed of two sections, a modulo 2 and a modulo 8 counter

When the DOWN ENABLE signal is 1, the counter counts 15, 14, 13, ...

Figure 4.24 shows a 4-bit counter available as an integrated circuit. The counter is constructed from JK flipflops whose J and K inputs are all tied to 1. The counter is composed of two sections; flipflop Q_1 is a modulo 2 counter, and flipflops Q_2, Q_3, and Q_4 are a modulo 8 counter. The sections may be used independently, or Q_1 can be connected to $\overline{C}_1$ to form a modulo 16 counter. The R input is a RESET or CLEAR input.

4.6.2   BCD Counters

Since digital computers frequently process decimal information, it is useful to have counters that count modulo 10 rather than modulo 2^n. BCD (binary-coded-decimal) counters count in the usual binary fashion from 0 to 9 but then reset to 0 while giving a CARRY OUT signal of 1. Thus they count in decimal. Figure 4.25 shows a BCD counter stage composed of four JK flipflops. The unconnected inputs are assumed to be 1 signals. The small circles on the CLOCK inputs show that the inputs are negative edge triggered.

The counter counts in normal binary sequence until it reaches 1001. At the next CLOCK pulse the counter is reset to 0000. Q_0 becomes 0 because the Q_0 flipflop is a toggle flipflop and hence changes from 1 to 0. Q_1 stays 0 because $J_1 = \overline{Q}_3 = 0$ and $K_1 = 1$. Q_2 stays 0 because it does not receive a CLOCK pulse. Q_3 becomes 0 because $J_3 = Q_1Q_2 = 0$ and $K_3 = 1$. The counting sequence is shown in table 4.5. While the counter resets to 0, a negative-going CARRY

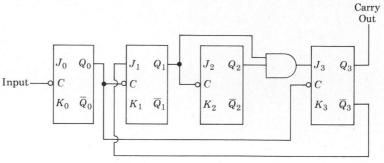

a)   Composed of *JK* flipflops

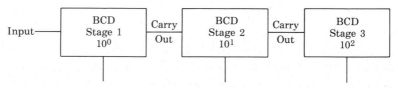

b)   Cascaded

Fig. 4.25   BCD counter stages

OUT signal occurs that can be used as the input to another BCD counter stage, as shown in figure 4.25b.

4.6.3 Decoders

The outputs of each flipflop in a counter are often used to drive a display to show the counter state or to provide control signals for some event that should start on a given count. Decoders, like those discussed in chapter 3, provide these functions. For example, the outputs of the four flipflops of the modulo 16 counter can be connected to a 1-of-16 decoder to provide control signals. Alternatively, the counter could be connected to another type of decoder to provide the signals for a display. Similarly, the outputs of each BCD counter could be connected to a BCD-to-seven-segment decoder to light a seven-segment display.

4.7 STATE NOTATION

Our discussions of flipflop circuits until now have been largely descriptive. In this section we introduce concepts from state theory

TABLE 4.5

COUNTING SEQUENCE OF BCD COUNTER

Q_3	Q_2	Q_1	Q_0
0	0	0	0
0	0	0	1
0	0	1	0
0	0	1	1
0	1	0	0
0	1	0	1
0	1	1	0
0	1	1	1
1	0	0	0
1	0	0	1
0	0	0	0

that will help clarify sequential circuit analysis and design. In later sections we will use these ideas for analysis and design and will examine more complex counters. (The rest of this chapter is not needed to understand the rest of the book so it may be omitted.)

Our discussions of flipflop circuits have centered on the behavior of each flipflop. Often, however, we are more interested in the behavior of the entire circuit. We can develop a transition table for a flipflop circuit that is much like the transition table of each flipflop. From it we can develop a state table that shows changes of state of the circuit, and a state diagram that graphically displays changes of state. We will leave formal analysis of sequential circuits to the next section and just show here the use of transition tables, state tables, and state diagrams for simple sequential circuits.

Example 4.1

The circuit of figure 4.26 has two JK flipflops with simple inputs. The first flipflop, Q_0, has both inputs J_0 and K_0 tied to 1. Hence this flipflop changes state or toggles at each clock pulse. The second flipflop has inputs J_1 and K_1 taken from the output of the XOR gate. Hence $J_1 = K_1 = \text{INPUT} \oplus Q_0$. We can construct a transition table that shows the current input to the circuit, the current state of each flipflop, and the next state of each flipflop. Table 4.6a shows this transition table. The next state entries for each flipflop are determined from its characteristic equation, $Q^n = J\overline{Q} + \overline{K}Q$. The transition table of table 4.6a is hard to read because it contains too much information and some entries are redundant.

A more helpful description is the modified transition table shown in table 4.6b. It shows the next state of each flipflop given the current

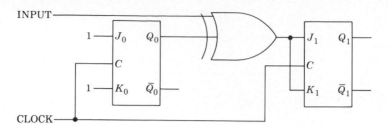

Fig. 4.26 Sequential circuit of example 4.1

state and the current circuit input, INPUT, which is the only independent input for the circuit. The column headings are the current value of INPUT; the row headings are the current states Q_1 and Q_0. The entries of the table are the next states, Q_1^n and Q_0^n. Although the states are written adjacent, multiplication is not intended. The notation means only the individual value of each state. This modified transition table more clearly shows circuit behavior; we will continue to use this form and call it simply a transition table.

The transition table shows the states of each flipflop in a circuit. Often we are more interested in the overall behavior of a circuit than in the behavior of individual flipflops. For this reason we introduce a notation for circuit state that uses either numbers or letters for each circuit state. Table 4.6c shows a state table derived from the transition table of table 4.6b. We have assigned states 0, 1, 2, and 3 to flipflop states 00, 01, 10, and 11, respectively. The state table shows that when INPUT is 0, the circuit moves to the next higher state, or counts up. Conversely, when INPUT is 1, the circuit moves to the next lower state, or counts down. The circuit is a modulo 4 up-down counter.

We can show state behavior graphically in a state diagram. (See figure 4.27.) Each state is shown as a circle, with connecting arrows corresponding to transitions between states. The arrow's tail shows the current state; the arrow's head shows the next state. The number written near each transition line is the input for that transition. On the state diagram, INPUT = 0 causes clockwise transitions as the circuit counts up. INPUT = 1 causes counterclockwise transitions as the circuit counts down.

In the preceding example we did not consider circuit outputs. For the circuit to be used as an up-down counter, circuit outputs would be taken from the flipflop outputs and decoded as discussed in the last section. More generally, we deal with circuits that have outputs that may be some combinational logic function of both circuit inputs

TABLE 4.6a

TRANSITION TABLE

Current input, INPUT	Current state Q_1	Q_0	Current control inputs J_1	K_1	J_0	K_0	Next state $Q_1{}^n$	$Q_0{}^n$
0	0	0	0	0	1	1	0	1
0	1	0	0	0	1	1	1	1
0	0	1	1	1	1	1	1	0
0	1	1	1	1	1	1	0	0
1	0	0	1	1	1	1	1	1
1	1	0	1	1	1	1	0	1
1	0	1	0	0	1	1	0	0
1	1	1	0	0	1	1	1	0

TABLE 4.6b

MODIFIED TRANSITION TABLE

Current state Q_1Q_0	Current input INPUT 0	1
0 0	0 1	1 1
0 1	1 0	0 0
1 0	1 1	0 1
1 1	0 0	1 0

Next state, $Q_1{}^n Q_0{}^n$

TABLE 4.6c

STATE TABLE

Current state S	Current input INPUT 0	1
0	1	3
1	2	0
2	3	1
3	0	2

Next state, S^n

and flipflop outputs. We want to be able to display outputs both in state tables and in state diagrams. Outputs of a sequential circuit may be associated either with the current state of the circuit or with transitions between states. In a *Moore circuit* the outputs are associated with circuit states and are level signals. The preceding example was a Moore circuit since the outputs of a counter circuit are ordinarily the decoded flipflop outputs. The outputs of a *Mealy circuit* are associated with the transitions between states and are pulse signals. The following example shows a Mealy circuit.

Example 4.2

The state diagram of figure 4.28a shows the behavior of an unspecified sequential circuit having one binary input. The four states—*A, B,*

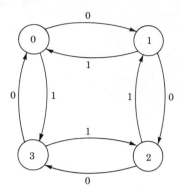

Fig. 4.27 State diagram of up-down counter

C, and *D*—are shown in circles. Transitions between states are shown by arrows. As before, the tail of the arrow identifies the current state; its head identifies the next state. Two numbers separated by a slash (/) are associated with each arrow. The left number shows the current input; the right number shows the output associated with the transition. This state diagram has only two 1 outputs. When the circuit is in state *B* or *C* and receives a 0 input, it returns to the same state and outputs a 1 pulse.

The state table can be written from the state diagram. Figure 4.28b shows the state/output table of this circuit, so-called because it shows both the next state and the output transition. The state/output table also shows that the only 1 outputs occur on the transitions from *B* or *C* back to the same state.

Example 4.3

A simple Mealy circuit that recognizes two consecutive 1 inputs, or outputs a 1 whenever two consecutive 1s have been inputted, is shown in figure 4.29a. The circuit starts in state *A*. If a 0 is inputted, it stays in state *A*. If a 1 is inputted, it goes to state *B*. In state *B* it returns to state *A* with a 0 output if a 0 is inputted or with a 1 output if a 1 is inputted. The circuit is in state *B* only when just one consecutive 1 input has been received. It outputs a 1 only when a second consecutive 1 input is received. Figure 4.29b shows the state/output table of this circuit. Similar circuits can be constructed to recognize any desired combination of input numbers or letters. This construction is basic to software devices that must recognize certain inputs as commands and data.

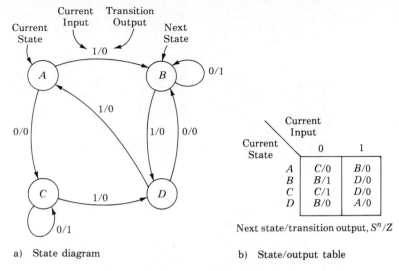

a) State diagram

b) State/output table

Fig. 4.28 A Mealy circuit

Example 4.4

A Moore circuit with four states is shown in figure 4.30a. Because the output of a Moore circuit is associated with the state instead of with the transition, both the state and output, separated by a slash, are shown within the state circle. The arrow shows the transition from the current state to the next state just as it did for Mealy circuits. Only the current input X is shown near the arrow. Figure 4.30b shows the state table of this circuit. Circuit outputs can be shown either by a column associated with the state table or as a separate output table, as shown in figure 4.30c.

A more general state diagram of figure 4.31 shows several types of states. *Regular states* (A, B, G, and H) can be entered from at least one other state and can exit to at least one other state. *Transient*

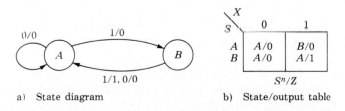

a) State diagram

b) State/output table

Fig. 4.29 A Mealy circuit that recognizes two consecutive 1s

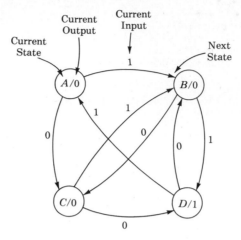

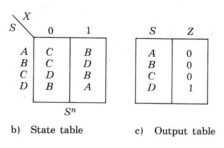

a)   State diagram

X			
S	0	1	
A	C	B	
B	C	D	
C	D	B	
D	B	A	

S^n

S	Z
A	0
B	0
C	0
D	1

b)   State table   c)   Output table

Fig. 4.30   A Moore circuit

states $(C$ and $E)$ cannot be entered from any other state but exit to at least one other state. A *persistent state* (D) can be entered from at least one other state but has no exit other than itself. An *isolated state* (F) cannot be entered from any other state and has no exit to any other state. Regular states G and H are isolated from the rest of the circuit; their entries and exits are only to each other.

4.8 SYNCHRONOUS SEQUENTIAL CIRCUIT ANALYSIS

The goal of sequential circuit analysis is to obtain a description of circuit behavior—either a statement or a state diagram—from the circuit diagram. To obtain both equations for the flipflop inputs and flipflop outputs and relations for the transitions between states re-

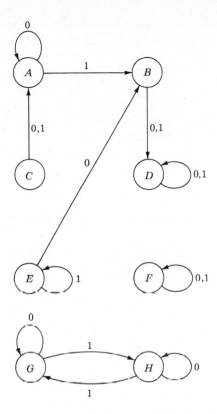

Fig. 4.31 State diagram showing regular states A, B, G, and H; transient states C and E; persistent state D; and isolated state F

quires several straightforward steps, most of which are now familiar. We consider a synchronous sequential circuit only. The flipflops in such a circuit change only during a CLOCK pulse. Between pulses combinational logic at the flipflop inputs and outputs can change, but the flipflop states cannot. Our discussion is brief and is illustrated by an example. Thorough discussion of sequential circuit analysis can be found in references at the end of the chapter. The procedure for sequential circuit analysis is:

1. Write equations for flipflop input functions and circuit output functions from the circuit diagram by combinational circuit analysis. Both the flipflop input or control functions and the circuit output functions may depend on circuit inputs and flip-flop outputs.

2. Develop control tables that display the flipflop input equations somewhat like a Karnaugh map. Control tables show flipflop control inputs as a function of circuit inputs and flipflop outputs.

3. From the control tables and the flipflop characteristic equation, develop a transition table for the circuit.

4. Assign circuit states to the combinations of flipflop states to construct a state table. At this point it is usually desirable to construct a separate output table or a combined state/output table from the output functions.

5. Graph the state table as a state diagram.

6. Describe the circuit behavior in words if desired.

This procedure is shown in figure 4.32. The blocks in the diagram are items produced during the procedure. The arrows between blocks show the method of analysis required between one block and the next.

Example 4.5

Figure 4.33a shows a circuit diagram for a sequential circuit with two JK flipflops. Analysis of the circuit proceeds as follows.

1. Combinational circuit analysis shows that the control inputs to the flipflops are:

$$J_0 = WY_1$$
$$K_0 = \overline{W}X + WY_0\overline{Y}_1$$
$$J_1 = W\overline{Y}_0$$
$$K_1 = \overline{W}X + WY_0$$

The output equations are simply $Z_0 = Y_0$ and $Z_1 = Y_1$.

2. The control inputs can be mapped into control tables, as shown in figure 4.33b. The control tables show control inputs for each flipflop in the circuit as functions of circuit inputs W and X and flipflop outputs Y_0 and Y_1.

3. The characteristic equation of a JK flipflop is:

$$Q^n = J\overline{Q} + \overline{K}Q$$

This equation is applied to the J and K control inputs in each cell of the control table to obtain the corresponding next state Y_0^n or Y_1^n. The next states of both flipflops are shown

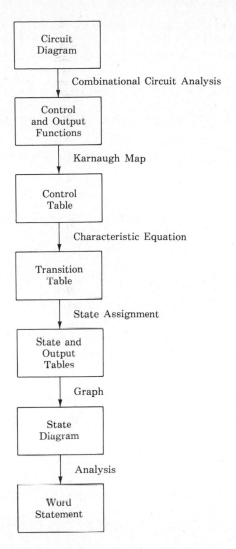

Fig. 4.32 Procedure for sequential circuit analysis

in a single transition table. (See figure 4.33c.) Each cell in the transition table shows the next state corresponding to the circuit inputs and current states.

4. States are assigned arbitrarily. *A, B, C,* and *D* are assigned to flipflop states 00, 01, 11, and 10. The resulting state table is shown in figure 4.33d. The output table, derived from the output functions, is shown as figure 4.33e.

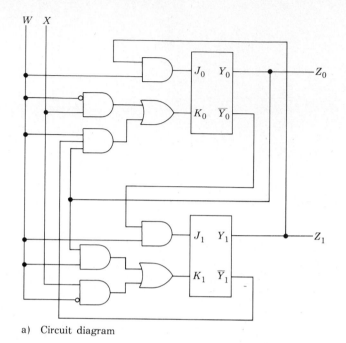

a) Circuit diagram

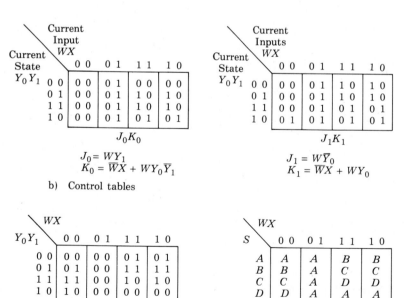

Current State $Y_0 Y_1$	Current Input WX 0 0	0 1	1 1	1 0
0 0	0 0	0 1	0 0	0 0
0 1	0 0	0 1	1 0	1 0
1 1	0 0	0 1	1 0	1 0
1 0	0 0	0 1	0 1	0 1

$J_0 K_0$

$$J_0 = WY_1$$
$$K_0 = \overline{W}X + WY_0\overline{Y}_1$$

Current State $Y_0 Y_1$	Current Inputs WX 0 0	0 1	1 1	1 0
0 0	0 0	0 1	1 0	1 0
0 1	0 0	0 1	1 0	1 0
1 1	0 0	0 1	0 1	0 1
1 0	0 1	0 1	0 1	0 1

$J_1 K_1$

$$J_1 = W\overline{Y}_0$$
$$K_1 = \overline{W}X + WY_0$$

b) Control tables

$Y_0 Y_1$	WX 0 0	0 1	1 1	1 0
0 0	0 0	0 0	0 1	0 1
0 1	0 1	0 0	1 1	1 1
1 1	1 1	0 0	1 0	1 0
1 0	1 0	0 0	0 0	0 0

$Y_1^n Y_2^n$

c) Transition table

S	WX 0 0	0 1	1 1	1 0
A	A	A	B	B
B	B	A	C	C
C	C	A	D	D
D	D	A	A	A

S^n

d) State table

Fig. 4.33 A sequential circuit based on two JK flipflops

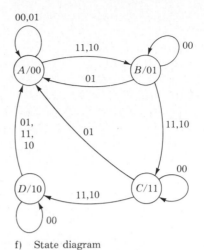

S	Z_0Z_1
A	0 0
B	0 1
C	1 1
D	1 0

e)   Output table

f)   State diagram

(Fig. 4.33 continued)

5. The state diagram is easily drawn from the state and output tables and is shown as figure 4.33f.

6. From the state diagram we can describe the circuit. The circuit counts modulo 4 in Gray code, that is, 00, 01, 11, 10, whenever it receives a W input. (Gray code, explained in chapter 3, is simply a method of counting that changes only 1 bit of a number at each count.) The $\overline{W}X$ input resets the counter to 00. The $\overline{W}\overline{X}$ input leaves the counter unchanged. In this example, assigning states tended to obscure the circuit behavior. It can be seen more easily from the transition table than from the state table. Fortunately, the counter outputs are still apparent from the state diagram.

4.9 SYNCHRONOUS SEQUENTIAL CIRCUIT DESIGN

Analysis of a sequential circuit is fairly easy and straightforward. It proceeds naturally from the circuit diagram. The converse problem—design of a sequential circuit given a statement of the desired behavior of the circuit—is much harder. Several aspects of sequential circuit design cannot be done algorithmically and hence require judgment from the designer. Other parts of the design involve choosing from a large number of possibilities. While it is possible to explore all possibilities, it is usually not desirable to take the time to do so. Hence again the designer must use his intuition and experience. Complications in circuit timing that may prevent successful operation can be eliminated only by detailed study of the circuit state tables; such problems, known as races and hazards, are beyond the scope of this text and will not be considered here.

In this section we outline the major steps of synchronous sequential circuit design and consider a simple example. We intend only to indicate the basic procedure and suggest some of the problems. The reader who is interested in sequential circuit design—both synchronous and asynchronous—should study the references of section 4.12.

Synchronous sequential design involves the following steps:

1. *Description of intended circuit behavior.* Sequential circuit design begins with determining the behavior desired for the circuit. Usually the designer is given a casual description of the desired behavior. The designer must turn the description into careful specifications of circuit inputs, outputs, and the relations between states.

2. *Construction of state table or state diagram.* The designer must then construct a state diagram or state table from the circuit specifications. Since state diagrams and state tables are equivalent, the designer may begin with either. Often it is easiest to begin by defining one state, considering transitions from it, and defining other states as needed. A state diagram may be more helpful in this approach.

3. *Minimization of the state table.* In sequential circuit analysis we were not concerned with minimization of either combinational logic or sequential logic. However, in sequential circuit design we must ensure that we are using no more gates or flipflops than are needed. We must examine the state table for possible redundant states that may be eliminated.

4. *State assignments.* The minimized state table from step 3 is written in terms of arbitrary states $A, B, C,$ and so forth. Coding these states into binary code and assigning them to the state variables of actual flipflops yields the transition table for the circuit. A large number of assignments is possible. If the flipflop table has m states, the number of flipflops, n, needed is given by

$$2^n \geq m$$

TABLE 4.7

NUMBER OF DISTINCT STATE ASSIGNMENTS

Number of states, m	Number of flipflops, n	Number of distinct assignments
2	1	1
3	2	3
4	2	3
5	3	140
6	3	420
7	3	840
8	3	840
9	4	10,810,800

If we choose the smallest n that will satisfy the inequality, there will be $(2^n - 1)!/((2^n - m)!n!)$ distinctly different possible assignments of states. (The notation $n!$ means $n \times (n-1) \times (n-2) \times \cdots \times 2 \times 1$.) For example, if we have four states and two flipflops, there will be three distinct state assignments. If we have three states and two flipflops, there will also be three distinct assignments. However, the number of assignments grows very rapidly with the number of states, as shown by table 4.7.

5. *Determination of flipflop control equations.* In the last two steps we determined the number of flipflops needed and the assignment of states to the flipflop variables. At this point we decide the type of flipflops that we will use. We learned earlier in this chapter that *JK, RS,* and *D* flipflops are equivalent in that, with suitable external circuits, we can make one of these flipflops resemble any other. Hence we can implement our sequential circuit design with any of these three flipflops, but one type might result in a design with fewer logic gates than the others. We may choose flipflops on the basis of availability or we may examine the designs we would get using each type. In either case we need the flipflop control equations for the flipflop under consideration. An easy way to determine the control equations is to develop flipflop control tables from the transition tables with the help of *excitation tables.* An excitation table is a variation of a flipflop transition table to show the inputs required for each possible transition. Table 4.8 shows excitation tables for *RS, JK,* and *D* flipflops. The *d* entries are don't cares, just as for combinational logic. The flipflop control tables developed

TABLE 4.8

EXCITATION TABLES FOR *RS*, *JK*, AND *D* FLIPFLOPS

a) *RS* Flipflop

Current state, Q	Next state, Q^n	Required inputs, S R
0	0	0 d
0	1	1 0
1	0	0 1
1	1	d 0

b) *JK* Flipflop

Current state, Q	Next state, Q^n	Required inputs, J K
0	0	0 d
0	1	1 d
1	0	d 1
1	1	d 0

c) *D* Flipflop

Current state, Q	Next state, Q^n	Required input, D
0	0	0
0	1	1
1	0	0
1	1	1

from the excitation tables and the circuit transition tables are minimized with Karnaugh map techniques to yield the flipflop control equations.

6. *Circuit implementation.* Once the flipflops and their controls (or inputs) have been determined, the circuit may be drawn. The output relations determined in the first step are used to design logic for the outputs, if any. The rest of the circuit has been determined.

The procedure for sequential circuit design is shown in figure 4.34.

Example 4.6

Two players, whom we will call W and X, control inputs to a clocked sequential circuit. At each CLOCK pulse a lamp lights if and only if the inputs matched at the two preceding CLOCK pulses. We wish to construct a sequential circuit for this game. Our design will follow the procedure just discussed.

1. From the problem statement we can specify two inputs, W and X, and one output, Z. We will need at least three states—cor-

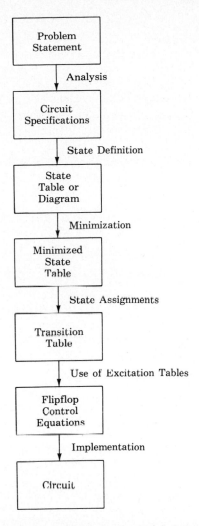

Fig. 4.34 Procedure for sequential circuit design

responding to mismatched inputs, inputs matched at one CLOCK pulse, and inputs matched at two or more CLOCK pulses. Only when the circuit is in the last state will the output be 1.

2. We can construct a state diagram as shown in figure 4.35a. Since the outputs are associated with the states, we will construct

a Moore machine. State A corresponds to the case of mismatched inputs, that is, inputs W and X that differ. State A has a 0 output. The circuit remains in state A as long as it receives differing inputs. State B corresponds to inputs that matched at the previous CLOCK pulse; that is, both W and X were 0 or both were 1. The output for state B is also 0. The circuit moves from state A to state B when the inputs first match. It returns to state A if it receives differing inputs. If the circuit receives matching inputs at a second consecutive CLOCK pulse, it moves to state C and outputs a 1. It stays in state C as long as it receives matching inputs and returns to A when it first receives differing inputs.

3. This state table has no redundant states and hence does not need minimization.

4. Since we have three states and will need two flipflops, table 4.7 shows that we can assign states in three distinctly different ways. Figure 4.35b shows the transition table and the output table that result from the assignment: $A = 00$, $B = 01$, $C = 11$. Other distinct assignments are $A = 00$, $B = 01$, $C = 10$ and $A = 00$, $B = 11$, and $C = 10$. The transition tables resulting from those assignments are left as an exercise for the reader. All other possible assignments can be shown to be the same as these three when complementation and permutation of the states are considered as the same.

5. We choose to implement the circuit with JK flipflops. Using the flipflop excitation table of table 4.8 and the preceding state table, we can derive the control tables for the JK flipflops shown in figure 4.35c. Treating them as we would a Karnaugh map, we can determine the flipflop control equations as:

$$J_1 = WXY_2 + \overline{W}\,\overline{X}Y_2$$
$$K_1 = \overline{W}X + W\overline{X}$$
$$J_2 = \overline{W}\,\overline{X} + WX$$
$$K_2 = \overline{W}X + W\overline{X}$$

Our choice of JK flipflops does not necessarily result in the best design. Use of RS flipflops would result in a different design and is left as an exercise for the reader.

6. The circuit can now be constructed and is shown in figure 4.35d.

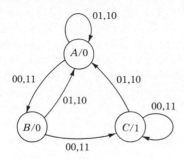

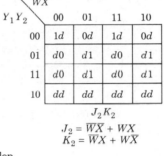

Y_1Y_2 \ WX	0 0	0 1	1 1	1 0
0 0	0 1	0 0	0 1	0 0
0 1	1 1	0 0	1 1	0 0
1 1	1 1	0 0	1 1	0 0

$$Y_1{}^n Y_2{}^n$$

Y_1Y_2	Z
0 0	0
0 1	0
1 1	1

a) State diagram

b) Transition table and output table

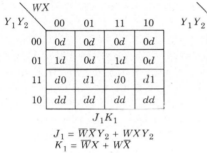

Y_1Y_2 \ WX	00	01	11	10
00	0d	0d	0d	0d
01	1d	0d	1d	0d
11	d0	d1	d0	d1
10	dd	dd	dd	dd

$$J_1K_1$$

Y_1Y_2 \ WX	00	01	11	10
00	1d	0d	1d	0d
01	d0	d1	d0	d1
11	d0	d1	d0	d1
10	dd	dd	dd	dd

$$J_2K_2$$

$$J_1 = \overline{W}\overline{X}Y_2 + WXY_2$$
$$K_1 = \overline{W}X + W\overline{X}$$

$$J_2 = \overline{W}\overline{X} + WX$$
$$K_2 = \overline{W}X + W\overline{X}$$

c) Control tables for JK flipflop

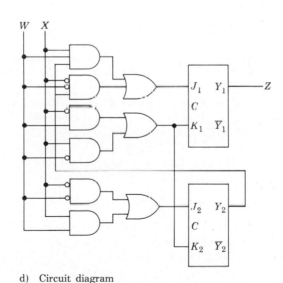

d) Circuit diagram

Fig. 4.35 Sequential circuit design for a two-person game

4.10   MORE COUNTERS

State diagrams can help us understand the operation of other counters besides the simple modulo 2^n and the BCD counters that we have already studied. The first additional counter we will consider is the *shift register counter*. These counters can be simply constructed from shift registers of any length. They have basic counting cycles of length n, where n is the number of flipflops. We will assume that D flipflops are used because they result in the simplest circuits. The output of the last flipflop (or the least significant stage) is fed back to the D input of the first flipflop. Figure 4.36 shows a three-stage shift register counter and its circuit diagram. Note that the counter is sensitive to the initial state of its flipflops. If the register initially contains all 0s or all 1s, the counter will stay in that state. If the counter initially holds any other number, it will count with a cycle of 3. We say the counter counts by 3 or counts modulo 3. Two cycles are possible—001, 100, 010, 001 and 101, 110, 011, 101. For this counter to be practical, we must be able to set it to a desired starting state and to decode the register contents into the desired counts, say 0, 1, 2.

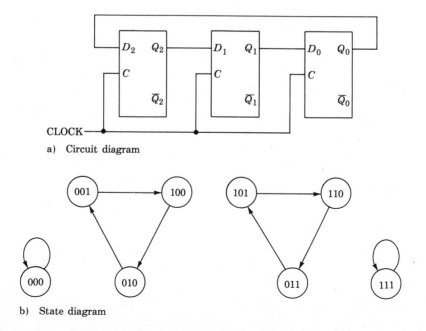

a)   Circuit diagram

b)   State diagram

Fig. 4.36   Three-stage, count-by-3 shift register counter

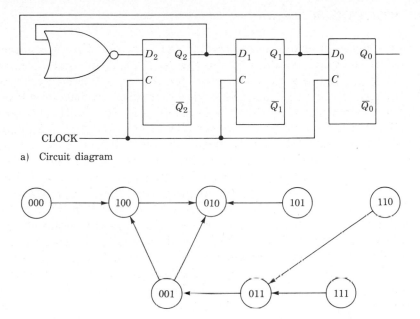

a) Circuit diagram

b) State diagram

Fig. 4.37   Three-stage, count-by-3, self-starting shift register counter

A *self-starting* counter is more useful. Because it has only one counting cycle, which is reached from any of its possible initial states, it will reach this cycle after, at worst, a few wasted steps. Figure 4.37 shows a three-stage self-starting shift register counter and its state diagram. The input to the first stage is the NOR of the outputs of the first two stages. The state diagram shows that the basic counting cycle is 100, 010, 001, 100. This counting cycle is reached after at most two steps, and the counter remains in it thereafter.

A variation of a shift register counter, called a *Johnson counter*, is shown in figure 4.38a. Johnson counters have basic counting cycles of length $2n$, where n is the number of flipflops. They are constructed by connecting the complement output of the last stage to the D input of the first stage. Figure 4.38b shows the state diagram of a three-stage Johnson counter. This counter has one basic cycle of length 2 times 3, or 6—000, 100, 110, 111, 011, 001, 000. It has another cycle of length 2—010, 101, 010. This Johnson counter, like the shift register counters, needs logic circuits to start it in a desired state and to decode the outputs.

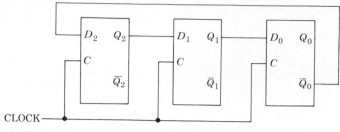

a) Circuit diagram

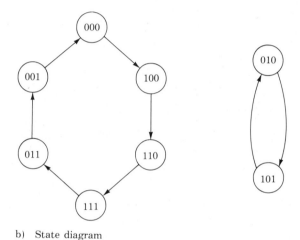

b) State diagram

Fig. 4.38   Three-stage, count-by-6 Johnson counter

4.11 SUMMARY

Flipflops are the main components of sequential logic circuits. They are bistable devices that provide complementary outputs. They may be controlled by pulse levels or be edge triggered; they may operate synchronously or asynchronously. The RS flipflop sets to 1 for an $S = 1$ input, resets to 0 for an $R = 1$ input, and stays in the same state for $R = S = 0$. Simultaneous 1 inputs to an RS flipflop are not allowed. The JK flipflop operates like the RS flipflop but changes state for simultaneous 1 inputs. The D flipflop simply delays the input until the next CLOCK signal. The T flipflop changes state when it receives a 1 input.

Sequential circuits that have flipflop outputs fed back through combinational logic to the flipflop inputs must have flipflops that are designed so that changes in one flipflop value cannot propagate back to the input and cause further changes. Master-slave flipflops prevent multiple changes during one CLOCK pulse by dividing the flipflop into two parts—one that is active when the clock is high and one that is active when the clock is low. Edge-triggered flipflops are also helpful in eliminating multiple changes since they are active only during the very short time of the edge transition.

Flipflops can be assembled into registers which can transfer information in and out in series or in parallel. A shift register transfers information serially. Parallel transfer circuits can transfer information in parallel from or to external devices or between registers.

Counters are important flipflop circuits. Modulo 2^n binary ripple counters require n stages to count to $2^n - 1$. BCD counters require four flipflops to count from 0 to 9; stages can be connected to count to any decimal number. Shift register counters use n flipflops for a counting cycle of length n; modified shift register counters (Johnson counters) use n flipflops for a counting cycle of length $2n$.

State diagrams show all circuit states, the transitions between them, and the associated inputs and outputs. Moore circuits have outputs that are associated with the states. Mealy circuits have outputs that are associated with transitions between states.

Sequential circuit analysis proceeds from a circuit diagram to a complete description of circuit behavior, either mathematically or verbally. Intermediate states, in order, are the construction of control and output functions, control tables, transition tables, state and output tables, and a state diagram.

Sequential circuit design is more difficult than analysis and requires more judgment from the designer. We considered only design of simple, clocked circuits. Design begins with a description of desired circuit operation and ends with a circuit diagram. Intermediate steps, in order, are the construction of a state table or state diagram, minimization of the state table, assignment of states to flipflops, determination of flipflop control equations, and circuit implementation.

Concepts

asynchronous
BCD counter
characteristic function
clock
control table
counter
current state

D flipflop
edge-triggered
excitation table
flipflop
isolated state
JK flipflop
Johnson counter
level

master-slave
Mealy circuit
modulo 2^n
Moore circuit
next state
parallel transfer
persistent state
pulse
race
register
regular state
reset
ripple counter
RS flipflop

self-starting counter
series transfer
set
setup time
shift register
shift register counter
square wave
state assignment
state diagram
state table
toggle flipflop
transfer clock
transient state
transition table
up-down counter

4.12   REFERENCES

Booth (1971) has much information on registers and on sequential circuit analysis and design at an introductory level. Bartee (1972) and Gschwind and McCluskey (1975) discuss counters in detail. Greene *et al* (1972) treat practical aspects of flipflop circuits. McCluskey (1965), Hennie (1968), and Hill and Peterson (1974) cover formal sequential logic analysis and design. Barna and Porat (1973) discuss integrated circuits, including counters. Blakeslee (1975) and Gschwind and McCluskey (1975) follow current industrial practice.

4.13   PROBLEMS

4.1   Describe the operation of the following circuit with

   a. a Karnaugh map for Y^n,
   b. a statement.

(4.1)

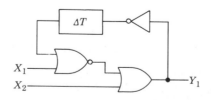

4.2 Describe the operation of the following circuit with

    a. a transition table,

    b. a statement.   (4.1)

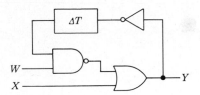

4.3 Describe the operation of the following circuit with

    a. a transition table,

    b. a statement.   (4.1)

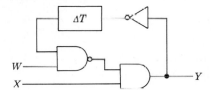

4.4 Describe the operation of the circuit below with

    a. a transition table,

    b. a statement.   (4.1)

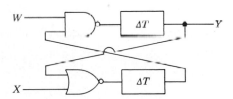

4.5 Model an *RS* flipflop with two NAND gates and two time delays ΔT.   (4.2)

4.6 Describe the operation of the circuit below with

    a. a transition table,

    b. a statement.   (4.4)

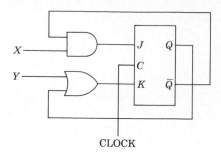

4.7   Sketch responses of the JK flipflop, as modeled below, to input J and K waveforms. Note the scale for ΔT.   (4.4)

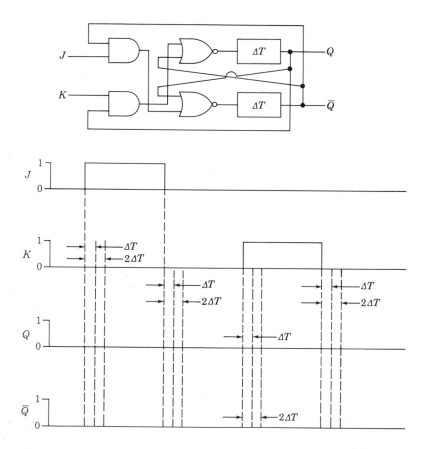

4.8   Model a D flipflop based on a JK flipflop   (4.4)

4.9   Model a T flipflop based on a JK flipflop.   (4.4)

4.10 Draw a circuit for a 4-bit shift-left register made of D flipflops.
      (4.5)

4.11 Draw a circuit of a four-stage register Y that accepts an input
      X serially and can transfer data to a four-stage register Z in
      parallel.   (4.5)

4.12 Draw the circuit for a modulo 8 ripple counter made of RS
      flipflops.   (4.6)

4.13 Draw a circuit for one 4-bit stage of a BCD counter made of
      RS flipflops.   (4.6)

4.14 The modulo 16 ripple counter of figure 4.21 is negative edge
      triggered.

      a. Construct a modulo 16 ripple counter that is positive edge
         triggered.
      b. Draw input and output waveforms like those in figure 4.22.
                                                                       (4.6)

4.15 Change the modulo 16 counter of figure 4.21 by connecting
      output $\bar{Q}_2$ instead of Q_2 to input T_3. Draw the input and output
      waveforms for this new circuit.   (4.6)

4.16 A candy machine sells candy for 20¢. It accepts nickels, dimes,
      quarters, and half dollars and gives correct change. A sequential
      circuit computes the change. Draw a state diagram for this
      circuit.   (4.7)

4.17 A sequential circuit gives a 1 output if and only if it has received
      three consecutive 1 inputs. Draw a state diagram for this circuit.
                                                                       (4.7)

4.18 A sequential circuit has two inputs, X_1 and X_2, and one output
      Z. If both inputs are 0 at any CLOCK pulse, the circuit enters
      a reset state, A. If for any five CLOCK pulses after the circuit
      is reset, the inputs X_1X_2 are 01, 10, 11, 10, 01, then the circuit
      goes to a set state, S, and outputs a 1. If the circuit receives

any inputs other than 00 or the sequence for the set state, it
goes to a wait state, W, until it is reset. Draw the state diagram
for this circuit.   (4.7)

4.19 Construct a state diagram for a circuit that has two transient
states, three persistent states, one isolated state, and no regular
states.   (4.7)

4.20 Analyze the circuit below. Show

    a. control equations,
    b. control tables,
    c. transition table,
    d. state/output table,
    e. state diagram.   (4.8)

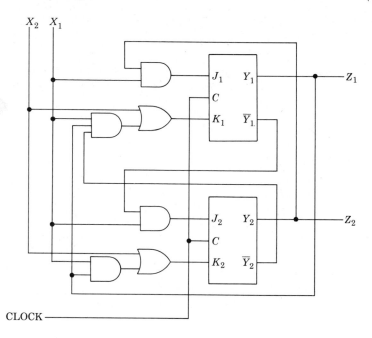

4.21 Analyze the circuit shown below. Show

    a. control equations,
    b. control tables,
    c. transition table,
    d. state/output table,
    e. state diagram.   (4.8)

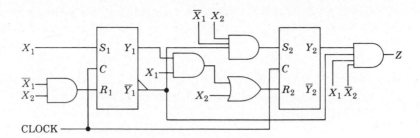

4.22 Construct the state table and output table for a clocked sequential circuit with inputs X_1 and X_0 and outputs Z_1 and Z_0. Inputs X_1 and X_0 can be interpreted as a 2-bit binary number X_1X_0 that is compared at each CLOCK pulse with the value of X_1X_0 at the preceding CLOCK pulse.

If (X_1X_0) current $> (X_1X_0)$ preceding, $Z_1 = 0$, $Z_0 = 1$;
If (X_1X_0) current $= (X_1X_0)$ preceding, $Z_1 = 1$, $Z_0 = 1$;
If (X_1X_0) current $< (Z_1X_0)$ preceding, $Z_1 = 1$, $Z_0 = 0$.   (4.9)

4.23 The transition and output table below describes the behavior of a clocked sequential circuit. Design the circuit with SR flipflops. Show

a. control tables,
b. control equations,
c. output equations.   (4.9)

Y_1Y_0 \ X_1X_0	00	01	11	10	Z_1Z_0
00	00	11	00	01	00
01	01	10	00	01	01
11	11	00	00	00	11
10	10	01	00	10	10

4.24 Example 4.6 showed three distinct assignments of two flipflop states to states A, B, and C. List all other possible assignments and show that they are equivalent within complementation ($Y_1\overline{Y}_0$ is equivalent to Y_1Y_0), permutation (Y_1Y_0 is equivalent to Y_0Y_1), or both.   (4.9)

4.25 Redesign the circuit of example 4.6 with RS flipflops.   (4.9)

4.26 Redesign the circuit of example 4.6 with the assignment $A = 00$, $B = 10$, $C = 01$.   (4.9)

4.27 Construct a modulo 12 counter from D flipflops to count eggs by the dozen. Show designs for

a. a shift register counter,
b. a Johnson counter,
c. (optional) a modified modulo 16 ripple counter.   (4.10)

4.28 Construct a pair of counters to count balls and strikes to a batter. Both counters should reset to 0 for a fourth ball, a third strike, or a new batter (i.e., a reset controlled by the umpire).
                                                        (4.10)

5 Register-Transfer Logic

5.1 OVERVIEW

Combinational logic and sequential logic are necessary parts of any computer or digital system, but they offer little insight into problems normally encountered. MSI and LSI technology has allowed us to build combinational and sequential logic components into larger blocks that can perform operations such as shifting and counting. Still we would like systems whose organization corresponds to the problem-solving steps that we ourselves might follow. We would like ways of describing systems that are powerful and economical in their expressions. Register-transfer-level systems offer such solutions.

We will first look at ways of describing registers and transfers between registers. With appropriate register-transfer notation we can describe large-scale systems with a relatively few statements, much fewer than are needed for the state descriptions of the last chapter. Moreover, the register-transfer descriptions will clearly and concisely explain the flow of control and the operations on data in the system. The state descriptions, in contrast, basically describe individual gate operations rather than the overall behavior of the system. We will look briefly at register-transfer languages to learn their capabilities (leaving detailed description to advanced texts), then examine one set of existing register-transfer components and the systems that can be built from them.

A central theme of this chapter is that sequential circuits can be divided into two parts—a data part and a control part. Figure 5.1 shows this division. The data part consists of data registers and the logic needed for the register inputs and outputs. Input data enter the data part; output data leave it. The control part consists of control

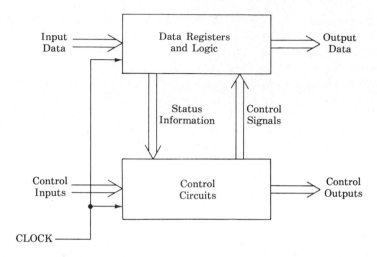

Fig. 5.1 A sequential circuit divided into data and control parts

circuits that may include registers and combinational logic. Control inputs enter the control part; control outputs leave it. The data and control parts are connected by status information sent from the data registers to the control circuits and by control signals sent from the control circuits to the data part. The figure shows common clock inputs to both parts that would be present in a clocked sequential circuit. However, the same division can be made for an asynchronous sequential circuit that operates without a clock.

5.2 REGISTER NOTATION

The last chapter considered the interconnection of flipflops to form registers, which are the basic information-storing devices in computers and other digital systems. The same operation is often performed on the contents of all flipflops or cells of a register. We need notations to describe a register, the contents of a register, and transfers between registers. A register is an ordered set of n flipflops or *cells*. We represent an n-cell register by a boldface letter, such as $\mathbf{A}$. Each cell of the register has a subscript that shows its order in the register, such as $\mathbf{A}_2$. We can also represent a register in terms of its cells. The four-cell register $\mathbf{A}$ can be represented as $\mathbf{A}_3\mathbf{A}_2\mathbf{A}_1\mathbf{A}_0$. More generally, the n-cell register $\mathbf{B}$ is represented as $\mathbf{B}_{n-1}\mathbf{B}_{n-2}\mathbf{B}_{n-3}\cdots\mathbf{B}_1\mathbf{B}_0$. Ordering the register from the highest-numbered cell to the lowest is convenient for performing arithmetic operations on registers.

The contents of each cell of a register is either a binary 0 or 1. The contents of an n-cell register is an n-bit binary number. For example, the contents of the four-cell register $\mathbf{A}$ can be any binary number from 0000 to 1111; thus the *value* of A is a 4-bit binary number. We can refer to the contents of an individual cell as, say, $\mathbf{A}_2 = 0$, meaning that the contents of cell $\mathbf{A}_2$ is 0.

The distinction between a register or cell and its contents is important. Registers and cells are physical devices that store information; their contents are that information. In the next section we will see that descriptions of transfers use the same symbols for both a register and its contents—the distinction is made only by the location of the symbols. Yet we must always remember whether we are considering information or the device that holds that information.

Registers may be divided into subregisters. For example, the four-cell register $\mathbf{A} = \mathbf{A}_3\mathbf{A}_2\mathbf{A}_1\mathbf{A}_0$ could be divided into two subregisters—a one-cell register $\mathbf{A}_3$ and a 3-bit register $\mathbf{A}_2\mathbf{A}_1\mathbf{A}_0$. Often a register that holds a number is divided into two subregisters—one cell to hold the sign bit and the remaining cells to hold the magnitude of the number. We will discuss this further in the next chapter.

The contents of a register, when treated by the computer as a single unit, is often called a *word*. A computer word may be either an instruction or data. Words are usually subdivided evenly into *bytes* consisting normally of 8 bits. Computer word lengths are not yet standard, but most computer words are multiples of 8 bits. Large computers may have word lengths of 64 bits or 32 bits, corresponding to 8 and 4 bytes, respectively. Small digital processors, such as microprocessors, may have words of only 4 or 8 bits.

The contents of a register may also be divided into *fields*, which may have any length. For example, the contents of the 4-bit register $\mathbf{A}$ that has a one-cell subregister for the sign bit and a three-cell subregister for the magnitude of a number has two fields—1 bit for the sign and 3 bits for the magnitude. The contents of the registers of the Hewlett-Packard pocket calculators have 56 bits, divided into 14 fields of 4 bits each. Ten fields are used for the mantissa, two for the exponent, and one each for the mantissa sign and the exponent sign. Each field of the mantissa and the exponent contains the BCD equivalent of one decimal digit. The sign fields could have been 1 bit each since the sign can only be positive or negative and thus can be represented by just 1 bit. However, the designer chose to make all fields the same length.

Information transferred from one register to another may be changed, for example, by complementing the contents of every cell of the register or, alternatively, only the contents of one field. We can consider any transfer or any transformation of register contents as a function. The notation $B = f(A)$ means that the contents of register B are a function of the contents of register A. This function assigns values to the contents of register B depending on the contents of register A. To distinguish between registers and functions of registers, we can call the former *independent registers* and the latter *dependent registers*. Here A is an independent register and B is a dependent register. Subregisters are a special case of dependent registers.

5.3 REGISTER TRANSFERS

To describe transfers between registers we introduce the following notation:

$$B \leftarrow A$$

which means that the contents of register A are transferred to register B and thus replace the former contents of register B. The contents of register A are not changed. The former contents of B are lost. More generally this notation means that the value on the right side of the arrow is transferred to the location on the left side. We can describe a *destructive transfer* from A to B (that is, a transfer in which the contents of A are destroyed or replaced by 0s) as

$$B \leftarrow A$$
$$A \leftarrow 0$$

The notation $A \leftarrow 0$ means that the contents of the n-cell register A become 0; that is, the value 0 is transferred into all cells of A.

Similarly, the transfer from one cell to another can be represented by

$$B_j \leftarrow A_i$$

where i and j may be different. Here the value of cell A_i is transferred to cell B_j. A destructive transfer from one cell to another is described as

$$B_j \leftarrow A_i$$
$$A_i \leftarrow 0$$

The distinction between regular transfers (nondestructive transfers) and destructive transfers is important. We must know whether the contents of the independent register remain or are cleared. The registers described in chapter 4 have nondestructive transfers. However, in later chapters, especially the chapter on memory, we will encounter devices that have destructive transfers. We will continue to use this notation for transfers and hence must always add a transfer of 0s into the independent register if the transfer is destructive.

We can also describe transfers of a function of one or more registers into a register. For example,

$$B \leftarrow \overline{A}$$

means that the complement of the value of A is transferred to register B. Likewise,

$$B \leftarrow A + B$$

means that the logical sum of the contents of registers A and B is transferred to register B. We can similarly describe transfers of other logical functions. In general,

$$C \leftarrow f(A,B)$$

means that the value of the logical function f of the contents of registers A and B is transferred to register C.

Transfers may involve subregisters. For example, suppose the eight-cell register A is divided into a three-cell subregister $A_7A_6A_5$ and a five-cell register $A_4A_3A_2A_1A_0$. We can refer to the first register as A_{7-5} and to the second as A_{4-0}. The subscripts show the cells that are involved. Then the transfer described as

$$B \leftarrow A_{7-5}$$
$$C \leftarrow A_{4-0}$$

means that the contents of cells 7 to 5 of register A are transferred to register B, while the contents of cells 4 to 0 of register A are transferred to register C. An obvious extension is the transfer of logical functions of subregisters.

Shift register transfers can also be easily described. In the usual shift register, as described in chapter 4, the contents of all but one cell move to the adjacent cell. Contents move right in a shift-right shift register and left in a shift-left. The contents of the remaining cell—the rightmost cell in a shift-right shift register and the leftmost cell in a shift-left shift register—are handled differently. In a serial shift register that accepts data at one end from some other register, the contents of the cell at the other end are shifted out of the register. If the source of data is a one-cell register B, this type of transfer in a shift-left register could be described as

$$A_0 \leftarrow B, \ A_1 \leftarrow A_0, \ A_2 \leftarrow A_1, \ A_3 \leftarrow A_2$$

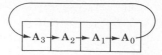

a)   Register cells and direction of transfer

b)   Contents of register at time t

c)   Contents of register after one shift,
$A_0 \leftarrow A_1, A_1 \leftarrow A_2, A_2 \leftarrow A_3, A_3 \leftarrow A_0$

Fig. 5.2   A circular, shift-right shift register

Circular shift registers shift data through the register and back around to the start of the register. Figure 5.2 shows a circular, shift-right shift register with its contents at two successive clock intervals. The contents of each of the leftmost three cells are shifted into the cell just to the right of it. The contents of the rightmost cell are shifted around to the leftmost cell. The shift is described as

$$A_0 \leftarrow A_1, \ A_1 \leftarrow A_2, \ A_2 \leftarrow A_3, \ A_3 \leftarrow A_0$$

5.3.1   Conditional Transfers and Sequencing

To implement a computer program at the register-transfer level we execute a sequence of register transfers. Sometimes, depending on the value of a logical variable or expression, we execute one of several possible transfers. (The notation describing such transfers depends on the condition of some variable of expression.) First, we number all steps of a register-transfer or control sequence. If when the sequence is executed, control always passes from step n to step $n + 1$, no conditional transfer or branching statement is necessary. If control can pass to any of two or more register transfers, a branching statement is necessary. The branching statement has the general form:

$$\rightarrow [(f_1 \cdot s_1) + (f_2 \cdot s_2) + \cdots + (f_n \cdot s_n)]$$

Each f_i is a logical variable or expression. Each s_i is a step in the register-transfer sequence. The f_i are chosen so that one and only one of them will be 1 at any time. Mathematically, this means:

$$f_i \cdot f_j = 0, \qquad i \neq j$$
$$f_1 + f_2 + \cdots + f_n = 1$$

Control transfers to step s_i when its corresponding f_i is 1. For example, the expression

$$\rightarrow [(f_1 \cdot 4) + (f_2 \cdot 6) + (f_3 \cdot 7)]$$

reduces to

$$\rightarrow 6$$

when $f_2 = 1$ and $f_1 = f_3 = 0$. Thus control transfers to step 6.

Example 5.1

The following control sequence describes a sequence of register transfers for a four-cell register X that accepts data from another four-cell register Y.

1. $X_0 \leftarrow Y_0, X_1 \leftarrow Y_1, X_2 \leftarrow Y_2, X_3 \leftarrow Y_3$
   $\rightarrow [(X_3 \cdot s_3) + (\overline{X}_3 \cdot s_2)]$
2. $X_0 \leftarrow \overline{X}_0, X_1 \leftarrow \overline{X}_1, X_2 \leftarrow \overline{X}_2, X_3 \leftarrow \overline{X}_3$
3. $Z_0 \leftarrow X_0, Z_1 \leftarrow X_1, Z_2 \leftarrow X_2, Z_3 \leftarrow X_3$

If the value of X_3 is 1, control passes to step 3. If the value of X_3 is 0, control passes to step 2, where the contents of X are complemented. After step 2 is executed, control passes to step 3. At step 3 the data are transferred to register Z.

Because these transfers are so simple, we can describe the control sequence more compactly with statements that show register transfer rather than cell transfers.

1. $X \leftarrow Y$
   $\rightarrow [(X_3 \cdot s_3) + (\overline{X}_3 \cdot s_2)]$
2. $X \leftarrow \overline{X}$
3. $Z \leftarrow X$

The sequence corresponds to the flowchart of figure 5.3. The data are transferred from Y to X. The value of X_3 is tested. If it is 0, each bit of X is complemented. If bit X_3 is 1, the data are not changed. Then the data are transferred to Z.

Register-transfer sequences are especially useful in describing large sequential circuits, such as those in computers and other large digital

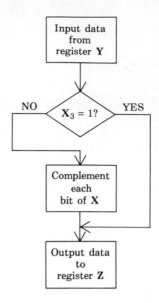

Fig. 5.3 Flowchart for the register-transfer sequence of example 5.1

systems. The state notation described in chapter 4 rapidly becomes unwieldy for descriptions as n (the number of flipflops in a sequential circuit) increases because the number of possible states is 2^n. Register-transfer descriptions concentrate on the transfers that occur between registers in response to control signals rather than all possible states of the registers. An example illustrates the usefulness of register-transfer descriptions.

Example 5.2

Figure 5.4 shows a sequential circuit composed of a four-cell register **X,** two control flipflops B_0 and B_1 and some combinational logic. The control part of the circuit includes control flipflops B_0 and B_1, some combinational logic, a decoder, control input SEQ, and control signals C_0 through C_3. The data part includes the four-cell data register **X,** the data inputs Y, and the combinational logic for the data register inputs. All flipflops are D flipflops. Data can be inputted from a four-cell register **Y** in another part of the circuit; only the input leads are shown. An input signal, SEQ, controls the sequencing of the circuit. A decoder presents four control signals—C_0, C_1, C_2, and C_3—to the data flipflops; the current control signal depends on the previous control signal and the current value of SEQ.

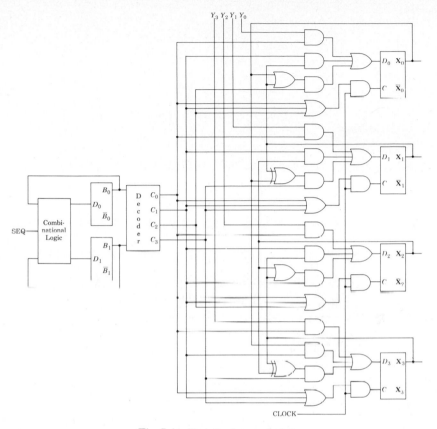

Fig. 5.4   Circuit of example 5.2

Table 5.1 shows an extended state table. The transfers between data registers depend only on the current state. The next state depends on the current state and the current value of SEQ. We consider the states of the circuit to be the states of the control signals. Although the circuit has six flipflops and hence 2^6 possible states, we are concerned only with states that occur in response to the control signals and their associated transfers. Thus we are interested only in the four states corresponding to the four control signals, C_0 through C_3. We do not consider the values stored in the **X** register.

The control signals are associated with simple transfers. C_0 causes data to be inputted from **Y** to **X**. C_1 shifts each bit to the adjacent cell with the lower subscript; the contents of $\mathbf{X}_0$ are shifted back to $\mathbf{X}_3$. C_2 replaces $\mathbf{X}_0$ with $\mathbf{X}_0 + \mathbf{X}_1$ and $\mathbf{X}_2$ with $\mathbf{X}_2 + \mathbf{X}_3$. C_3 replaces $\mathbf{X}_1$ with $\mathbf{X}_1 \oplus \mathbf{X}_0$ and $\mathbf{X}_3$ with $\mathbf{X}_3 \oplus \mathbf{X}_2$.

TABLE 5.1

EXTENDED STATE TABLE

Current state, S	Next state, S^n		Transfer associated with S
	SEQ = 0	SEQ = 1	
C_0	C_1	C_1	$X_0 \leftarrow Y_0$, $X_1 \leftarrow Y_1$, $X_2 \leftarrow Y_2$, $X_3 \leftarrow Y_3$
C_1	C_2	C_0	$X_0 \leftarrow X_1$, $X_1 \leftarrow X_2$, $X_2 \leftarrow X_3$, $X_3 \leftarrow X_0$
C_2	C_3	C_3	$X_0 \leftarrow X_0 + X_1$, $X_2 \leftarrow X_2 + X_3$
C_3	C_0	C_0	$X_1 \leftarrow X_0 \oplus X_1$, $X_3 \leftarrow X_2 \oplus X_3$

We can describe the circuit with the following control sequence:

0. $X_0 \leftarrow Y_0$, $X_1 \leftarrow Y_1$, $X_2 \leftarrow Y_2$, $X_3 \leftarrow Y_3$
1. $X_0 \leftarrow X_1$, $X_1 \leftarrow X_2$, $X_2 \leftarrow X_3$, $X_3 \leftarrow X_0$
   $\rightarrow [(\overline{SEQ} \cdot 2) + (SEQ \cdot 0)]$
2. $X_0 \leftarrow X_0 + X_1$, $X_2 \leftarrow X_2 + X_3$
3. $X_1 \leftarrow X_0 \oplus X_1$, $X_3 \leftarrow X_2 \oplus X_3$
   $\rightarrow (0)$

The control sequence shows that there is no branching after step 0; control always passes to step 1, corresponding to state C_1. After step 1, control passes to C_2 if SEQ = 0 and C_0 if SEQ = 1. After step 2, control passes to C_3. After step 3, control passes to C_0. This short control sequence describes the operation of the circuit more simply and economically than would the 64-state state diagram that shows all states of the six flipflops of **X** and **B**.

5.3.2   Register-Transfer Languages

The control descriptions discussed above are a variation of the language APL (A Programming Language) similar to the version described by Hill and Peterson (1973). Other register-transfer descriptions have been used for computer design. CDL (Computer Design Language) and DDL (Digital Design Language) are two of the more common languages used to describe register transfers. Some register-transfer languages resemble ALGOL and use IF-THEN-ELSE statements for branching. No register-transfer language is yet standard. Register-transfer languages and descriptions are likely to become increasingly more popular in the future because they describe the operation of large-scale systems simply and economically.

5.4 REGISTER-TRANSFER-LEVEL COMPONENTS

Register-transfer-level components more closely resemble the steps we take in solving a problem than do logic components at the combinational and sequential logic sublevels. For that reason, they seem more natural, and a system design at the register-transfer level is easy to understand.

There are six basic register-transfer-level components. *Memories* (*M*) store information without change. Registers are an example of memories. *Links* (*L*) send information between other components without changing the information. *Switches* (*S*) route data to other components by changing the links that connect components. *Transducers* (*T*) change the representation of information without changing its content or value. Transducers can interface between the digital system and the outside world. Thus they can receive a touch input from a keyboard and transform the information into the electrical bit pattern used within the system. They can also change data from one bit representation to another within the digital system.

Data operators (*D*) operate on information to produce new information. Data operators include arithmetic functions, such as addition, and logical functions, such as complementation, AND, and OR. *Controls* (*K*) cause the other components to operate at the right times and in the correct sequence. Controls are active; the other components are passive. These components are summarized in table 5.2.

The functions of these components can be seen from an example. Consider adding 43 and 36 on a calculator. The first step is to enter 43 by pressing the key 4 and then the key 3, followed by a key indicating that the number is completed. (In some calculators this would be an ENTER key to enter the number in memory; in others it would be an ADD key.) A transducer (*T*) changes the touch input into the bit pattern 00101011 to represent 43 in 8-bit binary. Then the number must be stored temporarily in a memory (*M*). A link (*L*) transfers the number from the transducer (*T*) to the memory (*M*).

Next we enter the number 36. The transducer (*T*) converts it from the touch inputs to the bit pattern 00100100. We then want to add the two numbers. The first number that we had stored in memory

TABLE 5.2

REGISTER-TRANSFER-LEVEL COMPONENTS

Component	Function
Memory (M)	Stores information without change
Link (L)	Sends information without change
Transducer (T)	Changes the form of information without changing its value
Data operator (D)	Produces new information
Switch (S)	Routes data
Control (K)	Controls other components

(M) must be sent from M via a link (L) to the data operator (D), an adder. This requires a switch (S) to reroute the number to the data operator (D). The second number is sent from the transducer (T) to the data operator, where the two numbers are added together. Their sum, represented as the bit pattern 01001111, is sent to the output transducer (T) that converts the number from its binary bit pattern to a visual display of the decimal number 79. Controls (K) direct the operations throughout.

Figure 5.5 shows the register-transfer components that perform the calculator addition of this example. The links between compo-

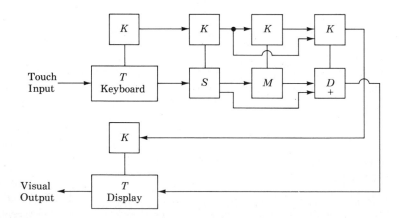

Fig. 5.5   Register-transfer level of calculator

nents are shown but are not labeled. Note that all other components have associated controls. While it would seem simpler for each component to control itself, we gain power and flexibility in digital systems by having separate controls.

5.5 REGISTER-TRANSFER MODULES

Now that we have studied the concept of register-transfer components and their arrangement to perform a simple calculation, we are ready to discuss a specific set of register-transfer components. *Register-transfer modules* (RTMs), manufactured by Digital Equipment Corporation (DEC), are the most widely used, commercially available register-transfer components. There are about 40 types of RTMs. We will discuss the four main types and a few specific RTMs so that we can assemble them into a simple system. The RTM system consists of the 16-bit register-transfer modules and a method of connecting them via a common *bus*. The bus is a link that carries information and timing signals for the register transfers. Three types of modules (T, M, and a hybrid of data operator with memory denoted DM) connect to the bus to transfer information. The fourth type, K modules, controls the data transfer.

5.5.1 Type T Modules (Transducers)

Transducers interface between the RTM system and the outside world. Thus they allow information transfer to and from teletypes, displays, switches, and other computers.

5.5.2 Type M Modules (Memories)

Memories consist of registers that store information temporarily. They correspond basically to variables, such as X and Y, in a computer program. The memory operations are mainly reading and writing. Reading transfers data from memory and is denoted $\leftarrow M$. Writing transfers data to memory and is denoted $M \leftarrow$.

5.5.3 Type DM Modules (Data Operation Combined with Memory)

DM modules combine data operation and memory. They are the heart of a digital system and act much like the arithmetic units discussed in the next chapter. They provide combinational logic for simple arithmetic and logical functions. The D or data operator part of a DM module evaluates simple arithmetic and logic expressions. To represent both types of expressions easily we will now use + for plus (addition) instead of for OR. We will use × for times (multiplication). We will spell out AND, OR, and XOR. For example, data operators can evaluate $A + B$, $A - B$, and A XOR B. After evaluation, the value is stored in a register of the M part of the DM module or transferred to other registers via the bus.

An important DM module is the DMgpa, the DM module for general purpose arithmetic. The DMgpa has two registers—**A** and **B**. It can calculate a wide variety of arithmetic and logical functions. These include A, B, $\overline{A}$, $\overline{B}$, $A + B$, $A - B$, $A + 1$, $A \times 2$, A AND B, A OR B, and A XOR B. The results can be transferred to other registers via the bus. Results can also be transferred to (written into) **A** and **B** (**A** ←, **B** ←). Data can be shifted right or left, and data can be shifted into the lefthand and righthand bits. This allows easy multiplication and division by 2. Individual bits of the **A** and **B** registers are available as outputs.

5.5.4 Type K Modules (Control)

K modules control the transfer of data among registers by *evoking* (executing) operations by DM and M modules. K modules resemble the control structure of a computer program. There are more varieties of K modules than there are of any other type. *K.evoke* modules control the times of execution of the operations of DM and M modules. *K.branch* modules decide which operations are to be executed next. *K.subroutine* modules connect together a sequence of operations as a subroutine. *K.serial-merge, K.parallel-branch,* and *K.parallel-merge* synchronize control flow over several control paths or for several operations. Clocks, delays, and manual start keys are other K modules. We will look at three control modules in more detail.

The K.evoke (Ke) module is the basic control module. It executes a function consisting of a data operation and a register-transfer operation. When the Ke module is evoked, it executes the function. When the function is complete, the Ke module evokes the next control module in the control sequence. Figure 5.6 shows the K.evoke module.

The basic Ke operation is the execution of data operation followed by a single register-transfer operation in the data-memory part of the RTM system, using the bus, such as $A \leftarrow A + B$. It may also evoke a data operation that does not use the bus (setting, complementing, or clearing a register), for example, $A \leftarrow \overline{A}$.

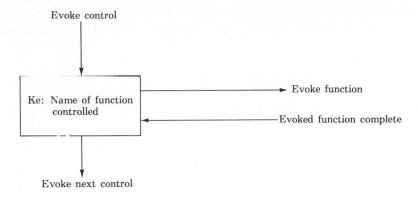

Fig. 5.6   K. evoke module

The sequence of the basic Ke is:

1. The Ke module receives an evoke signal as its input which evokes the control.
2. The module sends an evoke operation signal to the function it controls in the DM part of the system which executes the function.
3. When the operation is complete, the bus control module sends a done signal back to the Kc module.
4. The Ke module then sends an evoke next control signal to the next K module.

The K.branch two-way (Kb2) module routes control flow in either of two directions, depending on the value of an input logic variable. A diagram of Kb2 is shown in figure 5.7. When the control module is evoked, it in turn evokes one of the next controls, with the selection depending on whether the logic variable is 1 or 0.

A K.bus sense and termination module (Kbus) controls each independent data bus in an RTM system. Each data bus has a register (bus sense register, or BSR) that always holds the result of the last register transfer that occurred via the bus. The Kbus module monitors all register-transfer operations and sends an operation completion or done signal to the Ke modules when the requested function has been completed. It allows manual control of the RTM system when it is connected to the appropriate manual switches. It provides both a reset signal to initialize all modules and a zero signal, 0. It allows sense lights to be connected to the bus sense register to display data transfers.

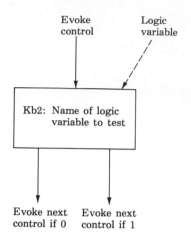

Fig. 5.7   K. branch two-way module

5.6 RTM SYSTEM EXAMPLES

An RTM system has two parts. The data part consists of data operations on explicitly declared data variables. The control part executes operations on the data part. Our first example will show the correspondence between these two parts.

Example 5.3—Summing Integers from 1 to N

We can build a small system to sum the integers from 1 to N (that is, $S = 1 + 2 + 3 + \cdots + N$) using the four modules we have discussed plus two more. We need a T.switch-register (Tsw) to enter N and a K.manual-start (Kms) to start operation of the system. Figure 5.8 shows the main parts of an RTM system. The general-purpose-arithmetic module (DMgpa) has registers to hold the sum S and the integer N. To start the system, we enter N in the switch register T and start the system manually. K.manual-start begins the control sequence. Instead of counting from 0 to N, we begin with N and count down to 0 while totaling our sum S. The first k.evoke gates T from the switch register onto the bus and then into the register N ($N \leftarrow T$). The second K.evoke initializes the sum S ($S \leftarrow 0$).

Next is a loop of three control functions. First, N is added to S, $S \leftarrow S + N$. Then N is decreased by 1, $N \leftarrow N - 1$. Then N is tested for $N = 0$. If $N = 0$, we are done. If not, we repeat the loop. A K.serial-merge module (Ksm) acts like an OR gate to channel the

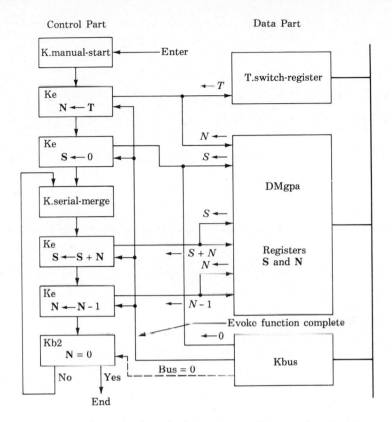

Fig. 5.8   RTM system for calculation of sum of integers from 1 to N

two incoming control paths into a single control flow link. The expression Bus = 0 is the logic input to a K.branch two-way module for this test.

Once we have seen one RTM system diagram, the connections between K modules and the M, DM, and T modules are usually obvious. Hence we use a simpler RTM diagram that shows the flow of control through the K modules. It shows the M, DM, T, and Kbus modules attached to each bus. It does not show the interconnections between the control part and the data part of the RTM system. Figure 5.9 is an RTM diagram for example 5.3.

Example 5.4—Counting the Number of 1 Bits in a Word

Since register-transfer modules are designed to be the hardware corresponding to the flowchart representation of an algorithm for solving

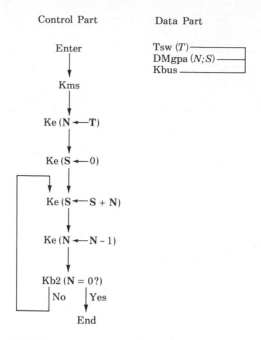

Fig. 5.9   RTM diagram for calculation of sum of integers from 0 to N

a problem, we may want to begin consideration of an RTM system with a flowchart. Figure 5.10 is a flowchart for an algorithm to count the number of 1 bits in a word. We start by initializing the total of 1 bits to 0, then enter a loop. We test to see if the word is all 0s. If it is, we are done since there are no 1 bits left to count. If the word is not 0, we shift all bits one position to the left and insert 0 in the rightmost position. Then we test the bit removed to the left. If it is 1, we add 1 to the total. In either case, we return to the start of the loop and test the word for 0.

The RTM diagram for a system corresponding to this algorithm is shown as figure 5.11. Although only two registers are needed—one for the total and one for the variable word—we have used two DMgpa (each of which has two registers) for simplicity. Initially one DMgpa holds the word for which the count of 1 bits is desired, the other holds the total, which is set to 0 in the first step of the control sequence. A Ksm (K.serial-merge) channels the three incoming control paths into a single control flow link.

Then we enter a loop. Word is transferred to the bus sense register (BSR). BSR is checked for 0. If it is 0, we are done since there are

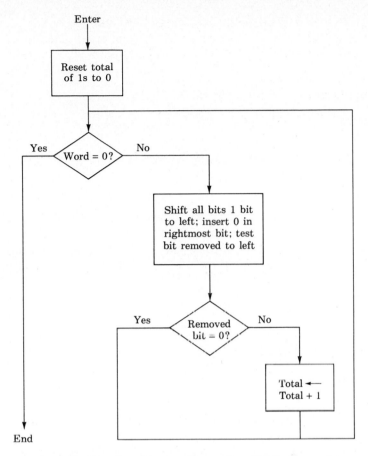

Fig. 5.10   Flowchart for counting number of 1 bits in a word

no 1s left to count. If not, we shift Word one bit to the left, enter a 0 at the right, and check the removed bit for 0. If it is 1, we increase Total by 1. Whether it is 1 or 0, we return to the start of the loop and check Word for 0 again.

5.7 SUMMARY

Digital systems may be divided into two parts—a data part that has data registers and combinational logic and a control part that controls operations on the data. The data and control parts communicate

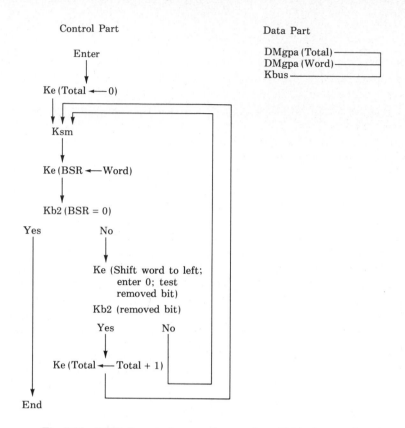

Control Part

Data Part

DMgpa (Total)
DMgpa (Word)
Kbus

Enter

Ke (Total ◄— 0)

Ksm

Ke (BSR ◄— Word)

Kb2 (BSR = 0)

Yes   No

Ke (Shift word to left;
    enter 0; test
    removed bit)

Kb2 (removed bit)

Yes   No

Ke (Total ◄— Total + 1)

End

Fig. 5.11   RTM diagram for counting number of 1 bits in a word

through status signals from the data part to the control circuits and through control signals from the control circuits to the data registers.

We represent registers by boldface letters such as **A** and their cells by subscripted letters such as $\mathbf{A}_1$. We represent transfers between registers by a statement such as

$$\mathbf{B} \leftarrow \mathbf{\bar{A}} + \mathbf{B}$$

which means that the value of $\mathbf{\bar{A}} + \mathbf{B}$ is transferred to register **B**. More generally the transfer statement means that the value of the expression on the right side is transferred to the register on the left side. We can represent conditional transfers by a statement of the form

$$\rightarrow [(f_1 \cdot s_1) + (f_2 \cdot s_2) + \cdots + (f_n \cdot s_n)]$$

that means control passes to step s_i if logical function $f_i = 1$. The conditional transfer statement must be written so that one and only one f_i can be 1 for each set of possible circuit conditions.

Register-transfer notations allow simple and powerful descriptions of circuit behavior with far fewer statements than state descriptions require. Several register-transfer languages have been developed for designing and describing digital systems.

Register-transfer-level components closely resemble the steps we would take in solving a problem. Basic register-transfer-level components are memories that store information without change, links that send information without change, transducers that change the form but not the value of information, data operators that produce new information, switches that route data, and controls that control other components.

Register-transfer-module systems comprise transducer modules, memory modules, data-memory modules, control modules, and a bus to interconnect the modules. All components except control modules have associated control modules. The control part of the system evokes operations on the data part.

Concepts

bus	field
byte	independent register
cell	link
control	memory
data operator	RTM
dependent register	subregister
destructive transfer	switch
DM module	transducer
evoke	word

5.8 REFERENCES

Bartee, Lebow, and Reed (1962) describe register operations and register transfers. Hill and Peterson (1973, 1974) discuss adapting APL to register-transfer design. Chu (1972) is an advanced discussion of computer organization using CDL. Bell, Grason, and Newell (1972) present the most detailed explanation of register-transfer modules.

5.9 PROBLEMS

5.1   **A** is a 12-cell register. **B** is a dependent register storing the number of 1s in the contents of **A**. What is the minimum number of cells in **B**? What is the minimum number of cells in another dependent register **C** that stores the information of the evenness or oddness of the value in **B**?   (5.2)

5.2   **A** and **B** are four-cell registers that hold binary integers. **S** is a dependent register that holds the sum of the integers stored in **A** and **B**. What is the minimum number of cells in **S**?(5.2)

5.3   A computer has 10 instructions, each coded as a binary integer with exactly two 1s. What is the minimum number of cells for an instruction register that can store these instructions?   (5.2)

5.4   Write a control sequence corresponding to the following extended state table.   (5.3)

| S | S^n | | Transfer |
	SEQ = 0	SEQ = 1	
C_0	C_0	C_1	$X \leftarrow 0$
C_1	C_3	C_2	$X \leftarrow Y$
C_2	C_0	C_3	$X \leftarrow \overline{X}$
C_3	C_2	C_0	$X \leftarrow X + Y$

5.5   Construct a sequential circuit for problem 5.4.   (5.3)

5.6   In a sequential circuit, control should transfer from step 5 to step 6 if $X = Y$, step 3 if $X = 1$ and $Y = 0$, and step 8 if $X = 0$ and $Y = 1$. Write a control statement for this transfer.   (5.3)

5.7   Devise an RTM system for the problem of example 5.3 that begins with $N = 0$ and increases until N equals the desired integer.   (5.5)

5.8   Devise an RTM solution for the problem of example 5.4 that omits the step of testing Word for 0.   (5.5)

5.9   Devise an RTM system for the problem of example 5.4 that uses just one general-purpose-arithmetic module.   (5.5)

5.10   Devise an RTM solution for the problem of example 5.4 that
shifts bits to the right.   (5.5)

5.11   Normalization determines the bit position of the most significant (leftmost) 1 in a word. Devise an RTM system to normalize
a word. The result is the word shifted so that the most significant bit is in the leftmost position.   (5.5)

6 Arithmetic Unit

6.1 OVERVIEW

Before proceeding to the discussion of the program level, we pause here to consolidate our knowledge of logic circuits by looking at the *arithmetic unit*. The arithmetic unit, sometimes called the *arithmetic and logic unit*, consists of logic circuits that perform basic arithmetic and logic operations. This unit and the control unit that generates timing and control signals for all computer operations combine to form the central processing unit (CPU). We will study the control unit and central processing unit in later chapters.

This chapter assumes a basic knowledge of binary arithmetic. Appendix A reviews binary arithmetic including conversions between binary numbers and decimal, octal, and hexadecimal numbers, as well as binary addition, subtraction, multiplication, and division. Readers who are unsure of their knowledge of binary arithmetic should review appendix A before reading this chapter.

The arithmetic operations performed by the arithmetic unit are the basic four of addition, subtraction, multiplication, and division. We will first consider ways of representing negative numbers for any computer operation. Next we will look at basic adder circuits that can be used either for addition or, with modification, for subtraction. Then we will study methods of multiplication and division of binary numbers and circuits that implement them. At the end of the chapter we will consider variations of these methods used for floating point numbers, that is, numbers with variable exponents.

The arithmetic unit also implements several logic operations. The simplest operations are the basic logic functions of AND, OR, and NOT. (We will consider practical applications of these operations.)

The arithmetic unit can also shift numbers in several different ways. (We will study types of shifting and their uses.) It can compare two numbers to determine five types of equality and inequality relationships. (We will study several simple comparators that implement these comparisons.) The arithmetic unit usually also detects simple errors by error-detecting circuits that we will examine.

In this chapter we use + for addition and × for multiplication; we do not use + for OR.

6.2   NUMBER REPRESENTATION

Before discussing arithmetic circuits, we consider three schemes for representing binary numbers for the computer: *signed-magnitude, ones complement,* and *twos complement representations.* The three methods represent positive numbers in the same way but differ in their representation of negative numbers. We first discuss *fixed point* representations, where the binary point (the binary analog of a decimal point) is fixed in one place for all numbers. In dealing only with integers, the binary point is assumed to be at the right end of each number. An optional section at the end of the chapter introduces floating point numbers that have exponents.

6.2.1   Signed-Magnitude Representation

Signed-magnitude representation most nearly resembles the representation chosen for hand calculations on binary numbers. We would probably represent each binary number as a numeral preceded by a sign, for example, +101 or −110. For signed-magnitude representation, we assign 0 to the positive sign and 1 to the negative sign. Thus +101 becomes 0101 and −110 becomes 1110 if 4 bits are used. If 8 bits are used, +101 is 00000101 and −101 is 10000101.

If n bits are available to represent a number in signed-magnitude form, $n-1$ bits can be used for the magnitude of the number and 1 bit can be used for the sign. Thus it is possible to represent numbers from $-(2^{n-1}-1)$ to $2^{n-1}-1$ in signed-magnitude representation. Numbers that can be represented are said to be in range.

While representation of numbers in signed-magnitude form is simple, addition in signed-magnitude is not simple. Consider, for example, the following addition:

$$
\begin{array}{ll}
+3 & 0011 \\
\underline{-2} & \underline{1010} \\
+1 &
\end{array}
$$

The rules for addition are not clear. If we simply add the two numbers, we obtain 1101, the signed-magnitude representation of −5. We will not try to devise rules for addition in signed-magnitude, but will consider other representations for which addition is simpler.

6.2.2 Ones Complement Representation

The *ones complement* of a binary number is its true or logical complement. Thus the ones complement of +5 or 0101 is 1010 or −5 if 4 bits are used. If 8 bits are used, +5 = 00000101 and −5 = 11111010. Ones complement representation allows a range of numbers from $-(2^{n-1}-1)$ to $2^{n-1}-1$ for n-bit binary numbers. While complementing a number is simple in ones complement representation, addition is not as simple as we would like.

6.2.3 Addition in Ones Complement

The procedure for addition in ones complement is:

1. Add the two numbers. Allow carries into and out of the sign bit.
2. If a carry out of the sign bit occurred, add 1 to the sum. (This is called an *end-around carry*.)
3. Examine carries into and out of the sign bit. If just one carry involving the sign bit occurred, overflow has occurred and the sum is incorrect. Otherwise the sum is correct.

The following examples illustrate addition in ones complement representation.

Example 6.1—Addition in Ones Complement

Addition of Two Positive Numbers

+3	0011	
+2	0010	
+5	0101	No sign bit carries, sum correct.

+6	0110	
+4	0100	
+10	1010	Carry into sign bit, overflow.

Addition of Two Negative Numbers

−2	1101	
−4	1011	
−6	1000	Two sign bit carries.
	1	End-around carry added.
	1001	Sum correct.
−7	1000	
−5	1010	
−12	0010	Only one sign bit carry.
	1	End-around carry added.
	0011	Overflow.

Addition of One Positive and One Negative Number

+4	0100	
−7	1000	
−3	1100	No sign bit carries, sum correct.
+7	0111	
−3	1100	
+4	0011	Two sign bit carries.
	1	End-around carry added.
	0100	Sum correct.
+5	0101	
−5	1010	
0	1111	No sign bit carries, sum correct.
		Negative zero.

In ones complement there are two zeros—a positive zero and a negative zero. For example, in the 4-bit numbers of the previous example positive zero is 0000 and negative zero is 1111. Having two zeros wastes a bit pattern that could be used to represent another number.

6.2.4 Twos Complement Representation

The *twos complement* of a number is the true (ones) complement of the number plus 1. Thus for 4 bits, the twos complement of +5 or 0101 is 1010 + 1 = 1011 or −5. If 8 bits are used, +5 = 00000101 and −5 = 11111011. With n bits we can represent numbers from -2^{n-1} to $2^{n-1}-1$ in twos complement.

Although taking the twos complement of a number is more difficult than taking its ones complement, addition of twos complement numbers is simpler than addition in ones complement or in signed-magnitude representation.

6.2.5 Addition in Twos Complement

The procedure for addition of numbers in twos complement form is:

1. Add the two numbers. Observe carries into and out of the sign bit.
2. If no or two carries occurred, the sum is in range. If just one carry occurred, the sum has overflowed and is incorrect.

Example 6.2—Addition in Twos Complement

Addition of Two Positive Numbers

+3	0011	
+4	0100	
+7	0111	No sign bit carries, sum correct.
+5	0101	Carry into but not out of sign bit,
+4	0100	overflow.
+9	1001	

Addition of Two Negative Numbers

−4	1100	Carry into and out of sign bit,
−1	1111	no overflow.
−5	1011	
−7	1001	Carry out of but not into sign bit,
−6	1010	overflow.
−13	0011	

Addition of One Positive and One Negative Number

−7	1001	No sign bit carries,
+5	0101	sum correct.
−2	1110	
−4	1100	Carry into and out of sign bit,
+4	0100	sum correct.
0	0000	

A variation of twos complement representation is the *excess-2^{n-1} representation*. (n is the number of bits in the number.) The representation of any n-bit number in excess-2^{n-1} form is the number plus 2^{n-1}. Thus the representation of +5 or 0101 in excess-2^3 is 0101 + 1000 or 1101. The representation of -5 in excess-2^3 is -0101 + 1000 or 0011. The magnitude of the number is represented the same in excess-2^{n-1} and in twos complement. Only the sign bit differs. In twos complement, a sign of 0 indicates a positive number and a sign of 1 indicates a negative number. In excess-2^{n-1}, a sign bit of 0 indicates a negative number and a sign bit of 1 indicates a positive number. The range of numbers that can be represented is -2^{n-1} to $+2^{n-1}-1$. Handling overflows is simpler in the excess-2^{n-1} system.

The main advantage of twos complement is that its addition rules are simple. When two numbers are added, the result is consistently the desired sum if the sum is in range—no extra additions need be made. The simplicity of twos complement representation has made it popular for digital computers. Even computers that use signed-magnitude representation usually convert numbers to twos complement form before adding negative numbers. Twos complement is the most common representation for minicomputers.

Table 6.1 compares the three main representations.

We can extend the concepts of ones complement and twos complements of binary numbers to numbers of any radix. The generalization of twos complement is the radix complement; the generalization of ones complement is the radix minus one complement. For example, for decimal numbers we can define a nines complement that is the result of subtracting each digit of the number from 9. Similarly, we

TABLE 6.1

COMPARISON OF NUMBER REPRESENTATIONS

	Signed-magnitude	Ones complement	Twos complement
Positive number $+XYZ$	$0XYZ$	$0XYZ$	$0XYZ$
Negative number $-XYZ$	$1XYZ$	$1XYZ$	$1\bar{X}\bar{Y}\bar{Z} + 1$
Range	$-(2^{n-1}-1)$ to $+2^{n-1}-1$	$-(2^{n-1}-1)$ to $2^{n-1}-1$	-2^{n-1} to $2^{n-1}-1$
Zero(s)	0000 1000	0000 1111	0000

can define a tens complement that is the nines complement plus one. Because these complements are not usually used in digital computers, we will not discuss them further here. The references provide discussions of these complements, and a few problems at the end of the chapter explore these concepts.

6.3 ADDITION

6.3.1 Half Adder

The half adder shown in figure 6.1 is a basic adder circuit. The half adder has two binary inputs, X and Y, and two outputs, a sum S and a carry C. The half adder sums the inputs arithmetically. If both inputs are 0, the sum and carry are also 0. If just one input is 1, the sum is 1 and the carry 0. If both inputs are 1, the sum is 0 and the carry is 1. These relations are shown in the truth table of figure 6.1c and can be summarized as

$$S = X\overline{Y} + \overline{X}Y = X \oplus Y$$
$$C = XY$$

Inputs to the half adder usually come from devices that store the numbers. If the devices are flipflops, both the inputs and their complements are available. Otherwise we would use inverters to complement the inputs as shown in figure 6.1b.

While a half adder performs the basic binary addition, it cannot by itself perform additions of numbers of more than 1 bit. It lacks provision for carries from preceding bits. As shown in example 6.3, carry inputs are necessary for each position in binary addition. Each carry input is the carry output from addition of the preceding bits, that is, the less significant bits on the right.

Example 6.3

11111110	Carry input
1101011	Addend
1011101	Augend
11001000	Sum

6.3.2 Full Adder

Full adders for binary numbers must receive carries as well as the addend and augend as inputs. A carry input, C_I, is the carry output,

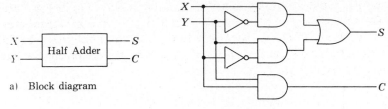

a) Block diagram

b) Logic diagram

Inputs		Outputs	
Addend	Augend	Sum	Carry
X	Y	S	C
0	0	0	0
0	1	1	0
1	0	1	0
1	1	0	1

c) Truth table

X	0	1
Y		
0	0	1
1	1	0

$S = X \oplus Y$

X	0	1
Y		
0	0	0
1	0	1

$C = XY$

d) Karnaugh maps for S and C

Fig. 6.1 Half adder

C_O, of the preceding addition. The full adder shown by the block diagram of figure 6.2a has these three inputs.

A full adder may be constructed from two half adders and an OR gate as shown in figure 6.2b. The first half adder sums inputs X and Y. The sum output of the first half adder is then added to the carry input C_I. The sum output of this second half adder is the sum S. The carry output of the second half adder is ORed with the carry output of the first half adder to produce the carry output of the full adder, C_O.

Constructing a full adder from two half adders may not be the most economical technique. Usually full adders are constructed directly from their input/output relations as shown in the truth table of figure 6.2d and the Karnaugh maps of figure 6.2e. The logical relations can be reduced to

$$S = X \oplus Y \oplus C_I$$
$$C_O = XY + XC_I + YC_I$$

The first form of the equations allows the outputs of several gates to be used twice as inputs. Figure 6.2c shows a full adder implementing these equations.

a) Block diagram

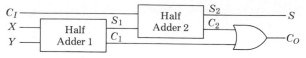

bı Block diagram with half adders

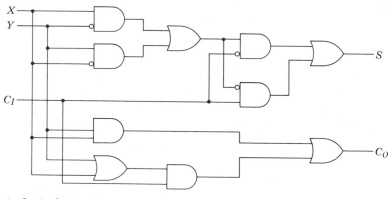

c) Logic diagram

Fig. 6.2 Full adder

6.3.3 Serial Adders

Adders may be used to add numbers serially (one bit at a time) or in parallel (several bits at once). The advantage of adding serially is that just one adder is needed. The inputs to a serial adder are two series of signals for the addend and the augend. The output S is a series of signals for the sum. The carry output C_O is delayed one clock pulse by a flipflop and fed back as a carry input C_I.

Figure 6.3 shows a serial adder constructed from a full adder and an RS flipflop. The adder is shown with inputs of 0011 and 0001 and sums them to give an S output of 0100. The bits are presented and added one at a time beginning with the least significant (right-most) bit. The carry output C_O from each addition is delayed one clock pulse by the RS flipflop and then becomes a carry input C_I for the next addition. The first carry input is always zero. All input and output signals are shown in figure 6.3.

We have not mentioned the representation of numbers for this

	Inputs			Outputs	
Addend	Augend	Carry in		Sum	Carry out
X	Y	C_I		S	C_O
0	0	0		0	0
0	0	1		1	0
0	1	0		1	0
0	1	1		0	1
1	0	0		1	0
1	0	1		0	1
1	1	0		0	1
1	1	1		1	1

d) Truth table

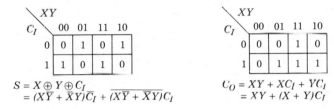

$$S = X \oplus Y \oplus C_I$$
$$= (X\overline{Y} + \overline{X}Y)\overline{C_I} + (\overline{X}\overline{Y} + \overline{X}Y)C_I$$

$$C_O = XY + XC_I + YC_I$$
$$= XY + (X + Y)C_I$$

e) Karnaugh maps for S and C_O

(Fig. 6.2 continued)

serial adder. Basically it adds magnitudes. We need a circuit to test the carries into and out of the sign bit if the numbers to be added are in twos complement. Using ones complement we not only have to test sign bit carries but also provide an end-around carry.

6.3.4 Parallel Adders

Parallel adders require more circuits than serial adders but allow all inputs to be presented at once instead of sequentially. A parallel adder for numbers with 4 bits of magnitude is shown in figure 6.4. The sign bit is handled separately, depending on the representation used for the numbers. The adder consists of four full adders, one for each bit. The OVERFLOW or CARRY line detects overflow from the most significant position. The END-AROUND CARRY line allows end-around carries for ones complement addition. Two passes through the adder are needed for ones complement if there is an end-around carry. We would also test both the carry into and the carry out of the final stage for addition in ones or twos complement by logic circuits that are not shown.

The operation of the adder can be explained through example 6.4, in which we consider all 4 bits as magnitude.

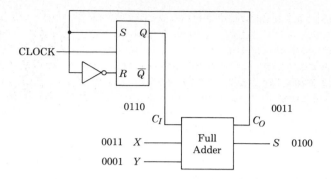

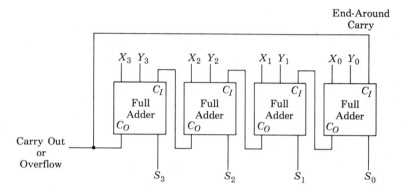

Fig. 6.3   Serial adder

Fig. 6.4   Parallel adder

Example 6.4

0101	$X_3 X_2 X_1 X_0$
0111	$Y_3 Y_2 Y_1 Y_0$
1100	$S_3 S_2 S_1 S_0$

Since X_0 and Y_0 are the least significant bits, there is no carry from a preceding stage. Since X_0 and Y_0 are both 1 in the example, the sum S_0 is 0 and the carry out C_{O0} is 1. The carry out C_{O0} is the carry in to the second adder, C_{I1}. The second adder sums $C_{I1} = 1$, $X_1 = 0$, and $Y_1 = 1$ to obtain $S_1 = 0$ and $C_{O1} = 1$. C_{O1} in turn becomes the carry in to the third adder, C_{I2}. The third adder sums $C_{I2} = 1$, $X_2 = 1$, and $Y_2 = 1$ to obtain $S_2 = 1$ and $C_{O2} = 1$. The fourth adder sums $C_{I3} = 1$, $X_3 = 0$, and $Y_3 = 0$ to obtain $S_3 = 1$ and $C_{O3} = 0$.

Although all addend and augend inputs are available to the parallel adder at the start, addition proceeds one step at a time because each adder must wait for the carry out from the preceding adder. This type of adder shows *carry ripple propagation* since carries propagate or ripple from the least significant bit to the most significant bit. A parallel adder for numbers with many bits may have to wait a long time for the final adder to receive its carry input. One solution to this problem is to generate the carry input to a later stage immediately through a *look-ahead carry* or *carry anticipation* circuit. Such a circuit for the carry input to the third adder is shown in figure 6.5. The carry anticipation circuit for the second carry out or the

				Inputs				Output
				X_1	Y_1	X_0	Y_0	C_{I2}
				0	0	0	0	0
				0	0	0	1	0
		C_{I2}		0	0	1	0	0
X_3	X_2	X_1	X_0 Addend	0	0	1	1	0
$+ Y_3$	Y_2	Y_1	Y_0 Augend	0	1	0	0	0
S_3	S_2	S_1	S_0 Sum	0	1	0	1	0
				0	1	1	0	0
a)	Addition with look-ahead carry			0	1	1	1	1
				1	0	0	0	0
				1	0	0	1	0
				1	0	1	0	0
				1	0	1	1	1
				1	1	0	0	1
				1	1	0	1	1
				1	1	1	0	1
				1	1	1	1	1

b)   Truth table for anticipated carry in, C_{I2}

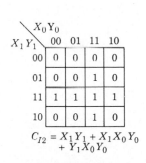

$X_1 Y_1$ \ $X_0 Y_0$	00	01	11	10
00	0	0	0	0
01	0	0	1	0
11	1	1	1	1
10	0	0	1	0

$$C_{I2} = X_1 Y_1 + X_1 X_0 Y_0 + Y_1 X_0 Y_0$$

c)   Karnaugh map

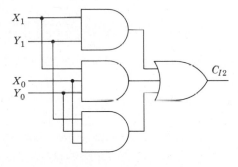

d)   Logic circuit

Fig. 6.5   Carry anticipation

third carry in requires four inputs, the two least significant bits of the addend and the augend. It generates the carry immediately. The equation for the look-ahead carry, C_{I2}, is

$$C_{I2} = X_1 Y_1 + X_1 X_0 Y_0 + Y_1 X_0 Y_0$$

Look-ahead carries become more complex as the number of bits considered increases. The look-ahead carry for the third stage requires only four inputs. The look-ahead carry for the final stage of a 16-bit parallel adder needs 30 inputs—the addend and augend bits of each of the preceding 15 stages. More gates are required. There is a tradeoff between speed and complexity.

We may decide to divide the adder into blocks of several adders. Within each block, look-ahead carries are available for each adder so that the block addition can be done immediately. Then each block adds in sequence, beginning with the least significant block. For example, a 16-bit adder can be divided into four blocks of four adders. Each block has carry anticipation for all bits. The look-ahead carry circuit for the most significant bit in the block requires seven inputs—the carry input to the block and the addend and augend bits from each of the three less significant stages. Figure 6.6 shows a block diagram of this adder.

Figure 6.7 shows a 4-bit parallel full adder with carry anticipation that is available as an integrated circuit. It may be used as one of the blocks of figure 6.6. A carry input to the adder, C_{I0}, allows cascading stages. Sum outputs are provided for each position, and a carry output is provided for the most significant position.

6.4 MULTIPLICATION

Since we can subtract by complementing the subtrahend and adding, we do not need separate circuits for subtraction. While subtracters can be built (see problems 6.12, 6.13, and the references), we will

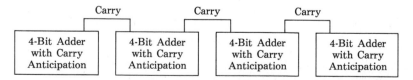

Fig. 6.6 A 16-bit adder constructed from four 4-bit adders, each with carry anticipation circuits

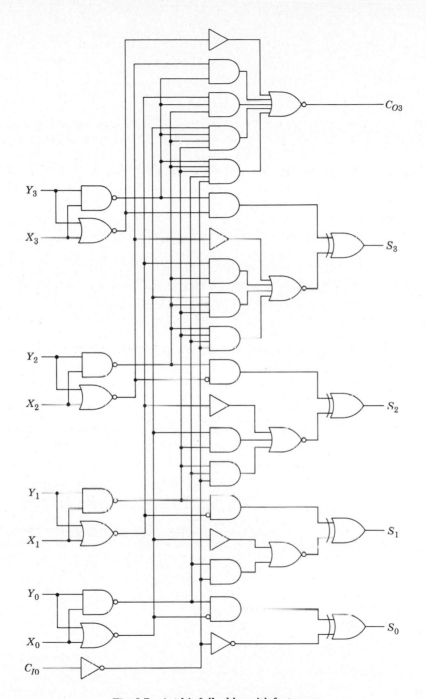

Fig. 6.7   A 4-bit full adder with fast carry

turn our attention to circuits for multiplication. We will consider magnitudes only; the sign can be handled separately.

All multiplication can be performed as repeated addition, but binary multiplication is particularly easy to perform as repeated addition. The example below makes this clear.

Example 6.5—Binary Multiplication

$$
\begin{array}{rl}
1010 & \text{Multiplicand} \\
\times \ 1011 & \text{Multiplier} \\
\hline
\left.\begin{array}{r} 1010 \\ 1010 \\ 0000 \\ 1010 \end{array}\right\} & \text{Partial products} \\
\hline
1101110 & \text{Product}
\end{array}
$$

Since binary arithmetic uses just two digits, there are just two rules for multiplying one multiple-bit binary number by a single binary bit.

1. If the multiplier bit is 1, the multiplicand is copied as a partial product.
2. If the multiplier bit is 0, the partial product is 0.

Thus, in example 6.5, since the least significant bit of the multiplier is 1, the multiplicand is copied for the first partial product. The second partial product is shifted left one place to represent multiplication by 10 (two) rather than just 1. Since the third bit of the multiplier is 0, the partial product is 0, or 0000. This zero partial product is also shifted left one place. Finally, the last partial product also copies the multiplicand and is shifted left one place.

This example suggests that a computer must perform three types of operations for multiplication:

1. It must determine whether a multiplier bit is 1 or 0 so that it can designate the partial product as multiplicand or 0.
2. It must shift partial products.
3. It must add partial products.

We need not wait until all partial products are formed before summing them. We can sum partial products two at a time. In fact, since our adders are designed to sum two numbers at a time, we prefer to do so. Thus in our example, we sum the first two partial products as soon as they are formed.

$$1010$$
$$\underline{1010}$$
$$11110$$

After the third multiplication, we add the third partial product.

$$11110$$
$$\underline{0000}$$
$$011110$$

We sum the fourth partial product to obtain our original result.

$$011110$$
$$\underline{1010}$$
$$1101110$$

Figure 6.8 shows a block diagram of a multiplier circuit that performs the multiplication just discussed. The circuit multiplies positive numbers only. Negative numbers must be put in positive form first. A separate circuit determines the sign of the product. The sign of the product is + if multiplier and multiplicand agree in sign and − if they differ in sign. For simplicity, the details of the control circuits are not shown. A special register, called the *accumulator*, accumulates the results of arithmetic calculations and other operations, i.e., holds the product. Both the accumulator and the register for the multiplicand must be twice the length of the register for the multiplier. Since the multiplier is 4 bits, both the accumulator and the multiplicand register must be 8 bits.

We begin multiplication by clearing the accumulator. We place the multiplicand into the four least significant positions of the multiplicand register **X** and place the multiplier into the multiplier register **Y**. A control circuit samples or tests the least significant bit of the multiplier, Y_0. Since Y_0 is 1 in this example, the contents

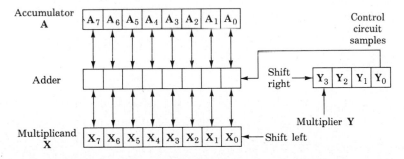

Fig. 6.8 Multiplier using two double-length registers and double-length adder

of the multiplicand register are added to the accumulator. The accumulator now holds the first partial product, 00001010. The multiplier is now shifted right one bit, and the multiplicand is shifted left one bit. Zeros are shifted into vacated positions. A control circuit tests Y_0, which now contains the second least significant bit of the multiplier. Since this bit is also 1, the shifted multiplicand is added to the contents of the accumulator so that the accumulator contains 00011110. Again the multiplicand is shifted left one bit and the multiplier is shifted right. The control circuit tests Y_0, which now is 0. Since there is no point to adding 0 to the accumulator, control circuits allow us to omit the addition. We again shift the multiplier to the right and the multiplicand to the left. A control circuit tests Y_0 which is 1. The shifted multiplicand is added to the accumulator to give 01101110, the final product. The multiplicand and multiplier are shifted again. A test circuit (not shown) shows that the multiplication is complete. We could use a counter to count the number of additions or a test of the Y register to see if the contents are 0.

We can summarize the multiplication procedure:

1. Clear the accumulator **A**. Place the multiplicand in **X** and the multiplier in **Y** with the least significant bits at the right.
2. Test Y_0. If $Y_0 = 1$, add contents of **X** to the accumulator **A**.
3. Shift contents of **X** left one position and contents of **Y** right one position. Enter 0s in vacated cells.
4. Check for completion. If not finished, go to step 2.

A flowchart of this procedure is shown in figure 6.9.

Although this scheme is simple conceptually, it is not the simplest to implement since two double-length registers are required. Figure 6.10 shows a variation of this scheme that uses only single-length registers. The least significant part of the accumulator is shifted into the multiplier register as the multiplier register is shifted out. A carry register connected to the accumulator holds any carry out from addition of the most significant bits. You should be able to explain the operation. Many other schemes are possible.

A similar scheme can be implemented for multiplication using RTMs. Consider multiplying two 8-bit numbers, using a single DMgpa for the multiplier and the multiplicand. We begin by entering the multiplier into the 8 least significant bits of the **A** register and the multiplicand into the 8 most significant bits of the **B** register of the DMgpa. We shift the multiplier to the right and allow the product to accumulate in the **A** register. We need a second DMgpa to count the times we need to shift and a memory constant (Mc) to store the constant 8. We also need K modules as shown in figure 6.11.

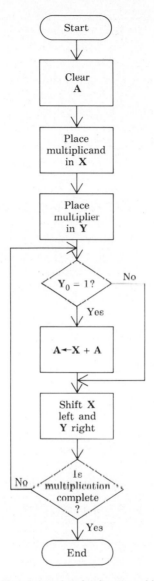

Fig. 6.9   Flowchart of multiplication of figure 6.8

We begin by testing the 0 bit (least significant bit of the multiplier). If it is 0, we shift the multiplier right one position. If it is 1, we add the multiplicand to the multiplier and then shift the multiplier right one position. We then decrease the count register by 1 and test to see whether the count is 0. If it is, we are done. If not, we

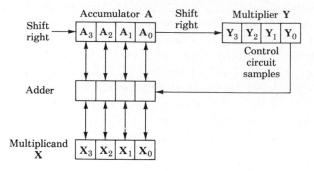

Fig. 6.10 Multiplier with single-length registers and adders

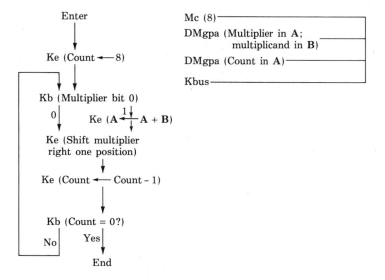

Fig. 6.11 Multiplier using RTMs

test the least significant bit of the multiplier again and continue through the loop.

6.5 DIVISION

Division is the most complex basic binary arithmetic operation. We consider two basic methods for binary division: *restoring division* and *nonrestoring division*. Restoring division is done as follows:

1. Place the divisor below the dividend with leftmost bits aligned.
2. Subtract the divisor from the dividend (or partial dividend).
3. Check the result. If it is positive or zero, the quotient bit just above the rightmost position of the divisor is 1. If the result is negative, the quotient bit is 0. Add the divisor back to the dividend to restore the original dividend.
4. Check to see if the quotient has the desired number of bits. If it has, the division is complete. Otherwise shift the divisor one place to the right and repeat steps 2 through 4.

A flowchart of this procedure is shown in figure 6.12.

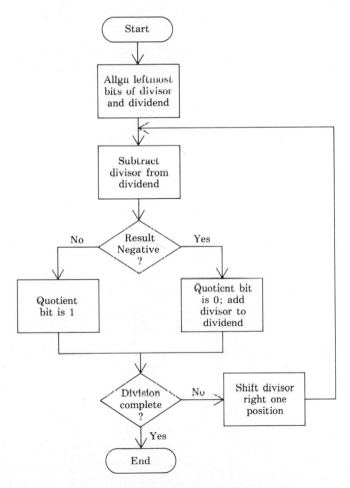

Fig. 6.12 Flowchart for restoring division

This process is best illustrated by an example, the division of 1001 by 1101. The binary point is at the right of the numbers. We extend the dividend with 0s as desired—for example, 1001.0000. We number the quotient digits with subscripts showing the exponent of 2 for each position. $Q_0 = 2^0$, $Q_{-1} = 2^{-1} = 1/2$, etc. We show addition and positive results with plus signs and subtraction and negative results with minus signs. You may wish to review binary subtraction in appendix A before proceeding.

Example 6.6—Restoring Division

$$Q_0\, Q_{-1} Q_{-2} Q_{-3}\, Q_{-4}$$

```
                    Q₀ Q₋₁ Q₋₂ Q₋₃ Q₋₄
                    0 · 1  0  1  1

   1101 | 1  0  0  1  0  0  0  0
         -1  1  0  1                    Subtract
         -0  1  0  0                    Negative, Q₀ = 0
         +1  1  0  1                    Restore
         +1  0  0  1  0
            -1  1  0  1                 Shift and subtract
            +1  0  1  0                 Positive, Q₋₁ = 1
            -1  1  0  1                 Shift and subtract
            -0  0  1  1                 Negative, Q₋₂ = 0
            +1  1  0  1                 Restore
            +1  0  1  0  0
               -1  1  0  1              Shift and subtract
               +0  1  1  1  0           Positive, Q₋₃ = 1
                  -1  1  0  1           Shift and subtract
                               +1       Positive, Q₋₄ = 1
                                        Remainder = 1
```

In nonrestoring division the step of restoring the dividend when the result of subtracting the divisor is negative is omitted. Instead the shifted divisor is added to the negative partial dividend. Thus the procedure becomes:

1. Place the divisor below the dividend with leftmost bits aligned.
2. Subtract the divisor from the dividend.
3. Check to see if the result is negative. If it is positive or zero, the quotient bit just above the rightmost bit of the divisor is 1. Shift the divisor to the right and subtract the divisor from the dividend. Go to step 4. If the result is negative, the quotient

bit just above the rightmost bit of the divisor is 0. Shift the divisor one place to the right and add to the dividend.
4. Check to see if the quotient has the desired number of bits. If it has, the division is complete. Otherwise, repeat step 3.

A flowchart of this procedure is shown in figure 6.13.

The step of shifting the divisor and adding to a negative partial dividend replaces the steps of restoring, shifting the divisor, and

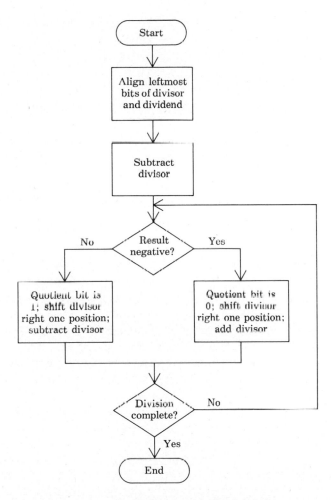

Fig. 6.13   Flowchart for nonrestoring division

subtracting. To justify this, let X be the negative partial dividend and Y be the divisor. Shifting the divisor one place to the right yields $1/2\ Y$. In restoring division, we restore the divisor to the negative partial dividend, shift, and then subtract. This yields $X + Y - 1/2\ Y = X + 1/2\ Y$. In nonrestoring division, we add the shifted divisor to the negative partial dividend. This yields $X + 1/2\ Y$ directly. Thus the two processes are equivalent.

Nonrestoring division of 1001 by 1101 is illustrated by example 6.7.

Example 6.7—Nonrestoring Division

$$Q_0\ Q_{-1}\ Q_{-2}\ Q_{-3}\ Q_{-4}$$

1101									
		0 ·	1	0	1	1			

```
        Q₀ Q₋₁ Q₋₂ Q₋₃ Q₋₄
         0 · 1  0  1  1

1101 │  1  0  0  1  0  0  0  0
       -1  1  0  1              Subtract
       -0  1  0  0  0           Negative, Q₀ = 0
         +1  1  0  1            Shift and add
           +1  0  1  0          Positive, Q₋₁ = 1
           -1  1  0  1          Shift and subtract
           -0  0  1  1  0       Negative, Q₋₂ = 0
             +1  1  0  1        Shift and add
               +1  1  1  0      Positive, Q₋₃ = 1
               -1  1  0  1      Shift and subtract
                +1  1  1  0  Positive, Q₋₄ = 1... 
```

$$
\begin{array}{r}
Q_0\ Q_{-1}\ Q_{-2}\ Q_{-3}\ Q_{-4} \\
0 \cdot 1 \quad 0 \quad 1 \quad 1
\end{array}
$$

1101 | 1 0 0 1 0 0 0 0
−1 1 0 1 Subtract
−0 1 0 0 0 Negative, $Q_0 = 0$
+1 1 0 1 Shift and add
+1 0 1 0 Positive, $Q_{-1} = 1$
−1 1 0 1 Shift and subtract
−0 0 1 1 0 Negative, $Q_{-2} = 0$
+1 1 0 1 Shift and add
+1 1 1 0 Positive, $Q_{-3} = 1$
+1 1 1 0 Shift and subtract
−1 1 0 1 Positive, $Q_{-4} = 1$
+1 Remainder $= 1$

Restoring division can be performed using the registers shown in figure 6.14. All registers are 5 bits long (sign + 4 bits). We place the dividend in the accumulator, the divisor in the **Y** register, and 0s in the **A** register. The quotient will be formed in the **A** register. Using twos complement arithmetic, we subtract by forming the twos complement and adding. At each stage we will subtract, restore if necessary, determine the quotient digit, and shift accumulator and the **A** register for the quotient left. The contents of all registers for restoring division of 1001 by 1101 are shown in table 6.2.

As with multiplication, we illustrated division with positive numbers. The sign can be determined separately.

6.6   LOGIC OPERATIONS

The arithmetic unit, in addition to arithmetic operations, can perform several logic operations. These include the basic logic operations of

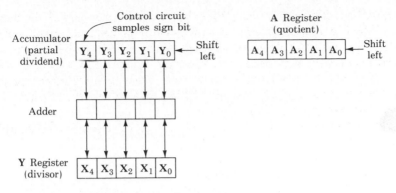

Fig. 6.14   Circuit for restoring division

AND, OR, and NOT; several types of shifts; several types of comparisons; and error-detecting circuits.

6.6.1 Basic Logic Operations

The basic logic operations of AND, OR, and NOT can be performed on either entire registers or individual bits. Since the implementation of these operations is straightforward, we will discuss the reasons why these operations might be performed.

The AND operation is often called an *extract* or *masking* operation when it is applied to a register. It extracts part of a word, or alternatively, it masks the remaining part of a word. Consider the ANDing of a computer word ABCDEFGH, where each letter may be either 0 or 1 with 00001111. The result of this logical multiplication is

$$ABCDEFGH$$
$$00001111$$
$$0000EFGH$$

The AND operation has extracted EFGH and has masked ABCD.

The AND operation is useful in extracting desired information from a computer word. We often save space in computer memories by packing several types of information in one word. For example, a single computer word might pack several pieces of information about a student—student number, year in school, sex, and home state as shown below. (The numbers are the bit numbers used to encode the information.)

STUDENT NUMBER	YEAR IN SCHOOL	SEX	HOME STATE
15	11 10	8 7 6	0

TABLE 6.2

CONTENTS OF ALL REGISTERS FOR RESTORING DIVISION OF 1001 BY 1101

Accumulator Partial Dividend	Y Register Divisor	A Register Quotient	Comments
01001	01101	00000	Start
01001	10011	00000	Y register is twos complemented
11100	10011	00000	Y register is added to accumulator; result is negative
11100	01101	00000	Y register is twos complemented
01001	01101	00000	Y register is added to accumulator to restore divisor
10010	01101	00000	Accumulator and A register are shifted left
10010	10011	00000	Y register is twos complemented
00101	10011	00000	Y register is added to accumulator; result is positive
00101	10011	00001	1 is added to rightmost bit of A register
01010	10011	00010	Accumulator and A register are shifted left
11101	10011	00010	Y register is added to accumulator; result is negative
11101	01101	00010	Y register is twos complemented
01010	01101	00010	Y register is added to accumulator to restore divisor
10100	01101	00100	Accumulator and A register are shifted left
10100	10011	00100	Y register is twos complemented
00111	10011	00100	Y register is added to accumulator; result is positive
00111	10011	00101	1 is added to rightmost bit of A register
01110	10011	01010	Accumulator and A register are shifted left
00001	10011	01010	Y register is added to accumulator; result is positive
00001	10011	01011	1 is added to rightmost bit of A register; quotient is .1101; remainder is 1

The home state of a given student can be extracted from this word by masking bits 7 through 15 and extracting bits 0 through 6. Extracting also is useful for testing a single bit for 0.

The NOT operation or logical complementation is also useful. As has been shown in the discussion of arithmetic operations, both ones complement and twos complement arithmetic liberally use NOT.

Most computers also provide the OR operation or logical addition for use in evaluating logic expressions.

6.6.2 Shifts

Generally, computers provide several types of shift operations. Shifts may be left or right; cyclic, logical, or arithmetic; and with or without a carry bit. A carry bit, sometimes called a *link* or *extend* bit, is a single bit that records carries in addition. Other variations are possible. The basic shift operation moves each bit one position or cell. The direction of the shift is predetermined and is the same for all bits; some shifts require additional operations on one or two bits.

Cyclic shifts move the bits around in a circle. Figure 6.15a shows a left cyclic shift for an 8-bit register with cells (bit positions) numbered from the right. Bits 0 through 6 move one cell to the left. Bit 7 shifts around to cell 0. A left cyclic shift of one position is the same as a right cyclic shift of seven positions. For this reason, computers may provide either the left cyclic shift or the right cyclic shift directly, but not both.

Cyclic shifts can be made with a carry bit as shown in figure 6.15b. Bits 0 through 6 move one cell left as in the straight left cyclic shift. Bit 7 moves into the carry cell; the carry bit shifts back to cell 0.

A *logical shift* moves bits over one cell and enters a 0 into the emptied cell. Bits shifted off the end are lost. Logical shifts can be made either without or with a carry bit as shown in figure 6.15c and d. Logical shifts can mask unwanted data by replacing all but the desired data with 0s.

Arithmetic shifts are so named because of their use in multiplication and division. Arithmetic shifts act like logical shifts except that the sign bit is not changed. Figure 6.15e and f shows arithmetic shifts. The left arithmetic shift corresponds to multiplication in twos complement. The right arithmetic shift corresponds to division in twos complement.

Other shifts can be used for arithmetic operations. Cyclic shifts can be used for multiplication and division of numbers in ones complement. The left arithmetic shift is multiplication by 2 for numbers

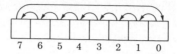

a)   Left cyclic shift

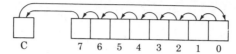

b)   Left cyclic shift with carry

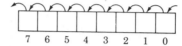

c)   Left logical shift

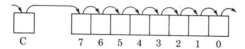

d)   Right logical shift with carry

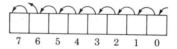

e)   Left arithmetic shift

f)   Right arithmetic shift

Fig. 6.15   Examples of shifts

represented by signed-magnitude. A right arithmetic shift that leaves the sign bit unchanged and enters a 0 into the most significant bit position (cell 6) divides by 2 for signed-magnitude representation.

6.6.3 Comparators

A *comparator* is a logic circuit that compares the magnitudes of two numbers. We will consider only binary comparators that compare the magnitudes of two numbers, expressed in natural binary form. We will ignore the sign of the numbers; that is, we will assume all numbers are positive. Signs may be compared separately.

When we compare two numbers X and Y, we wish to determine one of five possible relations:

$$X = Y, \quad X > Y, \quad X \geq Y, \quad X < Y, \quad X \leq Y$$

Ordinarily we test for one of the five relations and find that either the relation is true or its complement is true. The complements of the five relations can be expressed as follows:

$$\overline{(X = Y)} = (X > Y) + (X < Y)$$

$$\overline{(X > Y)} = (X \leq Y)$$

$$\overline{(X \geq Y)} = (X < Y)$$

$$\overline{(X < Y)} = (X \geq Y)$$

$$\overline{(X \leq Y)} = (X > Y)$$

The simplest case occurs when X and Y are 1-bit numbers. The magnitude relations then can be expressed in Karnaugh maps and implemented as logic circuits as shown in figure 6.16. The maps and gates are easily obtained. For example, $X = Y$ when $X = Y = 0$ and when $X = Y = 1$. The corresponding Karnaugh map is shown in figure 6.16a; the logic circuit uses the COINCIDENCE function. Similarly $X > Y$ only when $X = 1$ and $Y = 0$. The Karnaugh map and the logic circuit, an AND gate implementing $X\overline{Y}$, are shown in figure 6.16b.

Often we wish to compare two n-bit numbers X and Y. We express each number with positional notation; for example, $X = X_{n-1}X_{n-2} \cdots X_2X_1X_0$. The easiest comparison of two n-bit numbers is the test for equality. Two n-bit numbers X and Y are equal if and only if all corresponding bits of the two numbers are equal, that is, $X_i = Y_i$ for $i = 0$ to n-1. The equality test is easily implemented. The corresponding bits of the numbers are tested for equality with COIN-CIDENCE gates. The outputs of the COINCIDENCE gates are ANDed together. Figure 6.17 shows a 3-bit comparator that tests the equality of $X_2X_1X_0$ and $Y_2Y_1Y_0$. The extension to n bits is obvious. The equality comparison for any number of bits can thus be implemented by a two-level circuit. Implementation is limited only by the fan-in of the AND gate, that is, the number of inputs the AND gate can accept. Because the equality comparison is so simply implemented, computers and other digital systems tend to use equality comparisons more often than inequality comparisons.

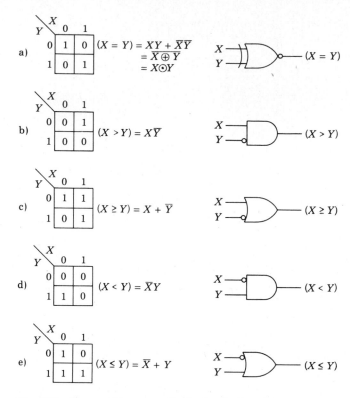

Fig. 6.16 Karnaugh maps and logic circuits for 1-bit comparators

Testing two n-bit numbers to determine whether they satisfy one of the four inequality relations is more difficult. For example, consider testing the n-bit numbers X and Y to determine if $X > Y$. If we were to do the comparison ourselves, we would inspect the two numbers, starting with the most significant bits. If X_{n-1} is 1 and Y_{n-1} is 0, we know immediately that $X > Y$; if X_{n-1} is 0 and Y_{n-1} is 1, we know that $X < Y$. In either case, the process is finished. However, if $X_{n-1} = Y_{n-1}$, we must inspect the next most significant bits in the same way. The comparison is finished as soon as we first encounter $X_i \neq Y_i$. For that value of i, if $X_i > Y_i$, then $X > Y$; if $X_i < Y_i$, then $X < Y$.

We can illustrate this procedure for two 3-bit numbers, X and Y. X is greater than Y if

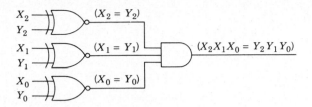

Fig. 6.17   A 3-bit comparator implementing $X_2 X_1 X_0 = Y_2 Y_1 Y_0$

1. (X_2 is greater than Y_2) OR
2. (X_2 equals Y_2) AND (X_1 is greater than Y_1) OR
3. (X_2 equals Y_2) AND (X_1 equals Y_1) AND (X_0 is greater than Y_0).

We can write these relations as an equation:

$$(X_2 X_1 X_0 > Y_2 Y_1 Y_0) = (X_2 > Y_2) + (X_2 = Y_2)$$
$$[(X_1 > Y_1) + (X_1 = Y_1)(X_0 > Y_0)]$$

Remembering that $(X_i = Y_i)$ is implemented as $X_i \odot Y_i$ and that $X_i > Y_i$ is implemented as $X_i \overline{Y}_i$, we can rewrite this equation as:

$$(X_2 X_1 X_0 > Y_2 Y_1 Y_0) = X_2 \overline{Y}_2$$
$$+ (X_2 \odot Y_2)[X_1 \overline{Y}_1 + (X_1 \odot Y_1) X_0 \overline{Y}_0]$$

This equation is implemented by the 3-bit *ripple comparator* of figure 6.18. Ripple comparators resemble ripple adders in that the results of comparing the least significant bits must propagate or ripple through the circuit. Ripple comparators are slow because they require many levels; the 3-bit ripple comparator for $X > Y$ requires five levels. If the COINCIDENCE function is implemented by an XOR gate followed by an inverter, as it often is, the circuit actually has six levels and hence six propagation delays.

A faster circuit can be obtained by rewriting the equation for $X > Y$ as follows:

$$(X_2 X_1 X_0 > Y_2 Y_1 Y_0) = (X_2 > Y_2) + (X_2 = Y_2)(X_1 > Y_1)$$
$$+ (X_2 = Y_2)(X_1 = Y_1)(X_0 > Y_0)$$
$$= X_2 \overline{Y}_2 + (X_2 \odot Y_2) X_1 \overline{Y}_1$$
$$+ (X_2 \odot Y_2)(X_1 \odot Y_1) X_0 \overline{Y}_0$$

This equation is implemented as the 3-bit *look-ahead carry comparator* of figure 6.19. This comparator is so named because it supplies "carry" information from the comparison of the least significant bits

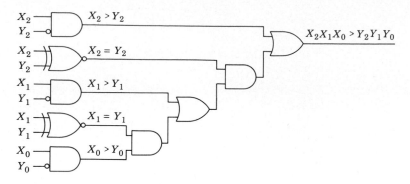

Fig. 6.18 A 3-bit ripple comparator implementing $X_2 X_1 X_0 > Y_2 Y_1 Y_0$

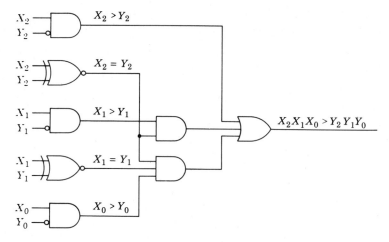

Fig. 6.19 A 3-bit look-ahead cary comparator implementing $X_2 X_1 X_0 > Y_2 Y_1 Y_0$

directly to gates involving the most significant bits. It has only three basic levels as shown, or four if implementation of the COINCIDENCE function requires two propagation delays. We can also construct a 3-bit comparator with only two basic levels; this is left as an exercise.

Integrated circuit comparators are available. Figure 6.20 shows the logic circuit for a common integrated circuit comparator that implements 4-bit versions of three comparisons: $A = B$, $A > B$, and $A < B$. Note the use of AND-OR-INVERT gates to reduce propagation

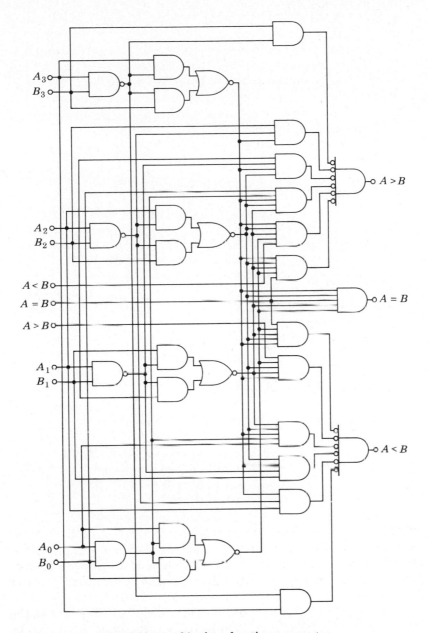

Fig. 6.20   A 4-bit, three-function comparator

delays. The comparators can be cascaded to allow comparing numbers of any length, limited only by loading characteristics of the integrated circuits.

The comparators just considered act on all bits of the numbers in parallel. The advantages of parallel comparators are that all bits are inputted at once and that the comparison can be fairly rapid, at least for the look-ahead carry and two-level comparators. The disadvantages of parallel comparators are that the number of gates required grows rapidly with n (the number of bits in the numbers) and that the number of inputs required may exceed the fan-in capability of the gates for large n.

Sequential comparators are an alternative to parallel comparators. Inputs to a sequential comparator are taken from shift registers that hold the numbers to be compared; the most significant bits may be inputted first. The comparison procedure resembles the procedure that we use for visual inspection, as described earlier in this section. The numbers are compared one bit at a time, starting with the most significant bits. The comparison ends as soon as $X_i \neq Y_i$ for some i. At that point if $X_i > Y_i$, then $X > Y$; if $X_i < Y_i$, then $X < Y$.

A sequential comparator requires two data flipflops. One flipflop, G, is 1 if X is Greater than Y and 0 otherwise. The other flipflop, E, is 1 when the comparison procedure has Ended and 0 otherwise. We begin the comparison procedure by resetting flipflop E to the 0 state. Flipflop G may be in either state. While flipflop E is 0, each clock pulse sets flipflop G to 1 if $X_i > Y_i$ for the ith bits being compared and resets G to 0 otherwise. As soon as X_i first is unequal to Y_i, flipflop E is set to 1. The comparison then ends, and the output of the G flipflop gives the result. If $X_i = Y_i$ for all n bits, the comparison ends after the nth clock pulse as determined by a counter that we will not consider. In either case the output G is 1 only if $X > Y$.

From this description of the comparator operation, we can write the extended state table of figure 6.20a. We choose JK flipflops, although we could also implement the circuit with RS or D flipflops. The values of the control inputs are taken from the excitation table for JK flipflops in chapter 4. Most entries for the control inputs are don't cares. The control inputs are mapped in figure 6.20b, and their equations are determined. $J_G = X_i \overline{Y_i} \overline{E}$; $K_G = (\overline{X_i} + Y_i)\overline{E}$; $J_E = X_i \oplus Y_i$; $K_E = 0$.

The logic circuit for the sequential comparator is shown in figure 6.20c. Circuit inputs are taken from the last stage of the shift registers holding **X** and **Y**. At each clock pulse the next most significant bits

Current Inputs		Current States X > Y End		Next States X > Y End		Current Control Inputs			
X_i	Y_i	G	E	G	E	J_G	K_G	J_E	K_E
0	0	0	0	0	0	0	d	0	d
0	0	0	1	0	1	0	d	d	0
0	0	1	0	0	0	d	1	0	d
0	0	1	1	1	1	d	0	d	0
0	1	0	0	0	1	0	d	1	d
0	1	0	1	0	1	0	d	d	0
0	1	1	0	0	1	d	1	1	d
0	1	1	1	1	1	d	0	d	0
1	0	0	0	1	1	1	d	1	d
1	0	0	1	0	1	0	d	d	0
1	0	1	0	1	1	d	0	1	d
1	0	1	1	1	1	d	0	d	0
1	1	0	0	0	0	0	d	0	d
1	1	0	1	0	1	0	d	d	0
1	1	1	0	0	0	d	1	0	d
1	1	1	1	1	1	d	0	d	0

Fig. 6.20a Extended state table for sequential comparator

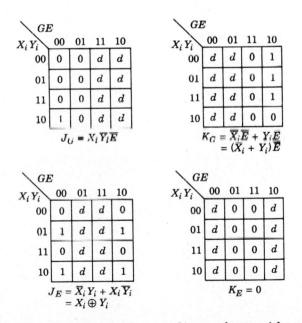

Fig. 6.20b Karnaugh maps for control inputs of sequential comparator

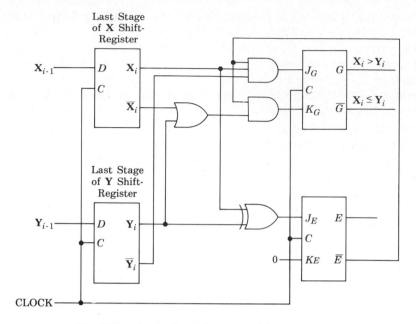

Fig. 6.20c   Logic circuit for sequential comparator

of **X** and **Y** are clocked into the comparator, and the states of flipflops G and E are allowed to change.

Some sequential comparators compare the bits in reverse order, starting with the least significant bit. This procedure is useful in serial systems that process the least significant bit first, as necessary for adders.

6.6.4 Error-Detecting Circuits

The simplest way to detect errors is to check parity. *Parity* is the oddness (*odd parity*) or evenness (*even parity*) of the number of 1s in a computer word. Usually an extra bit, called a *parity bit*, is appended to the basic computer word. The parity bit may be appended before the word is stored in memory or before it is added to another word. If the extra bit is selected to make the total number of 1s in the extended word even, the computer system has *even parity*. If the extra bit is selected to make the total number of 1s in the extended word odd, the system has *odd parity*.

Parity of the extended word can then be checked each time the word is used to ensure that it still has the desired parity. If an error occurs in just one bit of the extended word, the parity changes from odd to even or from even to odd. However, if errors occur in two bits, parity remains the same. Hence a parity check can determine if a single error occurred in the word but cannot determine which bit is in error. A parity check can also detect the presence of three, five, or any odd number of errors. Usually we assume that just one error occurred if the parity check shows a change in parity. More complex error-detecting systems check parity on several subsets of the bits of the computer word. Proper selection of the bits for parity checks allows identification of the incorrect bit. References at the end of the chapter discuss error-detecting and error-correcting codes, such as Hamming codes, that can be tested by parity checks.

Parity check generation and testing is easily done by XOR gates. Figure 6.21a shows a 6-bit parallel parity checker. Bits X_5 through

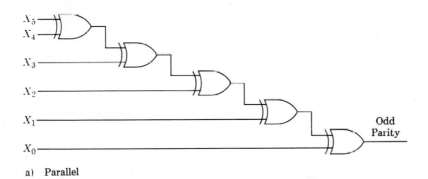

a) Parallel

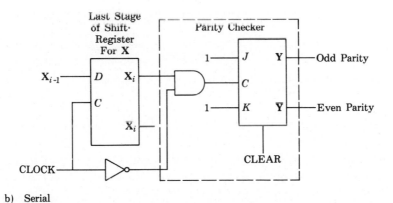

b) Serial

Fig. 6.21   Parity checkers

X_0 are applied simultaneously to the inputs shown. The output is 1 if the parity of the 6 bits is odd, that is, if the number of 1s is odd. The circuit shown has five levels of gates and consequently five propagation delays. A simpler circuit with three levels of two-input XOR gates can be designed.

Figure 6.21b shows a serial parity checker constructed from a JK flipflop. The flipflop J and K inputs are the bits of the word to be checked, presented in sequence. To start the parity check, the number to be checked is placed in the shift register and the JK flipflop is cleared to 0. At each clock pulse one bit of the number is shifted out of the shift register and into the flipflop J and K inputs. The flipflop changes state for every 1 bit in the shift register. The flipflop is in the 1 state whenever it has received an odd number of pulses and in the 0 state whenever it has received an even number of pulses. Thus the basic flipflop output Q shows odd parity, and its complement shows even parity.

Parity generators and checkers are available as integrated circuits. A typical integrated circuit parity generator and checker is shown in figure 6.22. The circuit checks the parity of an 8-bit data input. The EVEN and ODD inputs change the parity. If the parity of the 8 data bits is even, a 1 at the ODD input changes the parity to odd. A 1 at the EVEN input leaves the parity even. If the parity of the 8 data bits is odd, a 1 at the EVEN input changes the parity to odd. A 1 at the ODD input leaves the parity odd. The word length can be expanded by cascading two or more of these integrated circuits.

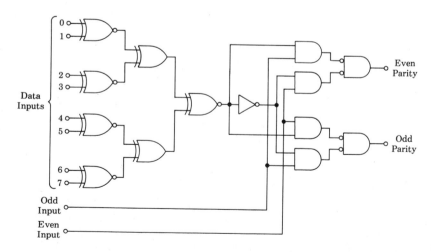

Fig. 6.22   An 8-bit parity generator and checker

6.7 BCD ADDERS

Since most calculations involve decimal numbers, it often is convenient to add numbers without converting them to binary form. Calculators and microprocessors often have adders that are designed
to work with decimal numbers represented in BCD form. In BCD
each digit is represented by its 4-bit binary equivalent as discussed
earlier. We add two digits with a 4-bit adder constructed from four
full adders and modified by extra logic circuits to convert the addition
from base 16 to base 10. The modification is necessary whenever the
sum of the two digits is greater than 9. For an example of the need
for the modification, consider the addition examined in example 6.8.

Example 6.8

$$
\begin{array}{r r}
9 & 1001 \\
+4 & 0100 \\
\hline
13 & 1101 \\
\end{array}
$$

The result of the addition of the binary forms of 9 and 4 is the
binary equivalent of 13. However, the binary form of 13 is not a
possible BCD digit. We need to convert the sum so that we have
one BCD digit representing 3 and another BCD digit representing
10. Thus we need to correct the least significant BCD digit to 3
and provide a carry to the next more significant position. We make
this correction by adding the binary equivalent of 6 (0110) to the
sum.

$$
\begin{array}{r r l}
9 & 1001 & \\
+4 & 0100 & \\
\hline
13 & 1101 & = 13_2 \\
& +0110 & +6 \\
\hline
1 \quad & 0011 & = 13 \text{ in BCD} \\
\end{array}
$$

carry

This correction, called a *decimal adjustment,* is needed in two cases:

1. When the sum outputs of the 4-bit adder hold a sum greater
   than 9; or
2. When there is a carry out of the highest full adder (this occurs
   when eights and nines are added as shown in example 6.9).

Example 6.9

$$
\begin{array}{rr}
8 \\
+9 \\
\hline
17
\end{array}
\qquad
\begin{array}{r}
1000 \\
1001 \\
\hline
1 \quad 0001 \\
+ \quad 0110 \\
\hline
1 \quad 0111 \\
\end{array}
\qquad
\begin{array}{l}
= 17_2 \\
+6 \\
= 17 \text{ in BCD}
\end{array}
$$

carry

Decimal adjustment also ensures that a carry goes to the next more significant stage when the result of the original addition exceeds 9. Adding 6 when the first result exceeds 9 yields a result that exceeds 15 and hence gives a carry, as shown in the first example.

We can design a BCD adder stage to provide decimal adjustment. Figure 6.23 shows a BCD adder stage that accepts 4-bit BCD-coded inputs X and Y and a CARRY from the preceding stage and produces their 4-bit sum Z and a CARRY to the succeeding stage. The basic addition is done by the 4-bit binary adder, constructed from four full adders. Decimal adjustment is provided by the logic gates and by the two half adders and fifth full adder. We can determine when and how the decimal adjustment must be made. Adding 6 does

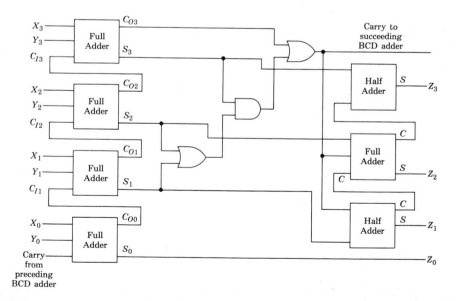

Fig. 6.23   BCD adder stage

not affect the least significant bit of the sum, Z_0, in any case. We add 6 (0110) only when there has been a CARRY out of the adder for the most significant bit or when the sum exceeds 9. We handle the first case by adding 1s to S_1 and S_2, the sum outputs of the addition of the middle 2 bits, whenever C_{O3}, the carry from the most significant bit, is 1. This requires a half adder for S_1 plus 1 and a full adder for S_2 plus 1 plus the carry from the half adder for S_1 plus 1. We must also add the carry from the full adder to S_3.

We also adjust the CARRY to the next BCD adder stage. The CARRY will be 1 whenever C_{O3} is 1. The CARRY will also be 1 whenever the result of the addition of the 4-bit adder is 10 or more. That sum will be 10 or more whenever S_3 is 1 AND either S_2 OR S_1 is 1. Hence we provide a carry that is $C_{O3} + S_3(S_2 + S_1)$.

Logic expressions for the terms of the decimally adjusted sum Z are left as an exercise.

BCD adder stages can be combined in parallel in much the same way as full adders. However, parallel adders require one BCD adder stage per digit and also have problems of carry propagation delay. Hence BCD addition is often performed using just one BCD adder stage with the digits to be added shifted in serially. Figure 6.24 shows such an adder. The adder is described as bit-parallel, digit-serial because the 4 bits of each digit are provided to the adder in parallel while successive digits are provided in series. Bit-parallel, digit-serial addition is common in small calculators and in microprocessors. The input digits are taken from shift registers with the least significant digits presented first. At each clock pulse (not shown in the figure) the 4 bits of the BCD code for X and the 4 bits of the BCD code for Y are presented to the adder. The CARRY from the previous addition has been held in a D flipflop and is also presented to the adder. The output sum Z is stored, and the CARRY enters the D flipflop.

Similar adders can be constructed for digits encoded in other codes, such as the excess-3 code described in chapter 3. One solution is to subtract 3 from each of the two numbers to be added and then to add 3 to the sum. Corrections for the sum and carry can be made in the same way as for the BCD adder. More ingenious solutions that deal with excess-3 numbers directly use fewer components.

6.8   FLOATING POINT BINARY ARITHMETIC

Floating point numbers are characterized by a mantissa M and an exponent E. Just as we can express decimal numbers in floating point,

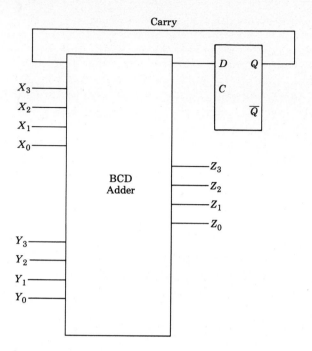

Fig. 6.24 Bit-parallel, digit-serial BCD adder

for example $23,142,67 = .2314267 \times 10^8$, we can express binary numbers in floating point, for example $1101.01 = .110101 \times 2^{100}$ or $.110101 \times 2^4$ if we choose to express the exponent as a decimal number. The fractional part of the floating point representation is the *mantissa;* the power of 10 or 2 is the *exponent.* We use the convention that the first bit of the mantissa of a binary floating point number is always 1. Thus the mantissa always represents a fraction, $\frac{1}{2} \leq M < 1$. The general form of a floating point binary number is

$$M \times 2^E$$

The exponent E is a binary integer. E ordinarily is limited to values in the range $-2^k + 1 \leq E \leq 2^k - 1$.

Some examples of binary floating point numbers are:

$$.101101 \times 2^{101} = .101101 \times 2^5 = 10110.1$$
$$.111011 \times 2^{1101} = .111011 \times 2^{13} = 1110110000000$$

6.8.1 Multiplication and Division

Multiplication and division are much easier to do in floating point than are addition and subtraction, hence we will consider them first. To multiply two numbers we form the product of the two mantissas and the sum of the two exponents; we then represent the result in standard floating point form. That is, multiplying $X = M_x \times 2^{E_x}$ and $Y = M_y \times 2^{E_y}$ yields $Z = X \cdot Y = M_x \cdot M_y \times 2^{E_x + E_y}$. This result holds for both positive and negative exponents E_x and E_y. If the resulting mantissa is outside the range $\frac{1}{2} \leq M < 1$, the exponent must be adjusted to move the mantissa in range.

Example 6.10

$$X = .101 \times 2^{110}$$
$$Y = .1001 \times 2^{-10}$$
$$Z = X \cdot Y = (.101 \times .1001) \times 2^{110-10}$$
$$Z = .0101101 \times 2^{100}$$

After adjusting the exponent to bring the mantissa in range,

$$Z = .101101 \times 2^{11}$$

The rule for adjusting the exponent is that the exponent is decreased by one for every place that the binary point must be moved right to bring the mantissa within range, $\frac{1}{2} \leq M < 1$.

A flowchart of binary floating point multiplication is shown in figure 6.25.

To divide two binary floating point numbers we form the quotient of the two mantissas and the difference between the exponent of the dividend and the exponent of the divisor. We then represent the result in standard floating point form. Thus, dividing

$$X = M_x \times 2^{E_x} \qquad \text{by} \qquad Y = M_y \times 2^{E_y}$$

yields $\qquad Z = X/Y = (M_x/M_y) \times 2^{E_x - E_y}$

As for multiplication, if the mantissa of the result is out of range, the exponent must be adjusted.

Example 6.11

$$X = .101 \times 2^{110}$$
$$Y = .1001 \times 2^{-10}$$

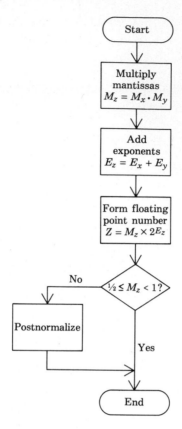

Fig. 6.25   Flowchart for binary floating point multiplication, $Z = X \cdot Y$

$$Z = \frac{X}{Y} = \frac{.101}{.1001} \times 2^{110 - (-10)}$$

$$Z = 1.00111 \times 2^{1000}$$

$$Z = .100111 \times 2^{1001}$$

The rule for adjusting the exponent is that the exponent is increased by one for each place the binary point must be shifted left to bring the mantissa within range. We can combine this rule with the one from the preceding example to form the general rule for adjusting the exponent, a process called *postnormalization* because it occurs after an arithmetic calculation:

Increase (decrease) the exponent by one for each place that the binary point must be shifted left (right) to bring the mantissa within range, $\frac{1}{2} \leq M < 1$.

A flowchart of binary floating point division is shown in figure 6.26.

6.8.2 Addition and Subtraction

We can add and subtract binary floating point numbers only if they have the same exponents. Thus the first step in addition or subtraction is to adjust the exponents so that they are the same. In order

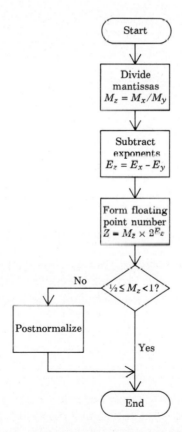

Fig. 6.26   Flowchart for binary floating point division, $Z = X/Y$

to keep the mantissas less than one, we increase the smaller exponent and simultaneously move the binary point of the corresponding mantissa to the left as many places as the difference between two exponents. Then we can add or subtract the mantissas, with binary points aligned. We express the result as a binary floating point number with the exponent equal to the original larger exponent. If necessary we adjust the exponent to bring the mantissa within range. This process is illustrated by the following example.

Example 6.12

$$X = .10001 \times 2^{110}$$
$$Y = .101 \times 2^{100}$$

Since $E_x = 110$ is larger than $E_y = 100$, we adjust Y to have an exponent of 110 by increasing E_y by two and shifting M_y right two places.

$$Y = .00101 \times 2^{110}$$

Now that the binary points are aligned we can add X and Y as follows:

$$\begin{aligned} X &= .10001 \times 2^{110} \\ +Y &= .00101 \times 2^{110} \\ \hline Z &= .10110 \times 2^{110} \end{aligned}$$

No further adjustment or postnormalization is necessary because the mantissa of the sum Z is in range.

We can also subtract Y from X.

$$\begin{aligned} X &= .10001 \times 2^{110} \\ -Y &= .00101 \times 2^{110} \\ \hline Z &= .01100 \times 2^{110} \end{aligned}$$

We must postnormalize the difference Z by decreasing the exponent by one and moving the binary point right one place.

Flowcharts of binary floating point addition or subtraction are shown in figure 6.27.

6.9 SUMMARY

Numbers can be represented for computer arithmetic as signed-magnitudes, ones complements, or twos complements. The representations are the same for positive numbers but differ for negative numbers.

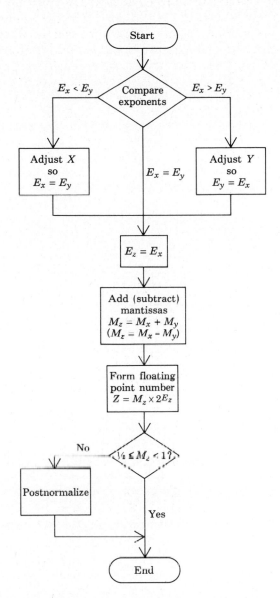

Fig. 6.27 Flowchart for binary floating point addition (subtraction),
$Z = X + Y (Z = X - Y)$

Ones and twos complement representations permit simpler calculations than signed-magnitude representation permits. A ones complement negative integer is the true complement of the positive integer; a twos complement negative integer is the true complement of the positive integer plus 1.

A half adder adds two binary inputs and gives sum and carry outputs. A full adder adds two binary inputs and a carry input from a preceding stage and gives sum and carry outputs. Serial adders use shift registers to add numbers presented in time sequence. Parallel adders use several sets of full adders to add numbers of several bits presented at one time. Carry propagation limits the speed of parallel addition; carry anticipation circuits can increase speed at the cost of extra complexity.

Multiplication is performed as repeated addition with two simple rules: (1) if the multiplier bit is 1, copy the multiplicand; (2) if the multiplier bit is 0, record 0s. Division is calculated either as restoring division in which the dividend is restored by adding the divisor when negative results are obtained or as nonrestoring division in which the divisor is shifted and added whenever negative results are encountered.

The arithmetic unit also performs several logic operations. The AND operation masks part of a computer word and extracts the remaining part. Other basic logic functions such as OR, NOT, and XOR can be performed.

Cyclic shifts move bits through all cells of a register in a circle. Logical shifts enter 0s into empty cells and lose bits shifted off the end. Arithmetic shifts leave the sign bit unchanged; they permit multiplication and division by 2. These shifts can be performed to the left or right and can occur with or without a carry bit.

Comparators are logic circuits that compare the magnitudes of two numbers. The equality comparison is the easiest to implement and can be done with a two-level circuit. Inequality comparisons are more difficult and can be implemented either in series or in parallel.

Errors can be detected by checking the parity of a computer word or of subsets of bits of the word. Even parity is an even number of 1s; odd parity is an odd number of 1s. Parity generators add one or more bits to make the parity of the extended word either odd or even as desired.

Floating point binary numbers have mantissas that are fractions in the range $\frac{1}{2} \leq M < 1$ and exponents that are expressed either as binary or as decimal numbers in some allowable range. Floating point multiplication and division are easy to perform. The mantissa of the product (quotient) of two binary floating point numbers is the product (quotient) of their mantissas; the exponent is the sum (difference) of the exponents. Binary floating point addition and subtraction of two numbers require (1) increasing the smaller exponent to make it equal the larger exponent, and (2) corresponding shifting of the mantissa to align the binary points. Then the numbers can be added or subtracted.

Concepts

arithmetic shift	mantissa
arithmetic unit	mask
carry anticipation	nonrestoring division
circular shift	odd parity
end-around carry	ones complement
even parity	overflow
excess-2^{n-1}	parity
exponent	postnormalization
extract	restoring division
fixed point	ripple adder
floating point	ripple comparator
logical shift	signed-magnitude
look-ahead carry	twos complement

6.10 REFERENCES

McCluskey (1965), Scott (1970), Bartee (1972), and Stone (1972) discuss basic number representation and arithmetic and logical operations. Flores (1963) and Gschwind and McCluskey (1975) examine arithmetic circuits in more detail. Bell, Grason, and Newell (1972) present RTM systems for multiplication and division. Barna and Porat (1973) discuss comparators. Peterson and Weldon (1972) provide an advanced discussion of error detecting and error correcting codes.

6.11 PROBLEMS

6.1 Which of the three number representations discussed in this chapter have both positive and negative zeros?   (6.2)

6.2 Describe the rules for addition of two numbers in signed-magnitude representation.   (6.2)

6.3 Calculate $+53 - 61$ using 8-bit binary numbers (sign + 7 bits) in

a. ones complement representation,
b. twos complement representation. (6.2)

6.4 Calculate $-47 + (-75)$ using 8-bit binary numbers (sign + 7 bits) in

a. ones complement representation,
b. twos complement representation

6.5 Which of the following expressions will generate overflow or an end-around carry for 4-bit ones complement representation:
a. $-6 + (-6)$
b. $+7 + 3$
c. $+7 + (-5)$
d. $+6 + (-7)$ (6.2)

6.6 Form the five-digit nines complement of the following decimal numbers:

a. 54306
b. 39109
c. 34790
d. 10000 (6.2)

6.7 Form the five-digit tens complement of the decimal numbers of problem 6.6.

6.8 Form the 6-bit sevens complement of the following octal numbers:

a. 1723516
b. 777000
c. 345621
d. 543620 (6.2)

6.9 Form the 6-bit eights complement of the octal numbers of problem 6.8. (6.2)

6.10 Show an example of subtracting a negative number from 0 in twos complement representation causing overflow. (6.2)

6.11 Divise rules for addition in excess-2^{n-1} representation. (6.2)

6.12 Construct a half subtracter circuit from ANDs, ORs, and NOTs that accepts inputs X and Y and calculates a DIFFERENCE, $X - Y$, and a BORROW output.   (6.3)

6.13 Construct a full subtracter circuit from ANDs, ORs, and NOTs that accepts inputs X, Y, and a BORROW input and calculates a DIFFERENCE, $X - Y$, and a BORROW output.   (6.3)

6.14 Construct a full adder using only NAND gates.   (6.3)

6.15 Construct a full adder using only NOR gates.   (6.3)

6.16 Show by example whether overflow can occur in a binary multiplier that multiplies numbers in signed-magnitude representation and has a double-length product.   (6.4)

6.17 Construct a flowchart for the multiplication procedure of figure 6.10.   (6.4)

6.18 Show the contents of all registers of figure 6.8 for each step in the multiplication of 1101 by 1001.   (6.4)

6.19 Show the contents of all registers of figure 6.10 for the multiplication of 1101 by 1001.   (6.4)

6.20 Divide 10101 by 11101 using restoring division.   (6.5)

6.21 Divide 10101 by 11101 using nonrestoring division.   (6.5)

6.22 Divide 1010 by 1100 using restoring division.   (6.5)

6.23 Divide 1010 by 1100 using nonrestoring division.   (6.5)

6.24 The numbers below are in twos complement form. Shift all numbers one place to the right (arithmetic right shift) and state the decimal equivalent.

   a. 01010
   b. 11101
   c. 10110
   d. 11111   (6.6)

6.25 Repeat problem 6.24 for ones complement representation. (6.6)

6.26 Register **A** contains 11010110. Register **B** contains 01111001. Calculate:

a. **A AND B**
b. **A OR B**
c. **A XOR B** (6.6)

6.27 Determine the parity of the following binary numbers:

a. 1110101011
b. 1000001010
c. 1110111101
d. 1010101010 (6.6)

6.28 Show the circuit of a 3-bit parallel comparator that determines if $X \geq Y$. (6.6)

6.29 Construct a two-level 3-bit comparator for $X > Y$. (6.6)

6.30 Express the following numbers in binary floating point:

a. 101.1101
b. 11111011
c. .00001011
d. .00000011 (6.7)

6.31 Express the following binary floating point numbers as fixed point numbers, that is, without an exponent:

a. $.111011 \times 2^{11101}$
b. $.111101 \times 2^{-110}$
c. $.10000001 \times 2^{101}$
d. $.11001101 \times 2^{-1101}$ (6.7)

6.32 Add the following pairs of binary floating point numbers:

a. $.1101101 \times 2^{110}$ and $.1010101 \times 2^{11}$
b. $.1011101 \times 2^{-100}$ and $.1000011 \times 2^{0}$
c. $.1110111 \times 2^{10}$ and $.1110110 \times 2^{1}$
d. $.1000010 \times 2^{-10}$ and $.100101 \times 2^{-1}$ (6.7)

6.33 For each pair of numbers in problem 6.32, subtract the second number from the first. (6.7)

6.34 Multiply the pairs of numbers in problem 6.32. (6.7)

6.35 For each pair of numbers in problem 6.32, divide the first number by the second. (6.7)

part II
The Programming Level

7 Machine Language Programming

7.1 Overview

Our study of the programming level begins with a look at the machine language level. Machine language is the set of instructions for the computer. Each instruction is represented by a pattern of 0s and 1s that direct the computer, through the logic circuits that we have already studied, to perform some action. Each instruction must specify two things either directly or implicitly—the operation to be performed and the address(es) of the operand(s) involved.

A major concept in machine language programming is specifying the address or addresses. We will see how many addresses are needed for various types of instructions and consider several ways that they may be specified. Machine language programming is complicated because of the number of details that we must specify in writing a program. After we have studied machine language programming, we will move on to assembly language and to high-level languages, letting the computer do some of the housekeeping details for us. Machine language programming is no longer important in itself; hence we will spend little time writing machine language programs. While studying machine language we will see the tradeoffs involved in the selection of instructions and will realize the relationship between programs and computer structure.

We will illustrate machine language programming with the PDP-8. We will also briefly look at the instruction sets of a wide variety of computers, ranging from a 4-bit microprocessor to a 32-bit large computer, so that we can see the ways in which the concepts of addressing and instruction set design are implemented in computers. The distinctions between microprocessors, minicomputers, and large computers are not well defined. A *microprocessor* is a central process-ing unit on a single integrated circuit; microprocessors range from 2 to 16 bits, overlapping with minicomputers at the higher end. A *minicomputer* is a small computer. Minicomputers once were defined as computers costing less than $20,000, but the decreasing cost of hardware has made that definition obsolete. Minicomputers are pri-marily computers with words of 12 to 16 bits, although they are now available with 32-bit words. Minicomputers can be contrasted with large, general purpose computers that have word lengths typi-cally of 32 bits or more.

7.2 Instructions

Machine language is the set of instructions for the computer. The instructions are n-bit binary numbers divided into sections called *fields*. Typical fields are an *operation code field* that states the operation to be performed and one or more *address fields* that give the address(es) of the operand(s) needed for the calculation. Most arithmetic operations require two operands, that is, two numbers to be operated on. Bits of the instruction can be numbered from right to left as shown below or from left to right. Both methods are used in the computer industry.

OPERATION CODE	ADDRESS
N-1	K K-1 0

Although we usually program in a high-level language such as FORTRAN, we are limited by the machine language instructions. The instruction set, in turn, is limited by the hardware design of the computer, including such features as the number of registers, the types of shifts available, and the presence or absence of a carry bit. Thus we wish to examine the characteristics of instruction sets and the types of instructions that may occur on computers we will encounter.

Word Length One important characteristic of a computer is its word length or the largest number of bits the computer processes in one operation. Word length of an instruction affects both the number of locations that can be addressed and the number of different operations that can be performed. An n-bit instruction that has k bits in the address field and m bits in the operation code field can address 2^k locations directly and perform 2^m different operations. For example, a 16-bit word that has 12 bits in the address field and 4 bits in the operation code field can directly address $2^{12} = 4096$ locations and perform $2^4 = 16$ different operations. For a given word length, there is a tradeoff between the number of *directly* addressable locations and the number of operations. (In another section we will look at addressing methods to increase the number of addressable locations for a fixed address field.) Longer words have more bits and thus need more cells of storage. Longer registers are also needed to hold longer words. If operations such as addition are to be performed in parallel, increasing the word length means providing more copies of basic circuits such as adders.

The length of instructions and data is not always limited to the length of the basic computer word. We will see later in this chapter that we can have some of the advantages of a longer computer word—greater addressing capabilities and more types of operations—by using instructions and data, each of which takes two or more computer words. For very small computers double-length or triple-length instructions are necessary to give flexibility of addressing and specifying instructions. For larger computers double length data allows twice the precision in arithmetic calculations. Increasing the effective word length by using two or three words for one instruction or datum avoids the disadvantages of longer registers and memory words and more complex arithmetic units. However, double- or triple-length words take two or three times as long to be processed.

Address Types Instructions may specify from zero to four addresses. Computers can be found that use each of these five types of addressing. Many computers have two or more address types and are classified according to which one predominates. In this section we compare address types, noting the length required and the relative efficiency for coding a particular arithmetic calculation for each type. We consider this calculation a *benchmark* since we use it to compare the five address types.

Instead of trying to find one computer that uses all five address types and copying its instructions, we will construct our own instructions. The instructions and addresses will be symbolic rather than the actual binary instructions and addresses used later in the chapter. We will also use three-letter abbreviations, called *mnemonics,* for each instruction; mnemonic means that the abbreviation is chosen to remind us of the instruction. For example, throughout this discussion we will use the following mnemonic codes for arithmetic operations:

Code	Meaning
ADD	Add
SUB	Subtract
MPY	Multiply
DIV	Divide

We will also use symbolic operands. For example, the instruction

ADD X,Y

means add the values of X and Y. Each of the variables X and Y is stored in a location, either in memory or in a register. Later in this chapter we will see that in machine language programming we must specify the numeric addresses of the locations. We understand that we add the contents of the two locations not their addresses. As mentioned in chapter 5, we must always know whether we are dealing with addresses or the contents of the numbers stored at the locations with those addresses.

We will use the notation introduced in chapter 5 to describe the instructions. The general form of the notation is

$$\text{left side} \leftarrow \text{right side}$$

which means that the value of the right side is transferred to the location named by the left side. Thus the statement

$$Z \leftarrow X \cdot Y$$

means that the value of the product of the contents of locations X and Y is transferred to location Z. Throughout this discussion we will use + to indicate arithmetic addition; we will indicate logical addition by OR. Similarly, we will use $\cdot$, $\times$, or adjacency (for example, XY) to mean arithmetic multiplication; we will use AND for logical multiplication.

7.2.1 Four-Address Instructions

A four-address instruction has address fields for the two operands of the instruction (sources), the address where the result is to be sent (destination), and the address of the next instruction. This format is shown below.

OPERATION CODE	SOURCE 1	SOURCE 2	DESTINATION	NEXT INSTRUCTION

A four-address instruction to add two numbers specifies the operation code for addition, the locations of the two numbers to be added, the location where the result is to be stored, and the address of the next instruction. Such an instruction has the form:

Instruction	*Description*
ADD X,Y,Z,P	$Z \leftarrow X + Y$; next instruction in P

We could similarly define the other arithmetic instructions. However, with the introduction of one simple device, we can convert four-address instructions to three-address instructions. We find no difference in the number of instructions required to code our benchmark program so we will introduce the device and move rapidly on to three-address instructions. A special register, called a *program counter,* holds the address of the next instruction. Because instructions either occur in sequence or branch to another part of the program, the program counter is updated by increasing its contents by 1 or replacing its contents by the branch location, respectively. If we know that we can always find the address of the next instruction in the program counter, we do not need to specify it in our instruction. We can thus save the length of the address field for the next instruction.

7.2.2 Three-Address Instructions

A three-address instruction gives the operation code and the locations of the operands (sources) and the result (destination). Its format follows.

OPERATION CODE	SOURCE 1	SOURCE 2	DESTINATION

Possible instructions for a three-address computer include:

Instruction	*Description*
ADD X,Y,Z	$Z \leftarrow X + Y$
SUB X,Y,Z	$Z \leftarrow X - Y$
MPY X,Y,Z	$Z \leftarrow X \cdot Y$
DIV X,Y,Z	$Z \leftarrow X/Y$

We can code our benchmark problem, the calculation of $Y = A + B(CD/E - F)$. We will use a temporary register, **T**.

Instruction	Description	Result
MPY C,D,T	$T \leftarrow C \cdot D$	$T \leftarrow C \cdot D$
DIV T,E,T	$T \leftarrow T/E$	$T \leftarrow CD/E$
SUB T,F,T	$T \leftarrow T - F$	$T \leftarrow (CD/E) - F$
MPY B,T,T	$T \leftarrow B \cdot T$	$T \leftarrow B((CD/E) - F)$
ADD A,T,Y	$Y \leftarrow A + T$	$Y \leftarrow A + B((CD/E) - F)$

Five instructions were needed to code this calculation which has five operations—two multiplications, one division, one subtraction, and one addition. In general, the number of three-address instructions needed will be the same as the number of binary operations in the expression.

7.2.3 Two-Address Instructions

If we insist that one operand be in a fixed location such as an accumulator and also use a program counter, we need only two addresses. A two-address instruction gives the operation code, the location of one operand (source), and the intended location of the result (destination). The second operand is assumed to be stored in the destination. Thus addition is performed by adding the number stored in the source to the number stored in the destination and sending the result to the destination. The format for two-address instructions is:

OPERATION CODE	SOURCE	DESTINATION

Two-address arithmetic instructions with X denoting the accumulator have the following form:

Instruction	Description
ADD X,Y	$X \leftarrow X + Y$
SUB X,Y	$X \leftarrow X - Y$
MPY X,Y	$X \leftarrow X \cdot Y$
DIV X,Y	$X \leftarrow X/Y$

We have lost some flexibility in going from a three-address instruction to a two-address instruction. One example is that we now find it difficult to perform the operations $Y - X$ and Y/X where X is the value stored in the destination. This problem does not arise in addition and multiplication because they are commutative. We could solve this problem by introducing inverse subtraction and inverse division operations. However, a simpler and common solution is to introduce a MOVE instruction. The MOVE instruction transfers the contents of one location to another location. That is,

$$\text{MOV X,Y} \qquad \text{means} \qquad X \leftarrow Y$$

We can now code our benchmark calculation $Y = A + B((CD/E) - F)$ (assuming that we have just one accumulator X which is used in every operation) as follows:

Instruction	Result
MOV X,C	$X \leftarrow C$
MPY X,D	$X \leftarrow C \cdot D$
DIV X,E	$X \leftarrow CD/E$
SUB X,F	$X \leftarrow (CD/E) - F$
MPY X,B	$X \leftarrow B((CD/E) - F)$
ADD X,A	$X \leftarrow A + B((CD/E) - F)$
MOV Y,X	$Y \leftarrow A + B((CD/E) - F)$

Seven instructions are needed to code this calculation with two-address instructions.

7.2.4 One-Address Instructions

We can simplify our address field still further by specifying only one source address. The other source is understood to be the accumulator. The result is placed in the accumulator. A separate instruction is needed to store the result in another location. A one-address instruction thus gives only the operation code and one source address. Most minicomputers use one-address instructions. The format of one-address instructions is:

OPERATION CODE	ADDRESS

Arithmetic one-address instructions with X denoting the accumulator have the following form:

Instruction	Description
ADD A	$X \leftarrow X + A$
SUB A	$X \leftarrow X - A$
MPY A	$X \leftarrow X \cdot A$
DIV A	$X \leftarrow X/A$

Again inverse subtraction and inverse division instructions are useful, and some computers have them. Instead of a MOVE instruction, LOAD and STORE instructions are usually found in one-address computers. The LOAD instruction moves a number to the accumulator; the STORE instruction moves a number from the accumulator to some other location. They have the following form:

Instruction	Description
LOD A	$X \leftarrow A$
STO A	$A \leftarrow X$

We can code the benchmark calculation $Y = A + B((CD/E) - F)$ in one-address instructions as follows:

Instruction	Result
LOD C	$X \leftarrow C$
MPY D	$X \leftarrow CD$
DIV E	$X \leftarrow CD/E$
SUB F	$X \leftarrow (CD/E) - F$
MPY B	$X \leftarrow B((CD/E) - F)$
ADD A	$X \leftarrow A + B((CD/E) - F)$
STO Y	$Y \leftarrow A + B((CD/E) - F)$

Again seven instructions are needed to code the calculation. If the calculation had required storage of intermediate results (for example, if the expression had involved calculating a sum of products), more one-address instructions than two-address instructions would be required. Transfers of intermediate results require just one MOVE instruction in two-address instructions, but both a STORE and a LOAD instruction in the one-address case.

Variations of these one-address instructions are sometimes found. The STORE instruction can be a STORE AND CLEAR ACCUMU-LATOR instruction. The PDP-8 has such an instruction, abbreviated as DCA, for DEPOSIT AND CLEAR ACCUMULATOR. The instruction DCA Y means $Y \leftarrow X$ and $X \leftarrow 0$. The LOAD instruction, which means CLEAR ACCUMULATOR AND LOAD, may be named CLEAR AND ADD, since the effect is to add a number to the accumulator after it has first been cleared to 0.

7.2.5 Zero-Address Instructions

Finally we can use a zero-address or *stack* instruction. This instruction consists of operation code only as shown by the format below. The addresses of the operands and the result are implied. Because zero-address instructions and stacks have some unique features, we will discuss them at greater length than we did the other address types.

```
OPERATION CODE
```

7.2.6 Pushdown Stacks

A *pushdown stack* is an ordered list of numbers. It resembles a stack of trays in a cafeteria. Numbers are put on or taken from the stack on a last-in-first-out basis. We speak of putting a number in the stack as *pushing,* and of removing a number from the stack as *popping.*

Some pocket calculators have pushdown stacks. The stack instructions consist of operation codes only; the addresses are implied by the instructions without the use of an address field. We will program our benchmark calculation on this type of calculator. Since it does not have a program counter, the user or programmer provides the instructions in the proper order. This pocket calculator is not a *stored program computer* because it lacks the capability of storing instructions.

Table 7.1 shows the instructions for the pocket calculator. We offer eight (2^3) instructions so we need eight different binary codes. We can represent the instructions with 3-bit numbers. As an aid to our memory, we also give the *octal* equivalents of the binary numbers and mnemonics for the instruction. (Binary-to-octal conversion is reviewed in appendix A.) We have assigned the binary numbers arbi-

TABLE 7.1

INSTRUCTIONS FOR PUSHDOWN STACK

Binary assignment	Octal equivalent	Mnemonic	Instruction
000	0	LOD	LOaD stack (push data on stack; all entries move down one space)
001	1	ADD	ADD top two stack entries*
010	2	MPY	MultiPlY top two stack entries*
011	3	SUB	SUBtract top stack entry* from entry just below
100	4	DIV	DIVide top stack entry* into entry just below
101	5	POP	POP stack (top entry removed; all entries move up one space)
110	6	CMS	CoMplement top Stack entry
111	7	PSH	PuSH all entries down one space

*All binary arithmetic operations destroy the numbers in the top two stack positions and move all entries below the top two spaces up one space.

trarily. In practice, the choice of the numbers is important in simplifying the logic design of the calculator.

We can write a simple program with these instructions to calculate

$$Y = A + B((CD/E) - F)$$

We assume that our stack has enough spaces to make this calculation and that the numbers will be in range. Figure 7.5 shows the program and the stack contents at each step.

We start with an empty stack. We load A, B, C, and D into the stack with LOD commands. MPY multiplies C and D. LOD E loads E. DIV divides CD by E. LOD F loads F. SUB subtracts F from CD/E. MPY multiplies $(CD/E) - F$ and B. ADD adds A to $B((CD/E) - F)$. POP empties the stack. This program required eleven instructions besides the final POP instruction. More efficient programs for this calculation can be devised (see problem 7.1).

The pushdown stack for this pocket calculator has permitted the calculation without explicit addresses. The user inputs data to the stack. All instructions operate on the top stack entry or the top two stack entries. The results of all operations (except POP) are stored in the top of the stack. Housekeeping operations of pushing data down in the stack are handled automatically. No program counter is needed since the user presents instructions in sequence.

Yet we can see problems in stack operation. We have bought the absence of address fields at the price of programming complications. We must be careful of the order in which we input data. Once we have pushed data on the stack below the first entry, we cannot read them without popping the entries above them. Thus we do not have easy access to data. In the next section we will see that instructions that provide address fields solve some of these problems.

Although we have considered pushdown stacks for a calculator that operates without program counters and other accessories, pushdown stacks have other uses, such as for temporary storage of data in computers. Many algorithms require that data be stored on a last-in-first-out basis; hence stack organization is desirable.

7.3 Instruction Classes

The types of operations needed to perform on a computer can be categorized into three types, corresponding to three classes of instructions:

1. We need to be able to store a word in memory or to load a register with a word from memory. We may also want to add

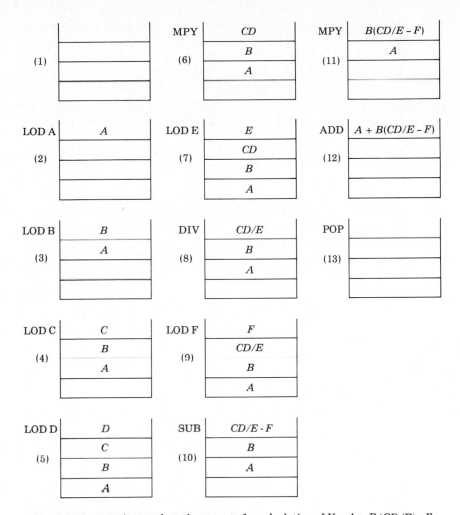

Fig. 7.1   Instructions and stack contents for calculation of $Y = A + B\,(CD/E) - F$

a word from memory to a sum already present in some register. These operations all deal with memory; instructions that require transferring words to or from memory are called *memory reference instructions*.

2. We need to operate on words that are already available in a register. We may need to complement the contents of a register or to increment the contents by 1. If our computer has more than one register, we may want to transfer a word between two registers or to add the contents of one register to the contents

of another. Instructions that deal only with words in registers are called *register reference instructions*. We will divide register reference instructions into two subclasses. *Register instructions* deal with operations involving only one register; they include complementing and incrementing the contents of a register. *Register-register instructions* involve operations between two registers; they include simple transfers and arithmetic operations.

3. We need to transfer words between the central processing unit of the computer and external devices, such as teletypes, tape units, and line printers. We also need to control these external devices and to determine when they are ready for information transfer. Instructions that deal with external devices are called *input/output* instructions.

While these three classes of instructions form a reasonable categorization of computer instructions, they do not suit all computers equally well. Computers that have only one register for holding data lack register-register instructions. Some computers are organized so that they treat memory and external devices in the same way. Such computers have memory reference instructions and input/output instructions that have the same form. The PDP-11, which we will look at briefly near the end of the chapter, is an example of a computer that lacks separate memory reference and input/output instructions.

In the rest of this section we will examine the three classes of instructions in more detail. We will look at the choices involved in determining the instructions for a hypothetical 16-bit computer. As a step toward preparing us to program in machine language for the PDP-8, we will look at PDP-8 instructions in each class. We have chosen the PDP-8 as an example because it is the most widely used minicomputer and because its organization is simple. Later in the chapter we will look at the instruction sets of several other computers.

7.3.1 Memory Reference Instructions

Memory reference instructions operate on information stored in one or more memory locations. These operations include:

1. Storing data in memory,
2. Reading data from memory,
3. Performing arithmetic and logical operations involving data stored in memory and data present in working registers or accumulators, and

4. Changing the order of execution of instructions in a program.

Memory reference instructions usually have the following fields:

1. Operation code—shows the type of operation.
2. Register designation—shows the register used for the operation if the computer has more than one register for holding data.
3. Address mode—states the type of addressing.
4. Address or displacement—displacement is used in determining the address.

A typical format for instructions in a 16-bit computer is shown below with the bits that might be assigned to each field.

OPERATION CODE	REGISTER	MODE	DISPLACEMENT

15   12 11   10 9   8 7   0

The operation code field of 4 bits allows $2^4 = 16$ memory reference instructions. However, one bit of the four is usually reserved to identify the instructions as a memory reference instruction. For example, bit 15 might be 1 for memory reference instructions and 0 for all other types of instructions. We might call bit 15 a *class code field* since it specifies the class of memory reference instructions. This approach leaves the other 3 bits of the operation code field for identifying one of eight memory reference instructions.

The register field of 2 bits allows the choice of any one of four registers, identified as 00, 01, 10, and 11. Register designations are not needed if the computer has just one accumulator because use of that accumulator is assumed. Register designations may be handled as part of the operation code, or implicitly if a particular operation can only use certain registers. Typical register assignments are:

A0	Accumulator 0
A1	Accumulator 1
A2/X0	Accumulator 2/Index Register 0
A3/X1	Accumulator 3/Index Register 1

Index registers aid in addressing and act as pointers to instructions or data; these functions will be explained later.

The mode field and the register field allow choice of the type of addressing. We will discuss five addressing techniques: direct addressing, indirect addressing, paging, register addressing, and immediate addressing. Few computers use all five techniques.

Many computers allocate one bit of the mode field as a direct/indirect bit (D/I bit). If the D/I bit is 0, the computer interprets the address as a direct address. Thus the address of the actual memory location is the address given in the displacement field. This is the *effective address* of the instruction.

We introduce some notation to explain this concept further:

$$EA = \text{Effective address or address of memory location}$$
$$D = \text{Displacement}$$
$$(M) = \text{Contents of memory location } M$$
$$(D) = \text{Contents of memory location } D$$

The distinction between a memory location (or register) and its contents is sometimes troublesome, as discussed in chapter 5. An instruction is usually stored in an *instruction register* while it is being executed. The register is a physical device. The contents of cells 7 through 0 of the instruction register for our example is the displacement D. D names a memory location. For example, if D is 11010011, it names the memory location 11010011. The contents of any memory location in this example is a 16-bit binary number. The contents of memory location 11010011 may be 0101110100010111.

Direct Addressing   Direct addressing means the effective address is the displacement, that is,

$$EA = D$$

If the displacement field has 8 bits as in our example, we can directly address only $2^8 = 256$ locations. The instruction below is an example of direct addressing.

Example 7.1—Direct Addressing

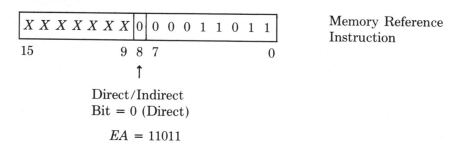

$$EA = 11011$$

We have adopted two conventions in showing this example. We denote bits that are irrelevant to the point we are discussing by X; here we assume only that these bits have values that are consistent with direct addressing. We also suppress leading 0s in giving the address; thus we express 00011011 as 11011.

Indirect Addressing   If the D/I bit = 1, the addressing is indirect. The computer interprets the displacement as a pointer to a memory location whose contents are the desired address. Indirect addressing means the effective address is given by the contents of the location named by the displacement, that is,

$$EA = (D)$$

We can address many more locations indirectly than we can directly. We are limited to 256 locations for an 8-bit displacement field when addressing directly, but can theoretically address 2^{15} locations when addressing indirectly with a 16-bit word. The reason for this is that the contents of the memory location given by the displacement field has 16 bits. One bit of the 16 may be reserved for higher levels of indirection as explained in the next paragraph. Our computer, however, may not have 2^{15} memory locations. We must be careful not to address a location not present in the memory of our computer. Indirect addressing is a powerful way to extend our effective addressing ability to access all available memory locations.

Indirect addressing can be cascaded to show higher levels of indirection. For example,

$$EA = ((D))$$

means that the effective address is the contents of the memory location that is given by the contents of the memory location given by D. More than two levels of indirect addressing are rarely used.

Example 7.2—Indirect Addressing

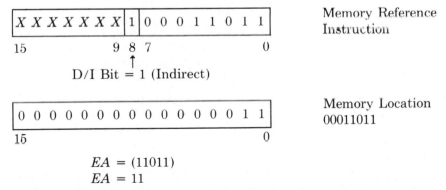

Memory Reference Instruction

D/I Bit = 1 (Indirect)

Memory Location 00011011

$$EA = (11011)$$
$$EA = 11$$

In this example the D/I bit is 1, meaning indirect addressing. The displacement is interpreted as the address of the location in memory whose contents are the desired address. Since the displacement is

11011, we go to memory location 11011 and examine its contents. The contents of location 11011 is 11, the effective address. We remember that bit 8 is reserved as a direct/indirect bit. In location 11011, bit 8 is 0 so we have no further levels of indirection.

Paging Another way to increase the number of locations that can be addressed is *paging*. We can picture the words of computer memory as arranged on pages. Each page has the same number of words. If the displacement field has 8 bits, each page has $2^8 = 256$ words. We can address more locations if we can address more than one page. Let us assume that we have $2^4 = 16$ pages, numbered from 0000 to 1111. The memory thus has $2^4 \times 2^8 = 2^{12} = 4096$ words. Figure 7.2 shows 16 pages of 256 words. The page with page number 0 is called the *base page* or page 0. We can address either of two pages in memory if we use 1 bit of the mode field of the memory reference instruction as a page bit. The page bit is often called a Z/C bit for page zero/current page.

If the page bit is 0, we address the words on the base page or page 0. The effective address is just the displacement as for direct addressing.

$$EA = D$$

If the page bit is 1, we address the words on the *current page* or the page containing the current instruction. The number of the current page is given by several bits of the program counter or memory

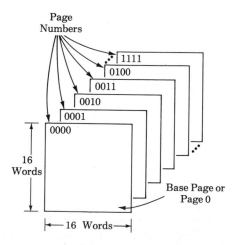

Fig. 7.2   Page addressing — 16 pages of 256 16-bit words

address register. The program counter, as explained earlier in this chapter, holds the address in memory of the next instruction to be executed. The *memory address register,* which we will discuss in more detail in chapter 9, holds the address in memory to which or from which a word is currently being transferred. In our case, the page number will be given by bits 11 through 8 of the program counter. The program counter of our example is a 12-bit register that keeps track of the address of each instruction of a program. Since we are limited to 4096 words, the program counter needs only 12 bits. When the page bit is 1,

$$EA = D + (PC_{11-8})00000000$$

The effective address is given by the displacement plus bits $11 - 8$ of the contents of the program counter followed by eight 0s. In other words, the address is the contents of bits $11 - 8$ of the program counter plus the displacement.

Example 7.3—Paging

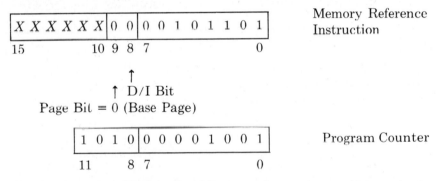

Since the page bit is 0 in this example, we ignore the contents of the program counter and leave the current page of 1010 to go to the base page. The effective address is

$$EA = 101101$$

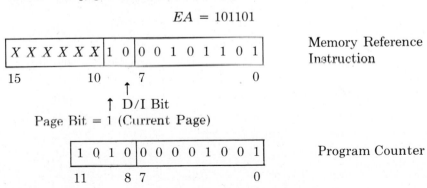

Since the page bit is 1, we stay on the current page. The current page number, given by bits $11 - 8$ of the program counter, is 1010. The effective address is

$$EA = 101000101101$$

Paging can be combined with indirect addressing. If the D/I bit of the example just discussed had been 1, the effective address would have been given by the contents of memory location 101000101101.

Many versions of paging exist. Some computers use several bits as page indicators to allow some choice of the register containing the page number. For example, a 3-bit page field allows choice of eight different registers for determining the page number.

The size of the page can be important in programming. We often want to keep the instructions and data for a program entirely on one page. Larger pages can, of course, contain larger programs. A program that fits entirely on one page of memory and contains no indirect references can easily be relocated to another page. This enhances building libraries of programs. Programs that can be executed on any page are called *page relocatable.*

Register Addressing Register addressing is much like paging. Addresses are modified by adding the contents of special registers, usually called *index registers,* to displacements. We will assume that we have two index registers X_0 and X_1. Bit 11 in our instructions refers to X_0 and bit 10 to X_1. If both bits are 0, the effective address is just the displacement as in the usual direct addressing.

$$EA = D \quad \text{if bit } 11 = \text{bit } 10 = 0$$

If either bit is 1, the contents of its associated register are added to the displacement. If both bits are 1, the contents of both registers are added to the displacement.

$$EA = D + (X_0) \quad \text{if bit } 11 = 1 \text{ and bit } 10 = 0$$
$$EA = D + (X_1) \quad \text{if bit } 11 = 0 \text{ and bit } 10 = 1$$
$$EA = D + (X_0) + (X_1) \text{ if bit } 11 = \text{bit } 10 = 1$$

Example 7.4—Register Addressing

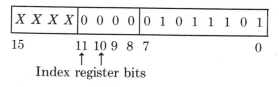

Memory Reference
Instruction

$$EA = 1011101$$

Since both index register bits are 0, the effective address is just the displacement.

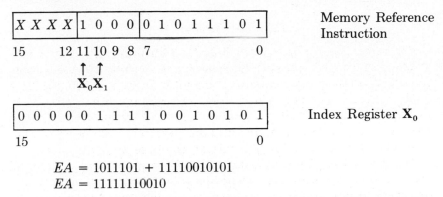

EA = 1011101 + 11110010101
EA = 11111110010

Since the bit for index register X_0 is 1 while the bit for index register X_1 is 0, the effective address is given by the sum of the displacement and the contents of index register X_0.

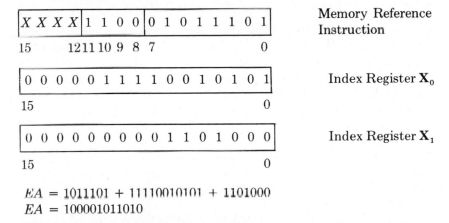

EA = 1011101 + 11110010101 + 1101000
EA = 100001011010

Since the bits for both index registers are 1, the effective address is the sum of the displacement and the contents of both index registers.

Another type of register addressing uses the register to hold the operand. We cannot show this with our basic memory reference instruction format since a different format is needed. A typical format is:

OPERATION CODE		MODE	REGISTER	D/I
15	6 5	4 3	1	0

If the D/I bit is 0 for direct addressing and the mode bits are 0 for register addressing, the effective address is

$$EA = \mathbf{R}$$

The desired operand is located in the register **R** specified by the register field; that is, the effective address is register **R**.

If the D/I bit is 1 for indirect addressing and the mode bits are 0 for register addressing,

$$EA = (\mathbf{R})$$

The effective address is given by the contents of register **R**.

The mode field permits different modes to, for example, let us automatically increase the address so that we can perform operations on a series of data stored in sequence. The mode field can also specify index register addressing in which the contents of an index register are added to a given address. Another possible mode is relative addressing in which the displacement or the contents of a register are added to the contents of the program counter. *Relative* addressing is the opposite of the *absolute* addressing which we have been discussing; in absolute addressing the address field shows the address independent of the contents of the program counter. Relative or absolute addressing can be combined with other modes such as direct or indirect to give such combinations as relative indirect addressing or absolute direct addressing, which we have previously called just direct addressing. Some of the references at the end of the chapter discuss the many variations of register addressing.

Register addressing is more versatile than paging since it can allow addressing any memory location instead of just the addresses on two pages. In this respect, it is much like indirect addressing. Computers are likely to use either register addressing or paging and indirect addressing.

Register addressing is commonly used to let an instruction operate on different data each time the instruction is executed. This address modification is called *indexing*. We can use indexing to complement each of a series of numbers that were stored in sequence by incrementing the index register after each operation. To do this we write a brief program to execute a series of statements repeatedly. For each number we (1) retrieve the number, (2) complement it, (3) store it in its original address, and (4) increment the contents of the index register to provide the address of the next number. The steps needed for this program will be more apparent after we have discussed machine language programming.

Another use of register addressing is to relocate a program in memory. We can simply add the contents of the register to every address in the program. We usually refer to the register involved in program relocation as a *base register* rather than an index register.

Immediate Addressing *Immediate addressing* is used by an instruction that shows the value of the operand. Often it is useful to be able to add or perform other operations with small constants. With immediate addressing we can specify the value of the constant directly; we do not have to give the address of a register or memory location that contains the constant. For example the immediate address instruction

ADD 9

means to add 9 to the contents of the accumulator. Of course, we must specify the base of the number (binary, octal, or decimal). There is no calculation of effective address in immediate addressing because the value of the operand is given by the instruction. Immediate addressing is frequently used in microprocessors.

Our discussion of addressing has been intended to show the most common schemes. Many variations of these schemes or more innovative schemes are used in modern computers.

Memory Reference Instruction Formats of the PDP-8 We will look at the memory reference instruction formats of the PDP-8, the computer we shall use to illustrate machine language programming. Our discussion will center on addressing rather than on the operation codes. Its instruction set is listed in appendix C.

The PDP-8 is one of the first minicomputers and the most widely used. It is a 12-bit, single address computer with one accumulator. Its memory reference instruction looks like this:

OP CODE	D/I	Z/C	DISPLACEMENT
0 2	3	4	5 11

The first three bits are the operation code. This allows eight different codes, but only six of the eight are used for memory reference instructions. Codes 110 and 111 are reserved for input/output operations and for microinstructions; we will discuss these later.

Bit 3 is a direct/indirect bit. It is 0 for direct addressing and 1 for indirect addressing. By convention, we show the bit D/I for 0/1. That is, 0 is associated with the first letter and 1 with the second.

Bit 4 is a page bit, Z/C. It is 0 for page 0 and 1 for the current page.

Bits 5 – 11 are the displacement or address on a page. Each page has 2^7 = 128 12-bit words. If the current memory reference instruction is located on any page except page 0, it can directly address 256 words, the 128 on the current page and the 128 on page 0. It can address 4096 words indirectly. In the PDP-8, 4096 or 4K words constitute a *memory field*. A memory field is a module of memory. We commonly express memory as so many K words, where K = 2^{10} = 1024, just a few more than 1000 words or a kiloword. The computer can provide eight memory fields for a maximum of 32K words of memory.

7.3.2   Register Instructions

Register instructions can be divided into register reference instructions and register-register instructions. Register reference instructions operate on just one register. The operations include:

1. Testing contents of a register, either the full word or a single bit;
2. Complementing the contents of a register;
3. Shifting or rotating the contents of a register (without a carry bit).

A typical format for register reference instructions is:

CLASS CODE	REGISTER	OP CODE 1	OP CODE 2	OP CODE 3
15 13	12 9	8 6	5 3	2 0

The class code designates the class of instructions as register instructions. It is part of the operation code. For example, we reserved bit 15 as 1 for memory reference instructions in our hypothetical example of formats of memory reference instructions. Bit 15 = 0 could designate all instructions other than memory reference instructions, including register instructions and input/output instructions. Bits 14 and 13 could designate register instructions; for example, 14 could be set to 1 for register reference, and bit 13 could be set to 1 for register-register. Bit 14 = bit 13 = 0 would then be reserved for input/output instructions. The register field, bits 12 through 9, shows the register for the operation.

We still have several bits left to name the operation. Usually these bits are grouped into several subfields for subinstructions, called *microinstructions* or *microprogrammed instructions,* that are executed in order from left to right. For example, one micro-operation might be to complement the accumulator. Another might be to increment the accumulator, that is, add 1 to the accumulator. Placing the operation codes for these two micro-operations in the fields for OP CODE 1 and OP CODE 2, respectively, causes complementing the accumulator followed by incrementing the accumulator. (The accumulator is the register designated by the register field.) Often these subfields for micro-operations are just 1 bit long.

Register-register instructions perform operations on two registers. They cannot be used on single-accumulator computers such as the PDP-8. Typical operations include:

1. Comparing the contents of two registers;
2. Moving contents from one register to another;
3. Shifting or rotating the contents of a register with a carry bit.

A typical format for register-register instructions is:

CLASS CODE	OP CODE	SOURCE	DESTINATION
15 13	12 8	7 4	3 0

The class code field, as part of the operation code field, shows the class of instruction as register-register. The operation code field names the operation to be performed. There are two register fields—the first to name the source and the second to name the destination. Arithmetic or other binary operations are performed by, for example, adding the source to the destination and storing the result in the destination.

You may have noticed that we have more bits available in register instructions than we had in memory reference instructions. In the example formats above, we were able to specify the register fields as 4 bits, thus allowing for 16 registers. We would have trouble finding available bits for a 4-bit register field in a 16-bit memory reference instruction. We could also allocate 5 bits as an operation code to designate 32 possible operations although we might have difficulty defining 32 operations. One problem of computer systems design is allocating the bits carefully to allow best use of the resources of the computer. In general, it is easier to design register and input/output instructions than memory reference instructions. The main problem with memory reference instructions is the large number of bits needed for the displacement.

Register Instructions of the PDP-8   Since the PDP-8 is a single-accumulator machine, it has only register reference instructions; it does not have register-register instructions except for operations dealing with the carry or link bit. It has three groups of microinstructions. Group 1 microinstructions perform primarily circular shifts (rotations) and operations involving the carry bit, called a *link* bit in the PDP-8. Group 2 microinstructions are primarily skip instructions that permit testing the link bit or the accumulator and skipping on certain outcomes. Group 3 microinstructions transfer data between the accumulator and the multiplier/quotient register used for multiplication. Table 7.2 shows the format of these three groups of microinstructions. The bits shown as 1 or 0 designate the type of instruction. Fields containing mnemonics are used only for the operation designated by the mnemonic; the operation is performed if the bit is 1 and not performed if the bit is 0. Only certain combinations of these microprogrammed instructions are allowed.

TABLE 7.2

PDP-8 REGISTER REFERENCE INSTRUCTIONS

Group 1 Microinstructions

1	1	1	0	CLA	CLL	CMA	CML	RAR	RAL	BSW	IAC
0	1	2	3	4	5	6	7	8	9	10	11

Group 2 Microinstructions

1	1	1	1	CLA	SMA	SZA	SNL	RSS	OSR	HLT	0
0	1	2	3	4	5	6	7	8	9	10	11

Group 3 Microinstructions

1	1	1	1	CLA	MQA	0	MQL	0	0	0	1
0	1	2	3	4	5	6	7	8	9	10	11

Mnemonics

CLA = CLear Accumulator
CLL = CLear Link
CMA = CoMplement Accumulator
CML = CoMplement Link
RAR = Rotate Accumulator Right
RAL = Rotate Accumulator Left
BSW = Byte SWap
IAC = Increment ACcumulator

SMA = Skip on Minus Accumulator
SZA = Skip on Zero Accumulator
SNL = Skip on Nonzero Link
RSS = Reverse Skip Sense
OSR = Or with Switch Register
HLT = HaLT
MQA = Multiplier Quotient into Accumulator
MQL = Multiplier Quotient Load

7.3.3 Input/Output Instructions

Input/output instructions transfer information between the computer and the outside world. Most computer systems include several peripheral devices to interface the computer with external devices. Input/output instructions must:

1. Show the peripheral device involved in the transfer.
2. Give the control information needed for the transfer.

The format for a typical input/output instruction is:

CLASS CODE	REGISTER	OP CODE	DEVICE
15 13	12 9	8 6	5 0

The class code shows that the instruction is an input/output instruction. The register designation states which register is involved in the transfer of information; most transfers are between a register and an external device. Some computers also have *direct memory access* (DMA) that allows direct transfers between memory and the outside world. The operation code shows the operation to be performed. Typical operations are:

1. Transferring the contents of a register to a device;
2. Transferring the contents of a device to a register;
3. Setting or clearing an I/O flag to control or check the operation of an external device;
4. Testing the status of a device.

We will discuss the reasons for some of these operations in chapter 10. The last field shows the device involved in the transfer.

Examples of PDP-8 Input/Output Instructions The input/output instruction of the PDP-8 has the following format:

1 1 0	DEVICE	OP CODE
0 2	3 8	9 11

The first 3 bits are the class code, 110, identifying the instruction as an input/output instruction. Bits 3 − 8 contain a device selection code. These 6 bits allow selection among 64 different input/output devices. The device selection code is transmitted to all input/output devices whenever the input/output instruction occurs. Device selectors within the input/output devices monitor the device codes. Whenever a device recognizes the device selection code as its own code, it accepts the instruction and performs the operation shown by the last 3 bits. The operation code of bits 9 – 11 permits eight different input/output operations.

7.4   Execution of Instructions

Now that we have looked at instruction types, we will consider execution and timing of instructions. The basic unit of time for most computers is called a *memory cycle*. A memory cycle for current minicomputers is about 1 microsecond. High-speed computers have faster memory cycles of the order of 100 nanoseconds. During a memory cycle, the computer may be in one of three states—FETCH, DEFER, or EXECUTE.

Much of the power of stored program computers results from their ability to store instructions along with data. In executing a program, the computer must be able to treat instructions differently from data. The three different states of computer action let the computer decode instructions and perform operations on data, thus distinguishing between instructions and data.

The FETCH state is used to retrieve an instruction from memory. The computer is in the FETCH state whenever an instruction was executed in the previous memory cycle. During a FETCH state, the central processing unit reads an instruction from the memory location whose address is in the program counter. It then decodes the instruction. If the instruction is not a memory reference instruction (MRI), it may be executed in the FETCH state. Direct address jump instructions (JUMP) may also be executed in the FETCH state. After the FETCH state has been completed, instructions using indirect addressing (that is, instructions whose D/I bit is 1) enter the DEFER state; memory reference instructions with direct addressing (except JUMP) enter the EXECUTE state.

Each state is divided into several segments called *time slices*. Different activities occur during each time slice. The FETCH state is divided into four time slices whose activities are roughly as follows:

1. Transfer the contents of the program counter into the memory address register so that the memory address register is ready to fetch the instruction.
2. Increment the contents of the program counter; that is, advance the program counter by 1.

3. Retrieve the instruction to be executed from the memory location shown by the memory address register. Decode the instruction. Restore the instruction in memory.
4. Perform the operation if JUMP direct or non-MRI instruction. Send the instruction to DEFER if indirect or to EXECUTE if direct MRI other than JUMP.

The DEFER state decodes indirect memory references. The processor enters a DEFER state only when an indirectly addressed instruction was read from memory in the previous memory cycle. During the DEFER state the processor computes the effective address from the contents of the memory location of the original instruction and retrieves the instruction located there. If the D/I bit of the contents is 1, the processor repeats the DEFER state in the next memory cycle. If the original instruction retrieved is a JUMP indirect, the instruction is executed in the DEFER state. Once the effective address is computed, the instruction enters the EXECUTE state.

Execution of memory reference instruction (except JUMP) is always completed in an EXECUTE state. An instruction enters the EXECUTE state from the FETCH state if it has a direct address. An instruction with an indirect address enters the EXECUTE state from the DEFER state after the indirect address has been decoded and the final instruction retrieved. After the EXECUTE state, the processor returns to a FETCH state to retrieve the next instruction.

Figure 7.3 shows the timing of execution of instructions.

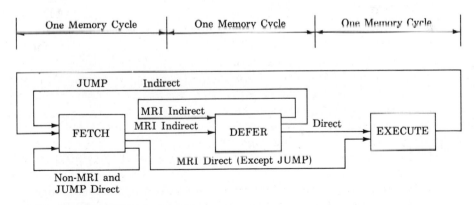

MRI = Memory Reference Instruction
JUMP = JUMP Instruction

Fig. 7.3 Timing of instructions

Some computers provide other states besides the three that we have mentioned. A direct memory access or DMA state is used to transfer data directly between memory and external devices. A programmed DMA state usually involves a maneuver called *cycle stealing,* in which the DMA transfer uses memory cycles that would otherwise be used by one of the other states. An *interrupt* state occurs in the processing of data from devices requesting service through interrupts. An interrupt state usually does not use any memory cycles. We will discuss these two procedures in chapter 10.

Although we have spoken of memory cycles as though they were always the same length, the lengths of memory cycles of most computers vary somewhat. Typically for current minicomputers a basic memory cycle is about 1 microsecond and a longer memory cycle, called a *slow memory cycle,* is about 1.2 microseconds.

7.5   Machine Language Programming

Machine language programming resembles programming at any other level except that it requires closer attention to housekeeping details like addresses of instructions and data. The procedure for machine language programming is:

1. Develop an algorithm or flowchart to describe the structure of the computation.
2. Select the instructions from the set available for the computer that we will use.
3. Decide where the data and instructions are to be located in memory.
4. Assign a memory location for each instruction and each piece of data. If our program generates additional data as it proceeds, we must assign memory locations for that data also.
5. Write the program.

In this section, we will consider a few simple programs and techniques used in machine language programming. We will write these programs in the machine language of the PDP-8, but similar steps are needed for programming in any machine language. Only the instructions differ. Our objective is not to perfect programming skills but simply to introduce the procedures of machine language program-

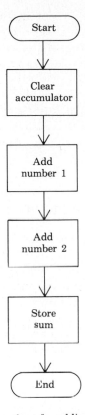

Fig. 7.4   Flowchart for adding two numbers

ming. Programming is best learned by writing and running programs
on a computer.

Example 7.5—Adding Two Numbers

Our first example is a program that adds two numbers. A flowchart
for this simple program is given as figure 7.4. The steps in this program
are simple. We must clear the accumulator to remove any number
that may have been left there, add the two numbers, store the sum,
and halt. All instructions and data are expressed as octal numbers.
A major advantage of octal numbers is that they are easier to remember than binary numbers. Conversion between octal and
binary numbers is shown as table 7.3. We need the following instructions:

Octal instruction	Mnemonic instruction	Explanation
7200	CLA	/CLear Accumulator to zero
10XY	TAD XY	/Twos complement ADdition of the number in memory location *XY* to the accumulator
30WZ	DCA WZ	/Deposit the Contents of the Accumulator in memory location *WZ* and clear the accumulator to zero
7402	HLT	/HaLT

To construct the actual instructions for a program, we must replace symbolic addresses, such as *XY* and *WZ*, by octal addresses. Determining the addresses of data is a major step in machine language programming.

We will arbitrarily start the program in octal memory location 010. We will store the two numbers to be added in memory locations 050 and 051 and store the sum in memory location 052. The program for adding the two numbers is shown in table 7.4.

Example 7.6—Adding Two Numbers and Checking for Overflow

In our first simple program we did not consider the possibility that the sum of the two numbers could be larger in magnitude than the maximum magnitude that the computer can handle. The 12-bit accumulator can only retain numbers less than or equal to $2^{12} - 1 = 4095$ in decimal or 7777 in octal. Numbers greater than 4095 will overflow and set the link bit to 1. The link is a 1-bit register just to the left of the accumulator; it is called a *carry register* on some computers. When overflow has occurred, the sum is out of range. A flowchart for a program that adds two numbers and checks for

TABLE 7.3

CONVERSION BETWEEN BINARY AND OCTAL NUMBERS

Binary	Octal	Binary	Octal
000	0	100	4
001	1	101	5
010	2	110	6
011	3	111	7

overflow is given as figure 7.5. The flowchart is basically the same as before except that we check for overflow. If overflow occurs, we set the accumulator to 7777 (all 1s in binary) and halt. Otherwise we store the sum as before. We need a few more instructions.

Octal instruction	Mnemonic instruction	Explanation
7300	CLA CLL	/CLear Accumulator and Link
7420	SNL	/Skip the next instruction if Non-zero Link
50XY	JMP XY	/JuMP to memory location XY
7240	CLA CMA	/CLear Accumulator and CoMplement Accumulator (or set the accumulator to 7777)

Again we must replace symbolic addresses, such as XY, by the actual memory locations in which the data will be stored.

Two of these instructions result from combining microinstructions. CLA CLL results from combining 7200 for CLA with 7100 for CLL. Note that the three rightmost digits of the octal numbers are added. Similarly, CLA CMA combines 7200 for CLA with 7040 for CMA. Here it is evident that the 200 comes from the CLA instruction, while the 40 comes from the CMA instruction. As noted in paragraph 7.3.2, only certain combinations of microinstructions are allowed. The rules for combining microinstructions are complicated and are discussed in programming manuals for the PDP-8.

TABLE 7.4

MACHINE LANGUAGE PROGRAM FOR ADDING TWO NUMBERS

Address	Octal instruction	Mnemonic instruction	Explanation
010	7200	CLA	/CLear Accumulator
011	1050	TAD 50	/ADd number 1
012	1051	TAD 51	/ADd number 2
013	3052	DCA 52	/Store sum and Clear Accumulator
014	7402	HLT	/HaLT
050	1020		/Number 1, 1020 octal
051	0471		/Number 2, 0471 octal
052	0000		/Sum will be stored here

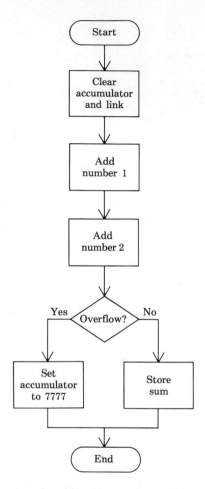

Fig. 7.5 Flowchart for adding two numbers with test for overflow

The program for adding two numbers and checking for overflow is shown in table 7.5. The program checks only for overflow into the link bit. Since numbers are represented in the PDP-8 in twos complement form, the link bit is 1 only when the sum of two negative numbers has a magnitude at least equal to 2^{11}. This program will not detect overflow that occurs when adding two positive numbers because two positive numbers that sum to 2^{11} or more look like a negative number to the computer. For example, consider adding $+2^{10}$ and $+2^{10}$. The binary representation of $+2^{10}$ is 010000000000. The sum of 010000000000 and 010000000000 is 100000000000, the

TABLE 7.5

MACHINE LANGUAGE PROGRAM FOR ADDING
TWO NUMBERS AND TESTING FOR OVERFLOW

Address	Octal instruction	Mnemonic instruction	Explanation
010	7300	CLA CLL	/CLear Accumulator and Link
011	1050	TAD 50	/ADd number 1
012	1051	TAD 51	/ADd number 2
013	7420	SNL	/Skip next instruction if link is 1 (Nonzero Link) (overflow)
014	5017	JMP 17	/JuMP to 17
015	7240	CLA CMA	/CLear and CoMplement Accumulator, i.e., set to 7777 to show overflow
016	7402	HLT	/HaLT
017	3052	DCA 52	/Store sum
020	7402	HLT	/HaLT
050	1020		/Number 1, 1020 Octal
051	0471		/Number 2, 0471 Octal
052	0000		/Sum will be stored here

12-bit twos complement representation of negative 2^{11}. Adding two larger positive numbers results in a negative sum. (Consider the examples of chapter 6.) To detect overflow during addition of positive numbers we could check the sign bit of the numbers. (See problem 7.17.)

7.6 Programming Techniques

If we wish to extend the program for adding two numbers to adding N numbers, we would soon tire of repeating instructions. We need programming techniques that will readily allow us to reuse instructions. Useful techniques are counters, pointers, loops, and subroutines.

7.6.1 Counters

Counters are used to count the number of times a calculation is done. We can construct a counter by storing $-N$ in some memory location; we will select memory location 50 for the counter in our example. After we complete each sequence of instructions that we want to count, we increment the counter by 1 with an ISZ instruction. The ISZ or Increment and Skip if Zero instruction is a common branching instruction. It increments (adds 1) to the contents of the memory location and then skips the next instruction if and only if the incremented contents are zero. Thus we begin with $-N$ in the counter, add 1 each time we perform the calculation, and skip the next instruction when the contents of the counter become zero. The instruction following the ISZ instruction is usually a JUMP instruction that causes the computer to repeat the calculation if the contents of the counter are not zero. Example 7.7, Multiplication of Two Numbers, illustrates use of the counter. The example is simplified and ignores problems of overflow.

Example 7.7—Multiplication of Two Numbers

Multiplication can be performed by repeated addition. The two numbers to be multiplied, A and B, are stored in locations 51 and 52, respectively. B is to be added to itself A times. The counter is initialized by forming the twos complement of A with a CIA or Complement and Increment the Accumulator instruction. Then B is added to the contents of the accumulator and the counter is incremented. The addition of B is repeated until the contents of the counter become zero, at which time operation halts. The program is shown in table 7.6.

TABLE 7.6

MACHINE LANGUAGE PROGRAM FOR MULTIPLYING
TWO NUMBERS, A AND B

Address	Octal instruction	Mnemonic instruction	Explanation
020	7300	CLA CLL	/CLear Accumulator and Link
021	1051	TAD 51	/ADd A
022	7041	CIA	/Complement and Increment the Accumulator
023	3050	DCA 50	/Store in counter
024	1052	TAD 52	/ADd B
025	2050	ISZ 50	/Increment counter contents and Skip next instruction if Zero
026	5024	JMP 24	/JuMP to 24 to repeat addition
027	7402	HLT	/HaLT; multiplication is complete; product is in accumulator
050	0000		/Counter will be here
051	0012		/A, 12 octal
052	0007		/B, 7 octal

7.6.2 Pointers

A *pointer* points to a memory location. Figure 7.6 shows the organization of memory for a pointer. The pointer is stored in memory location P. Somewhere else in memory is stored a series of data that we want to process. The pointer points to each data term as we process it. It points to the term by holding as its contents the address of the memory location of the current data term. We can increment the pointer by an ISZ instruction when we have finished processing one data term so that the pointer will point to the next data term.

Let us suppose that we wish to add a series of N numbers stored in memory locations 100 through $100 + N - 1$. (Recall that the numbers of all memory locations are octal and hence N is octal.) We arbitrarily assign memory location 53 to the pointer. We use indirect addressing to obtain the address of each desired data term. The instruction

TAD I 53

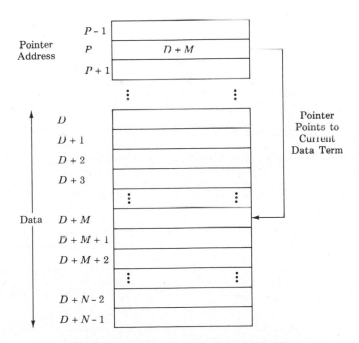

Fig. 7.6 Organization of memory for pointer

tells the computer to go to memory location 53 (the address of the pointer), retrieve the number contained there as address of the current data term, go to that address, and add its contents to the contents of the accumulator.

We next use the instruction

$$ISZ\ 53$$

to move the pointer to the next memory location. The ISZ 53 instruction increases the address of the pointer by one and thus moves the pointer to point to the next memory location. The ISZ instruction is often used as it is here to increment a memory word in situations where it is assumed the skip will never occur.

7.6.3 Loops

In building a program to add N numbers we repeat the operations of adding the numbers shown by the pointer and incrementing the pointer several times. For these repeated instructions we use a program *loop* with the general form shown in figure 7.7. We used a loop with a counter but no pointer in example 7.7.

Before we enter the loop, we must initialize all pointers and counters. We then enter the loop, which has three parts:

1. Perform all calculations;
2. Increment all pointers and counters;
3. Check the counters to see if all calculations are complete.

If all calculations have been finished, we exit to the rest of the program. If not, we go back to step 1 of the loop.

Example 7.8—Adding N Numbers

We now have all the techniques we need to write a program to add N numbers. For simplicity we will not check for overflow. The flow-chart of the program is shown in figure 7.8. The program has a new feature. Besides storing the sum in memory location 40, we will also restore it to the accumulator. The DCA command that we use to store the sum also clears the accumulator. If we wish to see the sum in the accumulator, we must use a TAD command to return the sum to the accumulator. The program is shown in table 7.7. A slightly shorter program can be written by placing the starting address in the pointer and $- N$ in the counter directly as data rather than having the program do those operations.

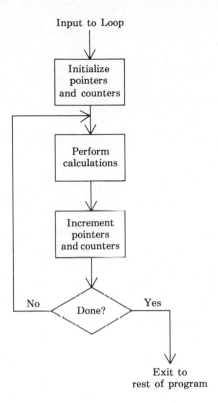

Fig. 7.7 Loop structure

7.6.4 Subroutines

Often we wish to divide a main program into subprograms called *subroutines*. Each subroutine performs a calculation that we want done several times in the program. It is convenient to write each subroutine just once and call for it as needed.

We call for a subroutine with a JuMp to Subroutine instruction,

$$JMS \ XYZ$$

where *XYZ* is the octal address of the subroutine. We must be able to return to the main program. Hence we use the first memory location of the subroutine to store the address of the instruction in the main program to which we wish to return. We want to return to the instruction immediately after the JMS instruction. We accomplish this by storing the contents of the program counter in the

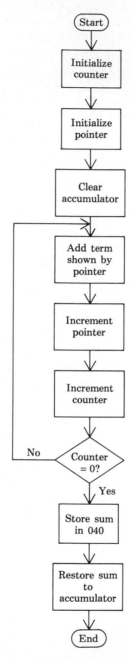

Fig. 7.8 Flowchart for adding N numbers

first memory location of the subroutine; the JMS instruction does this automatically. Since the FETCH cycle is finished before the JMS instruction is executed, the program counter has already been incremented. Hence the program counter contains the address of the instruction in the main program that follows the JMS instruction. Thus storing the contents of the program counter in the first memory location of the subroutine gives us the desired return address. The JMS instruction has two functions: (1) it transfers control to the subroutine, and (2) it stores the return address in the first location of the subroutine.

The instructions of the subroutine begin in the second memory location of the subroutine and proceed in order until the subroutine computations are complete. We then need to return to the main program. We accomplish this by a jump indirect instruction, JMP

TABLE 7.7

ADDITION OF N NUMBERS

Address	Octal instruction	Mnemonic instruction	Explanation
020	7200	CLA	/Clear Accumulator
021	1050	TAD 50	/Get − N (octal)
022	3051	DCA 51	/Initialize counter at − N
023	1052	TAD 52	/Get address of number 1
024	3053	DCA 53	/Set pointer to address of number 1
025	1453	TAD I 53	/Add term shown by pointer
026	2053	ISZ 53	/Increment pointer
027	2051	ISZ 51	/Increment counter and Skip next instruction if counter is Zero
030	5025	JMP 25	/Return to addition statement
031	3040	DCA 40	/Store sum in 40, clear accumulator
032	1040	TAD 40	/Show sum in accumulator
033	7402	HLT	/HaLT
⋮			
040	0000		/Sum will be stored here
⋮			
050	7770		/ − N = − 10 octal = 7770
051	0000		/Counter will be here
052	100		/Starting address of data
053	0000		/Pointer will be here
⋮			
100	0014		/Number 1 = 14 octal
⋮			
100 + N − 1	0417		/Number 10 octal = 0417 octal

I, to the memory location pointed to by the first memory location of the subroutine. This returns control to the desired location, the instruction following the JMS instruction.

For example, consider a simple subroutine that forms the twos complement of the contents of the accumulator. This calculation is so simple that in practice we might not bother with a subroutine. However, it illustrates the procedures of calling a subroutine and returning to the main program. This subroutine can be used in computing magnitudes. Let us suppose that 54 is the starting address of the subroutine and that 20 is the address of the JMS instruction.

The structure of the program using this subroutine is shown in table 7.8. When the instruction is fetched from memory location 20, the control unit places the incremented contents of the program counter (021) in memory location 54. The processor then executes the instructions of the subroutine. When memory location 57 is reached, we jump indirect using the address stored at the start of the subroutine, thus back to memory location 021. We then proceed with the second part of the main program.

If we wanted to call the subroutine from another section of the main program, we could do so. We would again need a JMS 54 command that would store the address of the next instruction in the main program in memory location 54. After finishing the calcula-

TABLE 7.8

STRUCTURE OF PROGRAM FOR CALLING SUBROUTINE
TO COMPUTE TWOS COMPLEMENT

Address	Octal instruction	Mnemonic instruction	Explanation
First part of main program			
020	4054	JMS 54	/JuMp to Subroutine, store 021 in 54
021			/Begin rest of main program
Second part of main program			
Subroutine			
054			/First location of subroutine, used to store return address
055	7040	CMA	/CoMplement Accumulator
056	7001	IAC	/Increment ACcumulator
057	5454	JMP I 54	/JuMP indirect to 54, return to address stored in 54, namely, 21

tions of the subroutine, we would jump back to the main program again.

The method of saving the return address for a subroutine by storing it in the subroutine is used mostly in simple, small computers. Saving the return address in the first location of the subroutine wastes space since every subroutine must have a reserved location for its return address. This scheme could not be used in a *multiprogramming* environment, in which many programs share the computer at one time. Each user of a multiprogrammed computer needs to save his own return address.

Two other methods can be used to save the return address for a subroutine on more complex computers. One method is to save the return address for the subroutine in a register. The second is to save the return address in a pushdown stack.

The programs and programming concepts discussed in this section merely introduce machine language programming. We have not dealt with input/output routines or with processing of nonnumerical data. We can use all these notions in developing assembly language programming that is similar to machine language programming but somewhat easier since we will no longer have to keep track of the addresses of all data and instructions.

7.7 Instruction Sets of Computers

As a bridge to the next chapter on assembly language programming and as a summary of the instruction types we have considered in this chapter, we will examine the instruction sets of various computers. Later in chapter 11 we will study the systems-level organization of these same computers and see the use of their instruction sets. Some of the computers we will study are 10 years old; others are relatively new. They are intended to represent a wide range of instruction types. New computers, of course, appear every year with features that obsolete many features of current machines. Nonetheless we can learn much from studying any computer since the basic principles of machine organization and instructions change much more slowly. The computers that we will examine here are the Intel 4004/4040, the Hewlett-Packard 2116, the Digital Equipment PDP-11, and the IBM 370.

4004/4040 The 4004 and the 4040 are 4-bit microprocessors. The 4004 was one of the earliest microprocessors; the 4040 is an updated version of the 4004 with a more powerful instruction set that includes all the instructions of the 4004. The basic registers of the 4004/4040 are 4-bit registers with transfers occurring as byte (4-bit) serial, bit parallel; that is, all 4 bits of a byte are transferred in parallel, but words are transferred in sequence. There are eight 4-bit registers that may be used as four 8-bit registers.

As our discussion of word length showed earlier, a 4-bit word is too short to contain both an operation code and an address of any complexity. The 4004/4040 solves this problem by working with 8-bit and 16-bit instructions composed of 2 and 4 bytes, respectively. A word is considered to be 8 bits, so the instructions are either one-word or two-word instructions. These instruction lengths allow instructions similar to those of minicomputers. However, the handling of transfers between the accumulator and memory is more complicated. The microprocessor has two types of memory—one similar to the memory of most computers called RAM in microprocessors, and the other whose contents can be read but not changed, called ROM. We will consider these memory types in chapter 9. Another difference is that many memory and input/output transfers are either made through special openings into memory, called *ports,* or are made with the use of special status characters. We will not consider these features.

Aside from these differences in memory reference and input/output instructions, most 4004/4040 instructions are fairly standard. There is a powerful set of register reference instructions, including both register-register instructions and register instructions, that deal with the accumulator. Arithmetic operations can be done between any register and the accumulator with the result stored in the accumulator. The adder and other arithmetic circuits are only 4 bits, so several steps are needed to add two 8-bit words. Indirect register addressing and incrementing of register contents are available. A stack is available with four levels for the 4004 and eight levels for the 4040, including the program counter. We will discuss these instructions further in chapter 11.

HP 2116 The HP 2116 is an early minicomputer designed at about the same time as the PDP-8. It resembles the PDP-8 but has two registers instead of one and a 16-bit word instead of a 12-bit word. The longer word length allows for more operation codes and larger pages. A page on the HP 2116 is 1024 or 1K words; the larger page simplifies programming because longer programs can be written on one page. The computer may have up to 32 pages for 32K 16-bit words of storage.

The instructions of the HP 2116 divide nicely into the categories of memory reference, register, and input/output instructions. The memory reference instructions resemble those of the PDP-8. Both paging and indirect addressing are available. The HP 2116 has two classes of register reference instructions—a shift-rotate class and an alter-skip group. Instructions for each type can provide two operations by microinstructions. A single instruction can refer to just one of the two registers; no true register-register operations can be performed. The input/output instructions are a little more complex than those of the PDP-8. Input/output transfers can involve either of the two basic registers. Eight operation codes are available for dealing with 64 devices. A special bit allows holding or clearing the device flag after the instruction is executed.

PDP-11 The PDP-11 is a newer 16-bit minicomputer that has eight registers in its basic version. The registers can be used so flexibly that all operations can be specified with only one class of instructions. The computer deals with memory in the same way that it deals with external devices; separate classes of memory reference and input/output instructions are not needed. In chapter 11 we will consider how the organization of the PDP-11 permits this flexibility.

The PDP-11 has indirect, index register, immediate, absolute, and relative addressing. It also has autoincrement and autodecrement features associated with its registers. *Autoincrement* means that the register points to data stored in sequence and is automatically incremented to give the successive addresses of additional data. *Autodecrement* is similar except that the register contents are automatically decremented to give successive addresses.

Most PDP-11 instructions are either one-address, two-address, or branching instructions. Three bits of the instruction are needed to specify which of eight registers is involved. Another 3 bits, called mode bits, show the type of addressing. Thus 6 bits are needed for the address field. One-address instructions need one 6-bit address field, thus leaving 10 bits for the operation code. Two-address instructions name two addresses—one for the source and one for the destination; two 6-bit address fields are required, leaving only 4 bits for the operation code. The branch instructions have a slightly different format divided equally into an 8-bit operation code and an 8-bit address field. The PDP-11 also has a few zero-address instructions.

IBM 370 The IBM 370 is a large and powerful family of computers. Its basic word length is 32 bits divided into four 8-bit bytes that can be addressed individually. Through complicated memory management techniques that we will discuss in chapter 9, its memory can be quite large, measured in millions of bytes. The maximum address length allowed within the computer is 24 bits.

The IBM 370 has 16 general-purpose registers (thus requiring 4 bits to name a general-purpose register) and eight registers reserved for floating-point arithmetic operations. The index register techniques of the 370 are complex; double indexing is allowed, that is, an address can be modified by the contents of two index registers. The 370 does not have indirect addressing; the complex indexing schemes allow ample flexibility of addressing.

The major arithmetic and logical processing instructions are divided into two groups—RX instructions and RR instructions. RX instructions (register-indexed-storage) are 32 bits (4 bytes) and specify a register, a memory location, and an operation code. RR instructions (register-to-register) take only 16 bits (2 bytes) and specify two registers and an operation code. The operation code field for both types of instructions is 8 bits. The 370 has several other instruction formats requiring from 32 to 48 bits; their descriptions can be found in the references.

7.8 Summary

Machine language instructions are n-bit binary numbers that have two basic fields—an operation code field to name the operation to be performed and an address field to show the operands. Instructions may be coded with four, three, two, one, or zero addresses.

Stacks operate with zero-address instructions. Stacks manipulate data on a last-in-first-out basis. The addresses of the operands are implicit in the stack operation since only numbers at the top of the stack can be manipulated.

Computers usually have three classes of instructions—memory reference instructions, register instructions, and input/output instructions. The main problem of memory reference instructions is addressing 2^n memory locations without using n bits for the address. Five addressing techniques are commonly used—direct addressing, indirect addressing, paging, register addressing, and immediate addressing. The first two techniques are usually handled by a direct/indirect bit that allows the computer to address the location named by the displacement, or the location referred to by the contents of the location named by the displacement. A paging bit is often used to allow addressing either the base page or the current page. Register addressing is a flexible technique that involves adding the contents of one or more registers to the displacement to calculate the effective address. Register and input/output instructions are less complex than memory reference instructions because they have ample bits available for designating registers or peripheral devices and operation codes. We looked at the instruction sets of five computers ranging from the simple 4004/4040 microprocessor to the IBM 370.

Execution of one instruction may require three or more memory cycles. All instructions are first processed in the FETCH state. Register, input/output, and jump direct instructions can be executed in the FETCH cycle. Indirect instructions must go through one or more DEFER cycles. Memory reference instructions (except for jumps) are executed in an EXECUTE cycle.

Machine language programming is much like programming in a high-level language except that more attention needs to be paid to housekeeping details like locations of instructions and data. Use of pointers, counters, loops, and subroutines can simplify coding of repeated calculations.

Concepts

absolute addressing
address
autodecrement
autoincrement
base page
base register
benchmark
class code
cycle stealing
DEFER state
direct addressing
displacement
DMA
effective address
EXECUTE state
FETCH state
field
immediate addressing
index register
indirect addressing
input/output instruction

instruction register
interrupt
memory address register
memory field
memory reference instruction
microinstructions
mnemonic
mode
octal
operand
operation code
paging
program counter
pushdown stack
register addressing
register reference instruction
register-register instruction
relative addressing
stored-program computer
time slices

7.9 References

When writing programs to be run on a particular computer, there is no substitute for programming manuals for that computer. Programming manuals for all the computers discussed in this chapter can be obtained from the computer manufacturers and are frequently updated. General information on machine language programming can be found in Booth (1971), Gear (1974), and Stone and Sieworek (1975). Soucek (1972) and Korn (1973) provide information on minicomputers.

7.10 Problems

7.1 Write programs using the instructions given in this chapter to calculate

$$Y = AB + CD + E(F + G)$$

Use three-address, two-address, one-address, and zero-address instructions. Compare the number of instructions required. (7.2)

7.2 Repeat problem 7.1 for the calculation of

$$Y = A + B(CD + EF - G/H) \tag{7.3}$$

7.3 Repeat problem 7.1 for the calculation of

$$Y = A(B + C(D + E/F)) \tag{7.2}$$

7.4 Compare the MOVE instruction for two addresses with the LOAD and STORE instructions for one address. Assume all data are initially in memory and that the result of a calculation must be stored in memory. What is the relation between the number of MOVE instructions and the number of LOAD and STORE instructions required for any general calculation? (7.2)

7.5 Write a more efficient program than the one given in this chapter to calculate $Y = A + B(CD/E - F)$ using the instruction set of the stack discussed in section 7.3. You should use either fewer instructions or fewer memory locations or both. (7.2)

7.6 Instructions for the stack of section 7.2 operated on data within the stack. For example, the ADS instruction added the two top numbers of the stack. Frequently, stack instructions for binary operations involve one operand at the top of the stack and another operand as external data.

a. Devise a set of instructions for a stack with the property that no instruction manipulates any piece of data below the top of the stack (except to push or pop).

b. Using your set of instructions, write a program to calculate

$$Y = A + B(CD/E - F) \qquad (7.2)$$

7.7 You are to calculate the effective addresses of the following instructions. The left bit of the instruction is a D/I bit. The remaining numbers are octal. The displacement of the instruction is the right two octal numbers. No paging or register addressing is involved. The table below gives the contents of selected memory locations in octal. Assume the computer has 2^{16} memory locations. Assume seven levels of indirect addressing. Calculate the effective addresses of the following instructions:

a. 000000
b. 100000
c. 100010
d. 000005 $\qquad (7.3)$

Table of Contents of Memory Locations

Location	Contents	Location	Contents
00	100002	05	100001
01	046710	06	063215
02	054304	07	077710
03	100000	10	100005
04	102543		

7.8 Assume an instruction has the following format:

D/I	OP CODE	I_1 I_2	Z/C	DISPLACEMENT
11	10	9 8 7	6	5 0

Register contents in octal are:

Program counter	0340
Register I_1	1111
Register I_2	0256

Assume there are 2^{12} memory locations, comprising 2^6 pages of 2^6 words. Assume seven levels of indirect addressing. Calculate the effective address of the following octal instructions, assuming index register addressing in which the contents of index registers named are added to the displacement:

a. 1046
b. 2433
c. 3615
d. 1111

(7.3)

7.9 The format for the PDP-8 memory reference instructions is:

OP CODE	D/I	Z/C	DISPLACEMENT

0   2   3   4   5   11

The contents of the program counter and selected memory locations in octal are: Program counter 1234

Location	Contents	Location	Contents
0020	0123	0120	1357
0021	1230	0121	0246
0022	2301	0122	3571
0023	3012	0123	2460
0024	4567	0124	5713

Determine the effective addresses of the following instructions in octal (Assume seven levels of indirect addressing.): (a) 4420; (b) 2224; (c) 1022; (d) 3521; (e) 5323.

(7.3)

7.10 A computer has 8-bit instructions with the format shown below.

OP CODE	D/I	DISPLACEMENT

0   3   4   5   7

Only one level of indirect addressing is allowed. The contents of several memory locations are as follows:

Location	Contents	Location	Contents
0 0 0	00000001	1 0 0	10100100
0 0 1	01011110	1 0 1	00010101
0 1 0	10011101	1 1 0	00000100
0 1 1	01110100	1 1 1	10100000

Calculate the effective address of the following instructions: (a) 11010111; (b) 11011111; (c) 11011110; (d) 11010010.

(7.3)

7.11 Assume an instruction has the following format:

OP CODE	I_1	I_2	Z/C	D/I	DISPLACEMENT
15 12	11	10	9	8 7	0

Register contents are (rightmost five digits in octal):

Register I_1	002543
Register I_2	063215
Program counter	004350

In register addressing the contents of the register named are added to the displacement. Assume there are 2^{16} memory locations comprising 2^8 pages of 2^8 words. Calculate the effective address of the following octal instructions: (a) 152301; (b) 074013; (c) 161123; (d) 140011.   (7.3)

7.12 Assume an instruction has the following format:

OP	D/I	I_1	Z/C	DISPLACEMENT
0 2	3	4	5 6	11

Register contents in octal are:

Register I_1	2222
Program counter	4444

Index register addressing for this computer means adding the contents of the index register to the displacement. Assume there are 2^{12} memory locations comprising 2^6 pages of 2^6 words each. Determine the effective address, in octal, of each of the following octal instructions: (a) 1225; (b) 3152.   (7.3)

7.13 A computer has 8-bit words and a memory of 256 words. Its instructions have the following format:

D/I	Z/C	OP CODE	DISPLACEMENT
0	1	2 4	5 7

Some of its registers and memory locations contain the following octal numbers:

Accumulator	364
Program counter	014

Locations

000	201	007	015	015	102
001	104	010	317	016	003
002	104	011	124	017	011
003	007	012	010	020	201
004	000	013	005	021	104
005	206	014	012	022	203
006	212				

Determine the effective addresses of the following instructions:
(a) 022; (b) 201; (c) 107; (d) 205; (e) 306.   (7.3)

7.14 Show the number of memory cycles required by each instruction
for the program of table 7.5.   (7.4)

7.15 Show the number of memory cycles required for each instruction
of the program of table 7.4.   (7.4)

7.16 Write a flowchart and a machine language program for calculating the absolute value of a series of numbers stored in locations
100 through $100 + N - 1$. Your program should calculate the
absolute value of each number and store the absolute value in
memory locations 200 through $200 + N - 1$.   (7.4)

7.17 Write a flowchart and a machine language program that will
detect overflow in the addition of any two numbers. Your program should test the sign bit to detect overflow from addition
of two positive numbers.   (7.4)

8 Assembly Language Programming

8.1 OVERVIEW

The last chapter acquainted us with the tediousness of machine language programming. We would like to find a way to program a computer that would keep the efficiency and close association with the logic design of the computer that machine language programming has. Assemblers do just that. They take care of the housekeeping details of looking up binary instruction codes and finding addresses for all instructions and data. Thus assemblers allow us to write programs using the basic machine language instructions of the computer without worrying about the details.

The assembler is a software routine that converts a program written in assembly language into binary code in two passes through the program. The assembler keeps a symbol table to record addresses of symbolic operands and statement labels. The assembler also interprets special instructions that are not translated into binary code.

In this chapter we also briefly discuss several other levels of programming and software programs. We consider loaders that load all other programs into the computer. We briefly discuss high-level languages that are independent of the hardware structure of a particular computer, as well as the translators that convert programs written in high-level languages into machine language. We mention microprogramming (the lowest and most complex programming level) that deals directly with the computer hardware. We mention executives and operating systems that control and coordinate other computer programs.

8.2 ASSEMBLY LANGUAGE

Our introduction to machine language in chapter 7 revealed some of its disadvantages. Programming in machine language can be tedious, primarily because of the following problems:

1. We must express all instructions in octal or hexadecimal code. The numerical form of instructions is hard to remember and using it leads to errors.
2. We must give a numerical address for every instruction and every piece of data in the program.
3. If we need to change the program, such as by adding or deleting an instruction, we must change the addresses on all subsequent instructions. This frequently requires further changes in addresses of data and in references to other instructions.
4. We cannot use parts of programs that we have previously written in a new program without recoding the addresses and instruction references to conform with the new program.

Assembly language programming was developed to solve these problems. It retains the use of instructions that correspond directly to machine operations and retains the efficiency of such programs, but adds the features of mnemonic operation codes and symbolic addresses to simplify programming.

We are already prepared for the use of mnemonic operation codes since, throughout the discussion of machine language programming in chapter 7, we included mnemonic forms of the instructions as well as octal. Machine language programs never used the mnemonic form because only numeric information was presented to the computer. The mnemonic form served only as an aid to our understanding. In assembly language programming, however, we will use only the mnemonic form for instructions. An *assembler* inside the computer will change the instructions from mnemonic form into binary.

We are also prepared to work with symbolic addresses from prior experience with programming in high-level languages such as FORTRAN. The symbolic addresses are names for the addresses of variables or constants that we wish to use in the program.

Our discussion of assembly language programming will use the PDP-8 as a running example, much as we did for machine language programming in chapter 7. The PDP-8 actually has a number of different assembly languages. We will use a composite of the features to show the characteristics of a simple assembly language. We will also point out some of the ways in which this assembly language differs from the assembly languages of other computers. The mnemonic instructions we will use are summarized in appendix C.

8.2.1 Instruction Format

Instructions in assembly language are represented on a single line, called a *statement,* that is divided into four fields: *label, operation code, operand,* and *comments.* The fields are distinguished by their order of appearance in the line and by the separating or delimiting characters that follow or precede the fields. Statements have the general format:

LABEL, OPERATION CODE OPERAND /COMMENT

A statement must contain at least one of these fields and may contain all four. Each field is separated from other fields (or delimited) by a comma, a space, or a slash as shown.

The label field is often empty. If present, the label represents the instruction address. It can be used to refer to the location of that instruction throughout the program. For example, the first instruction in a loop might be given the label, LOOP. At the end of the loop, a JMP LOOP instruction would return the program flow to the first instruction in the loop. Labels cannot be instruction mnemonics or the letter I by itself. They should have no more than six alphanumeric characters and must begin with a letter. Following are examples of legal and illegal labels:

Legal labels	*Illegal labels*	*Error*
NUMBR1	1ITEM	Does not begin with a letter
X0001	NUM 2	Contains a space
ITEM1	I	Single letter I
	NUMBER1	All letters beyond the sixth will be ignored
	CLA	Instruction mnemonic

The operation code field contains the mnemonics for instructions or *pseudo-instructions* that are special instructions for assembly language programs. Instructions with indirect references have the operator followed by a space and then I, e.g., TAD I. Pseudo-instructions are messages to the assembler. They are not translated into machine language code. Two PDP-8 pseudo-instructions are used for beginning and ending the program. The pseudo-instruction

$$*XYZ$$

means the starting address of the program; that is, the location of the first instruction is *XYZ*. The pseudo-instruction

$$\$$$

follows all instructions and data. $ is not a HLT instruction that stops processing after all instructions have been executed; instead it tells the assembler that it has processed all instructions and data. Other assembly languages usually use ORG XYZ to show the starting address and END to show the end of the program.

The operand field contains symbolic addresses or octal addresses for data or instructions referred to by the instruction. An octal number is the actual memory location. A symbolic address is subject to the same coding restrictions as a label. That is, a symbolic address should be a string of no more than six letters or digits, beginning with a letter. It must not be one of the instruction mnemonics or the single letter I. Operands may also be sums or differences of such strings; this will be explained further later.

The comment field contains descriptive remarks that document the program. A comment is separated from the remainder of the statement by a preceding slash (/) and is not operated on by the assembler, which just prints comments as part of the program.

Examples of Instructions

LOOP,	TAD I POINT	/ADD NUMBER SHOWN BY POINTER
	JMP LOOP	/RETURN TO START OF LOOP
	HLT	/HALT
	*100	/STARTING ADDRESS IS 100
	$	/END OF PROGRAM AND DATA
ADD,	TAD XX	/ADD NUMBER STORED IN LOCATION X

8.2.2 Data Format

The statement format just given is for instructions. We also need data statements. The format for data statements is simpler. It is:

LABEL,   DATA   /COMMENT

The label is still a symbolic address for the statement, in this case, the data. The data are usually a one-digit to four-digit octal number.

If the number is negative, the assembler converts the representation of the number to twos complement form.

Examples of Data Statements

SIX,	006	/DECIMAL NUMBER 6
NUM1,	0110	/DECIMAL NUMBER 72
POINT,	100	/ADDRESS OF FIRST DATA TERM

8.2.3 Special Characters

All the characters in any field in our version of PDP-8 assembly language are letters or numbers except for the special characters shown in table 8.1. We restrict use of the special characters to the purposes shown in the table.

8.2.4 Sample Programs

We can now write an assembly language program that will add two numbers and store the sum. This is the assembly language version of the machine language program of table 7.7. The program is shown in table 8.2.

We note that this program looks very much like the corresponding machine language program except that we did not need to worry about addresses other than specifying the starting address. We needed

TABLE 8.1

SPECIAL CHARACTERS

Character	Name	Use
Printing characters		
+	Plus	Combines numbers or symbols
—	Minus	Combines numbers or symbols
,	Comma	Assigns symbolic address
*	Asterisk	Begins assignment of starting address
.	Period	Equals value of current location counter
$	Dollar sign	Ends program
/	Slash	Shows start of comment field
Nonprinting characters		
	Space	Delimits
	Return	Ends statement

TABLE 8.2

ASSEMBLY LANGUAGE PROGRAM FOR
ADDING TWO NUMBERS

	*10	/STARTING ADDRESS IS 10
	CLA	/CLEAR ACCUMULATOR
	TAD NUM1	/ADD NUMBER 1
	TAD NUM2	/ADD NUMBER 2
	DCA SUM	/STORE IN SUM
	HLT	/HALT
NUM1,	1246	/NUMBER 1
NUM2,	0107	/NUMBER 2
SUM,	0000	/RESERVED FOR SUM
	$	

to refer to three items of data before we had defined them. This procedure is troublesome in machine language programs. We usually left blanks after each memory reference instruction while writing the instructions and then filled in the blanks with the correct addresses after we had assigned locations to the data. In assembly language programming, this procedure is easy since we assign symbolic names to the locations of reference. The assembler assigns addresses to the symbolic names. It keeps a *symbol table* in which it records the octal values for all symbolic addresses.

This program was quite simple. We did not need labels for instructions since we did not refer to any instructions. A somewhat more complex program that uses labels with instructions and also a subroutine is shown in table 8.3. This program doubles any number.

In the program to double a number we stated the starting address for the main program and for the subroutine. The return address of the subroutine was stored in the first location of the subroutine, just as it was in machine language programming.

Operands of instructions need not be limited to groups of alphanumeric symbols. Assemblers for powerful computers usually allow fairly complex arithmetic expressions. For our version of PDP-8 assembly language, we are restricted to operands that are either groups of alphanumeric symbols (with the restrictions already noted) or the sum or difference of two such groups. The assembler assigns an address to the expression that is simply the corresponding sum or difference of the addresses assigned to the groups of symbols. Examples are shown in table 8.4. The sums or differences must not include any spaces.

Jump instructions do not need a symbolic operand. Instead they refer to the contents of the *current location counter,* denoted by a

TABLE 8.3

ASSEMBLY LANGUAGE PROGRAM TO DOUBLE A NUMBER

	*200	/START PROGRAM IN 200
	CLA CLL	/CLEAR ACCUMULATOR AND LINK
	TAD N	/BRING N TO THE ACCUMULATOR
	JMS DOUBLE	/JUMP TO SUBROUTINE DOUBLE
	DCA TWON	/STORE TWON
	HLT	/HALT
N,	323	/ANY NUMBER N, EXAMPLE IS 323 OCTAL
TWON,	0000	/TWON WILL BE STORED HERE
	*40	/START SUBROUTINE IN 40
DOUBLE,	0000	/RETURN ADDRESS STORED HERE
	CLL RAL	/ROTATE LEFT, MULTIPLYING BY 2
	SNL	/SKIP IF OVERFLOW OCCURS (I.E., IF LINK = 1)
	JMP I DOUBLE	/NO OVERFLOW, RETURN TO MAIN PROGRAM
	CLA CMA	/OVERFLOW OCCURRED, SHOW 7777
	HLT	/STOP THE COMPUTER
	$	

TABLE 8.4

ASSEMBLED ADDRESSES

Operand	X1	X2	X1+X2	X1−X2
Address	0003	0006	0011	7775

period. This counter is kept by the assembler to show the address being assembled. JMP −3 means jump to the address located three before the current location. JMP .+1 can be a no operation instruction since it instructs the assembler to jump to the address that just follows the address of the instruction.

8.3 A TWO-PASS ASSEMBLER

To better understand assembly language, we will study the assembly process. We will consider *two-pass assemblers,* meaning that the assembler must scan the source program (that is, the program that we have written) twice. The reason the assembler makes two passes is clear from our previous example programs. Consider the following excerpt from the program in table 8.2:

```
                              . . .
                         TAD NUM1
                         TAD NUM2
                         DCA SUM
                              . . .

        NUM1,   1213
        NUM2,   0452
        SUM,    0000
```

The assembler had not assigned memory locations to NUM1, NUM2, and SUM before it encountered the instructions using them as operands. Thus assembly had to be postponed until NUM1, NUM2, and SUM were encountered in the label field. References like these to symbols that are defined later in the program are called *forward references*. One-pass assemblers handle forward references in a single pass. However, we will examine only two-pass assemblers because their division of activities is simpler.

The assembler has several tasks to perform:

1. It must recognize the various fields of a statement so that it can process the statement correctly. Since mnemonics for operations and pseudo-instructions are known, the assembler recognizes labels because they are followed by commas. It recognizes symbolic addresses since they follow operators, and it looks for them to appear in the label field. It does not need to deal with the comment field.

2. It must assign a unique memory location to each instruction and to each datum. The assembler accomplishes this by placing the first instruction in the location specified by the pseudo-instruction *XYZ at the start of the program. Thereafter, it places all instructions and data in sequential locations until it encounters the pseudo-instruction $ that ends the program or another *XYZ pseudo-instruction.

3. It must detect errors and give error messages. We like the assembler to detect as many different types of errors as possible and to give specific error messages. To simplify our discussion of the assembly process, however, we will not consider error detection.

In the first pass the assembler stores, in the symbol table, symbols found in the label field along with the addresses the assembler assigns to them. In the second pass the assembler finds codes for the address symbols in the symbol table and combines them with codes for the instructions to produce the assembled program.

Figure 8.1 shows some details of the assembly process. In the first pass the assembler scans the operation code of the instruction. The first operation code is the pseudo-operation * which sets the origin. The assembler sets the location counter equal to the operand of the * pseudo-instruction. The assembler then proceeds to examine the remaining instructions. Whenever it finds a label, it puts the label in the symbol table and assigns it an address equal to the contents of the current location counter. It then increments the location counter and is ready for the next instruction. When the assembler recognizes the pseudo-operation $, it ends the first pass.

The second pass begins with the assembler inspecting the first instruction. It recognizes the pseudo-operator * and sets the current location counter equal to its operand address. It then proceeds through the rest of the instructions. For each instruction it finds the operation code (that is, the binary code) associated with the instruction mnemonic. It then evaluates the operand address by substituting the address found in the symbol table for the symbolic operand. When it has retrieved the binary code for the instruction and the binary address for the operand, it assembles these codes in the proper positions for the instruction. Finally it sends the binary instruction to the output (or to temporary storage in memory) and increments the location counter. When the assembler recognizes the pseudo-operator $, it ends the assembly.

As an example of the assembly process, let us consider the assembling of the program to double a number (table 8.3). The assembled program is shown in table 8.5. In the first pass the current location

TABLE 8.5

ASSEMBLED PROGRAM TO DOUBLE A NUMBER

Octal location	Binary contents	Comments
200	111011000000	CLA CLL
201	001010000101	TAD N
202	100000100000	JMS DOUBLE
203	011010000110	DCA TWON
204	111100000010	HLT
205	000101010101	N = 341 DECIMAL
206	000000000000	TWON GOES HERE
⋮		
40	000000000000	BEGIN SUBROUTINE
41	111001000100	CLL RAL
42	111100010000	SNL
43	101100100000	JMP I 40
44	111010100000	CLA CMA
45	111100000010	HLT

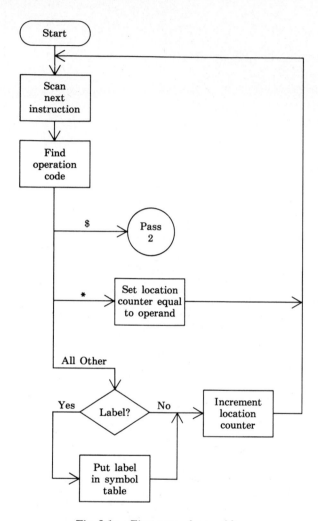

Fig. 8.1a First pass of assembler

counter is first set to 200. The next five instructions—CLA CLL, TAD N, JMS DOUBLE, DCA TWON, and HLT—have no labels and hence the program counter is simply incremented five times. The next two statements have labels N and TWON which are assigned addresses 205 and 206, respectively, and put in the symbol table. The current location counter is incremented after each address assignment. The *40 instruction resets the current location counter to 40. The label DOUBLE is put in the symbol table, and the current location counter is incremented. For the next five statements the

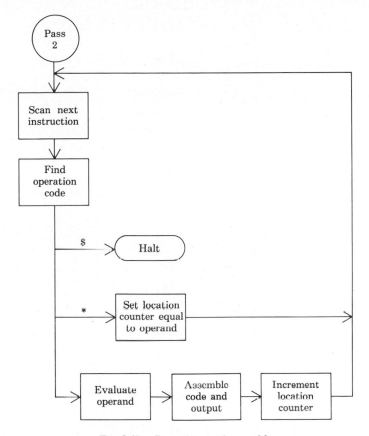

Fig. 8.1b Second pass of assembler

current location counter is merely incremented. Finally, the assembler recognizes the pseudo-operation $ and ends the first pass.

In the second pass the pseudo-instruction *200 again sets the current location counter to 200. Then the assembler begins assembling instructions. It finds the binary code for CLA CLL and assembles the instruction in location 200. It finds the code for TAD and the address of N and assembles the binary code for TAD N and places it in location 201. It proceeds in the same way throughout the main program.

When the assembler recognizes the pseudo-instruction *40, it resets the current location counter to 40. It then recognizes DOUBLE as a label and skips over it to assemble the datum 0000. Next it combines the operation codes for CLL and RAL to assemble that instruction in 41. It proceeds to assemble the rest of the instructions and data in a similar way until it recognizes the pseudo-operation $ and concludes the assembly.

8.4 OTHER PSEUDO-OPERATIONS

Most assembly languages have other pseudo-operations besides the two that we have discussed. We will discuss a few pseudo-operations available on the PDP-8, which require special processing during the assembly. We will not consider the nature of the special processing.

8.4.1 Macros

Frequently in assembly language programming we would like to perform a set of operations at several different points in the program. One way of doing this is to write a subroutine. Another way is to define a *macro-operation* or *macro*. PDP-8 assembly language allows defining macros with the pseudo-operation DEFINE. The format for the macro definition is

DEFINE   NAME   ARG1   ARG2

where NAME is the name of the macro and ARG1 and ARG2 are dummy arguments of the macro. The symbols used for dummy arguments must not have been defined at any point in the program before the macro. We reference the macro by giving its name, a space, and a list of the real arguments we wish to use, separated by spaces. We must list the same number of real arguments as the macro definition has dummy arguments. The assembler will substitute real arguments for the dummy arguments when it processes the program. For example, the following sequence of instructions would result in calculating the macro-operation for the values X and Y:

```
            *60
X,          0010
Y,          0004
            DIF  X  Y
```

We define the macro by specifying a series of operations and enclosing them in angle brackets < > . For example, the macro DIF could be defined as follows:

```
            DEFINE DIF  A   B
          < CLA
            TAD B
            CMA
            IAC
            TAD A >
```

Macros do not need arguments. For example, we could define the macro MASK4 that would mask the 4 left bits of the contents of the accumulator.

```
DEFINE MASK4
<CLL                    /CLEAR LINK
 RAL                    /ROTATE ACC. AND LINK LEFT ONE

 CLL
 RAL
 CLL
 RAL
 CLL
 RAL
 RTR                    /ROTATE ACC. AND LINK RIGHT
                        TWO
RTR>
```

Macros are handier than subroutines for shortening the writing of similar code segments that occur frequently in a program. For example, a PUSH macro can be defined for a computer that has no stack instructions. Macros are also useful in making programs easy to read.

8.4.2 Octal and Decimal

We want to be able to present data in either octal or decimal representations. The PDP-8 assumes that all data are octal. If we wish to enter decimal data, we can precede the list with the pseudo-operation DECIMAL. The assembler then interprets all numbers encountered in statements after DECIMAL as decimal numbers. We can return to using octal representation by using the pseudo-operation OCTAL. The following program segment shows how these two pseudo-operations can be used:

```
        *100
        DECIMAL         /ENTER DECIMAL DATA
TEN,    0010
X,      0239
Y,      0114
        OCTAL           /ENTER OCTAL DATA
EIGHT,  0010
Z,      0117
```

The assembler would produce the following object program from this segment:

Octal address	Octal contents	Comment
100	0012	/TEN
101	0357	/X
102	0162	/Y
103	0010	/EIGHT
104	0117	/Z

8.5 PROGRAMMED INPUT/OUTPUT TRANSFERS

We will further illustrate assembly language programming by considering input/output programs. We will consider only programmed input/output transfers, that is, transfers that are controlled by the user's program. Chapter 10 discusses another type of input/output transfer in which external devices are allowed to interrupt the main program.

Programmed input/output transfers involve 1-bit registers called *flags*. Each external device has one or more flags to show its condition. In the simplest case a device has one flag that can be either 0 or 1 to indicate NOT READY or READY. A slightly more complex device might have two flags used in combination as follows:

Flag bits	Meaning
0 0	Not ready
0 1	Ready
1 0	Error condition
1 1	Transferring information

We will consider devices that have only one flag apiece. More information on input/output devices and their flags is given in chapter 10.

The principle of programmed input/output transfer is to test the status of the device and to transfer information only when the device is ready for transfer. Figure 8.2 is a flowchart illustrating this procedure. The flag of the external device is repeatedly tested to see if it is 1, meaning that the device is ready. When the test first shows that the flag is 1, the information is transferred. Many external devices operate at speeds much slower than the computer, perhaps 1000 or more times slower. Hence the computer has to repeatedly loop through the device flag test until the external device is finally ready for transfer.

Teletype Transfer We will illustrate programmed input/output transfer by considering transfers involving the teletype, a common

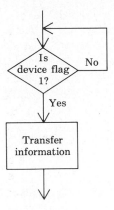

Fig. 8.2 Flowchart of programmed input/output transfer

input/output device for minicomputers. Operation for other devices, such as terminals, is basically the same although the commands are different. A teletype has two parts—a *keyboard/reader* used to input information to the computer and a *printer/punch* used to output information from the computer. The teletype keyboard resembles a typewriter keyboard but has extra symbols used for communication. The user can type a message on the teletype keyboard for transfer to the computer. The reader is a paper tape reader that can read information from the paper tape into the computer. The printer types information on a wide roll of paper. The punch is a paper tape punch that punches holes in the paper tape used by the reader.

Teletype information is coded into 8-bit characters of the ASCII code. Table 8.6 shows the ASCII code for letters, numbers, and common punctuation marks. The ASCII code is represented as holes or no holes on the paper tape and has electrical signals for the computer. In the PDP-8 the ASCII character is stored as bits 4-11 (the 8 rightmost bits) of a computer word. Minicomputers that have 16-bit words can store two ASCII characters to a word.

Teletype data transfer is very slow. Although somewhat faster models have recently been developed, most teletypes can transfer information no faster than 10 characters per second. Since the computer can execute most instructions, including checking a device flag, in a few microseconds, it must spend most of the input/output transfer time waiting for the teletype to transfer a character.

Commands for the keyboard/reader and for the printer/punch are similar. They include instructions to clear the device flag, to set the device flag, to skip the next instruction if the flag is 1, and to read (or write) a character. Reading or writing involves a device register,

TABLE 8.6

ASCII Representations of Selected Symbols

Character	ASCII representation (binary)	Octal	Character	ASCII representation (binary)	Octal
A	1100 0001	301	3	1011 0011	263
B	1100 0010	302	4	1011 0100	264
C	1100 0011	303	5	1011 0101	265
D	1100 0100	304	6	1011 0110	266
E	1100 0101	305	7	1011 0111	267
F	1100 0110	306	8	1011 1000	270
G	1100 0111	307	9	1011 1001	271
H	1100 1000	310	Blank	0000 0000	000
I	1100 1001	311	. Period, decimal pt.	1010 1110	256
J	1100 1010	312	+ Plus sign	1010 1011	253
K	1100 1011	313	$ Dollar sign	1010 0100	244
L	1100 1100	314	* Asterisk	1010 1010	252
M	1100 1101	315	; Semicolon	1011 1011	272
N	1100 1110	316	— Minus, hyphen	1010 1101	255
O	1100 1111	317	/ Slash, division	1010 1111	257
P	1101 0000	320	? Question mark	1011 1111	277
Q	1101 0001	321	= Equal sign	1011 1101	275
R	1101 0010	322	" Quotation mark	1010 0010	242
S	1101 0011	323	(Left parenthesis	1010 1000	250
T	1101 0100	324	) Right parenthesis	1010 1001	251
U	1101 0101	325	Space	1010 0000	240
V	1101 0110	326	CARRIAGE RETURN	1000 1101	215
W	1101 0111	327	LINE FEED	1000 1010	212
X	1101 1000	330			
Y	1101 1001	331			
Z	1101 1010	332			
0	1011 0000	260			
1	1011 0001	261			
2	1011 0010	262			

called a *buffer register,* that holds a character for the information transfer.

A flowchart for reading a single ASCII character and storing it in memory is shown in figure 8.3. The flowchart begins with clearing the keyboard/reader flag and the accumulator. It is always a good idea to begin an input/output transfer by clearing the flags of the external devices to be used and the accumulator if its contents are not needed. Next the flag of the keyboard/reader is tested to see if the device is ready. When the flag is 1 and the keyboard/reader is ready with the character to be read in its buffer, the character is read and then stored in memory.

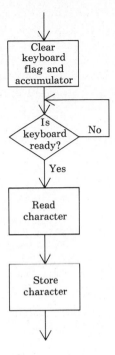

Fig. 8.3   Flowchart to read a character

Table 8.7 shows an assembly language program to read and store a single ASCII character, corresponding to the flowchart of figure 8.3. We have shown the pseudo-commands in the label field to correspond with usual practice for the PDP-8; however, we should remember that they are commands, not labels. The KCC command clears the accumulator and the keyboard/reader flag. The KSF in

TABLE 8.7

PROGRAM TO READ A CHARACTER

```
*200
        KCC             /CLEAR ACCUMULATOR AND
                          KEYBOARD/READER FLAG
        KSF             /IS KEYBOARD FLAG 1?
        JMP .–1         /NO, TRY AGAIN
        KRB             /YES, READ CHARACTER
        DCA CHAR        /STORE CHARACTER
        HLT             /STOP
CHAR,   0000            /CHARACTER WILL BE STORED HERE
$
```

struction checks the keyboard reader flag and skips the next instruction if the flag is 1; until the flag is 1, control remains in the KSF, JMP .—1 loop. When the flag is 1, the character is read from the keyboard/reader buffer by the KRB command. Then it is stored in memory location CHAR, and the program ends.

The procedure for writing a single character is similar. Figure 8.4 shows the flowchart and table 8.8 shows the program. The ASCII character is originally stored in the memory location CHAR. The first step is to clear the accumulator. Then a TLS instruction clears the printer/punch flag, loads the contents of bits 4–11 of the accumulator into the printer/punch buffer, and sets the printer/punch flag. (Since the accumulator holds all 0s—the ASCII code for a blank—the printer does not operate during the execution of the TLS instruction. If the accumulator had held any nonzero value in bits

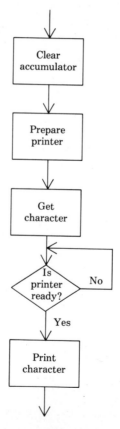

Fig. 8.4 Flowchart of program segment to print a character

4–11, the printer/punch would print it.) Then the character is moved from memory location CHAR to the accumulator. The computer then enters the TSF, JMP .–1 loop to test the printer/punch flag. When the printer/punch has completed the operations dictated by the first TLS instruction, the flag will be set to 1. When the flag is 1, the second TLS instruction commands the printer to clear the flag, transfer the last 8 bits of the accumulator into the printer/punch buffer, print the character transferred, and set the printer/punch flag when the transfer is completed.

Input/output transfer of numbers can be handled more efficiently. ASCII coding of a single octal digit requires 8 bits. Table 8.6 shows that the ASCII code for any number x is $26x$; for example, the ASCII code for 4 is 264. If we code numbers in ASCII, we can easily store only one octal number in a 12-bit word. Since an octal number requires only 3 bits, we want to store four octal numbers in a 12-bit word. We can write a subroutine to do this by using a mask to eliminate the 26 part of the ASCII code for the number and rotating the octal numbers thus obtained to pack four of them into one computer word.

The masking principle is simple. We read the contents of the keyboard/reader into the accumulator. Then we AND the contents of the accumulator with a mask that omits all but the 3 right bits of the contents, the bits of the octal number. For example, suppose we have read 266, the ASCII code for 6, into the accumulator. We will AND the accumulator contents with the octal mask 0007. The mask has 0s in the left 9 binary bits and 1s in the 3 right binary

TABLE 8.8

PROGRAM TO PRINT CHARACTER

*200		
	CLA CLL	/CLEAR ACCUMULATOR AND LINK
	TLS	/CLEAR PRINTER/PUNCH FLAG; LOAD BITS 5–11 OF ACCUMULATOR INTO PRINTER/ PUNCH AND OPERATE THE PRINTER/ PUNCH
	TAD CHAR	/MOVE THE CHARACTER TO THE ACCUMULATOR
	TSF	/IS THE PRINTER FLAG 1?
	JMP .–1	/NO, TRY AGAIN
	TLS	/YES, PRINT CHARACTER
	HLT	/STOP
CHAR,	124	/STORED CHARACTER
$		

bits. As a result, the product of the mask and the accumulator contents is:

	000 010 110 110	Accumulator contents
AND	000 000 000 111	Mask
equals	000 000 000 110	Result

or 0006 in octal, the desired result.

To read and pack four ASCII-coded octal digits in one computer word, we must rotate each octal digit into a different position in the word. We need to store the partial number temporarily while we read another ASCII-coded digit. The procedure, as shown in the flowchart of figure 8.5 and in table 8.9, requires a loop in which the accumulator contents are rotated three positions left and then stored temporarily. Then the keyboard/reader flag is tested, and when the flag is 1, the character is read and masked to extract the octal number. The contents of the temporary storage location TEMP are added to the accumulator. The counter, which has been initialized to −4,

TABLE 8.9

PROGRAM FOR SUBROUTINE TO READ AND PACK FOUR OCTAL
DIGITS INTO ONE MEMORY LOCATION

*400		
SUBRE	0000	/FIRST ADDRESS OF SUBROUTINE
	DCA POINT	/INITIALIZE POINTER
	TAD MFOUR	/GET MINUS FOUR, −4
	DCA COUNT	/INITIALIZE COUNTER AND CLEAR ACCUMULATOR
	CLL	/CLEAR LINK
ROTATE,	RAL	/ROTATE LEFT ONE
	RTL	/ROTATE LEFT TWO
	DCA TEMP	/STORE ACCUMULATOR CONTENTS TEMPORARILY
	KSF	/IS KEYBOARD/READER READY?
	JMP .−1	/NO, TRY AGAIN
	KRB	/YES, READ CHARACTER
	AND MASK	/MASK ACCUMULATOR
	TAD TEMP	/ADD TEMP TO ACCUMULATOR
	ISZ COUNT	/INCREMENT COUNTER, SKIP NEXT INSTRUCTION IF COUNTER IS ZERO
	JMP ROTATE	/GET NEXT CHARACTER
	DCA I POINT	/COUNTER IS ZERO; STORE BINARY NUMBER IN LOCATION SHOWN BY POINTER
	JMP I SUBRE	/JUMP INDIRECT TO MAIN PROGRAM
POINT,	0000	/POINTER WILL HOLD CONTENTS OF ACCUMULATOR ON SUBROUTINE ENTRY
MFOUR,	7774	/−4
COUNT,	0000	/COUNTER
TEMP,	0000	/TEMPORARY STORAGE
MASK,	0007	/MASK

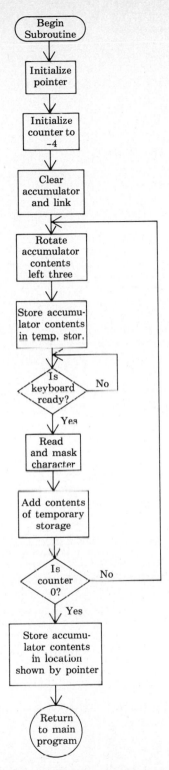

Fig. 8.5 Flowchart to read characters and pack four octal digits in one memory location

is checked to see if it is 0. If the counter is 0, the accumulator contents consisting of the four octal numbers are stored in a location shown by the pointer, which was initialized at the start of the subroutine.

8.6 SYMBOLIC PROGRAMMING

Now that we are familiar with ASCII characters, we can write assembly language programs that manipulate symbols instead of numeric data. We know that computers simply manipulate 1s and 0s; the 1s and 0s can represent characters as easily as numbers. In this section we consider some ways to store and handle symbols.

8.6.1 Storage of Characters

We have seen that ASCII characters require 8 bits and that they are stored in the 8 rightmost bits of the 12-bit PDP-8 word. Two ASCII characters can be stored in 16-bit words of many minicomputers, and four ASCII characters can be stored in 32-bit words. Storage of more than one character per word requires a procedure much like the one developed in the last section for packing four octal digits in one 12-bit word.

We may have a string of characters that we would like to store in adjacent locations in memory. For example, suppose we wish to store the character string representing the instruction

TAD 52

in memory beginning at memory location 220. We need six consecutive memory locations; note that the space between D and 5 must be stored. The contents of the memory locations after storage are as follows, using the ASCII code from table 8.6:

Memory location	Octal contents	Character
220	0324	T
221	0301	A
222	0304	D
223	0240	(space)
224	0265	5
225	0262	2

We have stored the two octal digits in their ASCII representation even though we could have stored them both in one memory location if we had packed them with the subroutine of the last section. It is usually best to store all parts of one message in the same format since doing so simplifies decoding on retrieval. If we wish to perform numerical calculations on the digits stored as characters, we must develop special routines for this purpose or else convert the numbers to a standard numerical form, for example, twos complement.

8.6.2   Reading Character Strings

We learned in the last section how to read and store a single ASCII character. Often we wish to read and store an entire string of characters, such as a line of characters terminated by a carriage return on a teletype or terminal. We can write a subroutine to read and store a string of characters until the carriage return symbol is encountered. Then the subroutine stores 0 in the next memory location and returns control to the main program. The flowchart of this program is shown in figure 8.6; the program is in table 8.10.

   The subroutine begins by initializing the pointer with the address held in the accumulator when the subroutine is entered. Then the character is read, stored, and checked to see if it is the carriage return symbol. For characters other than the carriage return symbol the

TABLE 8.10

SUBROUTINE TO READ AND STORE A STRING OF CHARACTERS

*300		
SUBSTO,	0000	/FIRST ADDRESS OF SUBROUTINE
	DCA POINT	/STORE CONTENTS OF ACCUMULATOR IN POINTER
READ,	KSF	/IS KEYBOARD FLAG 1?
	JMP .−1	/NO, CHECK AGAIN
	KRB	/YES, READ CHARACTER
	DCA I POINT	/STORE THE CHARACTER
	TAD I POINT	/RESTORE THE CHARACTER TO THE ACCUMULATOR
	TAD MCHECK	/ADD −215, THE COMPLEMENT OF THE CARRIAGE RETURN CHARACTER
	SZA	/ARE THE CONTENTS OF THE ACCUMULATOR ZERO? (IS THE CHARACTER A CARRIAGE RETURN?)
	JMP .+5	/NO, SKIP THE NEXT FOUR INSTRUCTIONS AND CONTINUE
	DCA I POINT	/YES, STORE 0
	ISZ POINT	/INCREMENT THE POINTER
	TAD POINT	/PLACE THE ADDRESS OF THE POINTER IN THE ACCUMULATOR
	JMP I SUBSTO	/JUMP INDIRECT TO THE MAIN PROGRAM
	ISZ POINT	/INCREMENT THE POINTER
	CLA	/CLEAR THE ACCUMULATOR
	JMP READ	/READ THE NEXT CHARACTER
POINT,	0000	/POINTER
MCHECK,	7563	/−215

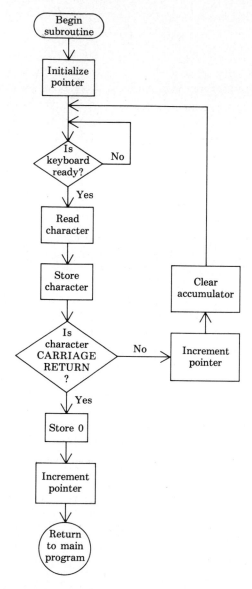

Fig. 8.6 Flowchart to read and store a string of characters that end with CARRIAGE RETURN

subroutine continues to increment the pointer, clear the accumulator, and read the next character. When the carriage return is encountered, 0 is stored in the location shown by the pointer, replacing the carriage return code. The pointer is incremented, the address of the pointer is placed in the accumulator, and control returns to the main program.

8.6.3 Tables

We often store symbolic information in tables. For example, suppose we wish to keep a record of the minimum total flying time from our local airport to other major airports. If we kept the information in a book, we would have a table like table 8.11. Since all the flying times are less than 8 hours, we can consider the table entries as hours and minutes in decimal, with a possible error of 2 minutes. (We could, of course, code the flying time in many ways.) To use this table, we would like to read in the mnemonic code for an airport (for example, ORD for O'Hare Airport in Chicago) and receive as output the flying time. To do this we must construct a second table that stores the ASCII code for each airport mnemonic and the value of flying time in successive memory locations. Table 8.12 shows this table. Each line of table 8.11 requires four memory locations—three to store the airport symbol and one to store the flying time.

We can write a subroutine to use this table. The subroutine should check any mnemonic term $M_1M_2M_3$ to see if it is in the table. If it is, the subroutine will place the associated flying time in the accumulator. The flowchart of this subroutine is shown as figure 8.7. The program is in table 8.13. We call this program a table lookup subroutine because it looks up entries in a table.

The subroutine assumes that M1, M2, M3, −N (where N is the number of airports in the table) and the first address of the table have already been stored in memory. First the subroutine initializes the pointer to the first address of the table and the counter to −N. Then it tries to match M1 to the first code in the table. If the match is successful, it tries to match M2 to the second code in the table. If this match is also successful, it tries to match M3 to the third code in the table. If all three matches are successful, the value of

TABLE 8.11

MINIMUM TOTAL FLYING TIME FROM LOCAL AIRPORT
TO OTHER AIRPORTS

Airport	Flying time in hours and minutes
BOS	0355
DCA	0325
JFK	0310
LAX	0545
ORD	0135
SFO	0600

flying time is placed in the accumulator, and control returns to the main program. If any match is not successful, the pointer and counter are incremented. If all entries have not been checked, the matching attempt continues with the next table entry. When all entries have been checked without finding a match of M1, M2, and M3, control returns to the main program with all 1s in the accumulator.

8.7   LOADERS

Once we have written an assembly language program, we face the problem of entering it into a computer. Entering a machine language program is simple. We simply enter the instructions directly in binary on the toggle or bit switches. To run an assembly language program, we must first enter the assembler program or check to see that the assembler program is in memory. The assembler program for mini-computers is usually punched on paper tape. A computer as it is delivered ordinarily has no way of loading programs from paper tapes. The computer's memory is just an array of storage cells. The first step, thus, is to provide a way to load programs from paper tapes. Loading is usually done in two steps:

1. First we enter a short program manually via the bit switches. This program, called a *bootstrap loader,* consists of the minimum steps necessary to allow loading another loader. The bootstrap

TABLE 8.12

Coded Table for Airports and Flying Time

Memory location	Octal contents	Symbol or number stored	Memory location	Octal contents	Symbol or number stored
200	0302	B	214	0314	L
201	0317	O	215	0301	A
202	0323	S	216	0330	X
203	0355	0355	217	0545	0545
204	0304	D	220	0317	O
205	0303	C	221	0322	R
206	0301	A	222	0304	D
207	0325	0325	223	0135	0135
210	0312	J	224	0323	S
211	0306	F	225	0306	F
212	0313	K	226	0317	O
213	0310	0310	227	0600	0600

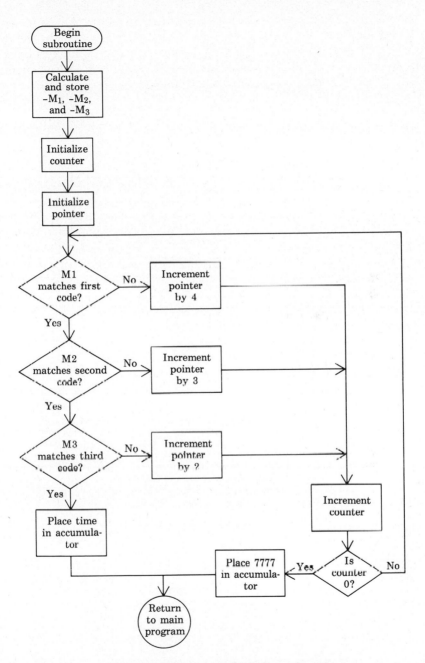

Fig. 8.7 Flowchart of table lookup subroutine

TABLE 8.13

TABLE LOOKUP SUBROUTINE

*300		
SUBTAB,	0000	/FIRST LOCATION OF SUBROUTINE
	TAD M1	/GET M1
	CMA IAC	/FORM COMPLEMENT
	DCA COMPM1	/STORE −M1
	TAD M2	/GET M2
	CMA IAC	/FORM COMPLEMENT
	DCA COMPM2	/STORE −M2
	TAD M3	/GET M3
	CMA IAC	/FORM COMPLEMENT
	DCA COMPM3	/STORE −M3
	TAD MNUMB	/GET −N; N IS THE NUMBER OF· AIRPORTS
	DCA COUNT	/INITIALIZE COUNTER WITH −(N−1)
	TAD ADDR	/GET FIRST ADDRESS OF TABLE
	DCA POINT	/INITIALIZE POINTER WITH FIRST ADDRESS OF TABLE
ENTRY,	TAD COMPM1	/GET −M1
	TAD I POINT	/ADD FIRST CODE OF TABLE ENTRY
	SZA	/SKIP THE NEXT INSTRUCTION IF M1 MATCHES CODE
	JMP DOWN1	/NO MATCH, TRY NEXT ENTRY
	ISZ POINT	/MATCH INCREMENT POINTER
	TAD COMPM2	/GET −M2
	TAD I POINT	/ADD SECOND CODE OF TABLE ENTRY
	SZA	/SKIP THE NEXT INSTRUCTION IF M2 MATCHES SECOND CODE
	JMP DOWN2	/NO MATCH, TRY NEXT ENTRY
	ISZ POINT	/MATCH INCREMENT POINTER
	TAD COMPM3	/GET −M3
	TAD I POINT	/ADD THIRD CODE OF TABLE ENTRY
	SZA	/SKIP THE NEXT INSTRUCTION IF M3 MATCHES THIRD CODE
	JMP DOWN3	/NO MATCH, TRY NEXT ENTRY
	ISZ POINT	/MATCH INCREMENT POINTER
	TAD I POINT	/GET FLYING TIME
	JMP I SUBTAB	/RETURN TO MAIN PROGRAM WITH FLYING TIME IN ACCUMULATOR
DOWN1,	ISZ POINT	/INCREMENT POINTER
DOWN2,	ISZ POINT	/INCREMENT POINTER
DOWN3,	ISZ POINT	/INCREMENT POINTER
	ISZ POINT	/INCREMENT POINTER
	CLA	/CLEAR ACCUMULATOR
	ISZ COUNT	/INCREMENT COUNTER; SKIP NEXT INSTRUCTION IF THE COUNTER IS 0
	JMP ENTRY	/COUNTER IS NOT ZERO, TRY NEXT TABLE ENTRY
	CLA CMA	/COUNTER IS ZERO, PUT 7777 IN ACCUMULATOR
	JMP I SUBTAB	/RETURN TO MAIN PROGRAM WITH 7777 IN ACCUMULATOR

TABLE 8.13 *continued*

M1,	0304	/FIRST SYMBOL, FOR EXAMPLE, D
M2,	0324	/SECOND SYMBOL, FOR EXAMPLE, T
M3,	0327	/THIRD SYMBOL, FOR EXAMPLE, W
COMPM1,		/COMPLEMENT OF M1 WILL BE HERE
COMPM2,		/COMPLEMENT OF M2 WILL BE HERE
COMPM3,		/COMPLEMENT OF M3 WILL BE HERE
MNUMB,	7772	/−N, WHERE N IS THE NUMBER OF
		AIRPORTS IN TABLE, HERE −6
COUNT,		/COUNTER
ADDR,	0200	/FIRST ADDRESS OF TABLE, HERE 200
POINT,		/POINTER

loader will load a program from a paper tape reader directly into memory without making any checks for errors.

The bootstrap loader is deliberately kept short so that it will be easy to load. On simple minicomputers, it must be reloaded fairly often as it is often destroyed by other programs that try to use its space. Some minicomputers provide a memory protect switch that protects the area of memory that holds the bootstrap loader and similar important programs. When the memory protect option is on, information cannot be stored in the protected section of memory. Other minicomputers have a loader that is permanently stored in read-only memory (described in chapter 9) so that it is always available.

2. We then use the bootstrap program to load another loader. This loader will load any binary program presented in a given format. Many minicomputer programs are written on paper tape; therefore, a paper tape loader is used for loading information from the paper tape reader.

The loader has several functions. It must load words into designated addresses in memory. It should be able to detect the most likely errors that could occur in transmission. Usually the loader does this by performing a *parity check,* as described in chapters 3 and 10. A parity check is a simple check on the number of 1 bits in each character read. Loaders may check to see that each word read is either part of an instruction or is data by checking special format codes built into the loader. The loader may check to see that the right number of words are read by verifying information given with the program.

Loaders may be *absolute* or *relocatable*. An absolute loader loads every instruction and data statement into fixed addresses in memory. An absolute loader can be used with an absolute assembler that calculates an absolute address for every source program instruction and data word. The assemblers discussed in the preceding sections are absolute assemblers.

A relocatable or *linking* loader is more sophisticated. It can modify addresses to load the program anywhere in memory. A linking loader can be used with a relocatable assembler. The relocatable assembler produces an object program that gives memory addresses in terms of their displacement from the program origin or from an external reference. The relocatable assembler contains a relative program counter that gives the displacements. Then the linking loader will complete the address when it loads the object program. The tenth statement of the program will be stored in the tenth address after the program origin, for example.

8.8 HIGH-LEVEL LANGUAGES AND TRANSLATORS

In the earlier sections of this chapter we learned the advantages that assembly languages offer—the relative freedom from tedious house-keeping chores and the convenience of mnemonic instructions. Yet, we can see that assembly language is still relatively difficult. Like machine language, it is closely tied to the hardware structure of the computer. If we use another computer, we must learn another assembly language. Its instructions accomplish relatively small and simple operations; we must write elaborate subprograms for the computer to evaluate arithmetic expressions.

We prefer to program in a language that is *machine independent,* that is, a language whose instructions are the same on every computer on which the language has been implemented. We also prefer to program in languages whose commands are as powerful as possible so that we can write one instruction to direct a sequence of operations. In addition, we like programming languages that require little training and experience of the user. *High-level languages* offer us these advantages. The most frequently used high-level languages are *procedure-oriented languages,* such as FORTRAN for scientific applications and COBOL for business applications. Procedure-oriented languages let the user write programs without requiring him (or her) to know the exact procedure the computer uses to compute. A special program, called a *translator,* changes the user's source program written in a procedure-oriented language to an object program written in machine language. Naturally the translators must be written specially for each type of computer, but the casual user does not need to worry about the details of the translation. The translators, like assemblers, are loaded by one or more loaders.

These advantages do not come without disadvantages. There is a loss of efficiency since the computer must translate the source program and may need to allocate memory for the source program and translator as well as the object program. This constraint is usually not troublesome on large computers, but may require a large percentage of the memory available for minicomputers and micro-computers. The object program may take more running time and memory space than a well-written machine language program. Modern translators for large computers are usually well optimized and produce efficient machine language code. Translators for minicomputers, and especially for microcomputers, are sometimes less optimal and may produce machine language code that is 20 percent or more longer than a good handwritten machine language program. Sometimes if a program is to be run many times, it is worth the programming time needed to write a program in machine or assembly language instead of a procedure oriented language. Another possibility is to examine the object program produced by the translator and attempt to hand optimize it by changing a few statements. Usually, however, the simplicity of procedure-oriented languages and the consequent savings in the programmer's time are more important than the cost of a small additional amount of running time.

Another disadvantage is that the available features of procedure-oriented languages differ somewhat from computer to computer despite attempts at standardization. This problem is particularly troublesome on small computers where manufacturers have discarded some capabilities of a language in order to fit the translator within available memory space. It is important to read the manufacturer's description of the implementation of a language on a computer, noting any deviations from the standard language.

Two types of translators are commonly used. A *compiler* translates an entire source-language program written in a procedure-oriented language into an object program written in machine language that can then be run on a particular computer. Typically, the translation is accomplished in two complete passes through the source program. The first pass results in an intermediate object program that resembles an assembly language program. The second pass performs many of the activities of an assembler and results in the complete object program. FORTRAN and COBOL are ordinarily translated by compilers.

An *interpreter* translates one or more source language statements into machine language code and then executes the machine language instructions before examining the next source language statements. It does not generate a complete object program that can be saved and reused. Thus, interpreters are most valuable when the source program will only be executed once, or perhaps just a few times. The interpreter can also show intermediate results as execution of the program proceeds, interlaced with inspection and translation of source language statements. Interpreter languages are often easier for beginners who like conversational programs (programs in which the computer interacts after every statement or so) since they can watch the translation and execution occur and identify errors as they happen. BASIC is usually translated by an interpreter.

Interpreters and compilers are more alike than different. Both can be used for most common procedure-oriented languages. We will next look at the construction and behavior of a simple compiler and should remember that the features of an interpreter are much the same.

8.8.1 A Simple Compiler

As mentioned above, a typical compiler translates in two separate passes. Early compilers required just one pass and generated an output program in assembly language that had to be processed by an assembler. The compiler that we will study resembles an early compiler followed by a modified assembler. Because we are already familiar with assemblers, we will concentrate on activities of the first pass of the compiler that result in an intermediate object program. Figure 8.8 shows some of the activities of the two passes.

The first pass of the compiler basically produces a program equivalent to the source program but written like an assembly language program. Activities performed in the first pass of the compiler include:

1. Classifying the type of each source statement. Source statements can be specification statements that identify the nature of source program labels (usually called *identifiers* in high-level language programs), assignment statements that require the computer to evaluate an expression and assign the resulting value to a variable, conditional or unconditional transfers, control statements, input/output statements, or others.
2. Detecting errors in the source program. Compilers usually have more powerful error-detection and error-diagnostic features than do assemblers. Each source statement is read into a statement buffer that inspects the statement for errors while classifying its type and noting any identifiers.

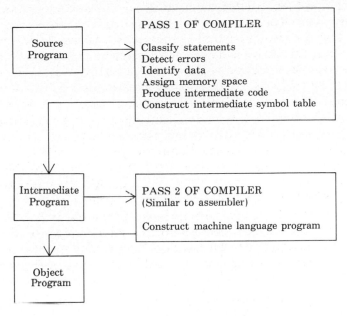

Fig. 8.8   Compiler operations

3. Assigning memory space for the intermediate object code needed for each source statement.
4. Identifying data.
5. Producing the intermediate object code for each source statement.
6. Constructing an intermediate symbol table. This table is more complex than the symbol table of an assembler. It records information about the type of term represented by each identifier (such as integer, real number, or statement number). It also accounts for the memory locations assigned to each identifier.

The compiler program has several control subprograms to perform the translation. For example, control programs allocate memory locations to the object program. It also has subroutines to translate specific kinds of source statements. For example, it has one subroutine to translate arithmetic expressions. More information on compilers can be found in the references.

8.8.2 Problem-Oriented Languages

Problem-oriented languages are even easier to use than procedure-oriented languages. A problem-oriented language is designed to solve a special type of problem, such as the analysis of electric circuits or the design of a building. The user of the language needs only to specify the structure of a model and its values. The language contains all the necessary information needed to analyze the system. Many problem-oriented languages are superimposed on procedure-oriented languages. For example, several circuit analysis programs are based on FORTRAN. However, the user does not need to know FORTRAN. Problem-oriented languages are rapidly increasing in popularity as they offer convenient solutions to problems while requiring a minimum knowledge of programming.

8.9 MICROPROGRAMMING

At the opposite end of the hierarchy of programming languages from high-level languages lies microprogramming. We encountered microinstructions in the chapter on machine language programming. A microinstruction is the lowest level of instruction that the computer can execute. In machine language programming we were able to assemble a few microinstructions into a single machine language instruction within constraints on the types and order of instructions that could be legally combined. Most machine language instructions, however, were already constructed for us. If we specified a twos complement add, TAD, the control unit of the computer would send signals to transfer information from the memory location we named and the accumulator to the registers of the arithmetic unit, to add the numbers, and to transfer the sum back to the accumulator. We were not able to control any individual part of this operation. The addition operation and most other machine operations are defined and implemented when the computer is constructed. Additions to the basic instruction set require rewiring the computer and possibly adding extra gates or registers. Hence the instruction set of computers is not ordinarily modified once the computer is installed in the user's location.

Microprogramming provides an alternative to this fixed instruction set. A microprogrammed computer provides a special memory, called a *control memory,* for decoding of instructions. The memory is usually one that can be read only, not written; we will study read-only memories in the next chapter. Whenever the machine language program names an instruction, the instruction is decoded by the control memory. Associated with the operation code of any instruction in the control memory is a list of micro-operations that should be executed to implement the machine language instruction. The micro-operations include register-to-register transfers and register-to-memory transfers as well as the basic arithmetic and logical operations of the computer. They deal not only with the registers accessible through machine language instructions, but also with the internal working registers of the computer. The microinstructions that implement any machine language instruction can be changed by changing the list of microinstructions associated with that instruction in the control memory.

A microprogramming instruction set must be able to describe all the computer hardware, including the control memory, other memories, registers, the arithmetic unit, and the bus or buses. It must provide exact timing so that it can designate operations that occur simultaneously and others that occur sequentially. It should generate efficient hardware operations.

Microprogramming lets the user get closer to the hardware structure of the computer. When the user is allowed to specify the micro-operations desired to implement a procedure, he or she has much more flexibility than is possible with a standard computer with a fixed instruction set. The instruction set of a computer can be changed by changing the associated sequence of microinstructions to make it emulate (act like) another computer. Microprogramming can also augment the capabilities of a computer. For example, a computer might have an option of hardware to perform floating point operations. If the computer can be microprogrammed, it is possible to write a sequence of microinstructions to perform floating point computations, even without the floating point equipment. Instead the program of microinstructions uses existing registers and arithmetic components to implement floating point operations. Thus, we can consider microprogramming as software that can implement functions not present in the hardware. Because of this capability of using software to accomplish former hardware functions, microprogramming is sometimes called *firmware*.

Microprograms can be changed in two ways. If the control memory is not a read-only memory, the user can write new sequences of microinstructions into it. The computer may have a program that can alter the microprogram stored in the control memory. Naturally this program must be protected from access by casual users. Usually, however, microprograms are changed by changing the control memory. The control memory typically consists of a card containing several chips of semiconductor memory. The microprogrammer may be able to change the chips in his own facility or may have to send specifications of the desired control memory to the manufacturer who will produce and deliver the new memory.

Microprogramming is the most difficult programming level that we have studied. Although it is becoming increasingly popular because of the power and flexibility it offers, it is only done by experienced and knowledgeable computer users. Some computers, called *microprogrammed computers,* have machine language instruction sets implemented through microinstructions and a control memory. The instruction sets of microprogrammed computers cannot be changed by the user. *Microprogrammable computers,* in contrast, allow the user to microprogram.

8.10   EXECUTIVES AND OPERATING SYSTEMS

We have now studied a number of system software programs—loaders, assemblers, compilers, and so forth—that enable us to run our user programs. To coordinate these system software programs computers have an *executive,* also called a *monitor* or *supervisor.* The executive is a program or set of programs that control and coordinate other computer programs. It increases the cost effectiveness of the computer. The executive normally resides in main memory while the computer is operating.

The executive performs several functions:

1. Scheduling jobs. The executive handles the sequence of loading and execution of programs and provides for orderly transition from one program to another.
2. Allocating storage. Depending on the complexity of the computer system, the executive may simply help the programmer determine where a single program should be stored or perform complex dynamic storage allocation for a *multiprocessing system* (a system that processes two or more programs during the same interval of time). The executive controls both main memory and secondary storage devices such as discs and drums that are discussed in the next chapter.
3. Handling input/output. The executive controls the operation of all input/output devices with the aid of their device controllers and assorted utility subroutines.
4. Monitoring. It checks for error conditions during program execution, such as infinite loops and numerical overflow. It provides error diagnostics.
5. Protecting. It protects the system programs of the computer from user interference and prevents users from accessing each other's programs.

6. Providing software services. It controls the use of software services, such as libraries of subroutines.

The executive is the key element of the system of programs called an *operating system*. A complex operating system, such as those of large computers and the more sophisticated minicomputers, can perform a variety of additional functions to enhance the efficiency of the computer.

1. It greatly improves the scheduling of computer programs by assigning priorities to programs. High-priority programs can interrupt other programs to be run immediately or to be put in a queue of waiting programs until programs of higher priority are executed. Lower-priority programs are run only as time becomes available.
2. It can group programs requiring similar system software programs, such as a FORTRAN compiler, so that they can be run together.
3. It can estimate the running time and memory needed by a program.
4. It can run a mixture of programs that use a lot of slow input/output operations along with those that primarily perform computations by the central processing unit so that the central processing unit is kept busy as much of the time as possible.

Operating systems are sufficiently complex to be the subject of entire books; the references list discussions on operating systems. We will not consider them further.

8.11 SUMMARY

Assembly language programming adds the features of mnemonic instructions and symbolic addresses to machine language. An assembly language statement can contain four fields: label, operation code, operand, and comments. The operations may be pseudo-operations that are messages to the assembler that are not translated into machine language. Special instructions called macros may be defined.

The assembler accepts a source program written in assembly language and produces an object program in machine language. A typical assembler requires two complete passes through the source program. On the first pass, the assembler builds a symbol table that records values for all symbolic addresses. On the second pass, the assembler combines address codes with instruction codes and assembles the program statements.

The assembled program is then ready to be loaded into the computer. Usually two loaders are required. A bootstrap loader is used to load an absolute or relocatable loader that can load the assembler and the object program.

High-level languages are machine independent, as contrasted with machine and assembly languages that are closely related to the computer hardware. Procedure-oriented languages let the user solve problems with little knowledge of the computer's operation. Problem-oriented languages are designed to solve specialized problems. High-level languages are translated by a compiler that translates the entire program before execution, or by interpreters that interweave translation and execution.

Microprogramming is the lowest level of programming and the one most closely related to hardware. Microinstructions allow individual operation of registers, including internal working registers, and other hardware devices. Microprograms are usually stored in a control memory.

Operating systems increase the efficiency of a computer by scheduling and controlling the running of other programs. An executive is the key element of an operating system. It schedules jobs, allocates storage, handles input/output, monitors errors during program execution, protects programs from illegal access, and provides a variety of software services. Complex operating systems, such as those on large computers, use a variety of scheduling procedures to allocate processing time efficiently among different types of programs.

Concepts

absolute loader	keyboard/reader
assembler	label
bootstrap loader	machine independent
comments	macro-operation
compiler	microprogrammable computer
control memory	microprogrammed computer
current location counter	microprogramming
executive	multiprocessing
firmware	operand
forward reference	operating system
high-level language	operation code
identifier	parity check
interpreter	printer/punch

problem-oriented language
procedure-oriented language
pseudo-instruction
relocatable loader
source program

statement
symbol table
translator
two-pass assembler

8.12 REFERENCES

Assembly language programming, like machine language programming, is best explained by the reference manuals for the computer
to be used. General references for assembly language programming
and assemblers include Gear (1974), Stone (1972), and Booth (1971).
Information on systems software can be found in Booth (1971) and
Abrams and Stein (1973). Colin (1971), Coffman and Denning (1973),
and Madnick and Donovan (1974) give advanced discussions of
operating systems.

8.13 PROBLEMS

8.1 Devise a simple scheme to sort a list of five three-digit octal
numbers and arrange them in ascending order. Write a flowchart
and an assembly language program to implement your
scheme.   (8.2)

8.2 Write a flowchart and an assembly language program that will
calculate the absolute value of N numbers.   (8.2)

8.3 Write the object program that would result from assembling
the following source program:

```
*20
CLA
TAD NUM
TAD NUM+1
TAD NUM+2
SZL
HLT
NUM,  20
NUM+1, 45
NUM+2, 177
$
```
                                                              (8.3)

8.4   Write the object program that would result from assembling
the program of table 8.2   (8.3)

8.5   Write a macro to calculate the sum of the absolute value of
two numbers.   (8.4)

8.6   Write a macro to calculate $X - Y + Z$.   (8.4)

8.7   Write a flowchart and an assembly language subroutine to read
one character from a teletype, store it in memory, retrieve it,
and output it to the teletype.   (8.5)

8.8   Using the subroutine of table 8.4, write a flowchart and assembly
language program to read $4N$ consecutive ASCII-coded octal
digits and store the octal digits in N consecutive memory locations.   (8.5)

8.9   Write a flowchart and assembly language subroutine that will
print your name on the teletype printer/punch.   (8.6)

8.10 Assume that a string of characters that ends with a carriage
return has been stored in memory. Write a flowchart and assembly language program to count the number of times the space
character appears in the string.   (8.6)

8.11 Write a flowchart and assembly language program that will
examine a sentence read in from a teletype, and count the
number of times the word THE apears in the sentence. Assume
that sentences end with periods and that periods are not otherwise used in the sentence.   (8.6)

8.12 Write a flowchart and an assembly language program that will
inspect a list of words separated by spaces read in from a teletype
and ending with the character /. The program should count
the number of letters in each word and print the word followed
by the letter count.   (8.6)

part III
The Systems Level

9 Memory

9.1 OVERVIEW

A computer memory stores instructions and data. Although some information can be held in registers, they are too expensive to use for large-volume storage. There is an increasing trend to store more information in registers or other high-speed memories (sometimes called *scratchpad memories*). Most information is stored in main memories where it can be easily retrieved when needed. Very large amounts of data that are not needed often (such as statistical information for a project that may be updated once a week) are stored on *mass memories* that offer inexpensive storage with relatively slow access. A central theme to the choice of the best type of memory for a given application is the tradeoff between speed and cost.

We will first consider the type of memory used for main computer memory, *random-access memory* (RAM), that requires the same length of time to access (that is, to select and read) any word within it. Most random-access memory is composed of either magnetic cores or semiconductors. Both can be organized with all bits of the words on one memory plane (word-organized or 2D) or with one bit of each of the words on a bit plane (bit-organized or 3D).

Mass memories are usually either *semirandom access* or *sequential access*. Semirandom-access memories can reach any word within one revolution of a drum or disc so access time is limited. Sequential-access memories store words in sequence, as on a tape, and access time may be long. Various techniques allow rapid trading of blocks of memory from mass memory into main memory or from main memory into scratchpad memory.

Most memories are *read/write memories* in which information can be both stored and retrieved. In contrast, *read-only memories* (ROMs) store information permanently and may only be read, as their name implies. ROMs are often used to hold tables or programs.

9.2 MAIN MEMORY ORGANIZATION

The basic memory of a computer—the memory referred to in chapters 7 and 8—is called *main memory*. It must be able to store the data and instructions needed for a program so that they can be accessed quickly and inexpensively. Since we want to both store and retrieve information, we need a read/write memory for our main memory. Later we will discuss read-only and read-mostly memories.

Memory size is usually measured in bits, although the information may be organized into bytes or words that can be individually addressed. A memory that holds W words of length B bits stores $W \times B$ bits of information. For example, a computer memory that holds 4K 16-bit words stores $4096 \times 16 = 65{,}536$ or 64K bits. Typical minicomputers store 4K to 32K words of 16 or 32 bits in their main memories. Large computers may have in main memory a few hundred K words of 32 to 64 bits in length for a total of several million bits.

Information is addressed as words or bytes. The *address* of a word or byte is its location in memory. The *content* of a word is the information stored in it. Some computers store information as bytes (usually 8 bits) as well as words (typically 16 to 64 bits). *Byte addressing* allows separate storage and recovery of smaller units of information. It also permits handling of variable lengths of information.

Computers use two registers to help store and retrieve information from memory. A *memory address register* holds the address of the word in memory with which the computer is working. A memory data register or *memory buffer register* holds the contents of that memory word. Figure 9.1 shows the relation of these two registers and memory. To store a word, we write it in memory by placing the desired address of the word in the memory address register and placing the contents of the word in the memory data register. We then transfer the contents of the word from this register to the memory location whose address is in the memory address register. Similarly, we can read a word from memory by placing the address of the word in the memory address register and transferring its contents to the memory data register. We can then move the contents of the word to any other register we wish. We will discuss these processes in more detail later.

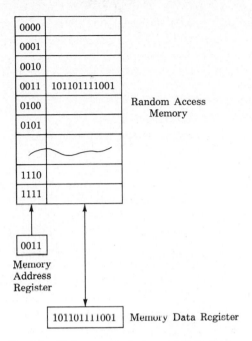

Fig. 9.1   Main memory and associated registers

Since speed is important, we are concerned with the times needed for reading and writing. *Access time* is the time required to select a word and read it. *Write time* is the time required to select a location and write a word into it. A *memory cycle* is the time required to read a word, erase it, and write or rewrite it in a magnetic core memory. A somewhat different definition applies to semiconductor memory in which the steps of erasing and rewriting are not necessary.

9.3   RANDOM-ACCESS MEMORIES

We will first be concerned with *random-access memories* (RAMs) since most main computer memories are random access. By random access we mean that we can access or reach any word in memory in the same amount of time or in the same number of operations.

Thus, in a random-access memory, access time and write time are constants. Other memories that we will discuss later, such as discs and tapes, require varying amounts of time to access a word of memory depending on its location. As stated earlier, random-access memories are usually composed of either semiconductors or magnetic cores. Although most main memories have been core in the past, semiconductor memories have been gaining rapidly in popularity. Semiconductor memories are faster and are less expensive for fairly small memories. Figure 9.2 shows approximate cost/bit relationships for semiconductor and core RAMs as a function of memory size. The main expense for core memories is the support circuitry. Thus the cost/bit for core is small when the cost of the support circuitry can be distributed over enough bits. Semiconductor memories have a more uniform cost/bit relationship with size. In the last few years, semiconductor memories have become relatively less expensive in the intermediate memory range. Semiconductor RAMs are likely to become more popular.

9.3.1 Semiconductor RAMs

Semiconductor RAMs may be either bipolar or MOS. In either case the basic storage element is one or more transistors. Bipolar RAMs have fast access times, typically less than 100 ns, but each memory cell requires a larger area and dissipates more power than an MOS memory cell. Access times for MOS RAMs are about 300 ns to 1 μs, which is comparable to magnetic core memories. MOS RAMs may be *static* or *dynamic*. Static memories are so named because they do not require attention. Dynamic memories require periodic

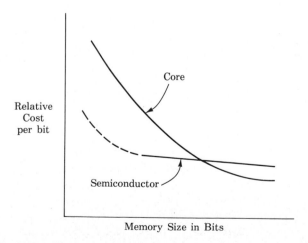

Fig. 9.2 Relative cost per bit as a function of size for core and semi-conductor memories

refreshing of the memory contents. Refreshing is usually done by periodically reading a subset of the memory locations, one at a time.

Semiconductor RAMs usually include the following circuits. *Address decoders* select the desired memory cell or cells. A *chip select* input (CS) enables the RAM's addressing and/or READ/WRITE circuits. A *bit driver* amplifies data that are to be written in memory. *Sense amplifiers* detect and amplify data that are read from memory. Sometimes *buffers* are needed to compensate for differences in level between memory and external circuits.

Semiconductor RAMs are organized as modules that are arrays of LSI circuits. Two addressing schemes are commonly used: *word organization* and *bit organization*. Word organization, as shown in figure 9.3, requires just one decoder. The memory is arranged as W words of B bits. The decoder selects one of W words. W is usually 2^n for some n so that n address inputs or $\log_2 W$ inputs are needed. To read from memory, all bits of the selected word are sensed and read by the sense amplifiers. To write a word into memory the location

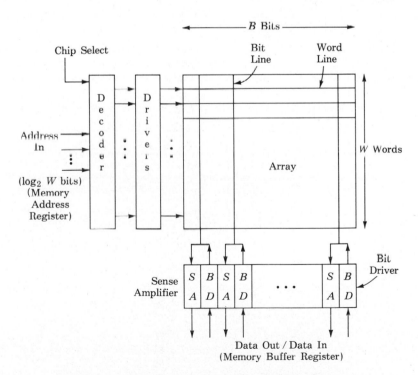

Fig. 9.3 Word organization of semiconductor RAM system

is selected by the decoder, and then data are written into the selected word through the B bit drivers. Sometimes a single line with a tristate output for reading that is disabled for writing is used instead of separate READ and WRITE lines.

A word-organized semiconductor RAM requires the following to store 2^n B-bit words:

1. $2^n \times B$ storage cells,
2. One 1-of-2^n decoder (with n input address lines and 2^n output WORD lines),
3. B bit drivers and amplifiers, and
4. B BIT lines.

For example, a 256-word by 6-bit word-organized memory requires:

1. $256 \times 6 = 1536$ cells,
2. One 1-of-256 decoder (with eight address lines and 256 WORD lines),
3. Six bit drivers and amplifiers, and
4. Six BIT lines.

Bit organization is often used in larger memories. Two decoders are needed to address $W = 2^n$ cells. Each decoder has $n/2$ inputs and can select one of $2^{n/2}$ lines. For example, a 1024-word by 1-bit memory is addressed by two five-input decoders, each of which drives 32 lines. One decoder selects the X address of the desired memory cell; the other selects the Y address. A cell is selected by the unique intersection, or coincidence, of the X and Y select lines. This scheme is illustrated in figure 9.4 for a 16-bit RAM.

Although *coincidence addressing* (as this scheme is sometimes called) requires smaller decoders, additional logic circuits are needed to detect the coincidences. Words of more than 1 bit can be addressed in this scheme by paralleling B identical copies of the memory for a B-bit word, as shown by figure 9.5. The X and Y select lines select the memory cell in the same position on each bit plane. Only one X decoder/driver and one Y decoder/driver are needed.

Figure 9.6 shows a complex organization of a 4096-word by 8-bit memory using 256-bit RAMs and separate decoder/drivers. Each bit plane has sixteen 256-bit RAMs. Eight 1-of-16 decoder/drivers address the RAMs. Six address bits are required for each of the X and Y axes. Two address bits acting as enable inputs select one of the four decoder/drivers for each axis. The other 4 address bits are the basic

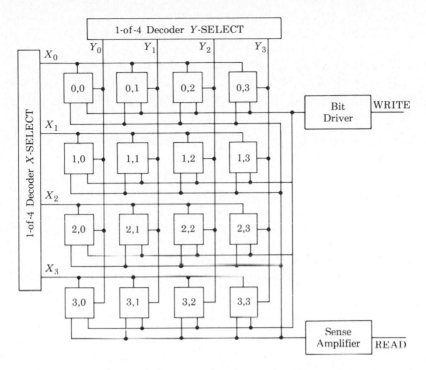

Fig. 9.4   A 16-bit RAM with coincidence addressing

address inputs to each decoder. Because the decoder/drivers are not part of the RAMs, the RAMs are said to be undecoded.

To summarize, a bit-organized semiconductor RAM requires the following for 2^n B-bit words:

1. $2^n \times B$ storage cells,
2. Two 1-of-$2^{n/2}$ decoders (each with $n/2$ input address lines and $2^{n/2}$ output word select lines that connect to all B planes),
3. B bit drivers and amplifiers for each of the B-bit planes, and
4. B BIT lines, one for each bit plane.

For the same example as used for word-organized storage, a bit-organized memory of 256 6-bit words would require:

1. $256 \times 6 = 1536$ storage cells,
2. Two 1-of-16 decoders (each with four input address lines and sixteen output word select lines that connect to all six bit planes),

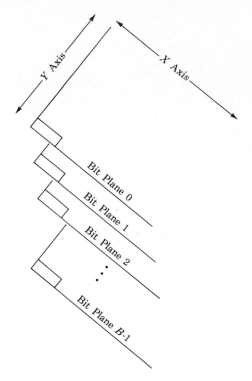

Fig. 9.5 Selection of one word of B bits with B identical bit planes

3. Six bit drivers and amplifiers, and
4. Six BIT lines.

Figures 9.7 and 9.8 show two bit-organized RAMs with coincidence addressing. The 1024-bit RAM has a *refresh amplifier* that refreshes (reenergizes) each bit every 2 ms. Both RAMs are fully decoded; that is, the decoder and driver circuits are on the chip.

9.3.2 Core Memories

In contrast to semiconductor memories, core memories are *nonvolatile*—the memory stores information even when the power is off. Core memories have *destructive* readout; the reading process destroys the information stored. A WRITE step must be included in the READ cycle to rewrite the information into memory so that it can be reread as desired.

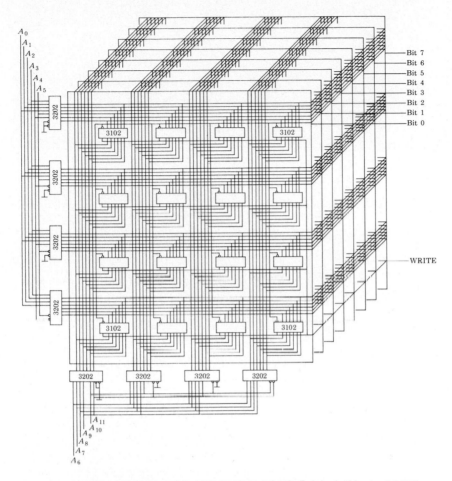

NOTE: Each plane has sixteen 256-bit RAMs (marked 3102). Each decoder/driver (marked 3202)
has 4 address bits to address 16 locations. Another 2 address bits on each axis select the
proper decoder/driver.

Fig. 9.6   Organization of a 4096-word by 8-bit memory. Each plane has 16 256-bit
RAMs (marked 3102). Each decoder-driver (marked 3202) has 4 address
bits to address 16 locations. Another 2 address bits on each axis select
the proper decoder-driver.

The basic core memory is constructed from small magnetic cores
with a wire or line threaded through them as shown in figure 9.9.
The outer diameter of the core is about 0.02 inch (0.05 cm). Core
size has continually decreased since the first magnetic core memories
were built, with the result that each new core could pass through

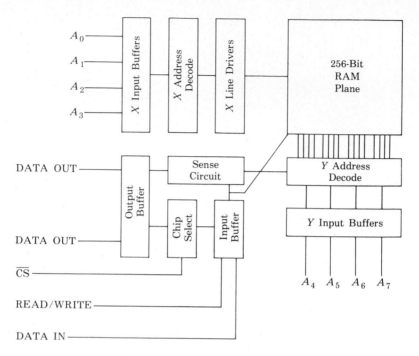

Fig. 9.7   256-bit random access memory

the hole in its predecessor. Cores are rapidly approaching the minimum size determined by the size of the wires that must pass through them. Naturally, the difficulty of wiring cores increases as the size of cores decreases. The core can be magnetized by passing a magnetizing current, I_M, through the center of the core perpendicular to the plane of the core. The direction of magnetization is given by the right-hand rule. If you point the thumb of your right hand in the direction of the magnetizing current, your curled right fingers will show the direction of magnetization. The core in figure 9.9a shows counterclockwise magnetization corresponding to the flow of current from left to right. If the direction of the magnetizing current is reversed, the direction of magnetization also reverses.

For storing information, four characteristics of magnetic cores are important:

1. There are two distinct directions of magnetization that we may call 0 and 1. The 1 state results from the magnetizing current, $+I_M$; the 0 state results from the opposite current, $-I_M$.
2. When I_M is removed, the core stays magnetized.

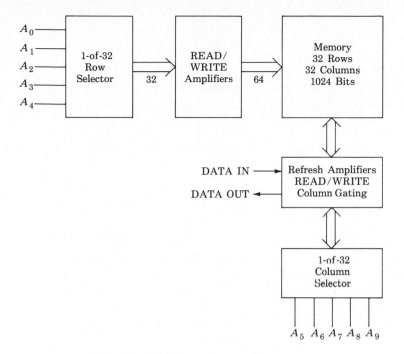

Fig. 9.8 1024-bit random access memory

3. The direction of magnetization can be reversed by reversing the magnetizing current.
4. Applying a current of half the magnitude of the magnetizing current, $I_M/2$, does not change the magnetization.

The behavior of a magnetic core is shown in figure 9.9b, which plots a hysteresis loop of magnetic flux density versus magnetizing current. If a current I_M is applied through the core when it is in the 0 state, the core will switch to the 1 state when the current is turned off. Similarly, the core will switch from the 1 state to the 0 state after an application of $-I_M$. However, currents of $+I_M/2$ or $-I_M/2$ do not move the core far enough along the hysteresis loop to switch state.

To read the information stored in a magnetic core, we need two lines as shown in figure 9.10. We apply a current to the INPUT line and sense a voltage on the SENSE line. By Faraday's law, the voltage induced in the SENSE line is proportional to the rate of change of the magnetic flux density. By convention the current applied to the INPUT line is $-I_M$, the magnetizing current required

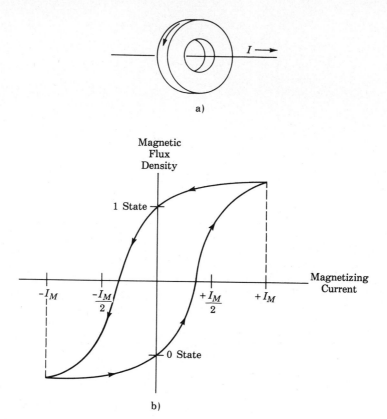

Fig. 9.9 A magnetic core (a) and a hysteresis loop (b)

to write a 0 into the core. If the core is already in the 0 state, a small pulse will appear in the SENSE line. If the core is in the 1 state, the magnetizing current will cause the core to switch to the 0 state. As it switches to the 0 state, a larger pulse than would have come from a 0 core appears in the SENSE line. The distinction between these two pulses is not as clear as we would like it to be and is one major disadvantage of magnetic core memories. Noise can obscure the difference between the 0 pulse and the 1 pulse and cause reading errors.

To use cores in a large memory, we need still more wires. Figure 9.11 shows a magnetic core with four wires. One is the SENSE line already discussed. The X-SELECT and Y-SELECT lines correspond to the previous single INPUT line. By applying a current of $I_M/2$ in the same direction through both select lines, we can write a 0

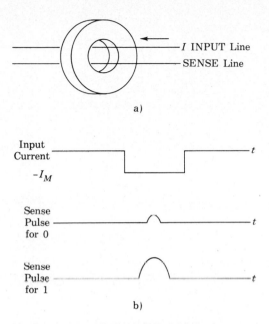

a)

Input
Current

$-I_M$

Sense
Pulse
for 0

Sense
Pulse
for 1

b)

Fig. 9.10a) Magnetic core with input and sense lines
   b) Input current and sense pulses if core was magnetized as 0 or 1

or a 1. If we apply currents of $I_M/2$ in opposing directions, the core
will not change. Alternatively, the INHIBIT line can be used to
oppose or inhibit the effect of currents in the SELECT lines.

Figure 9.11a shows writing a 1 into a core that has been in the
0 or counterclockwise state. Both SELECT lines carry a current $I_M/2$,
or half the magnetizing current. Figure 9.11b shows reading a 1. The
core has been in the 1 or clockwise state. Currents of $-I_M/2$ are
applied to both the X-SELECT and Y-SELECT lines causing the
core to switch to the 0 state. A 1 pulse appears on the SENSE line.

There are two ways to write a 0. The core is shown as being in
the 0 state because the READ process always returns the core to
the 0 state. In figure 9.11c, currents of $-I_M/2$ are applied to both
SELECT lines. The total current of $-I_M$ holds the core in the 0
state. In figure 9.11d, currents of $+I_M/2$ are applied to the X-SELECT
and Y-SELECT lines as if a 1 were to be written. However, the
INHIBIT line carries a current of $-I_M/2$. The net current is $+I_M/2$,
and the core stays in the 0 state.

Figure 9.11e shows reading a 0. Currents of $-I_M/2$ are applied to
the SELECT lines. The SENSE line reads a 0 pulse.

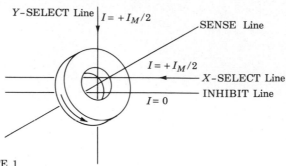

WRITE 1

a) Writing a 1 requires X and Y currents of $I_M/2$ and inhibit current of 0; magnetism is initially 0 and switches to 1.

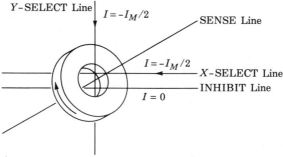

READ 1

b) Reading a 1 requires X and Y currents of $-I_M/2$ and inhibit current of 0; magnetism is initially 1 and switches to 0 with a large pulse output on SENSE line.

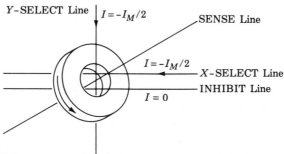

WRITE 0

c) Writing a 0 can be accomplished by X and Y currents of $-I_M/2$; magnetism is 0 and stays 0 with a small pulse output on SENSE line.

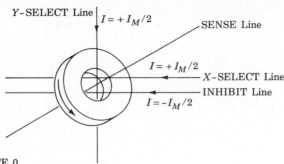

WRITE 0

d) Writing a 0 can be accomplished when the magnetic state is already 0 by X and Y currents of $+I_M/2$ and inhibit current of $-I_M/2$ for a total current of $+I_M/2$.

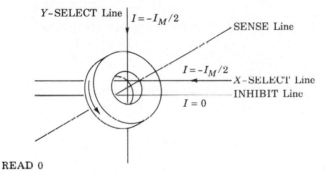

READ 0

e) Reading a 0 requires X and Y currents of $-I_M/2$; magnetism is 0 and stays 0 with a small pulse output on SENSE line.

Fig. 9.11   A magnetic core element with wires clockwise magnetism $= 1$; counterclockwise magnetism $= 0$

The timing of the READ and WRITE operations is shown in figure 9.12. Because the READ process is destructive, we must store the results of the READ operation in flipflops. During the WRITE operation, the outputs of the flipflops determine whether or not the INHIBIT line is enabled. If a 1 is read and stored in a flipflop, the flipflop output determines that the INHIBIT current should be 0 so that the net magnetizing current will write a 1 into the core. If the flipflop output is 0, the INHIBIT line is enabled to carry a current of $-I_M/2$. Then the total magnetizing current is $I_M/2$ and the core stays in the 0 state throughout the WRITE process.

Core memories are usually organized in one of three ways:

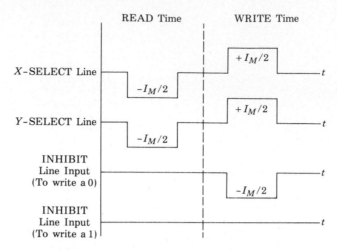

Fig. 9.12   Timing of currents for writing into magnetic core

1. 3D or coincident current memories;
2. 2D or word-organized memories; and
3. 2½D memories.

3D Memories   3D memories resemble bit-organized semiconductor RAMs. One bit plane is required for each bit of the word to be stored. Such a bit plane—one that stores 16 bits—is shown in figure 9.13. The 4-bit address of each cell is divided into its two X bits and two Y bits and presented to the decoder/drivers. One cell is selected as the coincidence of the X-SELECT and Y-SELECT lines. One INHIBIT line is common to the entire bit plane.

Let us suppose that we have six such bit planes and that we wish to write 101101 into the bits of word 1011. We assume the word is initially zero. It is customary to clear (write zeros into) a word before writing the desired information. We select 1011, the fourth bit in the third row of each bit plane, by the input X address 10 and the input Y address 11. We apply currents of $+I_M/2$ to the selected X and Y lines in all six bit planes. This allows us to write 1s in all bits of word 1011. Because we want 0s written into bits 1 and 4, we make the INHIBIT lines of bit planes 1 and 4 carry currents of $-I_M/2$. The cores of word 1011 in these two bit planes receive currents of $+I_M/2$, $+I_M/2$, and $-I_M/2$; the net current of $+I_M/2$ does not affect them. As a result, we write 1s into bit planes 0, 2, 3, and 5 and 0s into bit planes 1 and 4. Thus we write 101101.

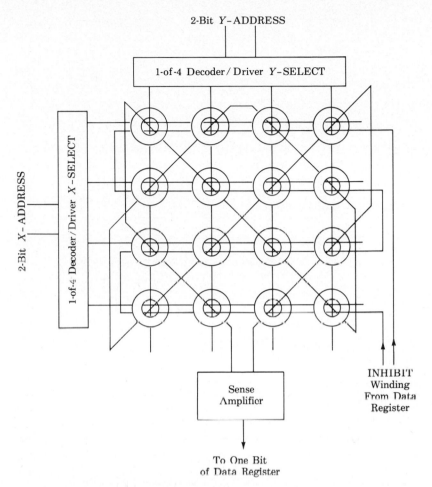

2-Bit Y-ADDRESS

1-of-4 Decoder/Driver Y-SELECT

2-Bit X-ADDRESS

1-of-4 Decoder/Driver X-SELECT

Sense
Amplifier

INHIBIT
Winding
From Data
Register

To One Bit
of Data Register

Fig. 9.13 Organization of 1-bit plane of a four-wire 3D or coincident current memory

We should check to be sure that we are not inadvertently writing into any other cores. All the cores in the third row of bit planes 0, 2, 3, and 5 receive a current of $+I_M/2$ from the X-SELECT line. This current is too small to cause magnetization. Similarly, all cores in the fourth column of those bit planes receive $+I_M/2$ and are not affected. Most cores in bit planes 1 and 4, except for the selected cores, receive a current of $-I_M/2$ and are not affected; cores that are in row 3 or column 4 (but not both) receive a net current of 0.

The READ process is similar but does not require the use of the INHIBIT line. We address the desired word by the X-SELECT and

Y-SELECT lines that are common to all bit planes. We then apply a current of $-I_M/2$ to all selected lines. The output of the SENSE line for each bit plane shows whether the bit was 0 or 1. All cores in the selected word receive a net current of $-I_M$ and are read. Other cores on the same X-SELECT or Y-SELECT line receive currents of $-I_M/2$ and stay constant.

The memory shown has separate lines for INHIBIT and SENSE. Since the INHIBIT line is used only for writing and the SENSE line only for reading, it is possible to have just three lines instead of the four shown in figure 9.13. Logic circuits can control the timing of the combination SENSE-INHIBIT line, also called a *BIT line*. The resulting memory is called a *three-wire 3D memory* as contrasted with the four-wire 3D memory shown.

A general 3D memory requires the following to store 2^n B-bit words:

1. $2^n \times B$ cores to store the information,
2. 1 X-SELECT decoder/driver with $n/2$ inputs and $2^{n/2}$ outputs,
3. 1 Y-SELECT decoder/driver with $n/2$ inputs and $2^{n/2}$ outputs,
4. B SENSE-INHIBIT lines, one for each bit plane.

For example, a 256-word 8-bit memory requires $256 \times 8 = 2048$ cores. The X-SELECT and Y-SELECT decoder/drivers each have four inputs and 16 output lines that are common to all 8-bit planes. Eight SENSE-INHIBIT lines are needed.

2D Memory   A 2D magnetic core memory is similar to a word-organized semiconductor RAM. Figure 9.14 shows a 2D memory that can store four words of 4 bits each. A 1-of-4 decoder is required to select the word. Each BIT-SENSE line runs through the same bit of all words in the memory. Writing can be done by applying half magnetizing current, $+I_M/2$, to the selected word and to each bit in the word that will be 1. The bits in the selected word that are to be 1 receive a net current of $+I_M$ and hence are magnetized to 1. The other bits in the selected word receive a current of $+I_M/2$ and stay 0. Similarly, the bits in all other words that receive a current of $+I_M/2$ in their BIT-SENSE lines are unchanged. Reading is done by sensing the response of each bit to a current pulse of $-I_M$ applied to the word. All cores in the selected word are changed to 0 and sensed for their previous state. No other cores get any current.

A general 2D memory for 2^n B-bit words requires:

1. $2^n \times B$ bits of storage,
2. 1 1-of-2^n decoder with an n-bit address and 2^n WORD lines,
3. B BIT lines.

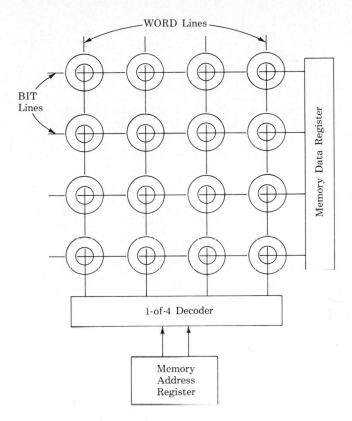

Fig. 9.14   A 2D or word-organized core memory

For example, a 2D memory for 256 × 8 bit words requires a 1-of-256 decoder and 256 WORD lines given a 16-bit address, 256 × 8 = 2048 bits of storage, and eight BIT lines.

2½D Memory   2½D memories, as shown in figure 9.15, are closely related to 2D memories. The main difference is that two words are associated with each WORD line. A BIT-SENSE line passes through the corresponding bit of all the words with positive direction through the first half of the words, and with negative direction through the second half. To WRITE a word, a half magnetizing current, $+I_M/2$, is applied to the word selected. Because of the organization, this current is actually applied to two words, both the word desired and the other word on the same word line. A current of $+I_M/2$ is applied to each BIT line for which the bit should be 1. In the second word, the current is in the opposite direction and hence is $-I_M/2$ for a

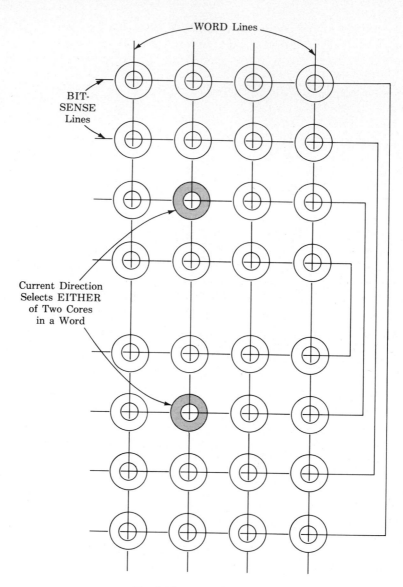

Fig. 9.15   A 2½D memory

net current to the bit of 0. No BIT line current is applied to the bits that are to be 0. Reading is also accomplished by applying currents to both the BIT lines and the WORD lines. A current of $-I_M/2$ is applied to the WORD line and the BIT lines of the selected word. Bits in the selected word are made 0, and the sense amplifiers detect their prior state. Bits in the other word on the same WORD line receive a net current of 0 and hence are not changed.

Another variation of 2½D memory closely resembles 3D memory. As in 3D memory, B bit planes are used and selection of the desired core is made by coincident currents. There is one X decoder/driver whose output lines are common to all B bit planes. There are B Y decoder/drivers, one for each bit plane. To WRITE, a current of $+I_M/2$ is sent through the chosen X-SELECT line, and a current of $+I_M/2$ is sent through only those Y-SELECT lines for which the bit is to be 1. The coincidence writes a 1 into the bits of the word that should be 1. Other cores on the same X-SELECT line receive only half the magnetizing current and are hence left unchanged. To READ, a current of $-I_M/2$ is sent through the X-SELECT line and through all Y-SELECT lines for that word. No INHIBIT lines are needed.

Other Magnetic Memory Technologies Other devices besides cores can store information magnetically. Thin-film memories and plated-wire memories are also used. A thin-film memory contains small dots of magnetic material on a glass surface. The dots can be magnetized in either of two directions—horizontal or vertical—and are usually organized as word-organized or 2D memories. Thin-film memories read nondestructively; thus a READ cycle does not require a WRITE step. They are faster than magnetic core memories, with cycle times from a few nanoseconds to, more typically, a few tenths of a microsecond. They are not used as extensively as core memories.

Plated-wire memories are a variation of thin-film memories. Instead of having magnetic dots on a flat surface, they have thin magnetic films on cylindrical rods or wires. Reading is nondestructive. They are somewhat slower than thin film memories but give larger output signals and are easier to manufacture. They can be organized as 2D or 3D memories.

9.4 READ-ONLY MEMORIES (ROMs)

Although we usually want to be able to change the information we have stored in memory, memories that can be read but cannot be written into are desirable for some applications. Read-only memories hold information permanently or near permanently. The information may be entered into them by the manufacturer or by the user. Programmable read-only memories (PROMs) are constructed so that the user can determine the program he wants stored in the memory.

The program is then permanently put in memory, usually electrically. If large quantities of ROMs with a particular program are needed, the information can be changed by LSI techniques at the time the memory array is constructed. Alternatively, some ROMs can have their information contents changed by some slow electrical process, although the information cannot be stored by normal computer operations. Such memories, sometimes called *read-mostly memories,* are useful if it is likely that small changes will be made in the programs. Such alterable ROMs are often used for storing micropro-grams, as we will discuss later in the chapter on system control.

Read-only memories can replace combinational logic. For example, consider the seven-segment decoder whose truth table is given as table 9.1. The inputs are the binary equivalents of the decimal digits, and the outputs are the seven segments of a seven-segment display for the numbers, shown in figure 9.16. We could construct a two-level AND/OR logic circuit that would realize this function. (See problem 2.27.) However, a simpler solution is to build a read-only memory that stores the information shown in the table. This memory will give the seven-segment outputs whenever the binary number is used as an address.

Other applications of ROMs include:

1. Library subroutines for frequently wanted functions, control routines, scale transformations, etc.
2. Special-purpose programs
3. System programs, such as bootstrap loaders
4. Function tables, such as logarithmic and trigonometric tables

TABLE 9.1

TRUTH TABLE FOR A SEVEN-SEGMENT DECODER

Inputs				Outputs						
W	X	Y	Z	A	B	C	D	E	F	G
0	0	0	0	1	1	1	1	1	1	0
0	0	0	1	0	1	1	0	0	0	0
0	0	1	0	1	1	0	1	1	0	1
0	0	1	1	1	1	1	1	0	0	1
0	1	0	0	0	1	1	0	0	1	1
0	1	0	1	1	0	1	1	0	1	1
0	1	1	0	0	0	1	1	1	1	1
0	1	1	1	1	1	1	0	0	0	0
1	0	0	0	1	1	1	1	1	1	1
1	0	0	1	1	1	1	0	0	1	1

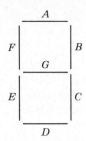

a) Display with segments lettered

b) Digits 0 through 9

Fig. 9.16 Seven-segment display

5. Emulation of other computers
6. Microprogramming

Programmed Logic Arrays A variation of read-only memory is a programmed logic array (PLA). Like a conventional read-only memory, a PLA is organized to provide an output of stored information in response to an input address. The difference between a PLA and a ROM is that the ROM is organized to provide outputs in response to all possible inputs, while a PLA can ignore some inputs and provide the same outputs for other groups of inputs. In other words, a PLA is like a condensed ROM that gives outputs for only some inputs. Its main advantage is the efficiency of providing storage for only certain desired inputs. As the cost of memory continues to decrease, this advantage becomes less important.

9.5 SEMIRANDOM-ACCESS AND SEQUENTIAL-ACCESS MEMORIES

Besides random-access memories, you may have encountered two other types of memory organizations. One is *semirandom-access memories,* such as discs and drums. The storage devices in semi-random-access memories rotate with a constant period. Any word can be accessed at some time within the period of rotation. Hence access time, while not constant, is limited by the period.

9.5.1 Magnetic Drums

Magnetic drums were among the first semirandom-access memories. A magnetic drum consists of a rotating cylinder coated with a thin layer of magnetic material. Several recording heads are mounted in a row along the surface of the drum. They write information on the drum by magnetizing small areas, and read information from it by sensing the magnetization of these areas. As the drum rotates, a thin strip called a *track* passes continually under each head. A track is divided into cells, each of which stores one binary bit. Figure 9.17 shows the general organization of a drum. Only a few heads and associated tracks are shown; a magnetic drum can have several hundred tracks. One track usually provides timing for the drum.

Capacities, sizes, and rates of rotation of magnetic drums vary widely. A small drum may have 15 to 25 tracks with 1000 or so cells per track for a total storage capacity up to 25,000 bits. A large drum may have 500 to 1000 tracks with as many as 100,000 cells per track for storage of as many as 10^8 bits. Rotation rates vary from 120 to more than 3600 rpm. Large drums ordinarily rotate more slowly than small drums. Access time decreases as drum speed increases. Access time can be decreased by mounting several heads on each track or by programming memory operations so that they occur just as the desired word is about to pass under the head.

Magnetic drums may be operated either in series or in parallel. With parallel operation all bits of a word may be read or written

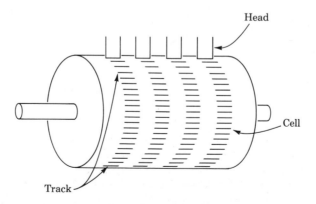

Fig. 9.17 Magnetic drum memory

simultaneously. For example, if a computer word has 32 bits, a magnetic drum with 32 tracks plus a timing track can store one word in each row along the drum. Separate READ and WRITE amplifiers for each track are needed for parallel operation. Words are located by the timing track. For example, if each track contains 1024 cells, a 10-bit counter can account for track position with respect to a reference 0 position. The counter is increased by 1 as each new timing mark (corresponding to a cell on the information tracks) appears. An address register can hold the address of a word to be read.

With series operation, only one track is read or written at a time; hence only one READ and WRITE amplifier is needed. Each word is stored in adjacent cells along a single track. Locating a word requires finding the correct track and the cell along the track that contains the first bit of the word. Usually in series operation each track is assigned a number and is divided into sectors. If a computer word has 32 bits, and a track has 1024 cells, the track is divided into 32 sectors, each of which can store a 32-bit word. Both track number and sector number must be specified to locate a word. Thus an address register with 10 bits (5 for the track number and 5 for the sector number) is needed to hold the address of a 32-bit word stored serially in the 32-track (plus timing track), 1024-cell track memory that we have described.

9.5.2 Magnetic Discs

Magnetic discs are also semirandom-access memories that operate much like magnetic drums. Their appearance resembles a coin-operated record player or jukebox. Several rotating discs coated with a thin layer of magnetic material are stacked with thin spaces in between. Magnetic heads positioned along a radius of each disc record information in a circular band. A disc may have several hundred of these bands or data tracks. Data may be recorded around each track with a density of a few thousand bits per centimeter. Because the outer tracks have greater circumference than the inner tracks, they can store more bits. The discs rotate at speeds on the order of 1000 rpm. Their diameters may be as large as 1 meter or more.

Various schemes have been developed for placing the magnetic head at the end of a mechanical arm in the correct position. Some disc memories have only one magnetic head for all the discs in the memory. Others have one or two heads per disc. Accurate positioning of the mechanical arms is difficult and limits the number of bits that can be stored on a disc. Information is usually stored on a magnetic disc in a manner comparable to serial storage for a magnetic drum. Thus each data track on the disc is divided into sectors, each of which can store one word. The word is located by finding the correct track and the correct sector.

9.5.3 Floppy Discs

A major recent advance in magnetic disc memories has been the development of *floppy discs*. These discs combine the head positioning technology of magnetic discs with the recording surface technology of magnetic tapes. The recording medium is standard computer Mylar tape fashioned into a disc instead of strips. Floppy discs look like flexible 45 rpm phonograph records. Each disc is enclosed in a square plastic envelope. The track and sector formats are the same as for magnetic discs (now called hard discs to distinguish them from floppy discs). In addition, floppy discs are much less expensive than hard discs.

A standard floppy disc holds about 3.1 million bits—about 250,000 bytes. Its data is recorded on 77 tracks at a maximum density of about 1260 bits/cm on the inside track. Any point on the disc can be accessed in less than a second.

9.5.4 Shift Register Memories

Shift register memories are another example of semirandom-access memories. The basic shift register principle was discussed in chapter 4. Recently, shift register memories have been constructed from *charge-coupled devices* (CCDs), which are MOS devices that transfer charges serially. One CCD memory stores 9216 bits arranged as 1024 words by 9 bits. The nine registers are shifted in parallel, thus allowing for handling of 9-bit bytes in a byte-serial mode. The main advantages of CCD memories are low cost and high bit density. CCD memories need only about 1% of the chip area per bit of bipolar memories. They are good candidates for mass memories of many megabits (millions of bits).

Another shift register memory technology is *magnetic bubbles*. Bubbles are small magnetic domains that can be made to drift along and hence transfer information in series. They are primarily used for mass memories.

9.5.5 Optical Memories

Information can be recorded optically on film. Current optical memories use a bit-by-bit serial storage that is accessed much like magnetic disc or tape. Current memories are primarily read-only and are limited by the mechanical techniques required for access. Holographic methods offer promise for future optical memories.

Sequential-access memories, such as tapes, have access times that may be quite long if the word to be read is at one end of the tape and the search is begun at the other end. Both sequential-access memories and semirandom-access memories are used for storage of large amounts of information that is not needed as quickly as the information in main memory.

9.5.6 Magnetic Tapes

Magnetic tape is the most common type of sequential-access memory. Its low cost permits storage of vast amounts of information. Unfortunately, its access time can be very long. Magnetic tape storage is not volatile; information on magnetic tape may be held almost indefinitely.

Magnetic tape systems may use reels, cassettes, or cartridges. The largest systems usually use reels; minicomputer systems often use cassettes. Cassettes are slower than reels but are more convenient to mount. The tape and the recording system look much like those used for home entertainment.

Data are recorded on magnetic tape with some coding system. Several data tracks or channels are recorded along the length of the tape. Typically, a partial word or byte can be stored in parallel across one row of the tape. Two types of parity checks can be used. Data can be checked for each row across the tape (transverse parity) or for several bits along one channel (longitudinal parity). Tape can be formatted or unformatted. *Formatted* tapes have a timing or reference track to locate data. *Unformatted* tapes have no reference marks; a block of data is located by identifying a header at the start of the block.

The characteristics of tape systems vary widely. Tapes can store from 6000 to a few hundred thousand bytes (8-bit characters) per second. Start and stop times can range from 1 to 20 ms. Tape speeds vary from 18.75 to 900 inches per second. Access times can be as long as 4 minutes. As many as a few million 16-bit words can be stored on large reels.

Paper tape can also be used for sequential-access memory. It is less satisfactory than magnetic tape because it is prone to tear and cannot be rerecorded. We will discuss paper tape input/output systems in the next chapter.

9.6 MAGNETIC RECORDING TECHNIQUES

Magnetic recording—whether on drums, discs, or tapes—requires storing a binary 0 or 1 on a small area of a moving magnetic surface. The recording technique should store data as densely as possible and be as reliable as possible. Unfortunately, there is a tradeoff between packing density and reliability. Three techniques are commonly used to store information magnetically:

1. Return-to-zero (RZ)
2. Return-to-bias (RB)
3. Nonreturn-to-zero (NRZ)

All three techniques change input current patterns to magnetic flux patterns when information is written. When information is read, the flux patterns are sensed and changed to current in the READ winding. The recorded magnetic flux pattern closely resembles the input current. The voltage in the READ winding responds to the rate of change of the magnetic flux. The voltage sensed in the READ winding is a positive pulse whenever the flux increases and a negative pulse whenever the pulse decreases. As a result the output current at the READ head changes polarity twice as often as the input current at the WRITE head does when writing the information. The three recording techniques differ in their ways of coding input information to provide easy reading of the output current.

9.6.1 Return-to-Zero Recording

In *return-to-zero* (RZ) recording a brief positive pulse represents 1 and a brief negative pulse represents 0, as shown in figure 9.18. Between pulses the input signal current returns to 0, whence the name. The flux pattern resulting from this pattern of input pulses also consists of brief pulses of either polarity. The output signal from the READ head consists of a positive pulse followed almost immediately by a negative pulse when the input is a 1, and the opposite when the input is a 0. A major difficulty in RZ recording is detecting the first of the two adjacent pulses in each time interval in order to detect a positive pulse for a 1 and a negative pulse for a 0. Synchronization signals aid in detecting the first pulse.

A major disadvantage of RZ recording is that it is difficult to rerecord or write over previously recorded information. The timing of each new pulse that is to replace the old information is critical.

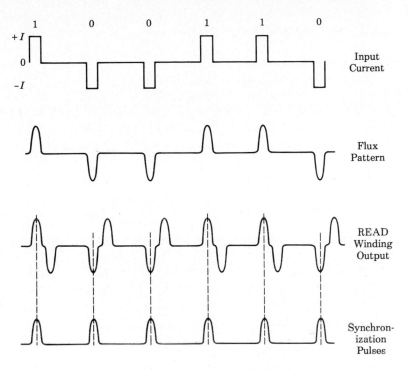

Fig. 9.18 Return-to-zero recording

Thus this system is usually used only with timing tracks. Alternatively, the information could be erased from the magnetic medium before recording new information.

9.6.2 Return-to-Bias Recording

Return-to-bias (RB) recording maintains input current constant at $-I$ except when 1s are to be represented by a brief pulse of $+I$ as shown in figure 9.19. Between 1 pulses the current returns to a bias of $-I$, whence the name. The flux pattern has a pulse for each 1 signal. The resulting READ winding output has double pulses—positive followed by negative—to represent 1 signals. The output stays constant for 0 signals. The detection problem is simpler than for RZ signals. Synchronization signals show the timing of the 1 pulses.

RB systems allow easier rerecording than do RZ systems. Timing of the new information is less critical inasmuch as the bias current

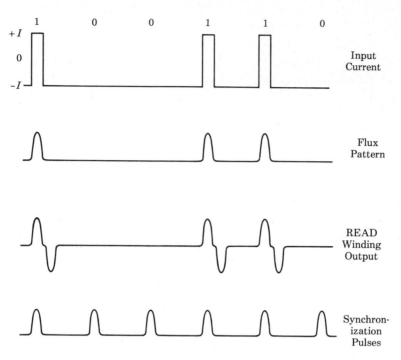

Fig. 9.19   Return-to-bias recording

of −I effectively erases all 1s. Long sequences of 0s can cause problems in RB systems because only 1s cause changes in flux and therefore outputs at the READ head.

9.6.3 Nonreturn-to-Zero Recording

All three types of *nonreturn-to-zero* (NRZ) recording share the common feature that the input signal does not return to zero—thus the name. They differ in their representations of input signals. All three use signals that hold a level longer than the brief pulses of the return-to-zero and return-to-bias methods.

The basic NRZ method (shown in figure 9.20a) represents 1s by +I and 0s by −I. The input current stays constant for strings of consecutive 0s or consecutive 1s. It changes only for transitions between 0 and 1. The READ winding output has positive pulses corresponding to input signal transitions from 0 to 1, and negative pulses for input transitions from 1 to 0. A decoder can change these transition signals into a copy of the input signal.

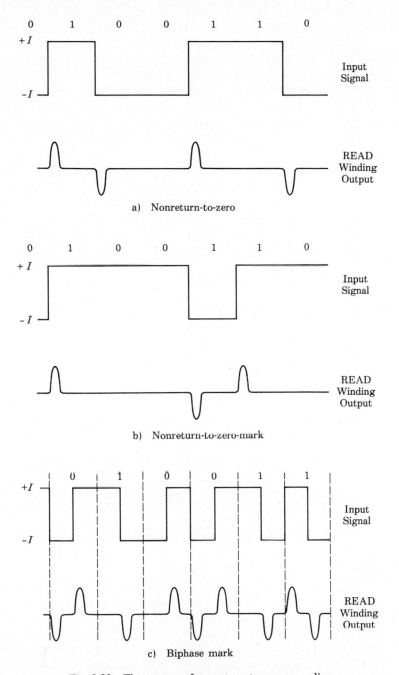

Fig. 9.20   Three types of nonreturn-to-zero recording

The NRZ-mark method (shown in figure 9.20b) has an input signal that changes from $+I$ to $-I$ or from $-I$ to $+I$ for 1s and stays constant for 0s. Hence 1s and 0s no longer have an absolute polarity. A reference signal, usually obtained from a timing track, is needed at the start of a signal sequence. The READ winding output alternates positive and negative pulses to show a transition between 1 and 0 or between 0 and 1. A decoder can change the transition signals into a copy of the input signal provided that it has an initial reference.

Biphase mark signaling represents 0 by a current of $-I$ followed by a current of $+I$, and 1 by the opposite signal as shown in figure 9.20c. In either case each current is on for half the signal period. The READ winding output has negative pulses that correspond to negative transitions of the input signal and positive pulses for positive transitions of the input signal. The output tends to have many more pulses than does the output of either of the two preceding NRZ methods. Decoding is more difficult and requires synchronization signals.

9.7 MEMORY HIERARCHIES

The various types of memory in a computer are arranged in a hierarchy. Information that is needed most often is kept in fast memory or in a specially fast semiconductor RAM, called a *scratchpad* or *cache memory*. Other information that will be needed for the operation of a program is kept in main memory. Information that may be needed only rarely is kept in mass memories that are semirandom or sequential access. The central problem of memory management is to keep information in the proper location according to the likelihood that it will be needed so that the computer will always be able to access information quickly. Various schemes have been devised to swap information between the scratchpad and main memory, bringing information that will be needed to the scratchpad and storing information that is not needed for the next few calculations in main memory.

Other similar schemes swap blocks of information between main memory and mass memory. If such schemes do not require the programmer to keep track of the absolute location of information, they are said to be *transparent* to the programmer. That is, the computer's operating system, rather than the programmer, handles the swapping of information. One such scheme, used on the IBM System 370, is called *virtual* memory.

9.8 SUMMARY

Random-access memories (RAMs) can be made from either semiconductors or magnetic cores. Semiconductor RAMs, especially bipolar RAMs, are faster but are more expensive except for small memories. Hence most memories now are magnetic core, but semiconductor memories are likely to acquire a much larger part of the market in the near future.

Semiconductor memories can be either word-organized or bit-organized. Word organization is simpler and holds the entire memory on one plane. However, it requires larger decoders. Bit organization requires one memory plane for each bit to be stored. Two sets of relatively small decoders are used to access the word.

Magnetic core memories can be organized as 3D (coincident current or bit-organized), 2D (word-organized), or 2½D (a hybrid). The relative advantages of the first two schemes are the same as for semiconductor RAMs. 2½D memories require fewer wires than the corresponding 3D memories.

Read-only memories (ROMs) are memories into which information is permanently or near permanently written. They can replace combinational logic and can store commonly needed programs or routines.

Semirandom-access memories, such as magnetic drums and discs, can access any word within a time determined by the period of rotation of the memory device. Sequential-access memories have information stored in sequence along a strip; access times can be as long as a few minutes. Magnetic tape, held either on reels, cassettes, or cartridges, is the most common sequential-access memory.

Return-to-zero magnetic recording systems use brief positive and negative pulses to represent 1s and 0s, respectively; the current returns to zero between pulses. Return-to-bias recording uses brief positive current pulses for 1s; 0s and intervals between pulses are represented by a bias of negative current. Nonreturn-to-zero recording uses three different schemes to code incoming information; all three schemes use relatively long pulses to represent both 1s and 0s.

The central concern of memory design is the tradeoff between speed and cost. Large computers have a hierarchical arrangement of memory from high-speed registers, through high-speed scratchpad or cache memories, through the main memory, to relatively slow mass memories. Memory management schemes attempt to arrange the information so that the information that is most likely to be needed is always in the fastest parts of memory.

Concepts

access time
address decoder
bit driver
bit organization
buffer
byte addressing
cache
charge-coupled devices
chip select
coincidence addressing
decoder/driver
destructive
disc drum
dynamic
floppy disc
formatted
fully decoded
inhibit line
magnetic bubbles
main memory
memory address register
memory cycle

memory data register
nonreturn-to-zero
nonvolatile
random-access memory
read-only memory
read/write memory
refresh
return-to-bias
return-to-zero
scratchpad memory
semirandom access
sense amplifier
sequential access
static
tape
timing track
transparent
undecoded
virtual memory
volatile
word organization
write time

9.9 REFERENCES

Riley (1971) discusses detailed aspects of memory technology. Booth (1971), Bartee (1972), and Abrams and Stein (1973) present elementary aspects of memory. Poppelbaum (1972) is an advanced computer hardware text that is especially strong on the physical principles of memory technology.

9.10 PROBLEMS

9.1   Consider a 2K 16-bit memory. How many bits are needed for the memory data register? How many for the memory address register? (9.2)

9.2   Consider a 16K 32-bit memory. How many bits are needed for the memory data register? How many for the memory address register?   (9.2)

9.3   Determine the number of storage cells, the number of bit drivers and amplifiers, the number of BIT lines, and the size of the decoder needed for a 512-word by 8-bit word-organized memory.   (9.3)

9.4   Determine the number of storage cells, the number of bit drivers and amplifiers, the number of BIT lines, and the size of the decoder needed for a 4K-word by 12-bit word-organized semiconductor memory.   (9.3)

9.5   What size decoder is needed for a chip select to increase a 256-word by 8-bit word-organized semiconductor memory to a 4K-word by 8-bit memory?   (9.3)

9.6   Determine the number of storage cells, the number of bit drivers and amplifiers, the number of BIT lines, and the number and size of the decoders needed for a 1K-word by 10-bit bit-organized semiconductor memory.   (9.3)

9.7   Determine the number of storage cells, the number of bit drivers and amplifiers, the number of BIT lines, and the number and size of the decoders needed for a 4K-word by 18-bit bit-organized semiconductor memory.   (9.3)

9.8   Determine the number of cores, the number of SENSE-INHIBIT lines, and the size of the X-SELECT and Y-SELECT decoder/drivers for a 3D 64K-word, 16-bit magnetic core memory.   (9.3)

9.9   Determine the number of cores, the number of SENSE-INHIBIT lines, and the size of the X-SELECT and Y-SELECT decoder/drivers for a 3D 1024-word, 12-bit magnetic core memory.   (9.3)

9.10 Determine the number of cores and BIT lines and the size of the decoder needed for a 512-word, 16-bit 2D magnetic core memory.   (9.3)

9.11 Determine the number of cores and BIT lines and the size of the decoder needed for a 4K-word, 8-bit 2D magnetic core memory. (9.3)

9.12 Determine the number of bits of ROM needed to implement an n-input, m-output function. (9.4)

9.13 Calculate the bit capacity and the maximum access time for a magnetic drum memory with 25 tracks plus a timing track of 1024 bits per track that rotates at 6000 rpm. (9.5)

9.14 Calculate the bit capacity and the maximum access time for a magnetic drum memory with 512 tracks (plus a timing track) of 4K bits per track that rotates at 3600 rpm. (9.5)

9.15 A magnetic drum memory has a circumference of 100 cm and a packing density of 500 bits/cm. It has 48 tracks plus a timing track. How many bits can it store? (9.5)

9.16 A magnetic drum memory has 64 tracks plus a timing track and 1440 bits per track. It is used in a serial mode to store 24-bit words. How many bits are required to address each word? How many bits are required to address a track? How many bits are required to address a sector? How many words can the memory store? (9.5)

9.17 A magnetic drum memory has 257 tracks including a timing track with 1280 bits per track. It stores 16-bit words in a serial mode. How many bits are required to address a word? How many bits are required to address a sector? How many words can the memory store? (9.5)

9.18 A magnetic tape memory has seven tracks per centimeter. If the packing density is 100 bits/cm and the tape moves at 20 cm/second, how many bits can be read per second from a 2-cm-wide tape? (9.5)

9.19 A magnetic tape memory has eight tracks per centimeter. If the packing density is 150 bits/cm and the tape moves at 10 cm/second, how many bits can be read per second from a 1-cm-wide tape? (9.5)

9.20 Draw flux and READ winding waveforms for storing 1110101 on return-to-zero, return-to-bias, and all three nonreturn-to-zero recording systems. (9.6)

9.21 Draw flux and READ winding waveforms for storing 0100111 on return-to-zero, return-to-bias, and all three nonreturn-to-zero recording systems. (9.6)

10 Input/Output

10.1 OVERVIEW

We are now ready to discuss input/output operations. You are probably familiar with many input/output devices such as card readers, teletypes, paper tape punches, and so forth. We will describe the principles of operation of some of these devices later in the chapter, but will begin by considering some of the requirements of any input/output transfer. How can a high-speed computer deal with a slow input/output device? How can the computer schedule the transfer of data? How are differences in information format handled? How can data be handled most efficiently in terms of both speed and memory?

There are a great number of input/output devices and a great variety of techniques for input/output transfers. We can choose between programmed input/output transfers (in which the program controls the transfer once the device is ready) and interrupt transfers (in which an input/output device is allowed to interrupt the computer). We can transfer information directly through the accumulator of the CPU or indirectly through special data paths into memory. Input/output systems are so diverse that all we can do in an elementary text is discuss a few input/output devices and techniques.

10.2 EXTERNAL DEVICES

We can think of an external, peripheral, or input/output device as having three main parts, as shown in figure 10.1. The *transducer* converts information from electrical to other forms of energy during output or from other forms to electrical during input. For example, the transducer of a paper tape reader converts information from mechanical or optical form to electrical signals. Similarly, the transducer of a paper tape punch converts electrical signals into punched holes. Later in this chapter we will discuss the physical behavior of several major input/output devices.

The *data register* or *buffer* momentarily holds information that is being transferred between the transducer and the computer. The register may be as long as a computer word to allow storing the contents of memory in auxiliary storage such as drums or magnetic tapes. (In the previous chapter we viewed such devices as memory, but in this chapter we consider them as input/output devices since they have much in common with other input/output devices.) The data register may be shorter than a computer word. For example, teletypes and paper tape readers have 8-bit registers that hold single characters. Information can be transferred between the data register and the computer either in series or in parallel as shown in chapter 4.

The device controller supervises the transfer of information between the device and the computer. It sends status signals to the computer to show the state of the device. Figure 10.2 shows two 1-bit status registers, called *flags*, in the device controller. The READY/NOT READY flag shows if the device is ready for information transfer. The BUSY/DONE flag shows if the device is transferring information. The device controller also accepts and executes control signals from

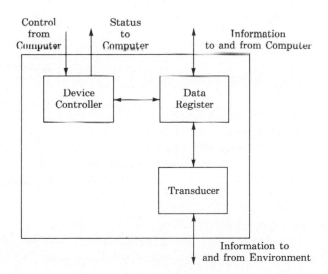

Fig. 10.1 An external device

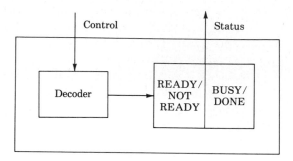

Fig. 10.2   Device controller

the computer, such as READ or REWIND TAPE. It has a decoder to decode control signals for the selection of the device being addressed, and to identify the command to be executed.

10.3 INPUT/OUTPUT REQUIREMENTS

There are three main requirements for communication between input/output devices and computers—timing, speed, and coding. External devices are not usually synchronized with the same clock that controls the computer. They operate *asynchronously* with respect to the computer. Thus there is a problem of synchronizing the times of information transfer between external devices and the computer. This problem can be partially solved by holding the data in a data register or buffer until the computer is ready for it. However, some devices cannot hold data for more than a few microseconds. For example, an instrument recorder that has no memory of its own must transfer its information to the computer before it takes the next reading or the information may be lost. Such devices should be allowed to interrupt the computer to transfer information. We will discuss this problem in more detail in the next section.

A second important requirement is the difference in speed of operation between an external device and the computer. Most external devices operate several orders of magnitude more slowly than do computers. Since the mechanical technology affecting peripheral device operation is not increasing in speed nearly as rapidly as the semiconductor technology governing computer processor and memory operation, the differences in speed are likely to increase. However, some nonmechanical peripheral devices, such as optical devices, may solve this problem.

Table 10.1 shows typical speeds of operation of various devices expressed as equivalent characters per second. One of the slowest is the number of actions that a human can take. Another example of a slow transfer involves an instrument such as a thermometer that needs to be read only every 5 minutes. Of all the devices listed, only magnetic discs and drums can transfer information at speeds comparable to the speed of operation of the computer, approximately one million operations per second. Because of this vast difference in speed, we must use information transfer techniques that minimize the amount of time the computer spends waiting for the input/output device to act. These techniques are discussed in the next two sections.

The third requirement affecting transfer between the computer and an input/output device is coding information. Numbers may be recorded in binary, binary-coded decimal (BCD), or in any of several other codes. Characters are recorded in Hollerith card code on punched cards and in ASCII or EBCDIC code on most other media. We discussed ASCII in chapter 8. EBCDIC is an 8-bit code used on IBM computers. We will discuss these codes in more detail when we consider specific devices later in the chapter. Now we are simply concerned with devices that code information in several different ways. We can solve this problem either by converting all device codes to one standard code or by recording the coded information in memory with a notation of the type of code used. For the first solution we would build a hardware code converter from either random logic or read-only memory as we have discussed earlier. Then the information from the device can be automatically coded into the form preferred

TABLE 10.1

TYPICAL OPERATING SPEEDS OF EXTERNAL DEVICES

Device	Device rate	Maximum equivalent characters/second
Man	1-10 actions/sec	10
Measuring instruments	0.01 to 100 samples/sec	1000
Teletypes (ASR-33)	10 characters/sec	10
Cathode ray tube displays	10–140 characters/sec	240
Paper tape readers	10–1000 characters/sec	1000
Paper tape punches	10–150 characters/sec	150
Card readers (80 columns)	100–2000 cards/min	2667
Card punches (80 columns)	100–250 cards/min	333
Line printers (150 columns)	100–4000 lines/min	10,000
Graphic plotters	Up to 700 characters/sec	700
Magnetic tape	15,000–320,000 characters/sec	320,000
Magnetic drum/disc	30,000–1,500,000 characters/sec	1,500,000

for the computer. The code converter could be located in the external device or between the device and the computer. The second solution tags the coded information with a notation of the type of code used. The computer then handles the information as it is coded, but the information can be converted to a different code by either software or hardware as desired.

10.4 MODES OF CONTROL

We can handle input/output transfers in two ways. We can have the computer program determine the time at which input/output transfer is needed. Then under control of the program, the computer determines if the input/output device is ready and handles the transfer. The advantage of this approach is that the computer program controls the transfer. We can use this approach for any input/output transfer in which the information can be held in a register until the computer is ready for it. However, in the event the information will be lost if it is not transferred to the computer quickly, we must allow the input device to interrupt the computer to transfer information at the demand of the device.

Similarly, if the external device has information that is urgent, it must be allowed to interrupt the computer. Control of operations in real time, such as for a steel mill or an oil refinery, also requires input/output transfers for which external devices can interrupt the computer to exchange information.

10.4.1 Programmed Input/Output

The first method, called *programmed input/output,* can be handled easily in software. Under control of the program, the CPU asks the external device if it is ready. That is, the computer sends a control signal to the device to sense the status of the READY/NOT READY flag. When the READY flag is 1, the computer sends the necessary control signals to accomplish the information transfer. We examined this type of transfer for the PDP-8 in the last chapter.

10.4.2 Interrupts

We can transfer information more efficiently by using program interrupts. An interrupt controlled input/output transfer means that the external device signals the CPU when it needs to transfer information. For example, a radar might signal the CPU that it had spotted an object whose position and velocity should be sent to the computer.

The device starts the transfer by sending a signal to the CPU that interrupts the program being processed after the computer finishes executing the current instruction. The computer then acknowledges the interrupt and enters an interrupt routine.

The interrupt process is much like the actions of a person answering a telephone. When he hears the telephone ring, he may need to do something quickly to the work he has been doing so that it will stay as it is until he can return to it. For example, if he is sawing wood, he might turn off the saw so that the wood is saved in its current state. He then answers the telephone and talks with the person who called him. After he has talked with the caller and perhaps done something the caller asked him to do, he returns to his work.

A simple interrupt process involves several steps, as shown in the flowchart of figure 10.3. After executing the instruction that was in the CPU when the interrupt occurred, the computer turns off the interrupt system so that the computer will not be interrupted again until it is ready to accept another interrupt. The computer must then save enough information about the program it has been executing so that it can return to the program and resume execution after processing the interrupt. It must save the contents of the program counter so that it may return to the next instruction. The contents of the program counter are often stored in a fixed location in memory, say location 0. Then the contents of the accumulator must be saved, say in location 1. If the computer has several registers, the contents of all of them must be saved either in fixed locations in memory or in a stack. After the contents of all registers have been saved, the computer starts an interrupt service routine that may be located in location 2. The interrupt service routine may be the same for all interrupts or it may direct the computer to different service routines depending on the type of interrupt. For example, the service routine for a simple input transfer might involve reading an input character and storing it in memory just as was done in programmed input/output. After handling the transfer, the service routine restores the contents of the accumulator and any other registers for continued use in the main program. The interrupt system is then turned on again so that other interrupts can be handled. Control then returns to the main program via an indirect jump through location 0, where the contents of the program counter had been stored.

Figure 10.4 diagrams the changes in the contents of memory and registers while an interrupt is processed. When the interrupt occurs, instruction N of the user's program is being processed. After instruction N has been executed, the contents of the updated program

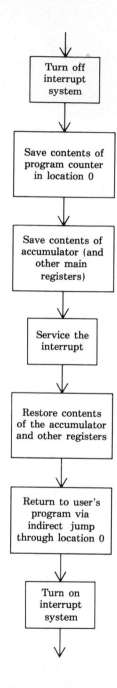

Fig. 10.3   Flowchart of interrupt procedure

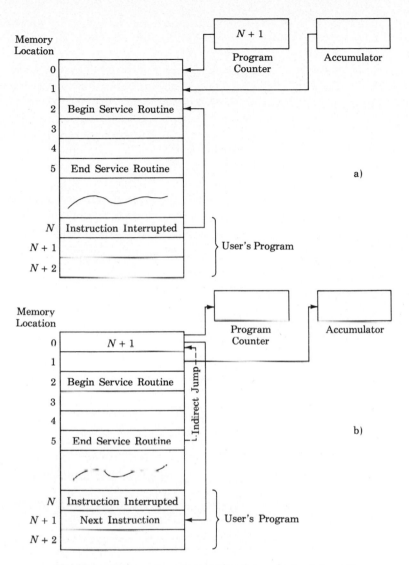

Fig. 10.4   Changes in memory and registers during interrupt

counter, $N + 1$, are stored in location 0. The contents of the accumulator are stored in location 1. The computer then processes the interrupt service routine, starting in location 2. When the service routine has been executed (fig. 10.4b), the contents of location 0 are returned to the program counter, thus transferring control back to instruction $N + 1$ of the user's program. The contents of location 1 are restored to the accumulator. The user's program resumes processing at instruction $N + 1$.

All but the simplest computers must handle a large number of interrupts of differing types and importance. In addition to interrupts for transfer of information to or from external devices, computers have interrupts that respond to other events. Most computers have interrupt procedures for emergency conditions such as power failure. When a sensor detects impending power failure, it interrupts the computer so that the computer may begin a power failure service routine. The power failure service routine may either transfer all important register and memory contents to a magnetic core memory that will not be affected by the power failure, or it may switch the computer to battery operation. A power failure interrupt may be handled entirely by hardware instead of by the programmed procedure just described.

Other important interrupts can occur when the user's program malfunctions. For example, an arithmetic operation in the user's program may result in a number that exceeds the range of numbers that the computer can handle; that is, it may overflow. Or the user may have attempted an illegal operation such as accessing protected areas of storage. When such irregularities occur, hardware in the CPU detects them and interrupts the user's program. (Interruptions caused by internal CPU conditions are often called *traps*.) The CPU then branches to an interrupt service routine to handle the condition. Typically it gathers and prints out information on the irregular condition. Depending on the severity of the problem, the computer might return to the user's program after servicing the interrupt or might abort the program if the error was one that prevents proper program execution.

Other types of interrupts include those for computer malfunctions and for timing. When error-detection circuitry in the computer detects an error, it notifies the control unit of the location and nature of the error. Errors are usually detected by adding one or more extra parity bits as discussed in chapter 6. When an error is detected, the computer branches to a service routine that attempts to determine if the error can be corrected. If the error cannot be corrected, the computer stops operation until it is fixed.

Interrupts for timing can regulate the amount of time each user can operate his program. A simple timing interrupt can end each user's program after it has run for a predetermined length of time. This scheme not only prevents one user from dominating computer time but also aborts programs that are stuck in an endless loop.

A similar timing interrupt method may be used on timesharing computers that allocate to each user the same small segment of time in rotation.

The existence of such a variety of possible interrupts requires the development of schemes to handle them. We can assign a priority to each external device and each possible interrupt from a user's program or from machine conditions. We can then build priority interrupt systems that will efficiently service interrupts according to the priority assigned. If two devices try to interrupt the computer at the same time, or a second interrupt occurs while the computer is still responding to an interrupt, the situation can be resolved according to the relative priorities. Resolution can be done by hardware or software. Hardware solutions require more expensive hardware but are usually faster; software solutions are less expensive but more flexible.

All interrupt systems, regardless of type, use much the same basic method for interrupts, as shown in figure 10.5. Two interrupt flipflops are used. When a device wants to interrupt the computer, its device control sets an *interrupt request* flipflop to 1 and sends a signal on the interrupt request line to the computer. When the computer is

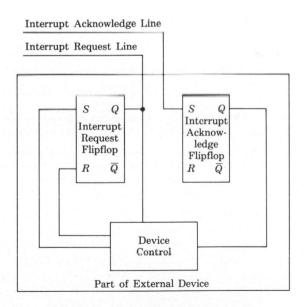

Fig. 10.5   Device controls for interrupts

ready to accept the interrupt, it sends a signal on an *interrupt acknowledge* line. The device can then transfer information. This procedure of having the computer acknowledge interrupt requests is known as *handshaking*. Variations of this scheme will be described for four types of systems. Additional hardware is required for device identification and priority determination.

The simplest but slowest priority interrupt system is a *single-level, single-priority system*. (*Level* refers to the number of interrupts that the processor can distinguish as occurring. *Priority* refers to the relative importance of each interrupt as implemented in hardware.) When an interrupt occurs in a single-level, single-priority system, the processor knows only that at least one interrupt has occurred. The interrupt request signal is the logical OR of the interrupt request signals of the external devices. To determine whether more than one interrupt occurred, and if so, which was more important, must be done by software. Thus, when the processor receives an interrupt request signal, it must ask each external device if it interrupted. If two or more devices have requested interrupts, the processor must decide which request to service first.

A slightly more complex system is a *multiple-level, single-priority system*. This system, besides having an interrupt request signal that is an OR of all device interrupt request signals, also has hardware that determines which device requested the interrupt. It has a device select code bus that allows the requesting device to identify itself. If a second device requests service before the processor has finished servicing the first interrupt request, the second device puts its select code on the device select code bus. The processor can then decide from some stored program which device has higher priority. In this system lower priority devices are allowed to interrupt processing of another interrupt request long enough to give the processor the device select code and to allow the processor to determine its priority. Because low priority devices can momentarily interrupt higher priority devices, the system's performance is degraded. The multiple-level, single-priority system has better performance than the single-level, single-priority system because device identification is handled quickly by hardware.

A *single-level, multiple-priority* interrupt system has devices arranged along an interrupt request line in order of their priority. When a device requests service, it opens a switch that breaks the interrupt request line from devices of lower priority. This line that passes through all the external devices is called a *daisy chain*. Thus a lower priority device cannot send an interrupt request signal to the processor until the processor has completed processing of a higher priority request. When the interrupt request has been serviced, the requesting device resets its interrupt request flipflop and thus completes the line to the lower priority devices. A lower priority device whose interrupt request flipflop has been set to request service can now send an interrupt request to the computer. Higher priority devices can interrupt lower priority devices in the system. This system is single-level because there is no hardware identification of the requesting device; the processor must identify the device. Such a system is not common since multiple-level systems are easy to construct.

The most advanced interrupt system is *multiple-level, multiple-priority*. It combines features of the two previous systems. External devices are arranged along a daisy chain according to their priority. A separate select code bus is used for device identification. When the device wants to interrupt the computer, it sends an interrupt request signal to the computer. When the computer is ready, it returns an interrupt acknowledge signal. Because of the daisy chain, all lower priority devices are prevented from interrupting the computer until the higher priority interrupt has been processed. When the device receives the interrupt acknowledge signal, it sends its select code on the select code bus so that the computer can identify it. It then transfers information.

The advantages of these four priority interrupt systems are summarized in table 10.2.

Even when interrupt priorities have been implemented in hardware, we may want to either change priorities by programming or ignore the interrupt system. Most interrupt systems let us do this through

TABLE 10.2

CHARACTERISTICS OF FOUR PRIORITY INTERRUPT SYSTEMS

System	Hardware complexity and cost	Programming effort required	Response time
Single-level, single-priority	Lowest	Highest	Slowest
Multiple-level, single-priority	Medium	High	Fast
Single-level, multiple-priority	Low	Medium	Slow
Multiple-level, multiple-priority	High	Low	Fastest

some hardware features that we have not yet described. One feature is an enable interrupt flipflop. When the enable interrupt flipflop is set, the interrupt system works as we have already described. When the enable interrupt system is reset or disabled, devices cannot request service. The system may have one master enable interrupt flipflop that can enable or disable all interrupts. Alternatively, each device may have its own enable interrupt flipflop that can be set or reset by control commands from the computer.

Another feature commonly used to control interrupts is an *interrupt mask register,* shown in figure 10.6. The bits of the interrupt mask register can be set by programmed commands to enable or disable interrupts. Each bit of the interrupt mask register that is 1 allows or enables interrupt conditions in that position. Each bit that is 0 inhibits interrupt conditions in that position. Each bit of the interrupt mask register is ANDed with the corresponding bit of the interrupt register. The outputs of the AND gates are masked interrupt signals that show interrupt requests from devices that the control unit has enabled.

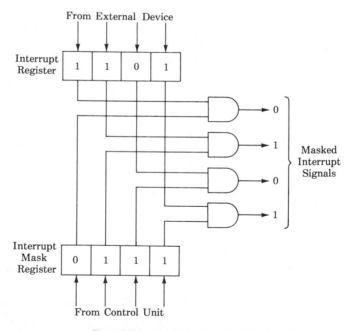

Fig. 10.6   Interrupt mask register

10.5 MODES OF TRANSFER

10.5.1 Direct Transfer

Although we have not mentioned it, we have so far been concerned with only one of the three common modes of input/output transfer, the direct transfer of information through the central processing unit. A block diagram of direct input/output transfer is shown in figure 10.7. Each data word is transferred between the external device and an accumulator of the CPU as controlled by the control unit. To transfer data between the external device and the computer memory, a second transfer is needed to transfer data between the accumulator and memory. This second transfer requires additional time. Direct transfer between an external device and computer memory is very slow, whether done by programmed commands or by interrupt systems. In programmed transfer we need a wait loop to wait until the device is ready for information transfer; repeated testing of the device status occupies the CPU and prevents its performing other tasks. Interrupt controlled transfer requires interrupting the main program, storing information, servicing the interrupt, and restoring the registers. The main program must usually be interrupted for each word. Often we want to transfer many words at one time. We also prefer to transfer information more rapidly while allowing the CPU to perform calculations. Two other modes of transfer—buffered information transfer and direct memory access—will accomplish this.

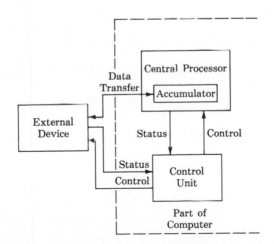

Fig. 10.7 Direct transfer of information through the CPU

10.5.2   Buffered Transfer

Buffered transfer is intended for transferring a block of words to or from a special area in memory, called the *buffer area*. Usually the user can specify the size and location of the buffer area, but some computers reserve one area of memory for buffer operations. Two words in memory are permanently reserved for each device using buffer transfer to store the addresses of the buffer area. Before the user starts buffer transfer, he stores in these two words the first location of the buffer area and either the last location or the number of words.

Input buffer transfer begins with the external device signaling the computer to request transfer of a block of stated length. The buffer control determines the starting and ending address of the storage area for the block. During buffer operation, as shown by the flowchart of figure 10.8, the external device starts buffer transfer of each word by sending a special signal when it is ready to transfer a word. This signal acts like an interrupt request signal and transfers control to a special buffer sequence at the end of execution of the current instruction. The buffer sequence reads the address for the word to be transferred, transfers the word, updates the count of words transferred, checks to see if all words have been transferred, and returns control to the user's program. Output buffer transfer is similar.

Buffer control is done exclusively by hardware or by microprogrammed control. No instructions are fetched. Thus the user's program is not affected except for the time needed to execute the buffer transfer. One or two memory accesses are needed for each buffer transfer to determine the storage location.

Buffer transfer is much faster than direct transfer because information is transferred between the external device and memory and because no wait loops or instruction fetches are needed. However, it is still not fast enough for transfer between a computer and very fast devices such as magnetic discs and drums. The speed of transfer is limited by the need to wait until the current instruction is executed before transferring each word. Thus if an instruction requires 3 microseconds to be executed in the worst case, and buffer transfer of each word requires 2 microseconds, then buffer transfers cannot be guaranteed to occur more often than every 5 microseconds. The speed of buffer transfer is also limited by the need for having one or two memory accesses to determine the current buffer address. We can eliminate these delays by providing separate registers for buffer addresses and enough logic to control the transfer entirely independently of the CPU. This transfer system is called *direct memory access* (DMA).

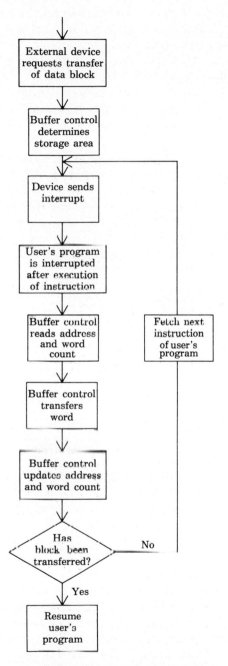

Fig. 10.8 Flowchart of buffer transfer

10.5.3 Direct Memory Access

A direct memory access system often has its own entrance to memory or *port* that is separate from the basic memory port as shown in figure 10.9. (Some DMA systems, such as that of the PDP-11, share the bus [and hence the memory port] of the CPU.) It has its own memory address register and memory data register inside the computer memory. The external device has three registers. A word count register keeps track of the number of words to be transferred. An address register holds the address in computer memory of the word being transferred; it connects directly to the DMA memory address register in the computer memory. A data register holds the word being transferred; it connects with the DMA memory data register.

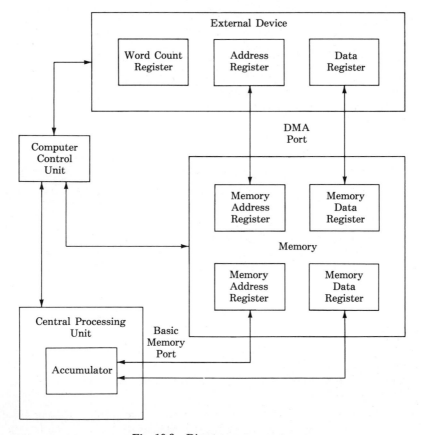

Fig. 10.9   Direct memory access

A direct memory access system operates on a principle of *cycle stealing*. Each transfer of a word occurs during a memory cycle "stolen" from the CPU. The CPU and the DMA system can share memory equally. A DMA transfer may occur under interrupt control. However, transfer of large blocks of information is initiated more often by the computer, so that the DMA transfer may occur under program control. The first step of the transfer is to determine the starting and ending addresses in computer memory for the transfer. This information is used to initialize the external device address register and word count register.

When the device is ready to transfer a word into memory, it loads the address where the word is to be stored from its address register into the DMA memory address register of the computer. The device transfers the word to be stored from its data register into the DMA memory data register. The external device then requests one memory cycle from the control unit. As soon as the memory is free, the word is transferred from the DMA memory data register into the desired memory location. The device then checks its word count register to see if the transfer of a block of information has been completed. If not, the transfer is continued. When the transfer has been completed, the CPU is interrupted to start a sequence to stop the DMA operation. A DMA output transfer is just the reverse process. Figure 10.10 is a flowchart of DMA transfer.

DMA transfers usually require external devices that have quite complicated controllers. These controllers are usually called *channels*. A channel has many CPU features such as registers, counters, etc. Because channels are expensive, often several external devices share one channel. A DMA system may have several channels, each connected to one or more external devices, as shown in figure 10.11.

A high-speed device such as a disc can keep a channel busy. A low-speed device such as a teletype or a card reader cannot keep a channel busy. Consequently, several low-speed devices can transfer data through one channel during the same period of time. The channel must have several registers and counters so that it can allocate separate registers and a counter to each device. Then it can transfer data from each device to the computer in rotation. For example, if each device requires 10 microseconds to transfer a character to the channel and then takes a delay of 500 microseconds before it can transfer the next character, one channel can service 50 devices in rotation. This system of mixing the transfers from several devices is called *multiplexing*.

The simplest multiplexing scheme consists of transferring one word from each device in turn. A variation of this scheme, called *byte multiplexing*, is to transfer 1 byte from each device in rotation. Some-

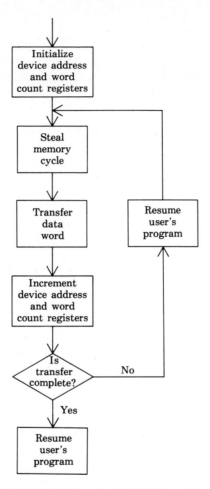

Fig. 10.10   Flowchart of DMA transfer

times we wish to transfer a block of information from one device before transferring anything from any other device. A channel that handles blocks of information from each device in sequence is a *block multiplex* channel.

A multiplex channel appears to the user as several channels because it services several devices. A multiplex channel is limited to a maximum rate of data transfer known as its *bandwidth,* measured in bits/second. The bandwidth thus limits the number of devices that one channel can service during the same period of time. The number

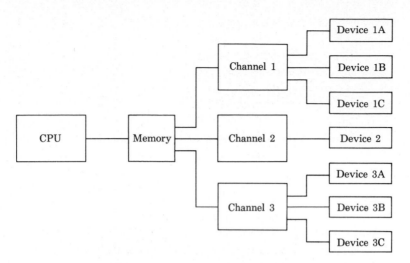

Fig. 10.11   A multichannel DMA system

of channels are limited by the speed or bandwidth of the computer memory. Because most input/output devices are much slower than memory, it is unusual for input/output transfers to saturate memory, that is, to take all of the memory cycles. However, very fast devices such as discs can take a significant percentage of memory cycles and thus slow execution of a user's program.

Some channels are so sophisticated that they are computers themselves. There is an increasing trend to use minicomputers connected to larger computers to process input/output. The minicomputer can execute its own instructions and can access memory of the main computer. Basically, it simply processes input/output in an offline mode. It is controlled by the CPU of the main computer. We will study this in more detail in the section on computer networks in chapter 11.

Our discussion of input/output processing must be understood as a simple discussion of the types of transfers commonly occurring. There is probably more variation in handling input/output procedures than in any other type of computer operation. Thus we may never encounter an input/output transfer that corresponds exactly to any one of the transfers discussed here. The distinction between programmed, buffered, and direct memory access transfers should be thought of as a range of possible procedures instead of as pure types. Similarly, the variety and types of interrupt systems are immense. Nonetheless, our discussion has covered most common input/output systems. We are now ready to discuss input/output devices.

10.6　SURVEY OF TYPICAL INPUT/OUTPUT DEVICES

The variety of input/output devices for computers is so large that it would take a book much longer than this one to list and describe them. Even categorizing input/output devices neatly is difficult. We can categorize them as input devices, output devices, or devices that are both input and output. This division may not be important since we can always choose to pair an input device with an output device to replace a device that does both. We can categorize devices as those that allow people to communicate directly (*online*) with computers, such as some typewriter devices; those that people use to communicate indirectly (offline) with computers, such as card readers; and those that send information directly to computers without human intervention, such as recording instruments. However, some devices, such as teletypes, can be used either to send information directly to a computer or to prepare a paper tape that will later be used as input to the computer. We can categorize devices according to speed, but we would find quite different speeds for the same basic devices. For example, a low-speed paper tape reader may read 30 characters a second, while a high-speed paper tape reader may read 2000 characters a second.

Instead of trying to discuss all possible input/output devices or to describe input/output devices as members of logical categories, we will in this section discuss a few common devices. We should remember that some of the bulk memory storage devices discussed in the last chapter can also be used as input/output devices. We will concentrate on the characteristics of speed, timing, and format of the devices. As we learned in section 10.2, these three characteristics of devices must be considered in interfacing them with computers.

10.6.1　Typewriters and Teleprinters

Typewriters and teleprinters are often used for slow-speed direct communication between a person and a computer. They are most often used for minicomputers and timesharing systems. The most common such device is the teletype.

Teletypes consist of a keyboard and a printer. Usually they also have a paper tape punch and reader, but we will defer discussion of paper tape operations until the next subsection. A teletype keyboard has letters and numbers and also some special abbreviations for communications such as WHO ARE YOU? Unlike ordinary typewriters, a teletype keyboard and its printer are not mechanically connected. In fact the keyboard and printer may be operated separately. It is possible to type on the keyboard while the printer is printing a message supplied it by the computer or some other source. We would probably not want to do this, but it is possible. We can also operate a teletype in a mode much like a typewriter so that the printer prints what we have typed.

Striking a key on the keyboard produces an 11-bit code word. Each code word begins with a 0 and ends with two 1s. In between are the 8 bits of some ASCII character, starting with the least significant bit. The bits are presented serially with each bit taking about 9 ms. The transmission of the entire code word thus takes approximately 11 × 9 ms or about 100 ms. Hence up to 10 ASCII characters can be sent in a second.

Other typewriter-like devices are often based on office typewriters, most frequently the IBM selectric "golf ball" typewriter. The terminal is known as a 2741 and may be used to communicate with equipment using EBCDIC or BCD codes.

10.6.2 Display Devices and Plotters

While printed output is enough for many purposes, we might like to plot and exhibit graphic displays. For example, we might want to plot a simple graph or draw a map with labels of the major features. For the graph a simple plotter will do. The map with labels requires both plotting and alphanumeric capabilities.

Plotters and graphic displays have two techniques of operation— random positioning and incremental plotting. In *random positioning* the pen may be moved to any point on the paper. (By pen we mean the writing device, and by paper the display medium; the pen may be a light beam or the paper a plasma panel, but the principle is the same.) Drawing a line in a random positioning plotter is usually done by specifying two points in a fixed *X-Y* coordinate system and issuing a CONNECT command to draw a line between them. The resolution of this system can be good. The coordinate system typically has 1024 × 1024 points or 4096 × 4096 points. This system is relatively easy to understand since the user specifies all points with respect to some absolute coordinate system. He can easily specify new points without considering the current location of his pen.

Incremental plotting is a technique that specifies a new position in terms of its distance and angle from the current position. Thus the user must know both where the pen is and where it should be next. Drawing a line is done by specifying the angle and distance from the current point. Incremental plotting is both more difficult and slower than random positioning. It is well suited to plotting graphs of continuous data such as the output of many instruments.

Cathode-ray tubes (CRTs) are often used as display devices. Their basic principle of operation is the deflection of an electronic beam much as in an oscilloscope or a television set. The simplest ones provide only for a limited number of lines of characters and print output much like a teletype. They are more convenient than teletypes since incorrect characters or lines can be erased. In addition, they save paper; paper copies (called hardcopies) are not needed for many applications. More complex displays plot points and lines by either the random positioning or the incremental plotting technique. One problem with CRT displays is that they usually need to be *refreshed,* that is, to have the graphic material electrically retraced on the display before it fades.

A recent competitor for the CRT display is the plasma panel. The plasma panel is one example of panel displays that operate from a wire grid connected to a material that lights when a point on the grid is excited. Plasma panels are somewhat slower but much less expensive than CRT displays.

A number of special devices have been developed to help users work with displays. The most common of these is the *light pen.* The light pen is a photoelectric device, shaped like a pen, that can be placed on the CRT display. The user can push a button on the pen to direct the computer to determine the location of the pen point on the display screen. The user can move the pen around the screen and "draw" on it by causing the computer to keep track of the position of the light pen.

Other devices, such as *joysticks* and *mouses,* can also be used to point to data on the display screen. A mechanical sensing device keeps track of the position of the device. Sometimes it is useful to input information without using the CRT display. *Electronic writing tablets* that respond to a special pen by the user can be used to input information.

10.6.3 Paper Tape

The format of paper tapes has varied over the years. An eight-channel format is now most common. Each channel is a position in which a hole may or may not be punched and which corresponds to 1 or 0, respectively. A line of sprocket holes, 0.1 inch apart, appears on the tape between channels 3 and 4. The sprocket holes are deliberately placed off-center to allow easy determination of the order of the channels. The channels may be used for coding in ASCII or some other code. Each character is represented by one line across the tape. A punch in all eight channels usually means TAPE FEED and is used for tape advancing. It also allows easy error correction since any character can be wiped out by punching holes in all eight channels with a RUB OUT command.

Paper tape is usually cheaper than paper cards for punching the same amount of information. However, paper tape is an unforgiving medium. When errors are detected in the middle of a program or set of data or when program changes are desired, an entire new tape must usually be punched. While some time and effort can be spared by duplicating the sections of the tape that do not need changes, the procedure is more complicated than changing a few cards. Paper tape is usually less desirable for high-speed batch operations since paper tapes cannot easily be combined to make one continuous tape.

Paper tape punching is usually done with a machine with a type-writer-like keyboard. In fact, as we have already noted, most teletypes have paper tape punches. Striking a key on the keyboard punches holes into the desired channels in one row of the tape and advances the tape one position. If the keyboard is also coupled to a printer, then the user can watch a typed copy of what is being punched. The printed copy is obviously easier to check than the punched paper tape. Teletype punches usually operate at the basic teletype speed of up to 10 characters per second. Faster punches can punch at rates up to 300 characters per second.

Paper tape readers may be mechanical or photoelectric. Mechanical readers read by sensing holes or the absence of holes with mechanical *sensing pins*. The motion of the pins actuates an electrical switch that converts the information into electrical signals. Mechanical sensing is slow, typically 10 to 50 characters per second. One disadvantage of mechanical sensing is that occasionally the pin will cause a hole to be poked in a position while it is reading the position. This erroneous hole may later be read as a 1 (hole). Because of this, tapes made of plastic or aluminum are sometimes used instead of paper tape for longer, troublefree life.

Photoelectric readers can run at much higher speeds, up to 2000 or more characters per second. They read holes by passing light through them and activating an electronic switch. Photoelectric readers are more expensive than mechanical readers. They are less likely to damage tape as they read it so that a given paper tape program will have a longer life when read photoelectrically.

Paper tape has been an important input/output medium for mini-computers. Because of its inflexibility and frequent mechanical problems in writing and reading, it is rapidly being replaced by more convenient and reliable media such as magnetic tapes.

10.6.4 Cards

Paper cards are the most common input medium. The most commonly used card is a 12-row, 80-column, 7¾ × 3¼ inch card. The code usually used for the cards is the *Hollerith code,* an alphanumeric code in which each character is represented in one column of the card. Each digit 0 through 9 is represented by a single punch in the corresponding one of the bottom 10 rows. A punch in any one of the top three rows of the card combined with a punch in one of the last nine rows represents a letter. Special characters, such as punctuation, are represented by combinations of three holes in one column.

Card punches operate much like paper tape punches. A typewriter-like keyboard is used for entering information. Striking a key punches holes in one column and advances the card to the next column. A hardcopy output may be simultaneously printed at the top of the card, directly above the corresponding punches. Individual card punches are limited by the typing speed of the operator rather than by mechanical limitations to perhaps 10 characters or so per second, comparable to paper tape speed. Cards can be duplicated or repunched at the rate of 200 to 400 cards per minute.

10.6.5 Line Printers

Printers are usually classified as *character printers* that print one character at a time, or *line printers* that print an entire line at a time. Character printers operate much like typewriters as discussed in paragraph 10.6.1. Line printers have some printing mechanism for each character on the line, typically from 80 to 150 characters. All characters on the line are printed simultaneously so that line printers are much faster than character printers.

Line printers may be classified as *impact printers* and *nonimpact printers.* Impact printers print mechanically. A set of all the characters to be printed and a decoder are available for each position on the line. Some line printers have separate bars for each character in each position; others have a constantly revolving print wheel that has all characters for each position. In either case, when the line is to be printed the decoders for each position select a character and the printing mechanism prints the characters by mechanically impacting the paper. Impact line printers can print about 1000 to 2000 lines per minute.

Nonimpact line printers use chemical, electrical, or hydraulic methods. Often characters are printed as an array of spots, with either 5 × 7 or 9 × 11 spots per character. One type of printer uses a jet process in which fine droplets of ink are sprayed on the paper to represent characters in arrays of 9 × 11 dots. Another printer works by pressing heated dots on special thermal paper. An electrostatic printer operates by blowing carbon dust on the paper in a 5 × 7 array and fixing it by heating. Other printers work much like Xerox copiers.

10.6.6 Analog-to-Digital and Digital-to-Analog Converters

The devices discussed so far have been designed to transfer information between computers and people. The inputs to teletypes, card readers, paper tape readers, etc., come from people who have information they want to be stored and operated on in a computer. Similarly, the outputs from teletypes, line printers, etc., are meant to be read by people. Often, however, we are interested in instruments and machines that communicate directly with the computer. We may want the computer to process data from a scientific instrument or control a machine tool without having a person intervene once the system has been designed and implemented.

Information from scientific instruments or from machines is either digital or analog. *Digital* signals may only have certain specified values. Binary signals are digital signals. The inputs to a calculator (any of the digits 0 through 9) are digital signals. *Analog* signals may have any value within a given range. For example, an analog voltage that is the output of a certain power supply may be any value between 0 and 150 volts, say 114.36 volts. Information in digital form can be processed very easily by a digital computer. The information may need to be coded to correspond to the format used by a program within the computer, but other changes are not usually needed. Information in analog form, however, must be converted to digital form or *quantized* before a digital computer can process it. Converting information from analog form to digital form requires an analog-to-digital (or A/D) converter. Converting information from digital to analog requires a digital-to-analog (or D/A) converter. A D/A converter is needed to convert any information transferred from a digital computer to an analog device.

Controlling an analog instrument or machine can be done by a digital computer with two converters as shown in figure 10.12. A system that can control an instrument or machine by responding to the current outputs or states of the machine is called a *real-time system*. Real-time computer systems control a wide variety of devices—traffic lights, radars, steel mills, etc. An A/D converter converts analog information from the instrument into digital data that a digital

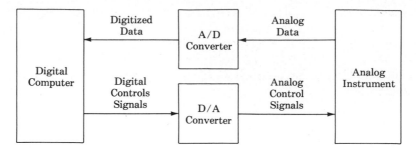

Fig. 10.12   Control of an analog instrument by a digital computer with A/D and D/A converters

computer can process. The digital computer returns digital control signals that are converted to analog control signals by a D/A converter. An alternative system uses an analog computer that processes information internally in analog form. However, digital computers are usually more precise so that it is desirable to convert analog information to digital for computation. Hybrid computers combine some of the features of analog and digital computers and employ A/D and D/A converters internally.

We will first consider an A/D converter that converts analog mechanical information into digital electric information. Many machines have rotating shafts. The degree of rotation of the shaft may need to be measured. For example, we may have a telescope mounted on a base and may need to know the angle at which the telescope is pointing. Two variations of a scheme to measure rotation are shown in figure 10.13 and table 10.3. A disc is mounted on the shaft. The disc has bands composed of segments of two different types of materials. A sensor that can distinguish the two types of materials on each band is mounted in a fixed position. The two types of materials might be electrically conducting and nonconducting; the device to sense or read them may be "brushes" like those in electric motors. The materials may be opaque and transparent; the device to read them may be a photoelectric reader. In either case the bands are shown in the figure as shaded or blank. The device that reads the bands is mounted at the top of the circles at about 360°. The reading or sensing device always requires some space so that the reading of the angle will not be exact in areas in which the segments in one or more bands change. The reader overlaps two segments where they join and may give either reading.

Figure 10.13a shows the bands coded in a simple binary coding of the angles. With four bands we can represent 2^4 or 16 different angular regions. As shown in table 10.3, we divide 360° of rotation

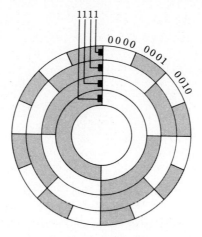

a)   Binary coded disc

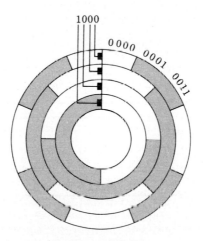

b)   Gray coded disc

Fig. 10.13   Two schemes for A/D conversion

equally into regions of 22.5°. We read the bands from the inside out considering a blank segment as 0 and a shaded segment as 1. Thus, the region from 0 to 22.5° is represented as 0000, and the region from 22.5° to 45° is represented as 1. The analog-to-digital conversion is the coding of each region of 22.5° into a 4-bit binary number.

A major problem with this method of coding occurs in trying to measure angles that are near the boundary between two segments.

TABLE 10.3

CODES FOR A/D CONVERTER OF FIGURE 10.13

Angle of rotation (degrees)	Decimal number	Binary code	Gray code
0 — 22.5	0	0000	0000
22.5— 45	1	0001	0001
45 — 67.5	2	0010	0011
67.5— 90	3	0011	0010
90 — 112.5	4	0100	0110
112.5— 135	5	0101	0111
135 — 157.5	6	0110	0101
157.5— 180	7	0111	0100
180 — 202.5	8	1000	1100
202.5— 225	9	1001	1101
225 — 247.5	10	1010	1111
247.5— 270	11	1011	1110
270 — 292.5	12	1100	1010
292.5— 315	13	1101	1011
315 — 337.5	14	1110	1001
337.5— 360	15	1111	1000

Because the reading device requires some space and may be slightly misaligned, it is easy to make reading errors near a boundary. For example, consider trying to read the angle 179.9°. This angle is between 157.5° and 180° and hence should be coded as 0111. However, if the innermost band is misaligned slightly, it will be read as a 1. The angle will then be read as 1111, the code corresponding to angles between 337.5° and 360° or the region 180° away from the correct region. Smaller errors will be made if any other single band is read incorrectly. The main problem in coding the disc in a simple binary code is that there are many boundaries in which two or more bands change at the same angle. Boundaries that have only one band change can be misread because of space or alignment problems in only one way. However, boundaries that have two band changes can be misread in three different ways because of space or alignment problems.

We can minimize the number of errors that can be made (because of the reader overlapping two bands or being slightly misaligned) by coding the disc in such a way that only one band changes at a time. A coding that will do this is called a *Gray code* and is shown in figure 10.13b and table 10.3. Gray code, as discussed in chapter 3, has the property that the representation of any number differs in only one bit position from the representation of either of its two adjacent numbers. For example, the Gray code representation for the region between 157.5° and 180° is 0100, which differs by only 1 bit from the 0101 for the region between 135° and 157.5° and the 1100 for the region between 180° and 202.5°. If the reader, because of misalignment or overlapping, misreads the most significant bit for 179.5° as a 1 instead of a 0, it will represent the angle as 1100, corresponding to the region between 180° and 202.5°. This is a much smaller error than the corresponding error for the binary-coded disc and is the only likely error at this boundary. Hence the Gray coded disc is more reliable for A/D conversion.

The corresponding digital-to-analog conversion to control the mechanical shaft is usually done by an electronic D/A converter coupled to an electric motor to drive the shaft. Hence we will not consider mechanical D/A converters but will look instead at electronic D/A and A/D converters.

Digital-to-analog conversion is simpler electronically than is analog-to-digital conversion, so we will consider D/A converters first. For digital-to-analog conversion we only need to generate an analog signal that equals the digital signal. For analog-to-digital conversion we must select a digital signal that is approximately equal to the analog signal. This process is called *quantizing*. As we saw in the shaft-coding A/D converter, we must represent a range of analog values as one digital value.

A basic method for A/D conversion is shown in figure 10.14. Digital signals in binary code are applied to the input of a resistor network. (If the digital signals are not already available in binary code, a coder can convert them.) Figure 10.14a shows four binary inputs. X_0 is the least significant bit. The output of the resistor network is a single analog voltage that is approximately equal to the number represented by the binary inputs. Figure 10.14b shows the resistor network that performs the conversion. The basis of operation of this resistor network is beyond the scope of this text, but readers who are familiar with circuit theory might want to work out the details. Basically, the circuit is a binary ladder. Each binary input may be 0 or some voltage V corresponding to logic 1. The ladder insures that voltage V applied to X_3, the most significant bit, results in twice the output voltage of V applied to X_2. Similarly, voltage V applied to X_3 results in four times and eight times the output voltage due to V applied to X_1 and X_0, respectively. The resistor network sums the contribution from each bit position and produces the output voltage.

Figure 10.15 shows a general n-bit D/A converter. The resistor network of figure 10.14 is the last stage of the D/A converter. The first stage applies some combinational logic to the input n bits, for example, to enable the inputs. The second stage is an n-bit register

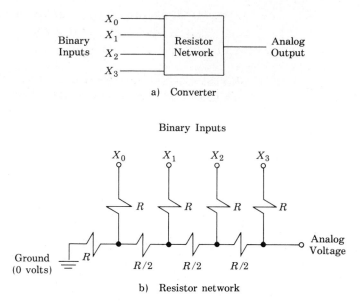

a)   Converter

Binary Inputs

b)   Resistor network

Fig. 10.14   D/A conversion

that holds the inputs. Amplifiers amplify the signals so that all 1 signals have the same magnitude. Finally, the resistor network converts the n-bit binary number to an analog voltage. The resolution of the D/A converter depends on the number of bits. The accuracy of the conversion depends on the precision of the components within the converter.

Analog-to-digital conversion can be done either simultaneously or sequentially. Figure 10.16 shows a simultaneous A/D converter to convert an analog input voltage to one of eight binary output voltages. The converter consists of seven analog comparators. In chapter 3 we studied binary comparators that produce a 1 output when the two inputs to the comparator are equal and a 0 output otherwise. We also studied binary comparators that produced a 1 output when one n-bit binary input exceeded the other input. The analog comparators in this A/D converter give a 1 output when the analog input voltage equals or exceeds the reference analog voltage into the comparator. Table 10.4 shows the comparator outputs for different ranges of the analog input voltage. This A/D converter can convert analog input voltages from 0 to more than 7 volts to binary outputs from 000 to 111. A voltage of 4.65 volts would produce 1 outputs from comparators C_1 through C_4 and 0 outputs from comparators C_5 through C_7. Simple combinational logic applied to the outputs of the compara-

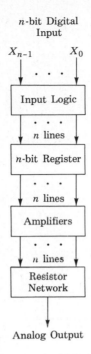

n-bit Digital
Input

X_{n-1} X_0

• • •

Input Logic

• • •
n lines

n-bit Register

• • •
n lines

Amplifiers

• • •
n lines

Resistor
Network

Analog Output

Fig. 10.15   General *n*-bit D/A converter

tors would convert these outputs to the binary numbers 000 through
111. The design of the logic circuits is left to the reader. (See problem
10.16.)

The main advantage of a simultaneous A/D converter is that it
converts quickly since all inputs are compared simultaneously. The

TABLE 10.4

COMPARATOR OUTPUTS

Analog input voltage	C_1	C_2	C_3	C_4	C_5	C_6	C_7
$0 < V < 1$	0	0	0	0	0	0	0
$1 \leq V < 2$	1	0	0	0	0	0	0
$2 \leq V < 3$	1	1	0	0	0	0	0
$3 \leq V < 4$	1	1	1	0	0	0	0
$4 \leq V < 5$	1	1	1	1	0	0	0
$5 \leq V < 6$	1	1	1	1	1	0	0
$6 \leq V < 7$	1	1	1	1	1	1	0
$7 \leq V$	1	1	1	1	1	1	1

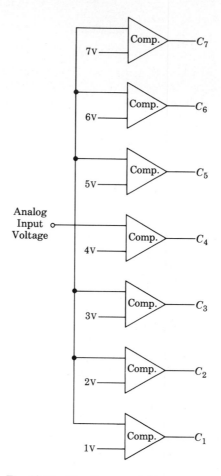

Fig. 10.16   Simultaneous A/D converter

main disadvantage is that to form an n-bit binary output, 2^{n-1} converters are required. As n becomes large, simultaneous A/D converters become uneconomical.

Sequential A/D converters require only one analog comparator, as shown in figure 10.17. A counter and D/A converter combine to produce an analog reference voltage that increases one step in each unit of time. The analog voltage thus looks something like a staircase. To operate the A/D converter, the counter is first set to 0. A clock advances the counter 1 bit on each clock pulse. The n-bit output of the counter is amplified and sent to a resistor network to produce

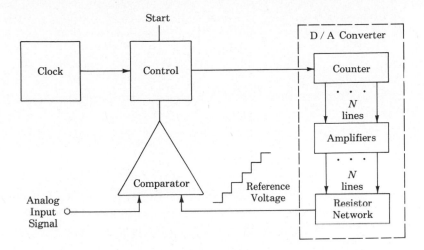

Fig. 10.17 Sequential A/D converter

the staircase reference voltage. During each clock pulse an analog comparator compares the reference voltage with the unknown analog input signal. When the reference signal first equals or exceeds the analog input signal, the comparator gives a 1 output and the control stops the A/D converter. The binary number in the counter when the converter stops corresponds to the desired digital voltage. The digital voltage is the value of the staircase reference voltage when the A/D converter stops.

10.7 SUMMARY

External devices have three main parts—transducers, device controllers, and data registers. The device controller contains flag flip-flops for maintaining status information and for receiving control signals from the computer.

Major input/output problems center around differences of speed between the external device and the computer, timing of input/output signals, and the format of encoding information.

Information can be transferred between an external device and the computer under programmed control or interrupt control. A programmed input/output sequence usually tests to see if the external device is ready and then transfers information when the device is ready. Interrupt control allows the external device to interrupt the computer when it is ready to transfer information. Interrupt control systems can be designed to allow hardware or software sensing of the priorities of a device and hardware identification of the interrupting device. Programmable mask registers can allow bypassing of hardware priorities.

Input/output transfers can be accomplished directly through the CPU, buffered through special buffer areas, or committed directly to memory via a cycle-stealing direct memory access system. Channels that may be as complicated as minicomputers can aid in multiplexing a large number of devices into one memory port and can perform many of the needed formatting and error-checking procedures.

The variety of input/output devices is immense and uses technologies ranging from mechanical to optical to thermal. D/A and A/D converters are needed for real-time control of analog instruments.

Concepts

analog	interrupt
analog-to-digital converter	interrupt acknowledge
asynchronous	interrupt request
bandwidth	joystick
block multiple	level
buffer	light pen
buffer area	line printer
buffered transfer	mouse
character printer	nonimpact printer
cycle stealing	peripheral device
data register	port
device controller	priority
digital-to-analog converter	programmed input/output
direct memory access	quantize
electronic writing tablet	random positioning
external device	real-time system
hardcopy	sensing pin
Hollerith code	teletype
impact printer	transducer
incremental plotting	trap

10.8 REFERENCES

Stone (1972), Gear (1974), Hellerman (1973), Hill and Peterson (1973), and Stone (1975) provide good descriptions of input/output transfers. Poppelbaum (1972) and Bartee (1972) have extensive discussions of input/output devices. Malvino and Leach (1969) discuss electronic D/A and A/D converters. Flores (1973) is a text written solely about peripherals.

10.9 PROBLEMS

10.1 Construct a combinational logic circuit whose input is the digits 0–9 in ASCII code and whose output is the digits 0–9 in BCD code. (10.3)

10.2 Construct a combinational logic circuit whose input is the digits 0–9 in Hollerith code and whose output is the digits 0–9 in BCD code. (10.3)

10.3 Write a flowchart and a program that will read a single teletype character and write it on a paper tape punch. (10.4)

10.4 Write a flowchart of servicing a single interrupt for which the program counter and accumulator are stored in a stack and the service routine is located in memory location 100. (10.4)

10.5 Write a flowchart of servicing multiple interrupts in a single-level, single-priority system that will store the program counter, accumulator, and two registers **X** and **Y** in a stack, branch to the correct service routine, and return. Assume there are four interrupting conditions—A, B, C, and D—with priorities given alphabetically (A has highest priority). All tests for priority must be shown in your flowchart. (10.4)

10.6 Write a flowchart for the problem of 10.5 for a multiple-level, multiple-priority system in which both select codes and priorities are determined by hardware. (10.4)

10.7 Sketch a diagram of an interrupt system with a mask register that can select from nine interrupts. One interrupt, the POWER FAILURE interrupt, should not be affected by the mask register. How many bits are needed for the mask register? How many bits are needed for the select code of the interrupting device? (10.4)

10.8 Sketch a diagram of a buffer area in memory. Your buffer area should be N bits long and should reserve two words for the initial address and the number of words to be transferred. Write a flowchart for operation of the buffer to transfer M words $(M < N)$. (10.5)

10.9 Sketch a flowchart for a channel that multiplexes one high-speed device that can transfer one 32-bit word every 4 microseconds with 40 low-speed devices that can transfer one 8-bit character every 400 microseconds. Assume that all transfers take 1 microsecond of the 4 microsecond or 400 microsecond interval. What is the maximum transfer rate of this channel in 8-bit characters per second? (10.5)

10.10 Sketch a flowchart for a channel that byte multiplexes one high-speed device that can transfer 4 bytes in parallel in 1 microsecond every 10 microseconds with 20 low-speed devices that can each transfer 1 byte in 5 microseconds every 100 microseconds. What is the maximum transfer rate of this channel in bytes per second? (10.5)

10.11 Explain the operation of the RUB OUT character for paper tapes. (10.6)

10.12 The EBCDIC code for digits consists of four 1s followed by a 4-bit code for the digit. Is this code BCD or binary? Why? (10.6)

10.13 An analog-to-digital disc like the one in figure 10.13 has a precision of eight decimal digits. How many bands are required? (10.6)

10.14 List the Gray code for a five-band disc similar to the one in figure 10.13b. (10.6)

10.15 List all possible errors for the disc in figure 13a that occur at transitions and classify them according to the distance of the erroneous region from the correct region. (10.6)

10.16 Design logic circuits for a 3-bit output A/D converter such as the one in figure 10.15 and table 10.5. (10.6)

10.17 If analog comparators cost 10 units each, and the control and timing circuits for a sequential A/D converter cost 60 units, and a D/A converter costs 15 units per bit, at what point does a sequential A/D comparator become more economical than a simultaneous A/D converter? (10.6)

11 Computer Systems

11.1 OVERVIEW

Now that we have examined computer levels from the logic to the programming level and have studied several main parts of a computer, we are ready to look at the top level, the computer systems level. This level is primarily concerned with the interconnection of the arithmetic unit, the control unit, memory, and input/output devices. However, while we are studying this level, we will also look into some of the lower levels in order to make some of the concepts discussed in earlier chapters more precise.

We begin by looking at the structure of a typical but hypothetical computer. We look at the organization of registers, interconnection of devices, and generation of control signals. Next, we look at a calculator, a microprocessor system, and three computers as examples of computer structures. Finally, we combine computers into networks.

11.2 ORGANIZATION OF A TYPICAL COMPUTER

We first consider the organization of a typical computer, as shown in figure 11.1. We are already familiar with the organization of some of the parts from discussions in earlier chapters. Now we can consider how the main parts of the computer interact.

The central processing unit (CPU) contains the arithmetic unit (usually several registers) and the control circuits of the computer. Usually the computer has some registers that can be accessed or programmed directly by the user, and other registers that are reserved

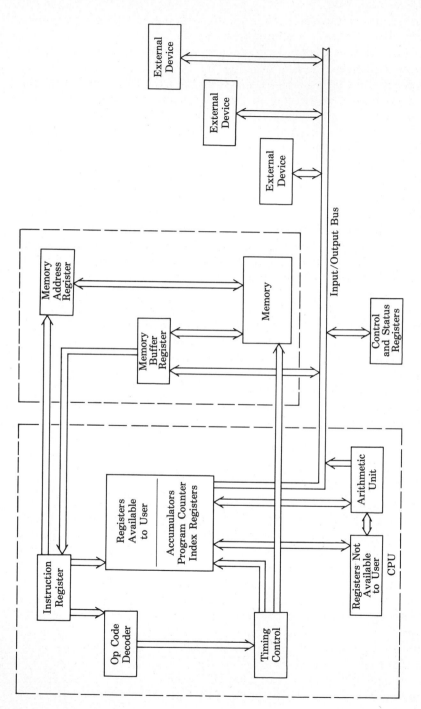

Fig. 11.1 Organization of a typical computer

for internal operations of the computer and cannot be programmed by the user. Figure 11.1 shows both types of registers.

The *instruction decoder, operation code decoder,* and *timing control* circuits implement the control functions of the CPU. The instruction register receives an instruction from the memory buffer register. The operation code decoder identifies the operation codes and signals the timing control unit to start timing pulses. It is connected to logic circuits in the computer that implement the instructions. The timing control unit generates the timing pulses for the FETCH, DEFER, and EXECUTE states as discussed in chapter 7. Ordinarily each of these states is divided into three or four parts so that separate actions can be started at different times within each state.

The memory shown in the figure is the main memory with an associated memory buffer register and memory address register just as discussed earlier. The memory address register receives an address from the address field of the instruction register. The memory buffer register holds information that is being transferred into or out of memory.

The *input/output bus* connects the main parts of the computer. A *bus* is simply a set of wires that interconnect registers of the computer. An n-bit word is usually transferred on a bus as n bits in parallel, but some small digital systems transfer bits or bytes of a word in series. The computer shown has the input/output bus connecting the *accessible registers,* the arithmetic unit, the memory buffer register, and the external devices. *Control* and *status registers* are also shown attached to the bus for monitoring of computer operations.

11.2.1 Bus Organization

The single input/output bus shown in figure 11.1 is one type of bus organization of a computer. Figure 11.2 shows two common bus organizations. In figure 11.2a the computer has two main buses—a *memory bus* and an *input/output bus*. The memory bus connects the CPU and the direct memory access (DMA) unit to memory. At any given time either the CPU or the DMA unit may transfer information to or from memory via the memory bus. The input/output bus is completely separate and connects the CPU and DMA unit to the external devices. At any given time one external device can communicate with either the CPU or the DMA unit; this communication can theoretically proceed independently of transfers on the memory bus. A computer that is organized with separate memory and input/output buses usually handles memory operations differently from

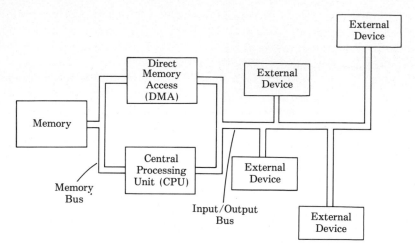

a)   Separate memory and input/output buses

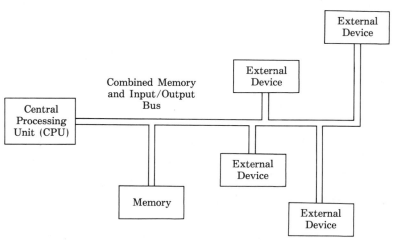

b)   Combined memory and input/output bus

Fig. 11.2   Two bus organizations

input/output operations. Such a computer usually has memory reference instructions with a completely different format from that for input/output instructions. The PDP-8 is an example. Usually, however, input/output bus operations are synchronized with CPU operations and memory bus operations. The need for synchronization effectively limits the length of the input/output bus to about 15 meters for high-speed computers. (Electric signals travel 15 meters in $15m/(3 \times 10^8$ m/sec) or 50 ns.)

Figure 11.2b shows a computer that has a combined or unified *memory and input/output bus*. The CPU, the memory, and all external devices are attached to a single bus. Transfer of information between memory and the CPU occurs in the same way as transfer of information between any external device and the CPU. Computers with a unified bus structure usually have the same format for memory reference instructions as for input/output instructions. Thus, all devices are addressed in the same way.

Computers with a unified bus structure often operate *asynchronously*. Instead of executing instructions at fixed intervals as determined by a master clock, instructions are executed in response to an event that occurs. Asynchronous operation frees the computer from limits on bus length and equipment placement since all parts of the computer do not have to be synchronized.

11.2.2 Instruction Control

In chapter 7 we discussed executing instructions. All instructions begin in a FETCH state. If the address field has an indirect bit that is 1, a DEFER state is also necessary. All but the simplest instructions are actually executed in an EXECUTE state. Each state has three or four intervals during which distinct operations are performed. We now take a closer look at the control of instructions.

Figure 11.3 shows a more detailed view of the CPU and memory of the hypothetical computer of figure 11.1. Control signals for the computer are underlined. The functions of the major registers of this computer can be summarized as follows:

1. *Memory address register* (MAR) holds the address of the memory location to which or from which information is being transferred.
2. *Memory buffer register* (MBR) holds the information being transferred to or from memory.
3. *Instruction register* (IR) holds the current instruction.
4. *Op code decoder* (OP) holds the operation code of the current instruction. It is only as long as the operation code field.
5. *Program counter* (PC) contains the address of the instruction being executed. The contents of the program counter may be transferred into the memory address register to allow program branching.
6. *Accumulator* (ACC) holds information being operated on.
7. *Register X* (XR) is a working register used with the accumulator. It holds operands.

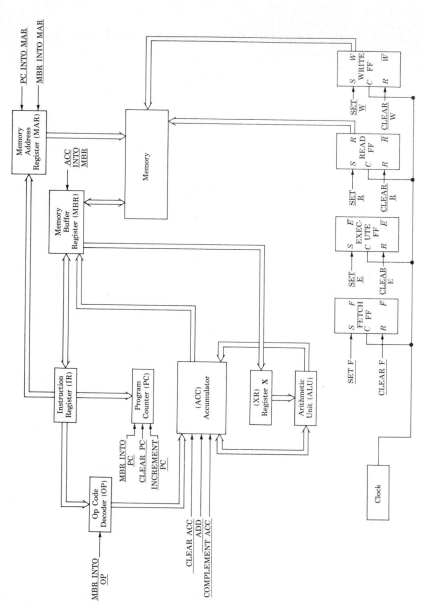

Fig. 11.3   Control signals and registers

8. *Fetch Flipflop* (F) is a 1-bit register that is set when the computer is in a fetch state.
9. *Execute Flipflop* (E) is a 1-bit flipflop that is set when the computer is in an EXECUTE state.
10. *Read Flipflop* (R) is a 1-bit register that is set to tell the memory to read a word.
11. *Write Flipflop* (W) is a 1-bit register that is set to write the contents of the memory buffer register into memory.

We now list some control signals with explanations and register-transfer descriptions that this computer might need to execute some simple instructions.

1. CLEAR PC sets the program counter to 0.

$$PC \leftarrow 0$$

2. MBR INTO PC transfers the contents of the memory buffer register into the program counter. This can be used to transfer control to an address located in a word in memory.

$$PC \leftarrow MBR$$

3. INCREMENT PC increases the contents of the program counter by 1 and is used to keep track of instructions that are stored in sequence.

$$PC \leftarrow PC + 1$$

4. MBR INTO OP transfers the operation code field of an instruction stored in the memory buffer register through the instruction register into the operation code decoder.

$$OP \leftarrow MBR_{op}$$

(The subscript shows the operation code field of the memory buffer register.)

5. PC INTO MAR loads the contents of the program counter into the memory address register to obtain the instruction stored at that address.

$$MAR \leftarrow PC$$

6. MBR INTO MAR loads the contents of the address field of the memory buffer register into the memory address register.

$$MAR \leftarrow MBR_{ADDR}$$

7. READ instructs the memory to read a word from the location shown by the memory address register into the memory buffer register.

$$MBR \leftarrow (MAR)$$

8. WRITE tells the memory to write the contents of the memory buffer register into the location shown by the memory address register.

$$(MAR) \leftarrow MBR$$

9. CLEAR ACCUMULATOR sets the accumulator to 0.

$$ACC \leftarrow 0$$

10. ADD adds the contents of the **X** register to the contents of the accumulator and puts the sum in the accumulator.

$$ACC \leftarrow ACC + X$$

11. COMPLEMENT ACCUMULATOR complements the contents of the accumulator.

$$ACC \leftarrow \overline{ACC}$$

12. MBR INTO XR sends the contents of the memory buffer register into the **X** register.

$$XR \leftarrow MBR$$

13. ACC INTO MBR transfers the contents of the accumulator into the memory buffer register.

$$MBR \leftarrow ACC$$

For the auxiliary flipflops (READ, WRITE, EXECUTE, FETCH) we need set and clear signals, such as

$$\begin{aligned} \text{SET R} \qquad & R \leftarrow 1 \\ \text{CLEAR R} \qquad & R \leftarrow 0 \end{aligned}$$

With these control signals we can generate simple instructions. We will assume that the computer does not have indirect addressing so that a DEFER state is not needed. We will assume that the computer memory and all registers are semiconductor and hence have nondestructive readout. Thus, we will not need to write information back into memory after we have read it. We will also assume that both the FETCH state and the EXECUTE state have four distinct intervals, as shown in figure 11.4. The clock sends out pulses at a

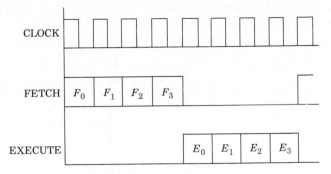

Fig. 11.4   Timing of control signals

constant rate. Counter and register circuitry generate the four intervals of the FETCH state—F_0, F_1, F_2, and F_3—and the four intervals of the EXECUTE state—E_0, E_1, E_2, and E_3. Details of the counter and register circuits are left as an exercise. (See problem 11.5.)

During any one interval of either the FETCH or EXECUTE state, two or three operations may be performed at the same time. For example, two flipflops might be set and information might be transferred between two registers during one interval, if these operations can be done independently. Sequential operations must usually occur, one at a time, in separate intervals. Exceptions are such brief pairs of operations as SET R and READ. We assume that the interval length is long enough to complete the operation started by any control signal.

The first instruction that we will examine is the ADD instruction, a twos complement addition of the number in the accumulator and the number in the memory location whose address is given by the address field of the ADD instruction. The result of the addition is returned to the accumulator. Table 11.1 shows the control signals that occur in each interval.

The FETCH state for all instructions begins in interval F_0 with setting the READ flipflop to control reading the instruction from memory into the memory buffer register. The memory location from which the instruction is read is determined by the contents of the memory address register. The contents of the program counter have been transferred into the memory address register during execution of the preceding instruction. In interval F_1 the operation code of the instruction is transferred into the op code decoder and decoded to identify the instruction as an ADD instruction. At the same time the READ flipflop is cleared to end the read operation. In interval

TABLE 11.1

SEQUENCE OF CONTROL SIGNALS FOR ADD INSTRUCTION

Time	Control signals	Explanation
F_0	SET R	Set READ flipflop. R ← 1
	READ	Read instruction from memory into memory buffer register. MBR ← (MAR)
F_1	MBR INTO OP	Transfer operation code of instruction into op code decoder. Decode. OP ← MBR_{OP}
	CLEAR R	Clear READ flipflop. R ← 0
F_2	INCREMENT PC	Increment the program counter to prepare for the next instruction. PC ← PC + 1
F_3	MBR INTO MAR	Transfer address field of contents of the memory buffer register into the memory address register. MAR ← MBR_{ADDR}
	CLEAR F	Clear FETCH flipflop to end FETCH state. F ← 0
	SET E	Set EXECUTE flipflop to begin EXECUTE state. E ← 1
E_0	SET R	Set READ flipflop. R ← 1
	READ	Read contents of the memory location addressed in F_3 into the memory buffer register. MBR ← (MAR)
E_1	MBR INTO XR	Transfer the contents of the memory buffer register into the **X** register. The **X** register now holds the number to be added to the contents of the accumulator. XR ← MBR
	CLEAR R	Clear READ flipflop. R ← 0
E_2	ADD	Add the contents of the **X** register to the contents of the accumulator and store the sum in the accumulator. ACC ← ACC + XR
E_3	PC INTO MAR	Transfer the contents of the program counter into the memory address register to prepare to fetch the next instruction. MAR ← PC
	CLEAR E	Clear the EXECUTE flipflop to end the EXECUTE state. E ← 0
	SET F	Set the FETCH flipflop to begin the FETCH state. F ← 1

F_2 the program counter is incremented by 1 to prepare for the next instruction. In F_3 three control signals operate at the same time. The contents of the address field of the memory buffer register are transferred into the memory address register to show the location of the number to be added to the accumulator. The FETCH flipflop is cleared to end the FETCH state, and the EXECUTE flipflop is set to begin the EXECUTE state. The computer then starts executing the instruction.

In interval E_0 for the ADD instruction, the READ flipflop is set and the contents of the memory location selected in F_3 are read into the memory buffer register. In E_1 the contents of the memory buffer register are transferred into the **X** register. The **X** register now holds the number to be added to the contents of the accumulator. The READ flipflop is cleared. In interval E_2 the contents of the **X** register are added to the contents of the accumulator, and the sum is returned to the accumulator. In E_3 the contents of the program counter are sent to the memory address register to prepare to fetch the next instruction. At the same time the EXECUTE flipflop is cleared to end the EXECUTE state and the FETCH flipflop is set to begin the FETCH state.

As a second example, we can consider the control signals needed to store information in memory. Table 11.2 shows the control signals for a STORE instruction for our hypothetical computer. In F_0 the READ flipflop is set and the instruction is read from memory into the memory buffer register. In F_1 the operation code field of the

TABLE 11.2

SEQUENCE OF CONTROL SIGNALS FOR STORE INSTRUCTION

Time	Control signals	Explanation
F_0	SET R	Set READ flipflop. R ← 1
	READ	Read instruction from memory into the memory buffer register. MBR ← (MAR)
F_1	MBR INTO OP	Transfer operation code of instruction into op code decoder. Decode. OP ← MBR_{OP}
	CLEAR R	Clear READ flipflop. R ← 0
F_2	INCREMENT PC	Increment the contents of the program counter to prepare for the next instruction. PC ← PC + 1
F_3	MBR INTO MAR	Transfer the address field of the instruction from the memory buffer register into the memory address register. MAR ← MBR_{ADDR}
	CLEAR F	Clear FETCH flipflop to end FETCH state. F ← 0
	SET E	Set EXECUTE flipflop to begin EXECUTE state. E ← 0
E_0	SET W	Set WRITE flipflop. W ← 1
	ACC INTO MBR	Transfer the word to be written into memory from the accumulator into the memory buffer register. MBR ← ACC
E_1	WRITE	Write contents of memory buffer register into memory. (MAR) ← MBR
E_2	CLEAR W	Clear WRITE flipflop. W ← 0
E_3	PC INTO MAR	Transfer the contents of the program counter into the memory address register to prepare to fetch the next instruction. MAR ← PC
	CLEAR E	Clear the EXECUTE flipflop to end the EXECUTE state. E ← 0
	SET F	Set the FETCH flipflop to begin the FETCH state. F ← 1

instruction is sent to the op code decoder where it is decoded and identified as a STORE instruction. The READ flipflop is cleared. In F_2 the contents of the program counter are incremented by 1 to prepare for the next instruction. In F_3 the contents of the address field of the memory buffer register are transferred into the memory address register to show the location into which the information is to be stored. The FETCH flipflop is cleared to end the FETCH state, and the EXECUTE flipflop is set to begin the EXECUTE state.

In E_0 the WRITE flipflop is set to start the write operation. The word that is to be written into memory is transferred from the accumulator into the memory buffer register. In E_1 the contents of the memory buffer register are written into the location in memory determined in interval F_3. In E_2 the WRITE flipflop is cleared. Finally, in E_3 the contents of the program counter are transferred into the memory address register to prepare to fetch the next instruction. At the same time the EXECUTE flipflop is cleared to end the EXECUTE state and the FETCH flipflop is set to begin the FETCH state.

There are similarities in the control signals for these two instructions that we can expect to see in all memory reference instructions. The first interval of the FETCH state implements reading the instruction. Later in the FETCH state the program counter is incremented by 1 to show the address of the next instruction in sequence. At the end of the FETCH state the contents of the memory buffer register are transferred into the memory address register if the instruction is a memory reference instruction. If it is not, other operations would occur in this interval. The FETCH flipflop is cleared to end the FETCH state, and the EXECUTE flipflop is set to begin the EXECUTE state.

During the EXECUTE state of a memory reference instruction, the instruction is executed. At some time during the EXECUTE state the contents of the program counter are transferred into the memory address register to prepare to fetch the next instruction. At the end of the EXECUTE state the EXECUTE flipflop is cleared, and the FETCH flipflop is set to begin the FETCH state.

We can compare the control signals needed for memory reference instructions with those needed for nonmemory reference instructions. Table 11.3 shows the control signals needed for a typical nonmemory reference instruction, the CLEAR THE ACCUMULATOR instruction. This instruction is both fetched and executed in the FETCH state. At F_0 the READ flipflop is set and the instruction is read from memory. At F_1 the contents of the operation code field of the memory buffer register are sent to the decoder and decoded. At the

TABLE 11.3

SEQUENCE OF CONTROL SIGNALS FOR INSTRUCTION TO
CLEAR THE ACCUMULATOR

Time	Control signals	Explanation
F_0	SET R	Set READ flipflop. R ← 1
	READ	Read instruction from memory into memory buffer register. MBR ← (MAR)
F_1	MBR INTO OP	Transfer contents of operation code field of memory buffer register into the op code decoder. Decode. OP ← MBR$_{OP}$
	CLEAR R	Clear the READ flipflop. R ← 0
F_2	INCREMENT PC	Increment the program counter to prepare to fetch the next instruction. PC ← PC + 1
F_3	CLEAR ACCUMULATOR	Execute the instruction. ACC ← 0
	PC INTO MAR	Transfer contents of the program counter into the memory address register. MAR ← PC

same time the READ flipflop is cleared. At F_2 the program counter is incremented to prepare for fetching the next instruction. At F_3 the CLEAR THE ACCUMULATOR control signal clears the accumulator. At the same time the contents of the program counter are sent to the memory address register. The computer stays in the FETCH state. The next interval will be the F_0 interval of the next instruction.

Other nonmemory reference instructions have similar control sequences. In the F_0 interval the instruction is read. During F_1 it is decoded, and the READ flipflop is cleared. In the last two intervals of the FETCH state the basic command of the instruction is executed. The program counter is incremented, and its updated contents are transferred to the memory address register.

Although we have illustrated the sequence of control signals with a hypothetical computer, the operation of an actual computer would be similar. Some instructions are more complex. If indirect addressing is used, there must be a way of actuating the DEFER state, which will have its own control signals during its three or four intervals. Later in this chapter we will show examples of control sequences for actual computers.

11.3 THE HP-35 CALCULATOR

The first digital machine that we will inspect is the HP-35 calculator. It is not a computer because it cannot store user programs and lacks other characteristics of a computer. However, it does contain most of the major components of a computer, and it makes an interesting example.

The HP-35 is the earliest of a family of Hewlett-Packard devices that now include more powerful scientific calculators and business calculators. The calculators share many features, such as the basic instruction set, some integrated circuits, and basic input/output. Design of the HP-35 provided for easy extension to design more powerful or different calculators. By adding more integrated circuits or by using inputs left unconnected on the HP-35, design of other calculators was simplified.

The HP-35 calculator can perform the usual four arithmetic calculations (addition, subtraction, multiplication, and division) and a number of transcendental functions (trigonometric, logarithmic, exponential, square root). It has five registers for storing constants and intermediate results. Four of these registers form a stack.

The basic word length of the computer is 56 bits, encoding binary-coded-decimal digits. It is natural for calculators that deal entirely with decimal information to be BCD oriented. Each word has 10 digits for the mantissa, one for the mantissa sign, two for the exponent, and one for the exponent sign. The calculator is organized on a bit-serial basis; that is, a word is transferred as 56 bits in series. This minimizes interconnections.

The organization of the HP-35 is shown in figure 11.5. The calculator has five main circuits—an arithmetic and register circuit, a control and timing circuit, and three read-only memories. Three main bus lines connect the circuits. One bus synchronizes the calculator operation by carrying a word synchronization signal (SYNC) that is generated by a 56-step counter on the control and timing circuit. A second bus carries a word-select signal (WS) that is generated either on the control and timing circuit or on one of the ROMs and enables the arithmetic and register circuit for part of a word time. It thus allows operations on only part of a number such as the exponent. A third bus transmits instructions(I_s) as serial bits from the ROMs to either the arithmetic and register circuit or to the control and timing circuit.

Instructions for the HP-35 are only 10 bits long. Figure 11.6 shows the types of instructions and their organization. Note that the operation code field is at the left. The instructions include a jump to subroutine, a conditional branch, arithmetic operations with their own 5-bit op code, status operations with provisions for four operations on 16 flags, pointer operations also with four operations on

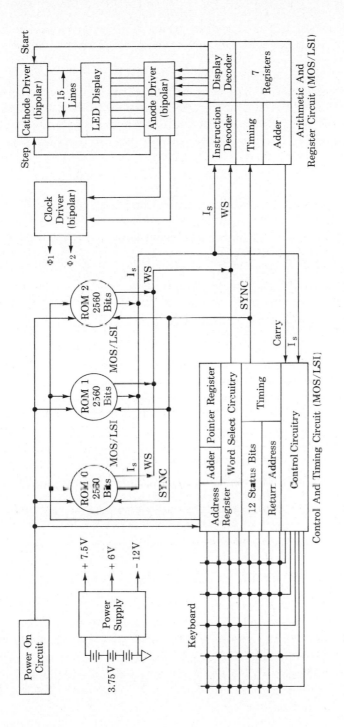

Fig. 11.5   Organization of the HP-35   (Courtesy Hewlett-Packard)

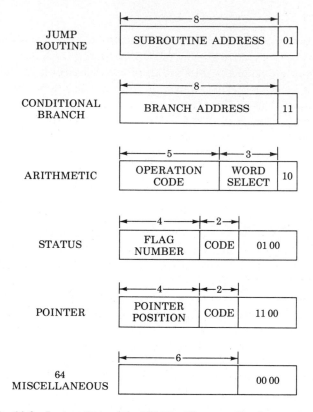

Fig. 11.6 Instructions of the HP-35 (Courtesy Hewlett-Packard)

16 pointers, and up to 64 miscellaneous operations. There is no unconditional jump instruction. This family of instructions was designed
to allow expansion for design of more powerful calculators.

11.3.1 Read-Only Memories

The mathematical routines for the functions of the calculator are
stored in the three ROM circuits. Each ROM chip holds 256 10-bit
instructions. Only one ROM circuit is used at any one time. A ROM
circuit is selected by a select code assigned for each ROM chip and
is decoded by a decoder within the ROM. Each ROM has a ROM
address register that receives the address sent by the control and
timing chip. When a ROM is selected, it responds to the address
by sending the corresponding instruction on the instruction bus to
the arithmetic and register circuit.

11.3.2 Control and Timing Circuit

The control and timing circuit performs the main housekeeping functions for the calculator. It keeps track of system status, synchronizes the system, identifies keyboard inputs, and modifies instruction addresses. The control and timing circuit has 12 status bits that can be set, cleared, or interrogated by microinstructions. It also has a pointer register that allows the calculator to point to a single digit of a number that should be operated on individually by the arithmetic and register unit. The pointer register can be set, incremented, or decremented by microinstructions. The control and timing circuit also generates a word-select signal that controls arithmetic operations.

The control and timing circuit has an address register to generate and update ROM addresses and to send them to the ROMs on the I_S line. During the execution of a branch instruction, the appropriate bit—carry or status—is tested to determine whether the conditional branch address should be followed.

The control and timing circuit also determines inputs from the keyboard. The keyboard is arranged as a five-column, eight-row matrix. Internally it is represented as a seven-column, eight-row matrix that allows for more input keys on more powerful calculators. The control and timing chip scans the keyboard continuously. When a key has been pressed, a code corresponding to the appropriate row and column is sent over the I_S line to the ROMs. The code gives the starting address of a program in ROM to service that key. A *lockout circuit* insures that only one key is identified at one time. A *key bounce circuit* insures that keys are read only once for each depression.

11.3.3 Arithmetic and Register Circuit

The arithmetic and register circuit executes instructions that enter on the I_S line. The word-select signal (WS) from the control and timing circuit, enables most arithmetic operations. The arithmetic and register unit contains an instruction decoder to decode instructions sent from the ROMs as 10 serial bits on the I_S line and the word-select signal (WS) from the control and timing circuit. It also has a timing circuit, seven 56-bit registers, and an adder. The output of the adder includes a carry signal that is sent back to the control and timing chip. Results to be displayed from the arithmetic and register circuit go through a display decoder on the circuit and then are sent on five lines to the two display drivers and then to the display. The display consists of 14 seven-segment lights (as discussed in chapter 3) and 14 decimal points. It can show numbers in fixed point or scientific (floating point) format.

Three of the seven registers in the arithmetic and register circuit are working registers. Two working registers are used only for internal storage and are not accessible by the calculator user. The other working register and three of the remaining four registers form a four-register stack. The seventh register is used independently for storage of constants. Many interconnections between the registers allow for operations such as: exchange two numbers, transfer a number, push the stack, etc. Because all numbers are transferred as serial bits, only one logic gate is needed for an interconnection.

Only whole words can be transferred into or out of the stack or the constant register. All other arithmetic instructions are governed by the word-select signal (WS) that permits selecting part of a word. Thus it is possible to add any two corresponding digits of numbers stored in two registers or to interchange their exponents or their mantissas.

An adder-subtractor is the core of the arithmetic and register circuit. It calculates the sum or difference of two decimal numbers. It has data inputs for two numbers, internal storage for carries and borrows, and sum/difference and carry/borrow outputs. The operations of addition and subtraction are done directly on each BCD digit, consisting of 4 binary bits. The operation begins with the least significant bit of each BCD digit. The first three additions are strictly binary. After addition of the fourth bit, the binary sum is checked. If the sum exceeds 9 (1001), the sum is corrected to the proper BCD result by adding 6 (0110). The resulting carry is then transmitted for the addition of the next BCD digit. For example, addition of 7 (0111) and 5 (0101) gives 12 (1100). This result exceeds 9, so 6 is added giving 2 (0010)—the correct result for that BCD digit—and a carry of 10 to the next BCD digit. This scheme for BCD addition is commonly used for calculators and was discussed in more detail in chapter 6. A similar correction is made for subtraction.

11.4 THE MCS-4 MICROCOMPUTER

As a second example, we will look at the MCS-4 microprocessor system. The Intel MCS-4 is an early microcomputer based on 4 bits and intended for BCD arithmetic and control of input/output devices. The MCS-4 consists of a CPU (4004 or the newer and more powerful

4040) and one or more attached memories that may be either RAMs or ROMs. Because microprocessors evolved after a few decades of computer architecture, even this small microprocessor has some interesting and significant architectural features. Although the MCS-4 is based on 4 bits and has only four data lines, it can work with 12-bit addresses and 8-bit or 16-bit instructions. The microcomputer accomplishes this by dealing with addresses and instructions as series of 4-bit words.

11.4.1   4004 CPU

The core of the MCS-4 microprocessor system is the CPU that contains the control unit and the arithmetic unit. It has five main functional blocks that communicate internally through a four-line bus. The blocks are:

1. Address register and address incrementer;
2. Index register;
3. Adder;
4. Instruction register, decoder, and control;
5. Input/output circuits.

Block diagrams of the CPU of the 4004 and 4040 are shown in figure 11.7. We will look at each functional block in detail, beginning with the 4004.

11.4.2   Address Register and Address Incrementer

Although the MCS-4 is a 4-bit system, it can address 2^{12} locations and hence uses 12-bit addresses. The address register is a stack of four 12-bit registers. One register holds the program counter; the other three registers are used for subroutine calls. The address register is made of dynamic RAM and hence is connected to a refresh circuit for refreshing of its contents. A control circuit and an effective address counter keep track of stack addresses that are sent to the address register through a decoder and multiplexer.

When an address is read, it is stored in a buffer register and is sent to the internal bus in three clock cycles. During each cycle 4 bits of the address are sent to the bus, starting with the 4 least significant bits. The address incrementer updates the address by 1 after each 4-bit segment, or *slice,* of the address is sent on the bus. When all three slices have been sent, the incremented address is sent back to the address buffer and then written back into the address register.

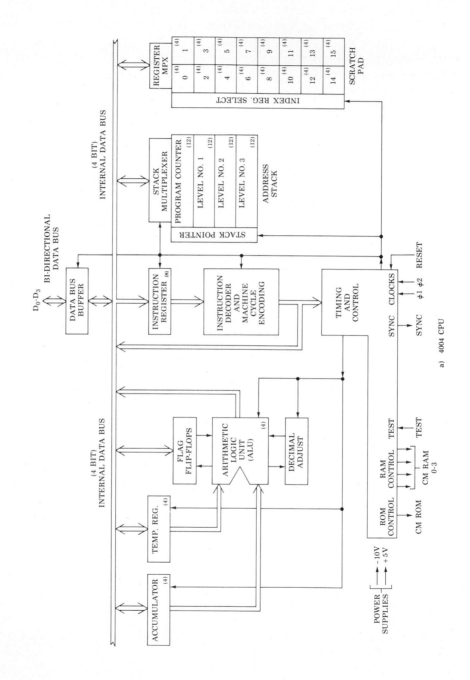

a) 4004 CPU

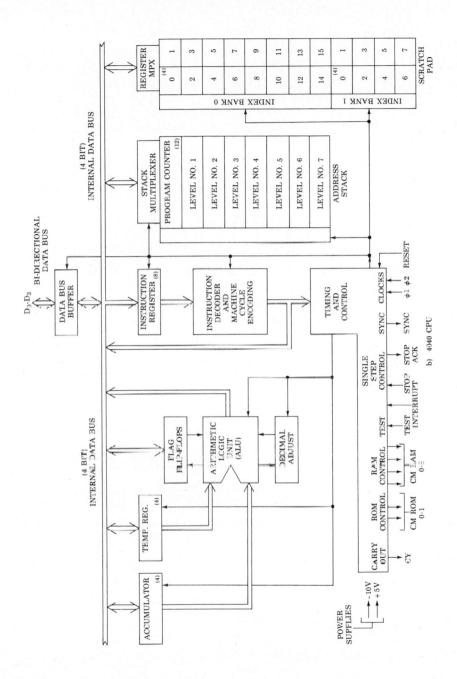

Fig. 11.7 Central processing unit of MCS-4 microprocessor system (Courtesy of Intel Corp.)

11.4.3 Index Register

The index register of the 4004 is an array of 16 × 4 bits that operate either as sixteen 4-bit words or as eight pairs of 4-bit words. In the first mode the index register can provide 16 storage locations for intermediate results that can be directly addressed. In the second mode the index register provides eight pairs of addressable locations for addressing the memories or for storing data. The index register is connected to the internal bus, the refresh counter, and an index register decoder in much the same way as the address register. Contents of the index register are transferred to the internal bus through a multiplexer. Data is inputted to the index register through a temporary register.

11.4.4 Adder

The adder of both the 4004 and the 4040 is an ordinary 4-bit ripple carry adder. The addend comes from the accumulator and carry flipflop. The augend comes from the ADB buffer register that receives data from the internal bus. The adder output is returned to the adder and carry flipflop. It contains a 4-bit accumulator and a carry flipflop. The accumulator has a shifter for right and left cyclic shifts.

The accumulator is connected to a command control register, special ROMs, a condition flipflop, and the internal bus. The command control register has a 3-bit code for switching lines between RAMs. The special ROMs convert numbers after addition to their proper BCD form by adding 6, just as in the HP-35. The condition flipflop senses a zero accumulator, the carry flipflop, and an external test signal (TEST) used for branching instructions.

11.4.5 Instruction Register

The instruction register of both the 4004 and the 4040 holds an 8-bit instruction in two 4-bit registers called OPR and OPA. Instructions are loaded from ROM via the internal bus and a multiplexer in two clock times. Instructions are decoded by the instruction decoder and combined with timing signals to control the CPU operations. A few instructions are double length or 16 bits. A double cycle flipflop controls the timing of the double length instructions. A condition flipflop controls branching instructions.

11.4.6 Input/Output Circuits

The main input/output circuit is a 4-bit input/output buffer and an associated input/output buffer control connected to the internal data bus. There are also output buffers that command four RAMs and one ROM. The timing circuit provides a signal (SYNC) for synchronizing external devices. A reset flipflop can clear all RAMs and static flipflops and set the data bus to 0.

11.4.7 System Organization

The organization of an MCS-4 microprocessor system is shown in figure 11.8. The 4004 CPU that we have just examined is in the upper left corner. The system can also contain up to 16 ROMs (4001), up to 16 RAMs (4002), and up to 128 input/output lines. The smallest possible system is one CPU and one ROM. The system shown here has two 4003 shift registers that can each convert three input/output lines to 10.

Each ROM is organized as 256 8-bit words for storing programs or data. Each ROM also has a 4-bit input/output port that can be used to send information to or from external devices. The ROMs can be microprogrammed before they are placed in the system, but cannot be changed during system operation.

The RAMs store data and instructions. Each RAM is arranged as four registers of 20 4-bit words for a total of 320 bits of storage. RAMs have four output lines that can control output operations.

The shift registers are 10-bit registers that receive data serially and can output data either in series or in parallel. Their main function is to increase the number of output lines to allow interfacing with external devices such as teletypes, displays, switches, etc.

The CPU transfers information to or from the ROMs and RAMs on the four-line data bus. It sends control signals to the ROMs and RAMs over five other lines. Four of these lines are used to control the RAM circuits. Since each line can control up to four RAMs, the four lines can control up to 16 RAMs. One line controls up to four ROMs.

11.4.8 Instruction Timing

Two separate clock signals must be applied to the CPU and to all RAMs and ROMs. Every eight clock periods the CPU generates a SYNC signal that it sends to the RAMs and ROMs to mark the start of an instruction cycle. The RAMs and ROMs then generate their own internal timing signals using the SYNC signal to the two clock signals. Figure 11.9 shows a basic instruction cycle.

A typical instruction cycle begins with three address times—A_1, A_2, and A_3. During A_1 the 4 least significant bits of the address are sent to the ROMs. Similarly, during A_2 and A_3 the middle 4 bits and the highest 4 bits are sent to the ROMs. The address selects

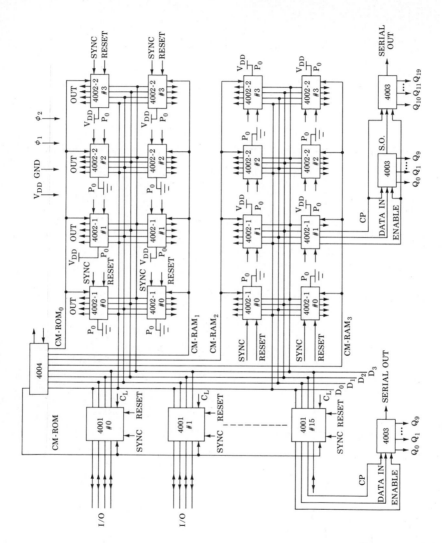

Fig. 11.8 An MCS-4 microprocessor system (Courtesy Intel Corp.)

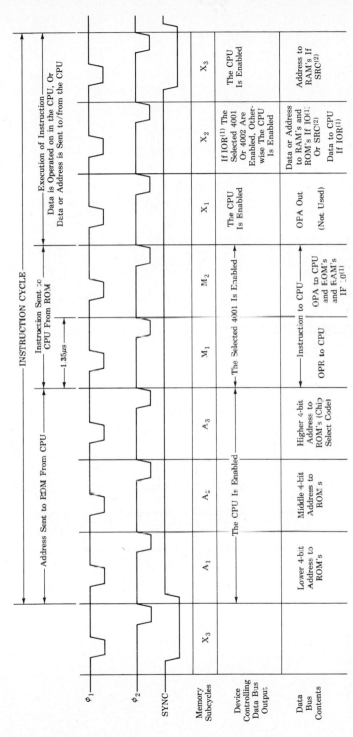

Fig. 11.9 Timing diagram for the MCS-4 (Courtesy Intel Corp.)

(1) IO instructions control the flow of information between accumulator in CPU, I/O lines in ROM's and RAM's and RAM storage. IOR stands for IO Read. In this case the CPU will receive data from RAM storage locations or I/O input lines of 4001's.

(2) The SRC instruction designates the chip number and address for a following IO instruction.

ONE WORD INSTRUCTIONS

D_3	D_2	D_1	D_0	D_3	D_2	D_1	D_0
X	X	X	X	X	X	X	X

OPR | OPA

OP CODE	MODIFIER

X	X	X	X	INDEX REGISTER ADDRESS
				R R R R

OR

X	X	X	X	INDEX REGISTER PAIR ADDRESS
				R R R X

OR

X	X	X	X	DATA
				D D D D

D_3	D_2	D_1	D_0	D_3	D_2	D_1	D_0
X	X	X	X	X	X	X	X

OPR | OPA

INPUT/OUTPUT & RAM INSTRUCTIONS

1	1	1	0	X	X	X	X

ACCUMULATOR GROUP INSTRUCTIONS

1	1	1	1	X	X	X	X

WHERE X = EITHER A "0" OR A "1"

TWO WORD INSTRUCTIONS

1st INSTRUCTION CYCLE

D_3	D_2	D_1	D_0	D_3	D_2	D_1	D_0
X	X	X	X	X	X	X	X

OPR | OPA

OP CODE	MODIFIER

X	X	X	X	UPPER ADDRESS
				A_3 A_3 A_3 A_3

OR

X	X	X	X	CONDITION
				C_1 C_2 C_3 C_4

OR

X	X	X	X	INDEX REGISTER ADDRESS
				R R R R

OR

X	X	X	X	INDEX REGISTER PAIR ADDRESS
				R R R X

2nd INSTRUCTION CYCLE

D_3	D_2	D_1	D_0	D_3	D_2	D_1	D_0
X	X	X	X	X	X	X	X

OPR | OPA

OP CODE	MODIFIER

MIDDLE ADDRESS	LOWER ADDRESS
A_2 A_2 A_2 A_2	A_1 A_1 A_1 A_1

MIDDLE ADDRESS	LOWER ADDRESS
A_2 A_2 A_2 A_2	A_1 A_1 A_1 A_1

MIDDLE ADDRESS	LOWER ADDRESS
A_2 A_2 A_2 A_2	A_1 A_1 A_1 A_1

UPPER DATA	LOWER DATA
D_2 D_2 D_2 D_2	D_1 D_1 D_1 D_1

one of 16 ROMs and one of 256 8-bit words on that ROM. During the next two clock times—M_1 and M_2—the 8-bit instruction stored at the memory location just addressed is sent from the ROM to the CPU. The instruction is sent over the four-line data bus as two 4-bit bytes (OPR and OPA). Finally during the last three clock times—X_1, X_2, and X_3—the instruction is executed.

11.4.9 Instructions

The 4004 has 45 instructions, five of which are double length and hence require two complete instruction cycles of eight clock times each. The format of some typical instructions is shown as figure 11.10. One-word instructions are stored in one location in ROM. Two-word instructions are stored in two adjacent locations in ROM. Each instruction word has two 4-bit fields. The upper 4 bits are called OPR and form the operation code. The lower 4 bits are called OPA and act as a modifier. The modifier can be a register address, a register pair address, 4 bits of data, or a modification of the operation code. In two-word instructions the modifier may also be part of a ROM address or a condition for jumping, and the second word is either the rest of an address or data.

11.4.10 4040 Features

The Intel 4040 CPU is compatible with the 4004; that is, it may be exchanged for the 4004 CPU in any system. It has several features that make it more powerful. For example, it has 14 additional instructions including halt, logical operations, and interrupt enable and disable. The address stack contains twice as many bits—8 × 12 bits—allowing seven levels of subroutine nesting. The index register array has been increased by eight 4-bit registers to 24 4-bit registers. An important hardware improvement is the addition of the hardware necessary for processing single-level interrupts. A STOP control allows the user to halt the processor or to *"single step"* the processor. (Single-step operation means that the CPU executes one instruction and then halts so that the user can easily check for program errors.)

11.5 PDP-8 MINICOMPUTER

Just as the MCS-4 was one of the first microprocessors, the Digital Equipment Corporation PDP-8 was one of the first minicomputers.

Fig. 11.10 MCS-4 instructions

Hence its organization is simpler than most current minicomputers. The PDP-8 is a single-address, 12-bit minicomputer that can readily address 2^{12} or 4K 12-bit memory words. Its memory can be extended to 32K bits. Its basic organization is shown in figure 11.11. The PDP-8 has two main buses—one that sends memory addresses and data between memory and the CPU, and one that sends input/output control information and data between external devices and the CPU.

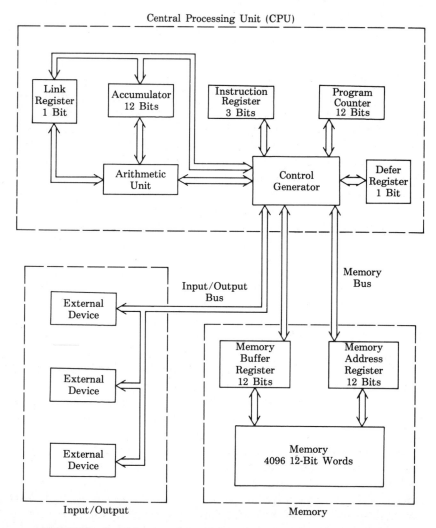

Fig. 11.11   Organization of the PDP-8 minicomputer (Courtesy Digital Equipment Corp.)

It uses twos complement arithmetic instead of the BCD arithmetic of the HP-35 and the MCS-4.

The CPU of the PDP-8 has a particularly simple organization. It has just one accumulator plus a 1-bit link register for handling carries and overflow. A master control generator develops all timing and control signals and sends them to all other parts of the computer. A 3-bit instruction register holds and decodes the 3-bit operation code of instructions. A 1-bit defer register holds the direct-indirect bit of the current instruction and shows when the computer needs to enter a DEFER state to find an indirect address. The program counter holds the address of the current instruction.

11.5.1 Instructions

The instruction set of the PDP-8 has been discussed in chapter 6, and we will quickly review it here. There are three types of instructions—memory reference instructions (six), register reference instructions, and input/output instructions. The operation code is the first 3 bits of the instruction. Memory reference instructions have an indirect bit as bit 3 and a page bit as bit 4. The last 7 bits are the address field. Input/output instructions have 6 bits for selecting one of 64 input/output devices and the last 3 bits for controlling the selected device. Register reference instructions are divided into three classes of microinstructions in which each bit generally specifies a specific micro-operation.

11.5.2 Timing

The control generator provides timing signals for the three main states—FETCH, DEFER, and EXECUTE—that may occur during each memory cycle. It produces four time state signals, $TS1$ through $TS4$, and four time pulse signals, $TP1$ through $TP4$. Figure 11.12 shows the relations between these signals for a fast memory cycle (1.2 microseconds). The PDP-8 also has a slow memory cycle in which $TS2$ is extended for 0.2 microsecond. These time state and pulse signals are used as controls throughout the computer.

Figure 11.13 shows the operations that occur in the FETCH cycle, which is always a fast cycle. During $TS1$ the program counter (PC) is incremented. At $TP1$ the current instruction is read from memory. During $TS2$ the operation code of the instruction is sent to the instruction register and decoded. During $TS3$ the instruction is executed if it is a register reference, input/output, or jump direct instruction. At $TP3$ the instruction is written back into memory. This step

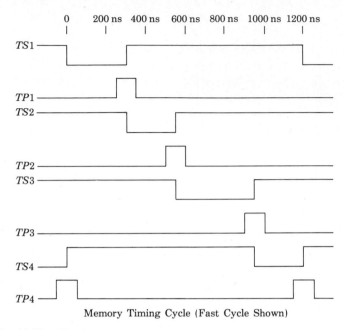

Memory Timing Cycle (Fast Cycle Shown)

Fig. 11.13   FETCH cycle of PDP-8 (Courtesy Digital Equipment Corp.)

is necessary since the memory is magnetic core and hence has destructive readout. During $TS4$ the CPU prepares for the next cycle. The direct/indirect bit (bit 3) is checked. If it is 1 the computer will enter the DEFER state after the FETCH state. If the next cycle is to be a FETCH cycle, the memory address register is incremented. Otherwise the CPU calculates the page address of the instruction and prepares for the EXECUTE state for direct commands and the DEFER state for indirect commands.

The DEFER cycle (shown in figure 11.14) is also a fast cycle except for a special feature, called *auto index,* that we will not consider. The CPU enters the DEFER cycle from the FETCH cycle when the current instruction has an indirect address. At $TP1$ the computer reads the address field from memory. During $TS3$ the CPU tests to see if the instruction is a jump instruction; if so, it sets the program counter equal to the operand address and thus executes the jump. At $TP3$ the address is written back into memory. If the instruction was a jump indirect, the CPU will next enter a FETCH cycle. Otherwise it places the operand address in the memory address register (MAR) and enters an EXECUTE cycle.

The EXECUTE cycle is used for execution of memory reference instructions. It is entered from the FETCH or DEFER cycle. At

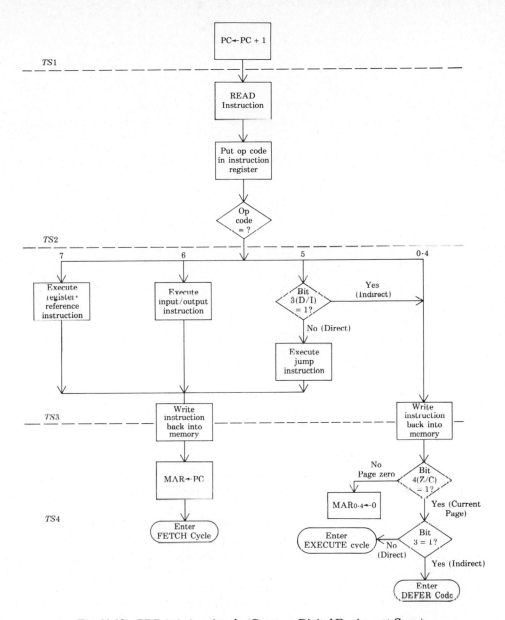

Fig. 11.12 PDP-8 timing signals (Courtesy Digital Equipment Corp.)

*TP*1 the operand is read from memory. During *TS*2 and *TS*3 the operation code is examined and the basic operation of the instruction is executed. At *TP*3 the operand is rewritten into memory. During *TS*4 the memory address register is updated, and the CPU prepares to return to the FETCH cycle.

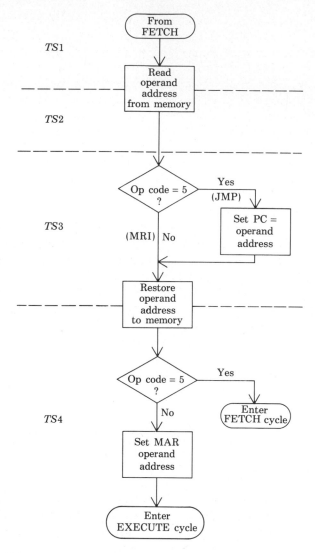

Fig. 11.14   DEFER cycle of PDP-8 (Courtesy Digital Equipment Corp.)

11.5.3 Interrupts

The PDP-8 has a simple single-level, single-priority interrupt system. Device status indicators for all input/output devices are ORed together on an interrupt request line. Whenever any device requests an interrupt, the line becomes 1. The system also has an interrupt enable flipflop that must be set to enable the interrupt system. The

CPU tests the interrupt enable flipflop and the interrupt request line during $TS4$ of every memory cycle in which an instruction was executed. If the interrupt enable flipflop is 1 and the interrupt request line is on, the CPU begins a program interrupt.

The program interrupt is simply a subroutine jump to memory location 0. During $TS4$ of the instruction during which the interrupt was discovered, the CPU clears the memory address register, places the subroutine jump operation code in the instruction register, and prepares to enter an EXECUTE cycle. During the EXECUTE cycle, the CPU first turns off the interrupt system so that no further interrupts can occur until the current interrupt is serviced. It then executes the subroutine jump instruction to memory location 0. It stores the address of the instruction which was in the program counter before the interrupt occurred and which was due to be the next instruction executed into memory location 0. The contents of the program counter then are incremented by 1 to begin servicing the interrupt. The user must provide the interrupt service routine as a program that begins in location 1. The program, as explained in chapter 10, ordinarily saves the contents of any registers that will be used by the interrupt service routine, identifies the interrupting device, corrects the interrupt condition, restores the register contents, turns on the interrupt system, and returns to the main program with a jump indirect to location 0 instruction.

11.5.4 Direct Memory Access

The PDP-8 also provides direct memory access for up to 12 devices. Each device that uses direct memory access has two registers—a current address register and a word count register. The 12-bit current address register holds the address of the memory location in which the last DMA transfer was performed. The contents of the current address register are incremented by 1 at the start of a DMA transfer and show the address of the memory location for the current transfer. The 12-bit word count register holds the twos complement of the number of words to be transferred. It is incremented by 1 during each transfer and sends a control signal to end the transfer when it becomes 0.

The DMA system is a priority system for up to 12 DMA devices. When the device is ready to transfer data, it sends its priority bit on the data bus. If no higher priority device is requesting service, the device sends two signals that disable the control generator, the instruction register, and the memory address register of the computer. The CPU enters a DMA cycle, and the external device can control the CPU logic circuits it needs for the transfer. When the transfer has been completed, program execution resumes at the point it was interrupted. The main registers of the CPU are not used during the DMA transfer so that no restoration of registers is needed.

11.6 PDP-11

The PDP-11 is a more recent minicomputer than the PDP-8. Although it is also made by the Digital Equipment Corporation, its features and organization are quite different. The PDP-11 is actually a family of computers. A typical PDP-11 has eight working registers instead of a single accumulator. It communicates with memory and input/output devices on a single bus. It has a 16-bit word that is organized as two 8-bit bytes that can be individually addressed and processed. It operates asynchronously; thus timing is limited by the response speed of each system component rather than determined rigidly by a master clock. Asynchronous timing allows easy updating of the system to incorporate faster components. It has direct memory access and a sophisticated multiple-level, multiple-priority interrupt system.

The basic structure of the PDP-11 is shown in figure 11.15. All components of the computer are connected to a single 56-line bus that carries addresses (18 lines), data (16 lines), and control information (22 lines). Each device attached to the bus communicates in the same way. Each device, including memory locations, CPU registers, and input/output device registers, is assigned an address on the bus. The CPU can manipulate input/output device registers in the same way that it does memory. All instructions can be applied either to memory or to data in input/output registers.

Communication between any two devices on the bus is done in a master-slave relationship. At any one time a single device, called

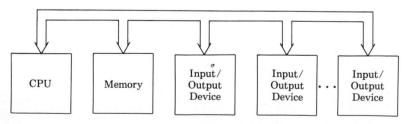

Fig. 11.15   Organization of the PDP-11

the bus *master,* controls the bus. The bus master can communicate with any other device on the bus, called the *slave.* For example, the CPU as bus master might fetch an instruction from the memory as slave. Master-slave relationships can change with time. The CPU might pass control to a disc, which would then be master. Some devices, such as main memory, can only be slaves.

A priority structure determines which device becomes bus master. Each device attached to the bus that is capable of being a master has a priority. When two such devices both want control of the bus, the device with the higher priority becomes the master.

Asynchronous operation of the PDP-11 is done through a handshaking relationship. When the master sends a control signal to a slave, the slave must respond to complete the communication. Thus, the time needed for a communication depends on the exchange of signals between the master and the slave. The time is independent of the length of the bus and does not need to be synchronized with clock pulses. Each device can operate at its highest speed.

11.6.1   CPU Structure

The CPU of most versions of the PDP-11 has eight registers, as shown in figure 11.16. The first six registers (**R0** through **R5**) are general registers that may be used as accumulators, index registers, pointers, etc. Arithmetic operations can be done from one general register to

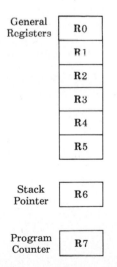

Fig. 11.16   PDP-11 registers

another, from one memory or input/output device register to another, or between a memory or input/output device register and a general register in the CPU. Register **R6** is usually used as a stack pointer to show the most recent entry in a stack. **R7** is used as the program counter.

11.6.2 Instructions

PDP-11 instructions have three main formats as shown in figure 11.17. Instructions for manipulating data are either one-address or two-address instructions. The addresses for these instructions have 6 bits, 3 for the register and 3 for the mode. The PDP-11 has eight addressing modes. One-address instructions name the destination register and have 9 bits for the operation code. Two-address instructions name both the source and destination registers and have only 3 bits for the operation code. Both one-address and two-address instructions reserve bit 15 to specify byte or word operation. The branch instruction has 8 bits for the operation code and 8 bits to specify the displacement from the program counter for the branch. The PDP-11 also has a few instructions that take two or three words each.

One-Address Instructions

Two-Address Instructions

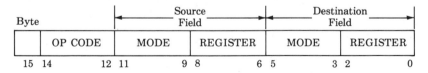

Branch Instructions

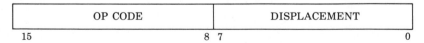

Fig. 11.17   PDP-11 instruction format

11.6.3   Control

The PDP-11 has a CPU status register with several condition flags. The 8 low-order bits of this register are shown as figure 11.18; we will not consider the rest of the register. Three bits of the CPU status register show the priority level of the CPU to control interrupts. The remaining bits are individual flags. T is a test bit that can be used in program debugging. N is a negative bit, Z a zero bit, V an overflow bit, and C a carry bit. These bits are set or cleared by most data manipulation operations. They can be individually tested by special instructions.

The general procedure for PDP-11 control is much like the PDP-8. Instructions are fetched in sequence, unless there is a branch instruction or an interrupt, and are executed. The timing is not as regular because of the asynchronous operation. An instruction time includes the time needed to fetch the instruction—one bus request and grant time plus one memory cycle that varies according to the speed of the memory used. It also includes the time needed to execute the instruction. If the instruction addresses a source or a destination other than one of the general registers, source or destination time must be added. Source and destination time includes time for access to memory or an input/output device register, and possibly memory time for indirect addressing.

11.6.4   Interrupts

The PDP-11 has a hardware multiple-level, multiple-priority interrupt system with four levels. Several devices can be attached to each level and each can individually send its service routine address. Thus, polling of devices to identify the interrupting device is not needed since the interrupt service hardware automatically selects and starts executing the appropriate service routine. The CPU automatically

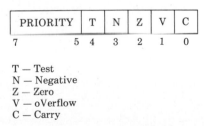

PRIORITY	T	N	Z	V	C
7	5	4	3	2	1	0

T — Test
N — Negative
Z — Zero
V — oVerflow
C — Carry

Fig. 11.18   Priority and control part of PDP-11 status registers

compares its own priority with the priority of an interrupting device and acknowledges the device with the highest priority level that exceeds the CPU's priority. Higher priority devices can interrupt the servicing of lower priority interrupts. All necessary registers and status information are automatically saved by hardware when multiple interrupts occur.

11.7   IBM 370

The IBM system 370 is a family of computers with more power and flexibility than the preceding computers. We will briefly consider some of its characteristics. The basic word length of the 370 is 32 bits. It is organized around 8-bit bytes, much like the PDP-11.

An 8-bit byte can represent one EBCDIC character, two BCD digits, or 8 binary bits. Bytes may be addressed and processed individually or may be grouped to form variable-length words or fields. Different word sizes are used for different purposes. A half word (16 bits) consists of 2 bytes and is the basic unit of instructions. Fixed point arithmetic can be done on half words. A word (32 bits) consists of 4 bytes and can be used for either fixed point or floating point arithmetic. Floating point arithmetic can also be done on double words (64 bits or 8 bytes) or on extended-precision words (128 bits or 16 bytes).

11.7.1   Data Formats

Four formats—two decimal and two binary—are used for numeric data. *Zoned decimal* format can be used with EBCDIC input and output; 4 bits represent the sign and each decimal digit. Typically, 1 byte encodes each digit of a number because a 4-bit representation of the sign precedes the 4-bit representation of each decimal digit.

Packed decimal format codes decimal numbers more efficiently. Variable field lengths are allowed up to 16 bytes that can encode 31 decimal digits and a sign. Numbers are treated as signed integers and are represented in signed-magnitude form. The sign is encoded only once per word.

Fixed point binary numbers can be stored in half words or full words, allowing 15 bits of 31 bits plus sign, respectively. Numbers are represented in twos complement form.

Floating point binary numbers, as mentioned above, can be represented in words, double words, or extended word. A short floating point number uses a full word for seven decimal numbers of precision.

A long floating point number uses a double word for 17 decimal numbers of precision. An extended floating point number is represented as two long floating point numbers for a precision of 34 decimal places. Floating point numbers are represented as fractions with the binary point at the far left. The exponent provides a range of -256 to $+252$ to represent numbers from 10^{-78} to 10^{+75}.

The CPUs of 370 computers have two different sets of registers for arithmetic or general-purpose operations, as shown by figure 11.19. They have eight 32-bit floating point registers. The eight 32-bit registers may be used as four double word or 64-bit registers if desired. There are also 16 general-purpose registers that can be used as sixteen 32-bit registers or as eight 64-bit registers.

11.7.2 Instructions

IBM 370 instructions may be 16, 32, or 48 bits long (or 2, 4, or 6 bytes). The 16-bit register-to-register (RR) instructions require 4 bits to specify each register for the transfer and 8 bits for the operation code. Register-and-indexed storage (RX) instructions also have an 8-bit operation code. They have 12 bits for the displacement and 4 bits each for register, index, and base. The RX instructions can use flexible forms of index and base register addressing. Register-and-storage (RS) operations also require 32 bits to specify operation code and three operands, two of which are in registers. Storage-and-immediate-operand (SI) instructions also take 32 bits, 8 of which are used as an immediate operand; that is, the number in bits 8 through 15 is used directly as data. The longest instructions are storage-to-storage (SS) instructions. SS instructions require 48 bits to designate operations between two operands located in memory. Figure 11.20 and table 11.4 show the formats and fields of representative IBM 370 instructions.

TABLE 11.4

FIELDS OF IBM 370 INSTRUCTIONS

Abbreviation	Meaning	Field length in bits
OP	Operation code	8
R	General register	4
B	Base register	4
X	Index register	4
D	Displacement	12
I	Immediate value	8
L	Length designation	4 or 8

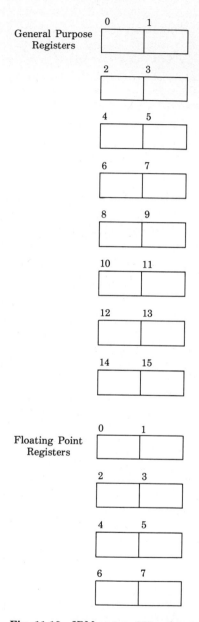

Fig. 11.19 IBM system 370 registers

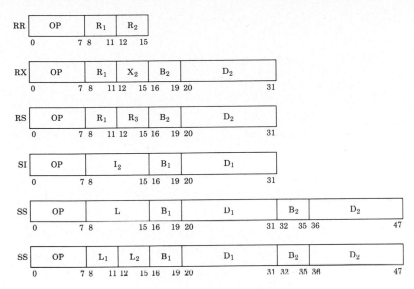

Fig. 11.20   IBM 370 instruction formats

11.7.3 Operation

Fetching of instructions for the IBM 370 is controlled by a 24-bit program counter. The program counter is part of a program status word (PSW), as shown in figure 11.21. The program status register contains several types of information on the status of the program, most of which do not concern us. It includes an instruction length code to show the number of 16-bit half words in the instruction. It also has a condition code to test results of arithmetic operations and logical comparisons.

Execution of a program depends on the status of the CPU. The CPU status has four alternatives—Problem/Supervisor, Wait/Running, Masked/Interruptible, and Stopped/Operating. When bit 15 of the PSW is 0, the CPU is in the Supervisor state. In this state all computer instructions are valid. When bit 15 of the PSW is 1, the computer is in the Problem state and only nonprivileged instructions—instructions other than input/output, protection, and status changing—are valid.

When bit 14 of the PSW is 0, the CPU is in the Running state in which normal operation proceeds. When bit 14 of the PSW is 1, the CPU waits for an interrupt and is in the Wait state. No instructions can be processed while the computer is in the Wait state.

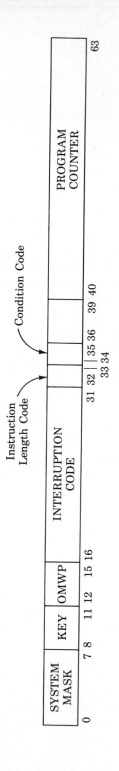

Fig. 11.21   IBM system 370 program status

The Masked/Interruptible alternative concerns interrupts. Mask bits in either the PSW or the control registers enable interrupts when the bit for a particular interrupt is 1 and mask off the interrupts when the bit is 0. Some interrupts are always enabled.

When the CPU is in the Operating state, it is either running or waiting. When it is in the Stopped state, instructions cannot be executed and interrupts cannot be handled.

11.7.4 Interrupts

The IBM 370 has powerful interrupt capabilities. It can handle five types of interrupts—input/output, program, supervisor call, external, and machine check. Two double-word locations in memory are associated with each type of interrupt to store the current PSW at the moment of interrupt and to obtain a new PSW containing the address of the interrupt service routine.

Input/output interrupts are similar to those discussed in chapter 10. Program interrupts result from illegal use of data or instructions or improper use of the computer. The supervisor call interrupt allows changing from the Problem state to the Supervisor state. External interrupts allow the CPU to respond to external occurrences transmitted through special lines. Machine check interrupts result from recoverable or nonrecoverable system malfunctions.

The preceding discussion has served just to introduce some of the features of the IBM 370. It is far more complex than any of the other computers we have studied. Readers interested in more information should consult the references at the end of the chapter.

11.8 COMPUTER NETWORKS

A *computer network* may be defined as an interconnection of two or more central processing units with associated memories, input/output equipment, etc. One example of a simple computer network is a PDP-11 system that has two or more CPUs attached to one bus with associated memory and input/output devices. In such a system one CPU would act as bus master and control the operation of the system. More complete computer networks often have several minicomputers acting as channel controllers (as explained in chapter 10) for a main central processing unit of a large computer.

Computer networks have two main organizations. They either have control centralized in one main computer or they have control distributed throughout the computers in the network with several computers having the capability of controlling the network. Each computer has input/output equipment that prepares the information for communication over the network. The preparation may involve coding, error checking, and conversion to the proper form for communication between computers.

Computer networks can be described graphically with the aid of the branch of mathematics called topology. Each main computer in the network is represented as a node of the graph. The communications connection between two computers is a link or branch of the graph. With topology, calculations can be done to determine the maximum communications capacity between any two computers and the best form of interconnections.

Figure 11.22a shows the structure of a centralized or star computer network. In a *centralized network,* one computer, called the *network controller,* controls the network. All other computers in the network can communicate only through the network controller. The computer performing network control may be dedicated to the control function or may alternate between the control function and other processing. The main advantage of a centralized network structure is that it is very simple. The main disadvantages are that communication lines cannot be shared and that only one route for messages between any two computers is possible.

A variation of a centralized network is a hierarchical or tree network, so called because it has branches like those of a tree, as shown in figure 11.22b. Tree networks are commonly used for industrial control of real-time systems. In the example shown, a host or main computer coordinates the actions of several minicomputers, which in turn process and control the actions of small real-time controllers—a balanced arrangement.

Figure 11.22c shows one example of a *distributed computer network* structure. In this structure no computer controls the network all the time. Instead, each computer is eligible for network control subject to priority constraints. Usually each computer is connected to at least two other computers. Communication between any two computers may either be direct if the two happen to be connected directly, or indirect if they are connected by several paths through other computers. Distributed networks are particularly attractive when all computers in the network are likely to act both as users of computer services and as providers of computer services. They are usually more complex and expensive than centralized computer networks. If the network includes a great number and variety of computers, standardization of interfaces between computers becomes difficult.

Figure 11.22d shows a variation of distributed network structure known as a loop or *ring* structure. In the loop each computer is connected to exactly two other computers. The form of the connections is a loop or ring; there are no other branchings or doubling backs in the structure.

An early version of the ARPA network of the Advanced Research Projects Agency of the Department of Defense is shown in figure 11.23. The ARPA network is a distributed structure that links several computers of varying sizes and types across the nation.

11.8.1 Network Communications

Network communications are handled in three basic ways—circuit switching, message switching, and packet switching. The commercial telephone system is an example of *circuit switching*. One or more switching centers establish a direct connection between two users, such as a terminal and a computer. When the circuit is established, communication can occur. If all feasible routes are in use, the caller receives a busy signal. Circuit switching requires time to establish a connection and ties up the connection for some time. However, once the circuit has been established, there is no further delay.

Message switching involves sending each message as a unit along a route through the network to its destination. The message has its destination address in a header preceding the text so that each node encountered enroute will know where to forward the message. Separate messages between the same source and destination may take different routes. If a node is busy when the message appears, it will store it for later transmission; such a system is called a *store and forward* system.

Packet switching is a special form of message switching in which messages are divided into fixed-length blocks, called *packets,* for transmission. Each packet of perhaps 4000 bits is sent individually along the best route at the time of transmission. At the destination a minicomputer reassembles the packets into the original message. Time can be saved in transmission because the several packets of a long message can be sent over several network paths simultaneously. In addition, communication can be more secure because only part of the message is sent along one path; thus the entire message is not available at intermediate nodes. Short messages may be grouped into a single packet.

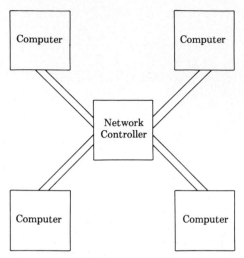

a) Centralized or star network

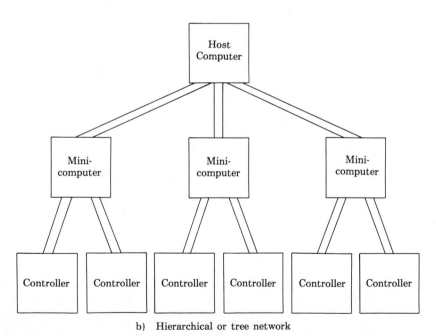

b)   Hierarchical or tree network

Fig. 11.22   Network structures

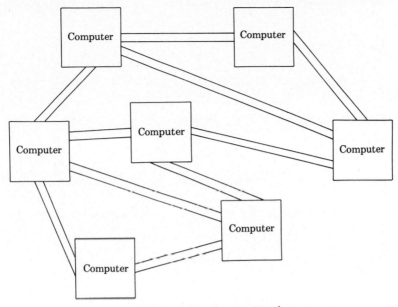

c) Distributed computer network

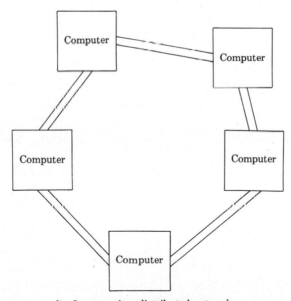

d) Loop or ring distributed network

(Fig. 11.22 continued)

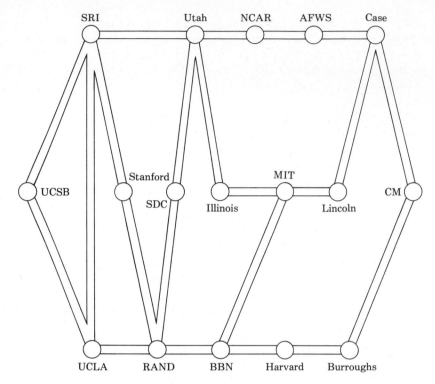

Fig. 11.23 An early version of the ARPA network

11.9 SUMMARY

The main parts of a computer are the central processing unit, memory, and input/output devices. The CPU includes an arithmetic unit, one or more working registers, and the control circuits for the computer. The control circuits include an instruction decoder, an operation code decoder, and timing generators to give timing pulses.

The registers and devices that comprise a computer are connected by one or more buses. Two typical organizations are the separate memory and input/output buses and a single combined memory and input/output bus. The first organization usually results in different instructions for memory reference instructions and for input/output operations. The combined bus structure allows addressing both memory and input/output devices in the same way.

Computers may operate either synchronously or asynchronously. In synchronous operation all control signals are started by timing pulses generated by a master clock. Regardless of the length of time actually necessary to complete a control operation, the next operation starts at a time determined by the master clock. In asynchronous operation a handshaking procedure governs control operations; one operation starts after it receives a signal that the preceding operation has been concluded. Asynchronous operation is more flexible since it takes advantage of faster speeds of new technologies, and it eliminates any limits on bus length.

Instructions are usually executed as a series of micro-operations that may be implemented either by standard logic or by microprogramming. Usually control of an instruction is done in one or more states, each of which is broken down into three or four intervals. During each interval one or more independent micro-operations may be performed. Operations that must be performed in sequence are done in separate intervals.

Some information was presented about five digital systems—the HP-35, the MCS-4, the PDP-8, the PDP-11, and the IBM 370. This selection ranges from a pocket calculator to a very powerful family of large computers. The HP-35 illustrated use of ROMs for control, BCD arithmetic, serial operation, and other concepts. The MCS-4 (an early microcomputer) showed the flexibility of using a basically 4-bit machine for 8- and 12-bit operations. The PDP-8 (an early minicomputer) showed the simple organization typical of a one-address, single-accumulator machine. The PDP-11 showed the more flexible operations possible for a minicomputer with several working registers and a single bus. Our discussion of the IBM 370 showed features of a typical large computer.

Computers may be linked together into computer networks. Networks are represented as graphs. Each computer is a node on the graph, and each interconnection is a branch. Centralized networks have one central computer that controls the network. Distributed networks share the control among various computers in the network.

Concepts

accessible register
asynchronous
bus
centralized network
circuit switching
computer network
control register
distributed network

input/output bus
instruction decoder
key bounce
lockout
master
memory and input/output bus
memory bus
message switching

operation code decoder	status register
packed decimal format	store and forward
packet switching	timing control
ring	zoned decimal format
slave	

11.10 REFERENCES

Good basic discussions on the principles of computer organization at the systems level may be found in Foster (1970), Abrams and Stein (1973), Bartee (1972), Gear (1974), and Stone and Sieworek (1975). Detailed analyses of many computers may be found in Bell and Newell (1971). The users manuals are the best source of information on the computers discussed here. Whitney (in Stone, 1975) has a good discussion of the HP-35. Katzan (1971) describes the IBM 370.

11.11 PROBLEMS

11.1 Design the counter and register circuits that will generate the four intervals for both the FETCH and EXECUTE states for the computer of section 11.2. (11.2)

11.2 Design a single stage of an accumulator and an **X** register that will have two basic operations. SHR will shift the contents right one position. ADR will add the corresponding bits of the accumulator and the **X** register and then shift right one position. Use SHR and ADR as control signals, a full adder, AND and OR gates, and *SR* flipflops. (11.2)

11.3 For the computer of section 11.2 show the control signals necessary for an unconditional jump operation. Assume the computer has a control signal JMP. Show the timing table. (11.2)

11.4 For the computer of section 11.2 show the control signals and the timing table for a CLEAR and ADD instruction. (11.2)

11.5 For the computer of section 11.2 show the control signals and the timing table needed for a SUBTRACT operation. Assume there is a SUB control signal that subtracts the contents of the **X** register from the accumulator and leaves the difference in the accumulator. (11.2)

11.6 Explain the sequence of operations of the HP-35 when the sine of an angle (entered in radians) is calculated. Assume the sine routine is stored in ROM 1. (11.3)

11.7 Explain the differences in the interrupt systems for the PDP-8 and PDP-11. (11.5)

11.8 Draw a block diagram of a PDP-11 with two CPUs. Discuss the procedure needed for exchanging bus master status between the two computers. (11.5)

11.9 Often minicomputers preprocess information for larger computers. Draw a block diagram of a possible system with four minicomputers used as preprocessors. Is this centralized or distributed control? Why? (11.8)

11.10 What are the advantages for one node in a computer network to have links connecting it directly with several other computers? What are the disadvantages? (11.8)

Appendix A
Review of Binary Arithmetic

A.1 OVERVIEW

Computers usually use the binary number system for calculations because physical variables that are binary or two-valued are easy to find. In writing programs, we often choose to condense binary numbers into groups of three to form octal numbers, or in groups of four to form hexadecimal numbers. In this appendix, we review conversion of decimal numbers into binary, octal, and hexadecimal; conversion of binary, octal, and hexadecimal numbers into decimal; and binary arithmetic.

All four number systems that we discuss are positional number systems. Each position of the number stands for a weight that is a power of the *base* or *radix* of the number system. In the decimal system, the base is 10. Hence all positions of a decimal number correspond to powers of 10. The digit present in each position is the coefficient by which the weight is multiplied. For example, the decimal number 527.16 means $5 \times 10^2 + 2 \times 10^1 + 7 \times 10^0 + 1 \times 10^{-1} + 6 \times 10^{-2}$.

The binary, octal, and hexadecimal systems have bases of 2, 8, and 16, respectively. We use a subscript to show the base when the base is not obvious. For example, 37_{10} means the decimal number 37, while 37_8 is octal. Because 8 and 16 are powers of 2, conversion between binary and octal or hexadecimal is simple.

The four basic arithmetic operations in binary are simple because the binary system has just two basic variables. Hence the tables for addition and multiplication have just four entries. Similarly, division and subtraction have only a few basic cases.

A.2   BINARY NUMBER SYSTEM

The binary number system is a positional number system, much like the decimal system. In the decimal system, the weights are powers of 10; in the binary they are powers of 2. The binary system is quite simple since the only digits used are 0 and 1. Thus, a given power of 2 is either present in a particular number as shown by a 1, or is absent as shown by a 0. We usually consider the parts of the number to the left and right of the binary point (analogous to a decimal point) separately. The powers of 2 increase from 0 to the left of the binary point, as shown below with their decimal equivalents. The leftmost bit of a binary number is called the *most significant* bit.

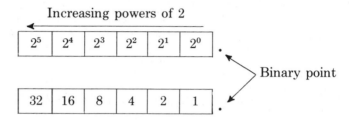

The powers of 2 decrease from −1 to the right of the binary point as shown below. The rightmost bit of a binary number is called the *least significant* bit.

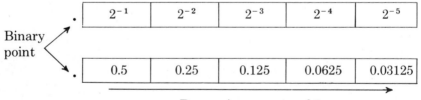

For powers of 2, it is convenient to refer to a table such as table A.1. As an example, consider the binary number below shown with its nonzero powers of 2.

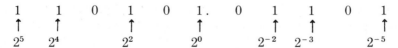

Binary-Decimal Conversion   As we might guess, changing binary numbers to decimal numbers is easy. We just add the powers of 2 for which the number has coefficients of 1.

TABLE A.1

TABLE OF POWERS OF 2

Zero and positive powers		Negative powers	
Power	$_2$Power	Power	$_2$Power
0	1		
1	2	−1	0.5
2	4	−2	0.25
3	8	−3	0.125
4	16	−4	0.0625
5	32	−5	0.03125
6	64	−6	0.015625
7	128	−7	0.0078125
8	256	−8	0.00390625
9	512	−9	0.001953125
10	1,024	−10	9.765625×10^{-4}
11	2,048	−11	4.8828125×10^{-4}
12	4,096	−12	$2.44140625 \times 10^{-4}$
13	8,192	−13	$1.220703125 \times 10^{-4}$
14	16,384	−14*	$6.103515625 \times 10^{-5}$
15	32,768	−15*	$3.051757813 \times 10^{-5}$
16	65,536	−16*	$1.525878907 \times 10^{-5}$
17	131,072	−17*	$7.629394535 \times 10^{-6}$
18	262,144	−18*	$3.814697268 \times 10^{-6}$
19	524,288	−19*	$1.907348634 \times 10^{-6}$
20	1,048,576	−20*	$9.536743170 \times 10^{-7}$

*Answer rounded to 10 significant figures.

Example A.2.1

Convert 110101.01101_2 to decimal.

$$110101.01101_2 = 1 \times 2^5 + 1 \times 2^4 + 1 \times 2^2 + 1 \times 2^0$$
$$+ 1 \times 2^{-2} + 1 \times 2^{-3} + 1 \times 2^{-5}$$
$$= 1 \times 32 + 1 \times 16 + 1 \times 4 + 1 \times 1$$
$$+ 1 \times 0.25 + 1 \times 0.125 + 1 \times 0.03125$$
$$= 53.40625_{10}$$

Thus, to convert a binary number to its decimal equivalent, we sum the powers of 2 for the positions in which the number has 1s.

Decimal-Binary Conversion Decimal-to-binary conversion is difficult. We must treat the integer and fractional parts of the decimal number separately. We convert the integer part by repeatedly dividing by 2 and the fractional part by repeatedly multiplying by 2.

We convert a decimal integer to a binary integer by the following steps:

1. Repeatedly divide the decimal integer by 2. Note the remainders.
2. Form the binary integer by writing the remainders, in decreasing order, starting with the last remainder as the most significant bit.

Example A.2.2

Convert 109_{10} to binary.

$$109 \div 2 = 54 + \text{remainder of } 1$$
$$54 \div 2 = 27 + \text{remainder of } 0$$
$$27 \div 2 = 13 + \text{remainder of } 1$$
$$13 \div 2 = 6 + \text{remainder of } 1$$
$$6 \div 2 = 3 + \text{remainder of } 0$$
$$3 \div 2 = 1 + \text{remainder of } 1$$
$$1 \div 2 = 0 + \text{remainder of } 1$$
$$109_{10} = 1101101_2$$

The binary equivalent of 109_{10} (1101101_2) is formed by writing the remainders in the order shown by the arrow; that is, the last remainder is the most significant bit. The first remainder, which shows whether the number is odd or even, is the least significant bit of the binary number.

Conversion of a decimal fraction to its binary equivalent is similar except that it uses multiplication and carries rather than division and remainders. We convert a decimal fraction to binary by the following steps:

1. Repeatedly multiply the decimal fraction by 2. Note carries to the left of the decimal point.
2. Form the binary integer by writing a 0 if the carry is 0 and a 1 if the carry is 1, starting at the right of the binary point.

Example A.2.3

Convert 0.78125_{10} to binary.

$$0.78125 \times 2 = 1.56250$$
$$0.5625 \times 2 = 1.1250$$
$$0.125 \times 2 = 0.250$$
$$0.25 \times 2 = 0.5$$
$$0.5 \times 2 = 1.0$$
$$0.78125_{10} = 0.11001_2$$

We write the binary fraction in decreasing order, starting with the first carry as the most significant bit. If the first carry is 1, the fraction is at least as large as one-half. Hence it should have a 1 in the 2^{-1} position just after the binary point. Similarly, if the second carry is 1, the fraction should contain an entry for the 2^{-2} position. We may continue the expansion to as many places as we want if the fraction does not convert evenly.

As mentioned before, we must convert mixed numbers by treating the integer and fractional parts separately. The next example shows the procedure.

Example A.2.4

Convert 121.34375_{10} to binary.

First we convert the integer part.

$$121 \div 2 = 60 + \text{remainder of } 1$$
$$60 \div 2 = 30 + \text{remainder of } 0$$
$$30 \div 2 = 15 + \text{remainder of } 0$$
$$15 \div 2 = 7 + \text{remainder of } 1$$
$$7 \div 2 = 3 + \text{remainder of } 1$$
$$3 \div 2 = 1 + \text{remainder of } 1$$
$$1 \div 2 = 0 + \text{remainder of } 1$$
$$121_{10} = 1111001_2$$

Next we convert the fractional part.

$$0.34375 \times 2 = 0.68750$$
$$0.6875 \times 2 = 1.3750$$
$$0.375 \times 2 = 0.750$$
$$0.75 \times 2 = 1.50$$
$$0.5 \times 2 = 1.0$$
$$0.34375_{10} = 0.01011_2$$

Thus, $121.34375_{10} = 1111001.01011_2$

Binary Addition   The rules for binary addition are:

$$0 + 0 = 0$$
$$0 + 1 = 1$$
$$1 + 0 = 1$$
$$1 + 1 = 10$$

In the fourth case, we have $1 + 1 = 0 +$ a carry of 1. We handle carries just as in decimal addition. Table A.2 summarizes binary addition.

TABLE A.2

BINARY ADDITION

+	0	1
0	0	1
1	1	10

Example A.2.5

Add 110101_2 and 10111_2.

$$\begin{array}{r} 110101 \\ +\ 101111 \\ \hline 1\ \ \ 100100 \end{array}$$

We can check this addition by noting that $110101_2 = 53_{10}$, $101111_2 = 47_{10}$, and $53_{10} + 47_{10} = 100_{10} = 1100100_2$.

Binary Subtraction The rules for binary subtraction are:

$$0 - 0 = 0$$
$$1 - 0 = 1$$
$$1 - 1 = 0$$
$$10 - 1 = 1$$

The fourth case could be stated that $0 - 1 = 1$ with a borrow of 1 from the next most significant bit. Alternatively, we can say that $0 - 1 = -1$. Borrows are handled as they are in decimal subtraction.

Example A.2.6

Subtract 101011_2 from 110100_2.

$$\begin{array}{r} 110100 \\ -101011 \\ \hline 1001 \end{array}$$

We can check this subtraction by noting that $101011_2 + 01001_2 = 110100_2$. We can also check the equivalent decimal subtraction, $52_{10} - 43_{10} = 9_{10}$.

Binary Multiplication The rules for binary multiplication are:

$$0 \times 0 = 0$$
$$0 \times 1 = 0$$
$$1 \times 0 = 0$$
$$1 \times 1 = 1$$

TABLE A.3

BINARY MULTIPLICATION

×	0	1
0	0	0
1	0	1

Table A.3 summarizes binary multiplication. We note the similarity between binary multiplication and the logical AND.

Example A.2.7

Multiply 1101_2 by 1001_2.

$$
\begin{array}{r}
1101 \\
\times\,1001 \\
\hline
1101 \\
0000 \\
0000 \\
1101 \\
\hline
1110101
\end{array}
$$

We can check the equivalent decimal multiplication, $13_{10} \times 9_{10} = 117_{10} = 1110101_2$.

As discussed more extensively in chapter 6, binary multiplication is a shift-and-add process. We begin multiplying with the least significant bit of the multiplier. If the multiplier bit is 1, we copy the multiplicand. If it is 0, we copy 0s. We then shift and take the next bit of the multiplier.

Binary Division The rules for binary division are:

$$
0 \div 1 = 0
$$
$$
1 \div 1 = 1
$$

Division by 0 is meaningless in the binary system as it is in the decimal system.

Division in binary can be done just as it is in decimal. Selecting a trial quotient bit, however, is much easier. We choose a quotient bit of 1 if the divisor is smaller than the partial dividend and 0 otherwise. Chapter 6 gives other methods of division.

Example A.2.8

Divide 10001111_2 by 1011_2.

$$\begin{array}{r} 1101 \\ 1011 \overline{)\ 10001111} \\ \underline{1011} \\ 1101 \\ \underline{1011} \\ 1011 \\ \underline{1011} \end{array}$$

The quotient is 1101_2. We can check the equivalent decimal division, $143_{10} \div 11_{10} = 13_{10} = 1101_2$. If the division does not come out evenly, there will be a remainder, just as in decimal division.

Example A.2.9

Divide 1001111 by 1001.

$$\begin{array}{r} 1000 + \text{remainder of } 111 \\ 1001 \overline{)\ 1001111} \\ \underline{1001} \end{array}$$

A.3   OCTAL NUMBER SYSTEM

In this positional number system each position of an octal number stands for a power of 8. The digit present in the position is the coefficient by which the power is multiplied. Eight digits—0, 1, 2, 3, 4, 5, 6, and 7—may be coefficients.

8^4	8^3	8^2	8^1	8^0	•	8^{-1}	8^{-2}	8^{-3}	8^{-4}

Octal
point

Octal numbers are used in machine language programming for many minicomputers because they are shorter and easier to use than their binary equivalents. The equivalence between octal and binary numbers is shown in table A.4. We can remember these equivalents easily with a little practice.

Binary-Octal Conversion   Conversion between binary and octal numbers is simple. To convert a binary number to octal, we separate the number at the binary point into its integer and fractional parts. Then we group the binary number into groups of 3 to the left and right of the binary point. Finally we substitute the octal equivalents for each binary group from table A.4. We may have to add 0s at the far left and right.

TABLE A.4

OCTAL-BINARY EQUIVALENTS

Octal	Binary
0	000
1	001
2	010
3	011
4	100
5	101
6	110
7	111

Example A.3.1

Convert $11110010101.01111100110_2$ to octal.

11	110	010	101	.	011	111	001	10
3	6	2	5	.	3	7	1	4

The octal equivalent is 3625.3714.

Octal-Binary Conversion   Conversion of an octal number to binary is equally easy. We substitute equivalent binary groups of three for each octal digit.

Example A.3.2

Convert 273.16_8 to binary.

$$
\begin{array}{ccccc}
2 & 7 & 3 & . & 1 & 6 \\
\downarrow & \downarrow & \downarrow & & \downarrow & \downarrow \\
010 & 111 & 011 & . & 001 & 110
\end{array}
$$

$$273.16_8 = 10111011.00111_2$$

Octal-Decimal Conversion   We can convert an octal number into decimal by multiplying the coefficients of each position of an octal number by the weight of the position.

Example A.3.3

Convert 423.15_8 to decimal.

$$
\begin{aligned}
423.15_8 &= 4 \times 8^2 + 2 \times 8^1 + 3 \times 8^0 + 1 \times 8^{-1} + 5 \times 8^{-2} \\
&= 4 \times 64 + 2 \times 8 + 3 \times 1 + 1 \times 0.125 + 5 \times 0.015625 \\
&= 256 + 16 + 3 + 0.125 + 0.078125 \\
&= 275.203125_{10}
\end{aligned}
$$

Decimal-Octal Conversion The simplest way to convert a number from decimal to octal is to convert it first to binary. Then convert the binary equivalent to octal.

Example A.3.4

Convert 139.43_{10} to octal.
First convert 139.43_{10} to binary.

$$139 \div 2 = 69 + \text{remainder of } 1$$
$$69 \div 2 = 34 + \text{remainder of } 1$$
$$34 \div 2 = 17 + \text{remainder of } 0$$
$$17 \div 2 = 8 + \text{remainder of } 1$$
$$8 \div 2 = 4 + \text{remainder of } 0$$
$$4 \div 2 = 2 + \text{remainder of } 0$$
$$2 \div 2 = 1 + \text{remainder of } 0$$
$$1 \div 2 = 0 + \text{remainder of } 1$$
$$139_{10} = 10001011_2$$

$$0.43 \times 2 = 0.86$$
$$0.86 \times 2 = 1.72$$
$$0.72 \times 2 = 1.44$$
$$0.44 \times 2 = 0.88$$
$$0.88 \times 2 = 1.76$$
$$0.76 \times 2 = 1.52$$
$$0.52 \times 2 = 1.04$$
$$0.04 \times 2 = 0.08$$
$$0.08 \times 2 = 0.16$$

At this point we arbitrarily truncate the fraction, noting that the next term would also be a 0.

$$0.43_{10} = 0.011011100_2$$
$$139.43_{10} = 10001011.011011100_2$$

Next convert 10001011.011011100_2 to octal.

10	001	011	.	011	011	100
2	1	3	.	3	3	4

$$139.43_{10} = 213.334_8$$

Another way is similar to the scheme for converting from decimal to binary. To convert directly to octal, we need to repeatedly divide the integer part of the number by 8 and to multiply the fractional part by 8. (See problem A.13.)

A.4 HEXADECIMAL NUMBER SYSTEM

The hexadecimal number system is another positional number system. Each position has a weight that is a power of 16. It is used in programming some computers—IBM computers, some minicomputers, and many microprocessors. It is especially convenient for programming computers that use words or bytes with lengths that are multiples of 4.

16^4	16^3	16^2	16^1	16^0	$\cdot$	16^{-1}	16^{-2}	16^{-3}	16^{-4}

Hexadecimal
point

The hexadecimal system requires 16 coefficients. Since we have only 10 decimal digits, we must use other symbols to represent the last six coefficients. We choose to use the first six letters of the alphabet as shown with their binary and decimal equivalents in table A.5.

Binary-Hexadecimal Conversion Because of the simple correspondence shown in table A.5, we can easily convert binary numbers to hexadecimal. We simply group the binary number into groups of four, starting at the binary point. Then we replace each binary group by its hexadecimal equivalent.

Example A.4.1

Convert 10111011001.10110100111 to hexadecimal.

$$
\begin{array}{cccccc}
101 & 1101 & 1001 & . & 1011 & 0100 & 111 \\
5 & D & 9 & . & B & 4 & E
\end{array}
$$

$$10111011001.10110100111_2 = 5D9.B4E_{16}$$

TABLE A.5

HEXADECIMAL-BINARY EQUIVALENTS

Hexadecimal	Decimal	Binary	Hexadecimal	Decimal	Binary
0	0	0000	8	8	1000
1	1	0001	9	9	1001
2	2	0010	A	10	1010
3	3	0011	B	11	1011
4	4	0100	C	12	1100
5	5	0101	D	13	1101
6	6	0110	E	14	1110
7	7	0111	F	15	1111

Hexadecimal-Binary Conversion Converting a number from hexadecimal to binary is just as easy. We replace each hexadecimal number by its binary group of four equivalent.

Example A.4.2

Convert $37C.B8_{16}$ to binary.

$$
\begin{array}{ccccc}
3 & 7 & C & . & B & 8 \\
\downarrow & \downarrow & \downarrow & & \downarrow & \downarrow \\
11 & 0111 & 1100 & . & 1011 & 01
\end{array}
$$

$$37C.B8_{16} = 1101111100.101101_2$$

Hexadecimal-Decimal Conversion The rather strange appearing number

$$AED.BF_{16}$$

can be converted to decimal in the same way that we converted binary and octal numbers to decimal.

Example A.4.3

Convert $AED.BF_{16}$ to decimal.

$$
\begin{aligned}
AED.BF_{16} &= A \times 16^2 + E \times 16^1 + D \times 16^0 + B \times 16^{-1} \\
&\quad + F \times 16^{-2} \\
&= 10 \times 256 + 14 \times 16 + 13 \times 1 + 11 \times 0.0625 \\
&\quad + 15 \times 0.00390625 \\
&= 2797.74609375_{10}
\end{aligned}
$$

Decimal-Hexadecimal Conversion The easiest way to convert a decimal number to hexadecimal is first to convert the decimal to binary. Then convert the binary number to hexadecimal.

Example A.4.4

Convert 167.45_{10} to hexadecimal.
First convert 167.45_{10} to binary.

$$
\begin{aligned}
167 \div 2 &= 83 + \text{remainder of } 1 \\
83 \div 2 &= 41 + \text{remainder of } 1 \\
41 \div 2 &= 20 + \text{remainder of } 1 \\
20 \div 2 &= 10 + \text{remainder of } 0 \\
10 \div 2 &= 5 + \text{remainder of } 0
\end{aligned}
$$

$$5 \div 2 = 2 + \text{remainder of } 1$$
$$2 \div 2 = 1 + \text{remainder of } 0$$
$$1 \div 2 = 0 + \text{remainder of } 1$$
$$167_{10} = 10100111_2$$

$$0.45 \times 2 = \underline{0}.90$$
$$0.90 \times 2 = \underline{1}.80$$
$$0.80 \times 2 = \underline{1}.60$$
$$0.60 \times 2 = \underline{1}.20$$
$$0.20 \times 2 = \underline{0}.40$$
$$0.40 \times 2 = \underline{0}.80$$
$$0.80 \times 2 = \underline{1}.60$$
$$0.45_{10} = 0.01\underline{1100}$$

The fraction will continue to repeat the underlined part 1100. We will use the first eight digits of the fraction.

$$0.45_{10} = 0.01110011_2$$
$$167.45_{10} = 10100111.01110011_2$$

Now convert 10100111.01110011_2 to hexadecimal.

1010		0111	.	0111	0011
A	-	7	.	7	3

$$167.45_{10} = \text{A7.73}_{16}$$

We could underline the 3 to show it repeats.

A.5 PROBLEMS

A.1 Convert the following binary numbers to decimal:

    a. 101101.101
    b. 110101.1101
    c. 100001.001
    d. 101011.10

A.2 Convert the following decimal numbers to binary:

    a. 35.1625
    b. 137.75
    c. 93.53125
    d. 224.40

A.3 Add the following binary numbers:

    a. 111011 and 100110
    b. 101011 and 110101
    c. 100001 and 100101
    d. 110101 and 100001

A.4 Subtract the following binary numbers:

    a. 100001 from 111011
    b. 100111 from 11001
    c. 101010 from 111000
    d. 1 from 1000000

A.5 Multiply the following pairs of binary numbers:

    a. 1011 and 1011
    b. 1001 and 1100
    c. 1101 and 1001
    d. 1010 and 1101

A.6 Divide the following binary numbers:

    a. 101 into 101101
    b. 1001 into 111111
    c. 1011 into 11101101
    d. 1011 into 10001101

A.7 Convert the following binary numbers to octal:

    a. 111011011.11010
    b. 1011011.1101101
    c. 101010101.00111
    d. 110011110.10101

A.8 Convert the following octal numbers to binary:
    a. 237.14
    b. 115.16
    c. 134.77
    d. 122.11

A.9 Convert the octal numbers of problem A.8 to decimal.

A.10 Convert the binary numbers of problem A.7 to hexadecimal.

A.11 Convert the following hexadecimal numbers to binary:

    a. 3ED.1F
    b. BCD.2A
    c. 12F.34
    d. 31A.97

A.12 Convert the hexadecimal numbers of problem A.11 to decimal.

A.13 Devise a method of converting decimal numbers directly to octal.

A.14 Devise a method of converting decimal numbers directly to hexadecimal.

A.15 Write the addition and multiplication tables in octal

A.16 Write the addition and multiplication tables in hexadecimal.

A.17 Write the numbers formed by adding 3 to each decimal number from 0 to 9 and then converting the decimal number to binary. This number system is called the *excess-three* system. Compare the representations for the decimal pairs 0 and 9, 1 and 8, 2 and 7, etc., in this system. What do you observe?

Appendix B
Answers to Selected Odd-Numbered Problems

2.1   0

2.3   0

2.7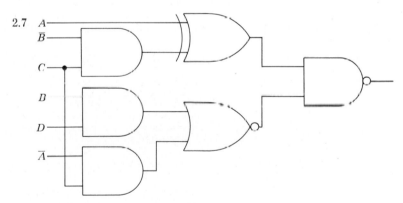

2.9   Valid

2.13 a. $f_d = (\overline{W} + X + Y)(W + XY + \overline{Z})$

   b. $\overline{f} = \overline{\overline{W}XY + W(X + Y)\overline{Z}}$

   c. $\overline{f}_d = (\overline{W} + X + Y)(W + XY + \overline{Z})$

   d. no

2.17 a.

	W	X	Y	Z	f
0	0	0	0	0	0
1	0	0	0	1	1
2	0	0	1	0	1
3	0	0	1	1	0
4	0	1	0	0	1
5	0	1	0	1	0
6	0	1	1	0	0
7	0	1	1	1	1
8	1	0	0	0	1
9	1	0	0	1	0
10	1	0	1	0	0
11	1	0	1	1	1
12	1	1	0	0	0
13	1	1	0	1	1
14	1	1	1	0	1
15	1	1	1	1	0

b. $f = \Sigma(1,2,4,7,8,11,13,14)$

$$= \overline{W}\overline{X}\overline{Y}Z + \overline{W}\overline{X}Y\overline{Z} + \overline{W}X\overline{Y}\overline{Z} + \overline{W}XYZ$$

$$+ W\overline{X}\overline{Y}\overline{Z} + W\overline{X}YZ + WX\overline{Y}Z + WXY\overline{Z}$$

c. $f = \pi(0,3,5,6,9,10,12,15)$

$$= (W+X+Y+Z)(W+X+\overline{Y}+\overline{Z})(W+\overline{X}+Y+\overline{Z})$$

$$(W+\overline{X}+\overline{Y}+Z)(\overline{W}+X+Y+\overline{Z})(\overline{W}+X+\overline{Y}+Z)$$

$$(\overline{W}+\overline{X}+Y+Z)(\overline{W}+\overline{X}+\overline{Y}+\overline{Z})$$

d. No further minimization possible

2.21 b. $Z = Y_1Y_2 + Y_1Y_3 + Y_2Y_3$

2.23 b. $g = X\overline{Y}\overline{Z} + \overline{X}\overline{Y}Z + \overline{X}Y\overline{Z} + XYZ$; 4 prime implicants

2.25 a.

YZ \ WX	00	01	11	10
00	0	1	0	d
01	1	1	1	0
11	1	0	1	0
10	1	1	1	d

b. $Y\overline{Z} + \overline{W}\overline{Y}Z + X\overline{Y}Z + \overline{W}\overline{X}Y + WX\overline{Z} + WXZ + \overline{W}\overline{X}Z + WXY$
   $+ \overline{W}X\overline{Y}$

c. $Y\overline{Z} + \overline{W}\overline{X}Z + \overline{W}X\overline{Y} + WXZ$

d. $(\overline{W} + X)(\overline{W} + Y + Z)(X + Y + Z)(W + \overline{X} + \overline{Y} + Z)$

e. No. $WXYZ$ gives 1 in c and 0 in d.

3.1 Positive logic: $1 = +12$ to $+15$ v
$0 = -5$ to -4 v
Negative logic: $1 = -5$ to -4 v
$0 = +12$ to $+15$ v

3.3 $5.75

3.9

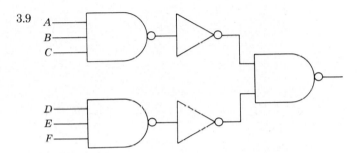

3.13 $f(A,B,C,D) = \overline{A}\,\overline{D} + \overline{B}\,\overline{D}$

3.19 $I_0 = 1,\ I_6 = 0,\ I_1 = I_4 = I_5 = I_7 = \overline{Z},\ I_2 = I_3 = Z$

3.21 $I_0 = 0,\ I_1 = Z,\ I_2 = 1,\ I_3 = \overline{Z}$

4.1 a.

Y \ $X_1 X_2$			
0	1	1	0
1	1	1	0

Y^n

b. The next state is 1 if X_2 is 1 or if X_1 is 0 and Y_1 is 1.

4.3 a.

W	X	Y	Y^n
0	0	0	0
0	0	1	0
0	1	0	1
0	1	1	1
1	0	0	0
1	0	1	0
1	1	0	0
1	1	1	1

b. A flipflop with set input X, reset input Y that retains its current state when both inputs are 1.

4.9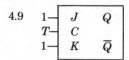

4.17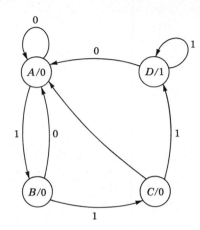

4.21 a. $S_1 = X_1$, $R_1 = X_1X_2$, $S_2 = X_1X_2$, $R_2 = X_1Y_1 + X_2$

b.

Current Input Y_1Y_2	Current Input X_1X_2 00	01	11	10
00	01	00	10	10
01	01	00	10	10
11	01	00	10	10
10	01	00	10	10

$$S_1R_1$$

Current State X_1X_2	Current State Y_1Y_2 00	01	11	10
00	01	10	00	01
01	01	10	00	01
11	01	10	01	01
10	01	10	01	01

$$S_2R_2$$

4.21 c.

Y_1Y_2 \ X_1X_2	00	01	11	10
00	01	10	10	10
01	00	01	11	10
11	00	11	10	10
10	00	11	10	10

$$Y_1{}^n Y_2{}^n$$

d.

S \ X_1X_2	00	01	11	10
A	$A/0$	$B/0$	$D/0$	$D/0$
B	$A/0$	$B/0$	$C/1$	$D/0$
C	$A/0$	$C/0$	$D/1$	$D/0$
D	$A/0$	$C/0$	$D/0$	$D/0$

$$S^n/Z$$
$$Z = X_1 X_2 Y_4$$

4.21 e.

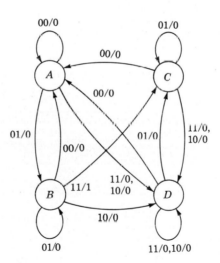

5.1   4, 1

5.3   4

6.1   Signed-magnitude and ones complement

6.3   a. $1110111 = -8$

b. $1111000 = -8$

6.5   a. end-around carry, overflow
b. overflow
c. end-around carry
d. neither

6.7   a. 45694
b. 60891
c. 65210
d. 90000

6.15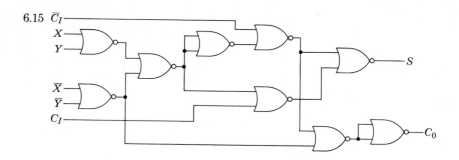

6.21

$$
\begin{array}{r}
0.10111 \\
\hline
11101 \overline{\smash{)}10101.00000} \\
11101 \\
-10000 \\
+11101 \\
\hline
11010 \\
-11101 \\
\hline
-\quad 110 \\
+11101 \\
\hline
101110 \\
-\quad 11101 \\
\hline
100010 \\
-\quad 11101 \\
\hline
101
\end{array}
$$

6.25 a. 00101, +5
b. 11110, −1
c. 11011, −4
d. 11111, −0

6.27 a. odd
    b. odd
    c. even
    d. odd

6.31 a. 11101100000000000000000000
    b. .000000111101
    c. 10000.001
    d. .000000000000011001101

7.7 a. 000000
    b. 054304
    c. 046710
    d. 000005

7.9 a. 0123
    b. 1224
    c. 0022
    d. 0246
    e. 1323

7.13 a. 002
    b. 011
    c. 007
    d. 015
    e. 016

7.15 CLA 1
    TAD 2
    TAD 2
    DCA 2
    HLT 1

8.5 DEFINE ABSUM X Y
```
    < TAD X
      SPA           /SKIP ON POSITIVE OR ZERO ACCUMULATOR
      CMA IAC    /COMPLEMENT AND INCREMENT ACCUMULATOR
      DCA X
      TAD Y
      SPA
      CMA IAC
      TAD X >
```

8.7   (program only)

```
          *200
          KCC
          KSF
          JMP .—1
          KRB
          DCA CHAR
          TAD CHAR
          TSF
          JMP .—1
          TLS
          HLT
CHAR,     1234
          $
```

8.9   Subroutine only

```
          *400
PRNAME,   0000
          CLA
LOOP,     TAD I POINT
          TSF
          JMP .—1
          TLS
          ISZ POINT
          ISZ COUNT
          JMP LOOP
          HLT
COUNT,    7773/—5 or —(LENGTH OF NAME)
POINT,    0420
          *420
S,        0323
L,        0314
O,        0317
A,        0301
N,        0316
          $
```

9.3   4096 cells, 8 bit drivers and amplifiers, 8 BIT lines, one 1-of-512 decoder

9.5   1-of-8

9.9   18,432 cores, 18 SENSE-INHIBIT lines, X-SELECT and Y-SELECT decoders with 5 inputs and 32 outputs (1 of 32 decoders)

9.13 2,097,152 bits, 1/60 second

9.15 2,400,000 bits

9.17 15, 7, 20, 480

9.19 22,500

10.11 The RUB OUT character punches holes in all channels, thus deleting any character. It functions as a NO OP (no operation).

10.13 27

10.17 at 4 bits

11.3 F_0 SET R
        READ
    F_1 MBR INTO OP
        CLEAR R
    F_2 MBR INTO PC
    F_3 PC INTO MAR

11.5 F_0 SET R
        READ
    F_1 MBR INTO OP
        CLEAR R
    F_2 INCREMENT PC
    F_3 MBR INTO MAR
        CLEAR F
        SET E
    E_0 SET R
        READ
    E_1 MBR INTO XR
        CLEAR R
    E_2 SUB
    E_3 PC INTO MAR
        CLEAR E
        SET F

Appendix C
Selected PDP-8
Instructions

Mnemonic Instruction	Octal Instruction	Description
AND XY	00XY	/ACC AND XY
TAD XY	10XY	/Twos complement addition of ACC and XY
TAD I XY	14XY	/Twos complement indirect addition of ACC and the number to which XY points
ISZ XY	20XY	/Increment XY and skip the next instruction if zero
DCA XY	30XY	/Deposit ACC at XY and clear ACC
DCA I XY	34XY	/Deposit ACC at the location to which XY points and clear ACC
JMS XY	40XY	/Jump to subroutine XY
JMP XY	50XY	/Jump to XY
JMP I XY	54XY	/Jump to the location to which XY points
RPE	6010	/Set reader/punch interrupt enable
RSF	6011	/Skip on paper tape reader flag
RRB	6012	/Read paper tape reader buffer
RFC	6014	/Reader fetch character
PCE	6020	/Clear reader/punch interrupt enable
PSF	6021	/Skip on punch flag
RCF	6022	/Clear punch flag
PPC	6024	/Load punch buffer and punch character
KCF	6030	/Clear Teletype keyboard flag
KSF	6031	/Skip on Teletype keyboard flag
KCC	6032	/Clear Teletype keyboard flag and ACC; advance reader
KRS	6034	/Read Teletype keyboard buffer
KIE	6035	/Set/clear interrupt enable
KRB	6036	/Read Teletype keyboard buffer; clear flag

TFL	6040	/Set teleprinter flag
TSF	6041	/Skip on teleprinter flag
TCF	6042	/Clear teleprinter flag
TPC	6044	/Clear teleprinter and print
TSK	6045	/Skip on printer or keyboard flag
TLS	6046	/Load teleprinter sequence
NOP	7000	/No operation—delay of 1.2 microseconds
IAC	7001	/Increment ACC by 1
RAL	7004	/Rotate ACC and link left one place
RTL	7006	/Rotate ACC and link left two places
RAR	7010	/Rotate ACC and link right one place
RTR	7012	/Rotate ACC and link right two places
CML	7020	/Complement link
CMA	7040	/Complement ACC
CIA	7041	/Complement and increment ACC; (form twos complement)
CLL	7100	/Clear link
STL	7120	/Set link to 1
CLA	7200	/Clear ACC
CLA IAC	7201	/Set ACC to 0001
STA	7240	/Set ACC to 7777
HLT	7402	/Halt
OSR	7404	/OR switch register with ACC
SKP	7410	/Skip unconditional
SNL	7420	/Skip if link is not zero
SZL	7430	/Skip if link is zero
SZA	7440	/Skip if ACC is zero
SNA	7450	/Skip if ACC is not zero
SMA	7500	/Skip on minus ACC
SPA	7510	/Skip on positive (or zero) ACC

Glossary

absolute characteristic of an address completely defined by a memory address number

absolute loader loader that puts information into *fixed* addresses in memory

accessible register register that can be used by the programmer

access time time required to select a word and read it

accumulator register in which numbers are added, changed, or stored temporarily

active low on, or 1, when the signal is low

address (noun) number that specifies a memory location; (verb) direct the computer to read the contents of a given memory location

address decoder circuit that selects desired memory location

ALGOL a high-level language

algorithm process for solving a problem in a finite number of steps

alphanumeric having to do with a character set that has letters, numbers, and usually other characters, such as punctuation

analog signal that may have any value within a given range

analog-to-digital converter device that changes analog signals into digital

AND logical product, a function that has value 1 only when all of its arguments are 1 and is 0 otherwise; a gate whose output is 1 only when all of its inputs are 1

AND-OR-INVERT (AOI) an integrated circuit consisting of AND gates followed by an OR gate followed by an inverter

argument variable partially determining the value of a function

arithmetic shift shift in which the sign digit is treated separately

arithmetic unit part of the computer that performs arithmetic and logic operations

ASCII abbreviation for American Standard Code for Information Interchange

assembler software package that translates programs from assembly language to machine language

associativity characteristic of functions that can be grouped or associated without changing their value, for example:
$$X + (Y + Z) = (X + Y) + Z$$

asynchronous characteristic of devices that operate at arbitrary times, possibly determined by the actions of other devices

autodecrement automatic subtracting of 1 from the contents of a register to give successive addresses

autoincrement automatic adding of 1 to the contents of a register to give successive addresses

auxiliary storage storage that supplements main memory, such as disc

background processing executing a low-priority program when high-priority programs do not need the computer

bandwidth measure of the maximum rate of data transfer

base total of different digits used in a particular number system, such as 10 in the decimal system

base page page zero

base register index register used to add a constant to every address

BCD counter decimal counter, usually constructed of separate stages, each capable of counting from 0 to 9

benchmark calculation used for comparison of computers or algorithms

binary number system based on base or radix 2

binary-coded-decimal (BCD) a system of coding decimal numbers in 4-bit binary in which each decimal number is represented by its 4-bit binary equivalent

binary point binary analog of a decimal point; separates the integer and fraction parts of a binary number

bipolar type of circuit constructed from conventional transistors

bistable having two stable states

bit single digit in a binary number; may have the value 0 or 1

bit density number of bits that can be recorded in a unit length, area, or volume

bit driver circuit that amplifies data to be written in memory

bit organization memory organization in which each bit of a word is on a separate memory plane

bit serial one bit at a time

block a consecutive set of data handled as a unit

block multiplex transfer blocks of information from each of several devices in sequence

Boolean algebra the mathematics of the laws of thought developed by George Boole

bootstrap loader simple loader, usually entered manually, that can load a more complex loader

buffer a register used for temporary storage of information during transfer between the computer and an external device; a device that compensates for differences in speed or voltage

buffer area region in memory used for buffered transfer

buffered transfer rapid transfer of a block of words to or from the buffer area of memory

bus group of wires that carry information

byte even subdivision of a word, typically 8 bits

byte multiplex transfer of 1 byte from each of several devices in rotation

cache memory very fast semiconductor memory in which information needed most often is kept; scratchpad memory

canonical form one of two standard forms by which a combinational logic function can be expressed

carry anticipation circuit in which carries are generated at one time for all pairs of bits

carry bit single bit that records carries in addition; also called a link or extend bit

carry ripple propagation characteristic of an adder in which carries can carry or ripple from addition of the least significant bits to the most significant bits

cathode-ray tube display device that resembles a television tube

cell smallest square on Karnaugh map

centralized network network in which one computer controls; star network

channel complex device that controls input/output transfers, usually for several peripheral devices

characteristic function function that shows the next state as a function of the current state and current input(s)

character printer device that prints characters one at a time

charge-coupled device (CCD) MOS device that transfers charges serially

chip select input that enables addressing or read/write circuits

circuit switching network communications like those of the commercial telephone network

class code part of operation code specifying the class of the instruction, such as memory reference

clear erase the contents of a register or memory location; reset

clock device that generates timing signals

CMOS circuits constructed with complementary metal-oxide-semiconductor components

COINCIDENCE function whose output is 1 whenever an even number of inputs are 1

coincidence addressing addressing scheme in memory in which the coincidence of two currents is required to select a bit

combinational logic   a logic system with output values that depend only on the logic structure and the current value of the system inputs

comment   documentation of a program statement

commutativity   characteristic of a function whose variables can be reordered without changing its value, for example:
$$X + Y = Y + X$$

comparator   logic circuit that compares the magnitudes of two numbers

compiler   software package that translates an entire source program into an object program before the program is executed

complement   (noun) a function whose value is 0 when its argument is 1 and conversely; (verb) change all 1s to 0s and 0s to 1s

complete set   a set of functions that can be combined to give any combinational logic function

complete sum   sum of all prime implicants

computer (digital)   electronic machine that can receive, store, and manipulate information coded in binary form

computer network   interconnection of two or more CPUs with associated memories, peripheral devices, etc.

computer systems level   the highest level in the computer hierarchy constructed from components such as the central processing unit, memory, etc.

console   front panel of a computer which has controls and signals for manual operation

contents   information stored in a register or memory location

control   device that governs the operation of other devices

control memory   special read-only memory in a microprogrammed computer used for decoding instructions

control table   table that shows flipflop inputs as a function of circuit inputs and flipflop states

core   small magnetic ring used to construct memories

counter   device that counts events such as pulses

current inputs   flipflop inputs now

current location counter   counter kept by assembler to show the address being assembled

current page   page containing the current instruction

current state   state of a flipflop now

cycle stealing   use of occasional memory cycles by the direct memory access system instead of by the CPU

cyclic shift   rotation of all bits of a register with or without an auxiliary carry register

daisy chain method of linking devices along a single line according to their priority such that lower priority devices are automatically prevented from interrupting the actions of higher priority devices

data general term denoting all numbers and characters processed by a computer

data operator device that transforms information, such as adding, complementing, etc.

data selector a multiplexer with n data select inputs that can select any of the 2^n data inputs to be connected to the output

decimal expression way of writing a canonical form of a logic function as the sum or product of rows of a truth table

decoder a circuit that converts information from n inputs to a maximum of 2^n outputs

decrement decrease, usually by 1

deduction application of postulates and previously proved theorems to prove a theorem

defer state state for decoding of indirect addresses

DeMorgan's theorem Product version: The complement of the sum of two variables equals the product of the complements of the two variables. AND version: The complement of the product of two variables equals the sum of the complements of the two variables.

demultiplexer decoder with a data input that can route input data to any one of 2^n outputs as selected by an n-bit input address

dependent register register whose contents are a function of the contents of another register

destructive readout reading from memory in which the information is lost to the memory so that it must be rewritten into memory

destructive transfer transfer of information from one device to another while permanently removing the information from the first device

D flipflop flipflop whose state copies the D (delay) input after a clock pulse

digital signal that may have only certain specified values

digital-to-analog converter device that changes digital signals into analog

direct address address that specifies the location of an operand

direct memory access (DMA) transfer of a block of information directly between an external device and memory without using a service routine

disc semirandom-access memory resembling a phonograph record

displacement   part of address field

distinguished 1 cell   1 cell covered by only one prime implicant

distinguished column   Quine-McCluskey analog to distinguished 1 cell

distributed network   network in which each computer is eligible to control subject to priority constraints

divide-by-2   characteristic of counter so arranged that each stage changes state at half the rate of the preceding stage

DM module   a register-transfer module that combines data operation and memory

dominance   characteristic of a prime implicant that covers the same remaining 1 cell(s) as another prime implicant and at least one other remaining 1 cell

don't care   a combination of inputs whose associated output does not matter

double-rail logic   a logic system in which both all variables and their complements are available for inputs

drum   memory constructed from a rotating cylinder coated with magnetic material

dual   the function formed by interchanging AND and OR and interchanging 0 and 1

dual in-line package   a common case for semiconductors with metal pins fixed in two parallel rows

dummy   an artificial address or instruction that stands for the actual item, such as a dummy variable

dynamic   characteristic of semiconductor circuits that require periodic refreshing to maintain their state

EBCDIC   abbreviation for expanded binary-coded-decimal interchange code

edge-triggered   responding to edge of signal

effective address   address of the actual memory location

electronic circuit level   the computer level in which electronic components such as resistors and transistors are combined to construct logic circuits such as AND and OR gates

electronic writing tablet   device used to input information to a CRT display

emitter-coupled logic (ECL)   a high-speed bipolar logic

enable   activate or turn on

end-around carry   addition of 1 to the least significant digit in ones complement addition when there is a carry out of the sign bit

equality   characteristic of two prime implicants that cover the same set of remaining 1 cells

essential prime implicant   prime implicant that contains a distinguished 1 cell

essential row   Quine-McCluskey analog to essential prime implicant

even parity   even number of 1s in a word

evoke   cause to operate

excess-three code   a code that represents numbers as the binary equivalent of the decimal digit plus three

excess-three Gray code   a code constructed by taking the Gray code of the decimal digit plus three

excess-2^{n-1}   representation of numbers in which the sign bit is the complement of the sign bit for the corresponding twos complement representation

excitation table   table that gives required flipflop input(s) as a function of current state and next state

EXCLUSIVE OR (XOR)   function whose value is 1 when an odd number of inputs are 1

execute   perform a given operation

execute state   state for executing memory reference instructions other than jump instructions

executive   program or set of programs that control and coordinate other computer programs; monitor; supervisor

exponent   power to which a base is raised (e.g., 5 is an exponent in 2^5)

external device   instrument or device electrically connected to a computer but not part of it; peripheral device

external noise immunity   resistance to external noise

extract   obtaining part of a word

falling edge   change of pulse from high voltage to low voltage

fall time   the time required for the voltage in a switching electronic circuit to drop from 90% to 10% of its nominal initial value

fan-in   the number of inputs of a particular gate

fan-out   the number of gates connected to the output of a particular gate

fetch state   first state in processing an instruction in which the instruction is fetched from memory, decoded, and—if short enough—executed

field   part of the contents of a register; unit of an instruction

firmware   microprogramming

fixed point   number system in which the binary point is fixed or in one place for all representations

flag   1-bit status register

flipflop   electronic device that has two stable states. A flipflop can be switched from one state to the other by a signal at a flipflop input; the state is sensed at the flipflop outputs.

floating point   scientific notation; representation of a number as an integer times an exponential

floppy disc   semirandom-access memory that combines the head positioning technology of discs with the recording surface technology of drums

formatted   having a predetermined structure, as tapes with timing or reference tracks

FORTRAN   widely used high-level language that allows programs to be written in an algebraic form

forward reference   reference to symbol defined later in the program

full adder   circuit that adds corresponding bits of two binary numbers plus a carry bit

gate   a logic device with one or more inputs and one output

Gray code   a binary code in which only one bit changes for the representation of two adjacent numbers

half adder   circuit that adds corresponding bits of two binary numbers

handshaking   method of acknowledging signals between two devices (or a device and a computer) such that both receive information of the action

high-level language   language that uses algebraic or English-like statements, each of which ordinarily corresponds to several machine language instructions

Hollerith code   alphanumeric code that represents a character on IBM cards as up to 3 punches in any of 12 rows in a column

identifier   label in a high-level language program

identity function   a function equal to its argument, for example, $f(X) = X$

immediate addressing   characteristic of an instruction whose address field contains the actual value of an operand rather than address

impact printer   device that prints mechanically

implicant   logical product that, if 1, implies the function is 1

implicate   logical sum that, if 0, implies the function is 0

increment increase, usually by 1

incremental plotting method of specifying a new position in terms of its location relative to the current position

independent register register whose contents are not a function of the contents of another register

index register special register used for modifying addresses

indirect address address in which the displacement is interpreted as a pointer to the memory location that holds the desired address

input (noun) information transferred from an external device to the computer; (verb) transfer such information

input/output instruction instruction concerning the operation of a peripheral device

instruction statement that tells the computer to perform an operation

integrated circuit a semiconductor chip containing one or more electronic circuits

internal noise immunity a characteristic of circuits that generate little noise

interpreter translator that translates one or a few source statements into machine language code and then executes them before translating the next statements

interrupt process initiated by an external device of interrupting the computer to transfer information

interrupt acknowledge external device flipflop or signal from a computer showing that an interrupt request signal has been received

interrupt mask register register that holds bits for masking or inhibiting undesired interrupts

interrupt request flipflop or signal from a device asking for service from the computer

inverter device that complements; NOT gate

isolated state state that cannot be entered and has no exit

JK flipflop variation of RS flipflop that allows for simultaneous 1 inputs

Johnson counter variation of shift register counter with counting cycle of length n, where n is the number of flipflops

joystick photoelectric device connected to a mechanical sensing device used for pointing to data on a CRT

K 1024

Karnaugh map graphic display of minterms and maxterms developed by Karnaugh

keyboard/reader input part of teletype consisting of type-writer-like keyboard and paper tape reader

key bounce circuit circuit that insures that an input key is read only once for each time it is depressed

label field of assembly language statement used for address of statement

large-scale-integration (LSI) integrated circuits with 100 or more gates per chip

leading edge change of pulse from low voltage to high voltage

least significant bit rightmost bit of a number

level characteristic of signals that are 0 or 1 for arbitrary (usually long) periods of time; number of interrupts that the CPU can distinguish by hardware

level mode operation of flipflops that are controlled by level signals

light pen photoelectric device that can write on a CRT

line printer device that prints a line of characters at a time

link a path between components over which information can be transferred without change

literal variable with or without an associated NOT

loader device to input information into computer memory

lockout circuit circuit that prevents more than one key at a time from being recognized as an input

logical equivalence characteristic of two logic functions that have the same value for all possible combinations of inputs

logical shift straight shift of all bits of a register with one or more bits lost off one end while zero(s) enter the other end

look-ahead carry circuit in which carries are generated at one time for all pairs of bits; carry anticipation

loop repeated series of instructions

machine independent characteristic of a language whose instructions are independent of the particular computer on which the program will run

machine language binary, octal, or hexadecimal coding of basic machine operations

macro a user-developed instruction consisting of two or more ordinary instructions in assembly language programming

magnetic bubble small magnetic domain that can be made to transfer information in series

mantissa fractional part of floating point representation

mask concealing part of a word

mass memory memory with very large capacity, exceeding one million words

master device with control of a bus; controlling flipflop in master-slave flipflop

master-slave flipflop with two separate parts arranged so that input changes cannot propagate through the flipflop

maximum fan-in the maximum number of unit load inputs that a given logic technology can handle

maximum fan-out the maximum number of unit loads that the output of gates of a given logic technology can drive

maxterm logical sum of the complements of all literals in one row of a truth table

Mealy circuit circuit whose outputs are associated with transitions between states and are pulses

medium-scale-integration (MSI) integrated circuits with 12 to 99 gates per chip

memory computer storage, usually in the form of an organized collection of storage elements

memory address register register used in association with memory that holds the address of the word involved in a memory transfer

memory buffer register register that holds the contents of the word whose address is in the memory address register; memory data register

memory cycle basic unit of time for a computer

memory data register memory buffer register

memory field module of memory

memory reference instruction instruction used for transferring information to or from memory

message switching communications in which each message is sent through the network as a unit

metal-oxide-semiconductor (MOS) a semiconductor technology based on field-effect transistors

microinstructions microprogrammed instructions

microprocessor central processing unit on a single integrated circuit

microprogrammable computer computer that a user can microprogram

microprogrammed computer computer with microprogramming whose instruction sets cannot be changed by the user

microprogramming use of a special set of computer instructions consisting of basic operations closely tied to the computer hardware

minicomputer small computer, usually with word lengths of 12 to 18 bits

minimal sum the simplest sum of prime implicants that is logically equivalent to a given logic function

minimization reducing a logic expression to its simplest form as measured by some minimization criterion, commonly the fewest literals in the fewest terms

minterm logical product of all literals in one row of a truth table

mnemonic abbreviation chosen to remind one of the words abbreviated, as by using initial letters

mode type of addressing

module-n characteristic of counter that counts 0, 1, 2, 3, . . . , n-1, 0, 1, . . .

Moore circuit circuit whose outputs are associated with circuit states and are level signals

most significant bit leftmost bit of the magnitude of a number

mouse small photoelectric device shaped like a mouse that can be used to point to data on a CRT display and to determine positions

multiplex mix electrical signals by dividing time or frequency intervals among them

multiplexer a device that connects one of 2^n inputs to an output

multiprocessing use of several computers to divide a set of jobs and execute them simultaneously

multiprogramming executing two or more programs held in main memory at the same time

NAND complement of AND; a function whose value is 1 except when all inputs are 1

negative-going edge change of pulse from high voltage to low voltage

next state the state to which a flipflop will switch given its current state and current inputs

NMOS a metal-oxide-semiconductor technology that uses n-channels

noise voltage fluctuations that can cause errors in digital circuits

noise margin guaranteed difference between output voltage levels and allowed input voltage levels

nonimpact printer device that prints by a chemical, electrical, or hydraulic method

nonrestoring division division scheme in which the shifted divisor is added to the dividend when the quotient bit is 0 and subtracted when it is 1

nonvolatile   stores information even when the power is off

NOR   complement of OR; a function whose value is 1 only when all inputs are 0

normalize   adjust the exponent and fraction of a floating point number so that the fraction has a standard format

NOT   complement, that is, NOT $X = 1$ when $X = 0$ and conversely

null function   a function of one variable with value 0, for example, $f(X) = 0$

object program   translation of a source program into machine language

octal   denoting a number system with base 8

odd parity   odd number of 1s in a word

offline   operating peripheral devices without computer control

ones complement   number system in which a negative number is represented by the true or logical complement of the corresponding positive number

online   operating peripheral devices under computer control

operand   value being manipulated; address or symbolic name in assembly language instruction

operating system   system of programs that governs the computer's operation

operation code   part of instruction that names the operation to be performed

OR   a function whose value is 1 whenever any of its arguments are 1; a gate whose output is 1 whenever any of its inputs are 1

overflow   result of arithmetic operation exceeding the capacity of the register

packet switching   variation of message switching in which messages may be divided or grouped into fixed length packets

page relocatable   programs that can be executed on any page

paging   addressing mode in which memory is effectively divided into pages, of which two can usually be easily accessed from any page

parallel transfer   transfer of data at one time; transfer of all bits of one word at once

parity   evenness or oddness of the 1 bits of a word

parity check   check on the number of 1s in a computer word

pass   complete process of reading a set of information through a device

perfect induction   display of the logical equivalence of two sides of an equation in truth tables

peripheral device device or instrument electrically connected to a computer but not part of the computer; external device

persistent state state that can be entered from at least one other but has no exit

photoelectric reader device that reads paper tape or cards by shining lights through the holes and sensing the presence or absence of the light

plated wire variation of thin-film memory consisting of thin magnetic films on wires

PMOS a metal-oxide-semiconductor technology that uses p-channels

pointer software means of pointing to a memory location or register

pop remove a number from the top of the stack

port electrical opening into memory

positive-going edge change of pulse from low voltage to high voltage

positive logic a logic system in which 1 is assigned to the more positive voltage and 0 to the other

postnormalization adjustment of the exponent after a floating point operation

precedence rules statements of the order in which operations must be performed

prime implicant an implicant that is implied by no other implicant; graphically the largest block that covers a given 1 cell

printer/punch output part of teletype consisting of character printer and paper tape punch

priority relative importance of an event or device

problem-oriented language high-level language designed to solve a specific type of problem

procedure-oriented language language that allows the user to write programs without understanding computer procedures

product-of-sums canonical form of a logic function consisting of the logical product of all maxterms for which the function is 0

program counter register that holds the address of the next instruction

programmable read-only memory (PROM) read-only memory with contents that can be altered by some relatively slow process

programmed input/output method of transferring information between the computer and external devices under control of a program

programmed logic array (PLA) variation of a read-only memory that can ignore some inputs and provide the same output for several inputs

programming   planning the solution of a problem for a computer

propagation delay   a measure of the time required for the output to respond to the input (e.g., the time between the 50% points on the input and output signals). Several types of propagation delay are commonly defined in semiconductor handbooks.

pseudo-instruction   special instruction for assembly language program

pulse   characteristic of signals that are 1 for specific (usually short) periods of time

pulse mode   operation of flipflops that are controlled by pulse signals

push   place a number on a stack

pushdown stack   ordered list of numbers arranged on a last-in-first-out basis

quantize   code analog signals into digital

Quine-McCluskey tables   tabular method of minimizing combinational logic functions

race   production of undesirable output sequences in response to change in circuit inputs

radix   base of a number system, such as 10 in the decimal system

random-access memory (RAM)   memory in which every location can be reached in the same amount of time or in the same number of operations

random logic   general logic functions

random positioning   a plotting method in which the position of the writing instrument is specified in terms of absolute coordinates

read-only memory (ROM)   memory from which information can be read but into which information cannot be written in ordinary computer usage

real-time system   system that responds to one set of inputs before receiving the next set

refresh   retrace electrical signals or restore the intensity of bits

register   row of associated flipflops

register instruction   instruction dealing with register only

register reference instruction   instruction dealing with word(s) in one or more registers

register-register instruction   instruction dealing with operations between registers

register-transfer language description of computer operation in terms of registers and the transfers of data between them, such as CDL and AHPL

register-transfer logic a logic system whose components are registers and paths between registers

register-transfer module (RTM) register-transfer component manufactured by Digital Equipment Corporation

regular state state that can be entered from at least one other and can exit to at least one other

relative addressing addressing in which the displacement or the contents of a register are added to the constant of some special register, such as the program counter

relocatable loader loader that can modify addresses to load a program anywhere in memory

reset input a 0; cause a flipflop to enter the 0 state

restoring division division scheme in which the shifted divisor is added back to the dividend whenever the quotient bit is 0

ripple adder adder in which carries propagate from the least significant bits to the most significant bits

ripple counter counter that propagates changes across all its stages instead of changing all stages simultaneously

rise time the time required for the voltage in a switching electronic circuit to rise from 10% to 90% of its nominal final value

rising edge change of pulse from low voltage to high voltage

RS **flipflop** flipflop with S (set) input and R (reset) input that cannot be 1 simultaneously

scratchpad memory very fast memory in which information needed most often is kept; cache memory

self-starting characteristic of counter that will enter the desired counting cycle from any initial state

semirandom-access memory memory with access times limited by the speed of rotation of some device, such as a disc or drum

sense amplifier circuit that detects and amplifies data that are read from memory

sensing pins mechanical wires that determine the presence or absence of holes in paper tape

sequential-access memory memory in which information is stored in sequence, as along a tape

sequential logic a logic system whose outputs depend on the structure of the system and both the current and past values of the inputs

serial transfer   transfer of each bit of a word in separate time intervals

set   input a 1; cause a flipflop to enter the 1 state

setup time   period during which inputs to an edge-triggered flipflop must stay constant

shift register   a set of flipflops arranged so that data can be shifted from one flipflop to another

shift register counter   counter constructed from a shift register, typically with counting cycle of length n, where n is the number of flipflops

signed-magnitude   number system in which representations of positive and negative numbers differ only in the sign bit—0 for positive and 1 for negative

simplified sum   sum equal to the complete sum but containing fewer literals

single-rail logic   a logic system in which only the uncomplemented values of inputs are available

single step   operation of the computer with the CPU halting after execution of each instruction or at the end of each memory cycle

slave   device controlled by master

small-scale-integration (SSI)   integrated circuits with from 1 to 11 gates per chip

speed-power product   a single figure of merit that measures both speed (or delay) and power

source program   program written by user, usually in a high-level language or assembly language

square wave   signal with equal periods of on and off

stack   see *pushdown stack*

state assignment   assignment of circuit states to state variables of flipflops as part of sequential circuit design

state diagram   map of state table showing state behavior graphically

statement   instruction or data

static   maintaining state without attention

store and forward   communications system in which messages are held for later transmission if a station is busy

stored program computer   computer with the capability of storing and executing programs that are input to it

subregister   distinct part of a register, such as a subregister that holds the magnitude of a number

subroutine   subprogram that is called by the main program and executed with return to the main program

sum-of-products (AND/OR)   canonical form of a logic function consisting of the logical sum of minterms for which the function is 1

switch   device for routing data between devices

switching algebra   the mathematics of digital technology derived from Boolean algebra

symbol table   table kept by assembler relating addresses to symbolic names

synchronous   characteristic of devices that operate at fixed time intervals, generally determined by a clock

table of combinations   truth table; a table displaying the output of a logic system for every possible combination of inputs

teleprinter   device that can print material received as electrical signals

teletype   popular teleprinter, consisting of a keyboard and printer

T flipflop   flipflop that changes state whenever it receives a T (toggle) input

thin film   memory constructed from small dots of magnetic material on a glass surface

three-state-logic (TSL)   logic with three stable states—0, 1, and a disabled state that prevents data transfer

time slice   segment of a memory cycle

toggle   enter information into a computer manually via bit switches

toggle flipflop T flipflop

track   one line of information on a drum

trailing edge   change of pulse from high voltage to low voltage

transducer   device that changes the representation of information without changing its content or value

transfer clock   clock used for transferring data

transient state   state that cannot be entered from any other but can exit to at least one other

transistor-transistor logic (TTL)   a popular type of bipolar logic technology

transition table   display of the next state(s) of a sequential circuit as a function of current state(s) and current input(s)

translator   program that changes a source program into an object program

transparent   characteristic of a computer scheme whose operations are not obvious to the computer user

truth table   display of the output of a logic system for every possible combination of inputs

two-level logic system with only two layers of gates, such as AND/OR or OR/AND

two-pass assembler assembler that takes two passes through an assembly language program to convert it into machine language code

twos complement number system in which a negative number is represented by the true or logical complement of the corresponding positive number plus one

unary function a function of one variable

unit load the power required for one specific gate

up-down counter a counter that can count in either ascending or descending order

virtual memory technique for swapping information between various types of memory to make the main memory appear larger

volatile loses information when the power is off

wired AND an AND gate constructed from wiring together the outputs of open collector TTL gates

word set of bits handled by the computer as one group

word length number of bits in a word

word organization memory organization in which each word is on one memory plane

write time time required to select a memory location and write a word into it

XOR a function whose value is 1 if and only if an odd number of its arguments are 1, a gate whose output is 1 if and only if an odd number of its inputs are 1

Bibliography

Abrams, M. D., and Stein, P. G. 1973. *Computer hardware and software.* Reading, Mass.: Addison-Wesley.

Abramson, N., and Kuo, F. F., eds. 1973. *Computer-communication networks.* Englewood Cliffs, N.J.: Prentice-Hall.

Adam Osborne & Associates. 1973. *The value of power.* Anaheim, Calif.: General Automation.

_____. 1974. *The value of micropower.* Anaheim, Calif.: General Automation.

American Micro-systems, Engineering Staff. 1972. *MOS integrated circuits.* New York: Van Nostrand Reinhold.

American National Standards Institute, Inc. 1973. *Graphic symbols for logic diagrams* [two-state devices]. New York: ANSI.

Bannister, B. R., and Whitehead, D. G. 1973. *Fundamentals of digital systems.* London: McGraw-Hill.

Barna, A., and Porat, D. I. 1973. *Integrated circuits in digital electronics.* New York: Wiley.

Barron, D. W. 1972. *Assemblers and loaders.* New York: American Elsevier.

Bartee, T. C. 1972. *Digital computer fundamentals.* New York: McGraw-Hill.

Bartee, T. C.; Lebow, I. L.; and Reed, I. S. 1962. *Theory and design of digital machines.* New York: McGraw-Hill.

Beizer, B. 1971. *The architecture and engineering of digital computer complexes.* New York: Plenum Press.

Bell, C. G.; Grason, J.; and Newell, A. 1972. *Designing computers and digital systems.* Maynard, Mass.: Digital Press.

Bell, C. G., and Newell, A. 1971. *Computer structures: readings and examples.* New York: McGraw-Hill.

Blakeslee, T. R. 1975. *Digital design with standard MSI and LSI.* New York: Wiley.

Booth, T. L. 1971. *Digital networks and computer systems.* New York: Wiley.

Breuer, M. A., ed. 1972. *Design automation of digital systems.* Englewood Cliffs, N.J.: Prentice-Hall.

Carr, W. N., and Mize, J. P. 1972. *MOS/LSI design and application.* New York: McGraw-Hill.

Chu, Y. 1972. *Computer organization and micro-programming.* Englewood Cliffs, N.J.: Prentice-Hall.

Clare, C. R. 1973. *Designing logic systems using state machines.* New York: McGraw-Hill.

Coffman, E. G., Jr., and Denning, P. J. 1973. *Operating systems theory.* Englewood Cliffs, N.J.: Prentice-Hall.

Colin, A. J. T. 1971. *Introduction to operating systems.* New York: American Elsevier.

Coury, F. F., ed. 1972. *A practical guide to minicomputer applications.* New York: IEEE Press.

Dietmeyer, D. L. 1971. *Logic design of digital systems.* Boston: Allyn and Bacon.

Drummond, M. E., Jr. 1973. *Evaluation and measurement techniques for digital computer systems.* Englewood Cliffs, N.J.: Prentice-Hall.

Eimbinder, J. 1971. *Semiconductor memories.* New York: Wiley.

Fitchen, F. C. 1970. *Electronic integrated circuits and systems.* New York: Van Nostrand Reinhold.

Flores, I. 1973. *Peripheral devices.* Englewood Cliffs, N.J.: Prentice-Hall.

Foster, C. C. 1970. *Computer architecture.* New York: Van Nostrand Reinhold.

Gallager, R. G. 1968. *Information theory and reliable communication.* New York: Wiley.

Gear, C. W. 1974. *Computer organization and programming.* New York: McGraw-Hill.

Greene, F. S.; Alfke, P. H.; Nichols, J. L.; and Watkins, B. G. 1972. *TTL/MSI applications and design with MSI.* Palo Alto, Calif.: Technology Learning Corporation.

Gruenberger, F., and Babcock, D. 1973. *Computing with minicomputers.* Los Angeles: Melville.

Gschwind, H. W., and McCluskey, E. J. 1975. *Design of digital computers.* New York: Springer-Verlag.

Hansen, P. B. 1973. *Operating system principles.* Englewood Cliffs, N.J.: Prentice-Hall.

Hellerman, H. 1973. *Digital computer system principles.* New York: McGraw-Hill.

Hennie, F. C. 1968. *Finite-state models for logical machines.* New York: Wiley.

Hewlett-Packard. (no date). *A pocket guide to Hewlett-Packard computers.* Palo Alto, Calif.: Hewlett-Packard.

———. 1970. *An introduction to Hewlett-Packard computers.* Palo Alto, Calif.: Hewlett-Packard.

Hill, F. J., and Peterson, G. R. 1973. *Digital systems: hardware organization and design.* New York: Wiley.

———. 1974. *Introduction to switching theory and logical design.* New York: Wiley.

Hnatek, E. R. 1973. *A user's handbook of integrated circuits.* New York: Wiley.

Husson, S. S. 1970. *Microprogramming: principles and practices.* Englewood Cliffs, N.J.: Prentice-Hall.

Iliffe, J. K. 1972. *Basic machine principles.* New York: American Elsevier.

Intel. 1974. *Intellec 8/MOD 80 operators manual.* Santa Clara, Calif.: Intel.

Katzen, H. 1971. *Computer organization and the system 370.* Cincinnati: Van Nostrand Reinhold.

Kohonen, T. 1972. *Digital circuits and devices.* Englewood Cliffs, N.J.: Prentice-Hall.

Korn, G. A. 1973. *Minicomputers for engineers and scientists.* New York: McGraw-Hill.

Lenk, J. D. 1973. *Manual for integrated circuits users.* Reston, Va.: Reston.

Lewin, Douglas. 1975. *Logical design of switching circuits.* New York: American Elsevier.

Logic Products Group. 1973. *Logic handbook.* Maynard, Mass.: Digital Press.

Madnick, S. E., and Donovan, J. J. 1974. *Operating systems.* New York: McGraw-Hill.

Malvino, A. P., and Leach, D. L. 1969. *Digital principles and applications.* New York: McGraw-Hill.

Marcus, M. 1975. *Switching circuits for engineers.* Englewood Cliffs, N.J.: Prentice-Hall.

Martin, J. 1967. *Design of real-time computer systems.* Englewood Cliffs, N.J.: Prentice-Hall.

McCluskey, E. J. 1965. *Introduction to the theory of switching circuits.* New York: McGraw-Hill.

Microcomputer Systems Group. 1972. *MCS-4 microcomputer set user's manual.* Santa Clara, Calif.: Intel.

_____. 1973. *MCS-8 microcomputer set user's manual.* Santa Clara, Calif.: Intel.

Microdata. 1972. *Microprogramming handbook.* Santa Ana, Calif.: Microdata.

Morris, R. L., and Miller, J. R., eds. 1971. *Designing with TTL integrated circuits.* New York: McGraw-Hill.

Nagle, H. T., Jr.; Carroll, B. D.; and Irwin, J. D. 1975. *An introduction to computer logic.* Englewood Cliffs, N.J.: Prentice-Hall.

Newman, W. M., and Sproull, R. F. 1973. *Principles of interactive computer graphics.* New York: McGraw-Hill.

PDP-8 Software Writing Group. 1972. *Programming languages.* Maynard, Mass.: Digital Press.

Peatman, J. B. 1972. *The design of digital systems.* New York: McGraw-Hill.

Peterson, W. W., and Weldon, E. J., Jr. 1972. *Error-correcting codes.* Cambridge, Mass.: MIT Press.

Poppelbaum, W. J. 1972. *Computer hardware theory.* New York: McGraw-Hill.

RCA. 1972. *COS/MOS integrated circuits manual.* Somerville, N.J.: RCA.

Rhyne, V. T. 1973. *Fundamentals of digital systems design.* Englewood Cliffs, N.J.: Prentice-Hall.

Richards, R. K. 1971. *Digital design.* New York: Wiley.

Riley, W. B. 1971. *Electronic computer memory technology.* New York: McGraw-Hill.

Schoeffler, J. D., and Temple, R. H., eds. 1972. *Minicomputers: hardware, software, and applications.* New York: IEEE Press.

Scott, N. R. 1970. *Electronic computer technology.* New York: McGraw-Hill.

Software Documentation Programming Department. 1973. *Small computer handbook.* Maynard, Mass.: Digital Press.

Software Writing Group. 1974. *Introduction to programming.* Maynard, Mass.: Digital Press.

Soucek, B. 1972. *Minicomputers in data processing and simulation.* New York: Wiley-Interscience.

Stone, H. S. 1972. *Introduction to computer organization and data structures.* New York: McGraw-Hill.

————. 1973. *Discrete mathematical structures and their applications.* Chicago: Science Research Associates.

————. 1975. *Introduction to computer architecture.* Chicago: Science Research Associates.

Stone, H. S. and Sieworek, D. P. 1975. *Introduction to computer organization and data structures: PDP-11 edition.* New York: McGraw-Hill.

Texas Instruments, Engineering Staff. (no date). *The integrated circuits catalog for design engineers.* Dallas: Texas Instruments.

Watson, R. W. 1970. *Timesharing system design concepts.* New York: McGraw-Hill.

Weitzman, C. 1974. *Minicomputer systems.* Englewood Cliffs, N.J.: Prentice-Hall.

Wilkes, M. V. 1972. *Time-sharing computer systems.* New York: American Elsevier.

Williams, G. E. 1970. *Boolean algebra with computer applications.* New York: McGraw-Hill.

INDEX

This book was set in 10-point Century Schoolbook with display lines in American Uncial Open Capitals and Vega Medium Extended. It was set by Computer Typesetting Services, Glendale, California, and printed by R. R. Donnelley, Crawfordsville, Indiana. Technical art was prepared by John Foster, Novato, California.

Acquisitions Editor   Alan W. Lowe and Paul Kelly
Project Editor   Gretchen Hargis
Designer   Judith Olson

67890/54321